THE PSYCHOLOGY OF CREATIVE WRITING

The Psychology of Creative Writing takes a scholarly, psychological look at multiple aspects of creative writing, including the creative writer as a person, the text itself, the creative process, the writer's development, the link between creative writing and mental illness, the personality traits of comedy and screenwriters, and how to teach creative writing. This book will appeal to psychologists interested in creativity, writers who want to understand more about the magic behind their talents, and educated laypeople who enjoy reading, writing, or both. From scholars to bloggers to artists, *The Psychology of Creative Writing* has something for everyone.

Scott Barry Kaufman, Ph.D., completed his doctorate in cognitive psychology at Yale University in 2009. He also holds an M.Phil. in experimental psychology from the University of Cambridge, where he was a Gates Cambridge Scholar, and a B.S. from Carnegie Mellon University, where he studied psychology, human–computer interaction, and voice performance. In his research, he combines various perspectives, including cognitive science, philosophy, and evolutionary psychology, to further an understanding of intelligence and creativity. In addition to publishing more than 20 book chapters and articles in professional journals such as *Intelligence* and *Journal of Creative Behavior*, he is co-editor of *The Cambridge Handbook of Intelligence* (with Robert J. Sternberg, forthcoming). Kaufman's work has been covered in media outlets such as *The Philadelphia Inquirer* and *Men's Health*. Additionally, he writes a blog for *Psychology Today* called "Beautiful Minds." He is the recipient of the 2008 Frank X. Barron student award from Division 10 of the American Psychological Association for his research on the psychology of aesthetics, creativity, and the arts.

James C. Kaufman, PhD, is an associate professor of psychology at the California State University at San Bernardino, where he directs the Learning Research Institute. Dr. Kaufman's research focuses on the nurturance, structure, and assessment of creativity. Kaufman is the author or editor of books either published or in press, including *Creativity 101*, *Essentials of Creativity Assessment* (with Jonathan Plucker and John Baer), *International Handbook of Creativity* (with Robert J. Sternberg), and *Applied Intelligence* (with Robert J. Sternberg and Elena Grigorenko). His research has been featured on CNN, NPR, and the BBC and in the *New York Times* and *New Yorker*. Kaufman is a founding co-editor of the official journal for the American Psychological Association's Division 10, *Psychology of Aesthetics, Creativity, and the Arts*. He is also the editor of *International Journal of Creativity and Problem Solving* and the associate editor of both *Psychological Assessment* and *Journal of Creativity Behavior*. He is the series editor of the Psych 101 series. He received the 2003 Daniel E. Berlyne Award from APA's Division 10, the 2008 E. Paul Torrance Award from the National Association of Gifted Children, and the 2009 Western Psychological Association Early Career Award.

The Psychology of Creative Writing

Edited by

Scott Barry Kaufman
Yale University

James C. Kaufman
California State University at San Bernardino

CAMBRIDGE UNIVERSITY PRESS
Cambridge, New York, Melbourne, Madrid, Cape Town, Singapore, São Paulo, Delhi

Cambridge University Press
32 Avenue of the Americas, New York, NY 10013-2473, USA

www.cambridge.org
Information on this title: www.cambridge.org/9780521707824

First published 2009

Printed in the United States of America

A catalog record for this publication is available from the British Library.

Library of Congress Cataloging in Publication data

The psychology of creative writing / edited by Scott Barry Kaufman, James C. Kaufman.
    p.   cm.
Includes bibliographical references and index.
ISBN 978-0-521-88164-7 – ISBN 978-0-521-70782-4 (pbk.)
1. Creative writing (Higher education) – Psychological aspects.   2. English language –
Rhetoric – Study and teaching – Psychological aspects.   3. Rhetoric and psychology.
I. Kaufman, Scott Barry, 1979–   II. Kaufman, James C.   III. Title.
PE1404.P77   2009
808′.0420711–dc22   2008051294

ISBN   978-0-521-88164-7 hardback
ISBN   978-0-521-70782-4 paperback

CONTENTS

CONTRIBUTORS

JOHN BAER
Memorial Hall
Rider University
Lawrenceville, NJ 08648
baer@rider.edu

MICHAEL V. BARRIOS
Department of Psychiatry
Yale University
105 Church Street
Guilford, CT 06437
michael.barrios@yale.edu

GENEVIEVE E. CHANDLER
School of Nursing
University of Massachusetts, Amherst
122 Skinner Hall
651 North Street
Amherst, MA 01003
gec@nursing.umass.edu

JAMES C. KAUFMAN
Department of Psychology
California State University at San
    Bernardino
5500 University Parkway
San Bernardino, CA 92407
jkaufman@csusb.edu

SCOTT BARRY KAUFMAN
Department of Psychology
Yale University

PO Box 208205
New Haven, CT 05620
scott.kaufman@yale.edu

ADÈLE KOHANYI
Psychology Department
Kwantlen Polytechnic University
12666 – 72nd Avenue
Surrey, B.C. Canada
V3W 2M8
adele.kohanyi@kwantlen.ca

AARON KOZBELT
Brooklyn College of the City
    University of New York
2900 Bedford Avenue
Brooklyn, NY 11210
AaronK@brooklyn.cuny.edu

E. THOMAS LAWSON
Institute of Cognition and Culture
School of History and Anthropology
Queen's University of Belfast
Belfast BT 7 1NN
Northern Ireland, UK
t.lawson@qub.ac.uk

MARTIN S. LINDAUER
College at Brockport, State University
    of New York
311 Oak Court
Daly City, CA 94014
mblindauer@earthlink.net

TODD LUBART
Université Paris Descartes
Institut de Psychologie
71 Avenue Edouard Vaillant
92100 Boulogne Billancourt Cedex
France
todd.lubart@univ-paris5.fr

DAVID JUNG McGARVA
Saybrook Graduate School
747 Front Street
San Francisco, CA 94111
dmcgarva@davidmcgarva.com

SHARON S. McKOOL
Department of Teacher Education
Rider University
2083 Lawrenceville Road
Lawrenceville, NJ 08648
smckool@rider.edu

DANIEL NETTLE
Centre for Behaviour and
   Evolution
Institute of Neuroscience
Henry Wellcome Building
Newcastle NE2 4HH, UK
daniel.nettle@ncl.ac.uk

JAMES W. PENNEBAKER
Department of Psychology A8000
University of Texas at Austin
1 University Station
Austin, TX 78712
Pennebaker@mail.utexas.edu

SUSAN K. PERRY
Los Angeles, CA
Susan@bunnyape.com

JANE PIIRTO
Ashland University
247 Dwight Schar College of
   Education
Ashland, OH 44805
jpiirto@ashland.edu

JONATHAN A. PLUCKER
Center for Evaluation & Education
   Policy
Indiana University
1900 East Tenth Street
Bloomington, IN 47406
jplucker@indiana.edu

SAMANEH POURJALALI
California State University at San
   Bernardino
Department of Psychology
5500 University Parkway
San Bernardino, CA 92407
pourjals@csusb.edu

STEVEN R. PRITZKER
Saybrook Graduate School
747 Front Street
San Francisco, CA 94111
spritzker@saybrook.edu

MARK A. RUNCO
Norwegian School of Economics and
   Business Administration
University of Georgia
323 Aderhold Hall
Athens, GA 30602
runco@uga.edu

SANDRA W. RUSS
Department of Psychology
Case Western Reserve University
Mather Memorial Building
Cleveland, OH 44106
sandra.russ@case.edu

R. KEITH SAWYER
Department of Education
Washington University
Campus Box 1183
St. Louis, MO 63130
ksawyer@wustl.edu

PAT SCHNEIDER
Theological Union

77 McClellan Street
Amherst, MA 01002
pat@amherstwriters.com

JANEL D. SEXTON
Department of Anesthesia and Critical
  Care Medicine Quality and Safety
  Research Group
The Johns Hopkins University School
  of Medicine
1909 Thames Street, Suite 200
Baltimore, MD 21231
janel@jhmi.edu

DEAN KEITH SIMONTON
Department of Psychology
University of California, Davis
One Shields Avenue
Davis, CA 95618
dksimonton@ucdavis.edu

JEROME L. SINGER
Department of Psychology
Yale University
PO Box 208205
New Haven, CT 05620
Jerome.Singer@yale.edu

E. M. SKRZYNECKY
Department of Psychology

California State University at San
  Bernardino
5500 University Parkway
San Bernardino, CA 92407

ROBERT J. STERNBERG
Tufts University
Ballou Hall, 3rd Floor
Medford, MA 02155
robert.sternberg@tufts.edu

AI-GIRL TAN
Department of Psychology
University of Munich
Martiusstr. 4, 80802
Munich, Germany
aigirl.tan@nie.edu.sg

GRACE R. WAITMAN
English Department
Washington University in St. Louis
1 Brookings Drive
St. Louis, MO 63130
gwaitman@indiana.edu

THOMAS B. WARD
Department of Psychology
University of Alabama
Box 870348
Tuscaloosa, AL 35487
tward@bama.ua.edu

FOREWORD

ROBERT J. STERNBERG

For many years, writing skills were treated as the ugly stepsister of reading skills. Tests of "verbal aptitude" and "verbal ability" comprised assessments of vocabulary, reading comprehension, and verbal reasoning. Writing was nowhere to be found. Even achievement tests of "English composition" created by the College Board often had no actual writing whatsoever. Although Louis Thurstone distinguished between verbal comprehension and verbal fluency in his early theory of primary mental abilities, the former has been widely measured, the latter only rarely. And when the latter was measured, it was typically by tests requiring writing at a basic level, such as writing down as many words beginning with a certain letter as an examinee could think of in a specific time period.

In 2008, as I am writing this foreword, the situation in practice has improved slightly. For example, the SAT Reasoning Test (as it is now called, after many name changes) includes a writing section, although it is so formulaic in its conceptualization and scoring that it is not clear how much it measures writing in a more creative sense. And educators are increasingly recognizing the importance of writing for success not only in school but also in later life. Writing has always been much harder to study and measure than reading, because it does not lend itself nicely to multiple-choice or other objective forms of scoring. But psychologists and others are rising to the challenge, as shown by the present book. And I am delighted and proud that the two psychologists who edited *The Psychology of Creative Writing* are both former graduate students of mine.

Creativity has been relatively little studied in psychology, creative writing even less so. It is hard to study. First, whereas participants can sit down at pretty much any time and answer reading comprehension questions or solve mathematics problems, they cannot do the same for creative writing: Sometimes the ideas just do not come! Second, it is hard to assess creativity. Third, the study of creative writing is interdisciplinary, involving cognitive, social, personality, and biological aspects of psychology – and phenomena that best lend themselves to interdisciplinary approaches are often the last to be studied, if only because no one person or team typically has the expertise to study the phenomena as a whole. Yet understanding creative writing is essential not only to psychology but to all of the humanities and many of the social sciences, most notably, psychology.

In the psychology of verbal processing, there are various levels of analysis, two of which are particularly salient. One is the study of what one might call the micro-processing of verbal material. In the study of reading, this would include how one processes phonetic information and decodes words. In the study of writing, it would include how one strings together words to form grammatical and meaningful sentences. Of course, even this micro level can be subdivided, but the main focus is on how writing is even possible in the first place. The other level is the study of what one might call the macro-processing of verbal material. In the study of reading, this would include how one understands a story or an essay. In the study of writing, this level would include how one writes a story or essay. The focus of this book is on the macro level of understanding writing, and the book limits itself to the creative side of writing.

The book is catholic in its approach to creative writing. Some of the chapters deal with the psychological processes involved in writing. Others deal with social processes, such as writing as a collaborative enterprise or how rewards can affect the creative writing process. Still others deal with the personalities of creative writers or how writing can help one's psychological state. The kinds of writing reviewed vary widely: from Shakespeare to screenwriters to the everyday writing we may all do as we face the tasks confronting us in our day-to-day lives.

Many themes run throughout this book. In a brief foreword, I cannot possibly cover them all. But I would like to mention one – namely, that many people become creative writers not by virtue of their education, but in spite of it. Indeed, many career creative writers showed no particular promise to be great writers in their school careers. Even when schools or assessments place some emphasis on writing, it is often the kind of writing that is largely expository and in which one is evaluated in terms of how well one meets the mechanical requirements of writing, rather than its creative ones.

If there is a single message to this book, I believe it is that schools need to place more emphasis on the creative side of writing (and everything else), and that in doing so, they will produce not only more creative writers but also people who are more creative as they go about their lives. Creativity is largely an attitude toward life. Creative people are those who are more willing to redefine the ways in which they look at problems, to take risks, to seek to overcome daunting obstacles, and to tolerate ambiguity even when its existence becomes psychologically painful. Teaching students how to write creatively helps teach them how to approach life in a creative way.

We live in a time of great challenges, in which the formulas of the past often fail when applied to the present. Indeed, as I write this foreword, Wall Street and much of the U.S. financial system are in a sort of meltdown the likes of which perhaps have not been seen since the Great Depression. If there ever has been a time for the encouragement of creativity in writing and thought, this is it. This book, I hope, will help lead us, as a society, toward that recognition. Arguably, with daunting threats to our survival as a species, our time for recognizing the importance of a creative approach to life is running out. We can only be grateful for books that celebrate the importance of creativity to our existence and survival.

PREFACE

> We laymen have always been curious to know... from what source that
> strange being, the creative writer, draws his material, and how he manages
> to make such an impression on us with it.
>
> — Freud (1908)

Who is this strange being that is the creative writer? How can we understand
the person behind the creative writer or what process a person may take to
write creatively? Can we use this knowledge to nurture aspiring creative writers
and even enhance the writing of already established creative writers? In *The
Psychology of Creative Writing*, we offer 20 chapters by top scholars musing on
the key components of creativity writing: the writer, the text, the process, the
development, and the education. These insights are bookended by our own
analyses and thoughts.

We have both been fascinated by creative writing and creative writers for as
long as we can remember. As a child, Scott would often peer into other worlds,
either through writing stories about time travel or reading science fiction such
as the Xanth series by Piers Anthony. Today, he works on stand-up comedy
writing whenever he has the time, and he tries to sneak away from his work
whenever he can to open up a psychological thriller or science fiction novel
and escape into another time and place.

As for James, he always wanted to be a writer – he was writing stories
by the fourth grade, always under the watchful eye of his first mentor, his
mother. He continued to write, becoming a sports journalist at age 14 for local
newspapers and slowly publishing his attempts at poetry, stories, humor, and
essays in a wide variety of tiny magazines and journals. In college he studied
under the famed novelist T. Coraghessan Boyle and realized he should find a
day job. Continuing to write plays and musicals to this day (and with the very
good fortune to see them often performed off-off-Broadway and around the
world), James initially began studying creativity itself as a way to understand
the creative writer.

We are not the only ones to harbor such fascination. A search on creative writers in PsycINFO returns 755 results; searches on creative mathematicians and creative painters return 58 and 97, respectively. In a world in which celebrities come and go like exploding supernovas, the writer has remained a constant. Stephen King, John Grisham, and J. K. Rawling have been stars for decades, with no sign of abatement. Literary giants (Joyce Carol Oates, the late John Updike, Margaret Atwood, Toni Morrison, Philip Roth) continue to be published and be discovered.

Perhaps because of this fascination with the creative writer as an individual, the first part of the book ("The Writer") is also the longest. Jane Piirto tackles the personalities of creative writers. Samaneh Pourjalali, E. M. Skrzynecky, and James C. Kaufman discuss the complex relationship among the creative writer, locus of control, and the tendency to dysphorically ruminate. Adèle Kohanyi takes on the related question of how mood variability and regulation affect different writers. Steven R. Pritzker and David McGarva write about eminent screenwriters; indeed, in addition to his accomplishments in psychology, Pritzker is a well-known screenwriter himself and has worked on such television shows as *The Mary Tyler Moore Show* and *Silver Spoons*. Finally, Scott Barry Kaufman and Aaron Kozbelt offer insight into the psychological characteristics of comedy writers.

In the second part of the book, "The Text," we begin with a chapter by Daniel Nettle on the evolution of creative writing. Martin S. Lindauer then argues for the importance of physiognomy, in which investigating the text itself can yield insights into a writer's thought process. Finally, Dean Keith Simonton analyzes the work of perhaps the best-known writer of all time, William Shakespeare.

The third part focuses on "The Process." Todd Lubart takes a delightful look at the creative process through the eyes of a certain young fictional girl named Alice. R. Keith Sawyer, known for his work on group creativity, applies that same lens to writing as a collaborative act. Mark A. Runco takes a broad look at many facets of writing and how these facets interact with many different ideas. Finally, Thomas B. Ward and E. Thomas Lawson offer a treat for science fiction/fantasy fans as they look at the role of creative cognition in this genre.

In the fourth part, our scholars focus on "The Development" of both the creative writer and creative writing. Susan K. Perry describes what it is like to write in flow, based on hundreds of interviews with eminent writers. Jerome L. Singer and Michael V. Barrios discuss perhaps the bane of a writer's existence – writer's block – and strategies for getting creativity kick-started again. Sandra W. Russ discusses how pretend play and emotional processes can play a role in developing narrative writing. Finally, Janel D. Sexton and James W. Pennebaker share their research on the curative powers of expressive writing (which serves as an alternate perspective to some of the chapters in the first section about creative writing and poor mental health).

In the fifth and final part, "The Education," we shift our focus to the classroom. John Baer and Sharon S. McKool describe two of the top creativity killers, rewards and evaluations, and propose ways to maintain a healthy enjoyment of creative writing. Grace R. Waitman and Jonathan A. Plucker share some of the myths of creativity, arguing that a successful approach to teaching writing could start by shattering some of these myths. Genevieve E. Chandler and Pat Schneider describe the Amherst Writers & Artists method of teaching creative writing, which has been applied to a number of nonartist populations. Finally, Ai-Girl Tan offers a cross-cultural spin on this topic by discussing ways of learning to write creatively in Chinese classrooms.

We are honored to have a foreword by Robert J. Sternberg, one of the true visionaries in creativity research and a mentor to both of us, to begin this collection. We have also written a final chapter that integrates and synthesizes the many suggestions and ideas proposed throughout the chapters.

We hope that, by bringing together the insights and research of these exemplary psychologists, this book will serve as a resource for many people. Certainly, psychologists who study creativity, writing, and creative writing may be the most obvious audience. But we hope that writers themselves – novelists, poets, playwrights, journalists, essayists, and bloggers – will find much to ponder (and, perhaps, disagree with) in the pages that follow. We also hope that people interested in writing can open the book to any chapter and find a discussion that introduces a new idea to ponder.

Scott Barry Kaufman
James C. Kaufman

ACKNOWLEDGMENTS

We would like to first thank our editors at Cambridge who shepherded this project through fruition, Eric Schwartz and Simina Calin. We would also like to thank Jeanie Lee for her tireless and cheerful work on this project; project manager Brigitte Coulton and copyeditor Gail Naron Chalew for a fantastic job; Thomas Neises for his assistance; and a terrific team of indexers led by David Loomis and including Ryan Holt and Anthony Sierra.

We appreciate the insight and help of Lori Handelman, Allison Kaufman, Paul Locher, and Genet Tulgetske.

We have both been lucky enough to be mentored by Robert J. Sternberg, who graciously wrote the foreword to this book. His support and accomplishments continue to inspire us both.

Jerome L. Singer was on both of our doctoral committees, and his imagination, wit, and joy for life are a constant delight.

We are continually inspired by our colleagues in the field of creativity research; we are also both especially invigorated by the stellar research and writing of a new generation of creativity scholars such as Ron Beghetto, Zorana Ivcevic, Aaron Kozbelt, and Paul Silvia (among many others).

Scott would like to thank his very supportive and wonderful friends: Elliot Paul (his twin brother from another mother, a man with a great mind and a big heart), Dr. Benjamin Irvine of jolly ol' England (thanks for the many stimulating conversations and fun times!), Eugene Ford, Markus LaBooty, Nienke Venderbosch, Brent Kyle, Jennifer DiMase, Louisa Egan, Candida Moss, Elise Christopher, Alia Crum, Yoona Kang, Adam Green, Bret Logan, Dave Roberts, Hillary Ruhl Dueñas, Erin Coulter, Justin Khoo, Mark Gerban, Avi Kouzi, Jamie Brown, and Balazs Aczar. He also owes a huge debt of gratitude to his terrific collaborators: James Kaufman (a constant mentor and friend, as well as his other twin brother from another mother), Colin DeYoung, Glenn Geher, Jean Pretz, and Luis Jiménez. As for his lifelong mentors, warm appreciation goes to Anne Fay and Nicholas Mackintosh for their continual guidance. Thanks to the late Herbert Simon for mentoring and inspiring him as an undergraduate and to Jeremy Gray for giving him a home at Yale. Cheers to his high school teachers Mary Acton, Regina Gordon, Tom Elliot, and Debra Hobbs for their fine teaching and warm encouragement and Mr. O for his stimulating and fun creative writing class.

And last, but certainly not least, acknowledgments go to his family. Thanks to his grandfather Harry Gorodetzer for showing him the importance of practice and sharing the cello with him (the most beautiful instrument in the world), his grandmother Jeanette Robbins Gorodetzer for the bear hugs, his Bubba for the warmth, and his Zeda for the toys. Scott's biggest acknowledgment and gratitude go to his parents, Barbara and Michael – thanks for encouraging all of his varied, sometimes zany creative pursuits and writings (remember *Roborky's Statue*?). Without their encouragement, love, and guidance, this book would hardly have been possible.

James would like to thank his many psychology mentors – those above and John Baer, Jeff and Lisa Smith, and Jonathan Plucker and his CSUSB colleagues (especially Mark Agars, Susan Daniels, Michelle Ebert Freire, and Allen Butt; chair Robert Cramer; and administrators Jean Peacock, Joanna Worthley, Jamal Nassar, Louis Fernandez, and Al Karnig). He would also like to thank his inner circle of friends – especially Nate, Amy, and Zachary Stone; Joshua Butler; and David, Aviva, and Jonah Hecht – and his family – the Bengels clan (especially Dennis and Barbara, Emily, and Jessica); Joseph, Jean, and Cindy Katz; Milissa, Matt, Josiah, and Mikaela Kaufman; Kate Singleton; Nicole Hendrix; Jennie, Mitch, Brianna, and Leo Singer; Alan and Nadeen Kaufman; and his wife, Allison, and son, Jacob.

PART I

THE WRITER

1

The Personalities of Creative Writers

JANE PIIRTO

Popular images of male novelists and poets show them professorially clad, in khakis or in tweed sport coats with leather patches on the arms, smoking pipes; or, as in the image of writers like Ernest Hemingway or Jim Harrison, cradling rifles or fly-fishing, wearing horn-rimmed glasses or swaggering beneath cowboy hats: They are writing from the ivory tower or writing from the field of battle. These two disparate images are, as we shall see, somewhat true. And what about the female writer? She is clad in mannish clothes, her hair cut in a butch, braless and strident, living with her male and female lovers in the Bohemian garrets of a large city; or she is whimsically virginal and intense, her long, tangled and flowing hair entwined with rosettes of wild flowers just picked, sitting in a meadow, her long delicate fingers slowly turning the pages of a leather-bound book with a ribbon for a marker. As we shall see, the personalities these images imply are also somewhat true.

Creative people are those who do creative acts. The creativity occurs in the becoming, the making. In the struggle to be creative, personality attributes are extremely important. Creative people seem to have certain core personality attributes. I have made personality attributes the base of my Piirto Piiramid of Talent Development (see Figure 1.1).

Many studies have emphasized that successful creators in all domains have certain personality attributes in common (cf. Feist, 1999). These attributes make up the base of the model and rest on the foundation of genes. Among these are the following: androgyny (Barron, 1968a; Csikszentmihalyi, Rathunde, & Whalen, 1993; Piirto & Fraas, 1995; Piirto & Johnson, 2004); creativity (Renzulli, 1978; Tannenbaum, 1983); imagination (Dewey, 1934; Langer, 1957; Plato, 1952; Prescott, 1920; Santayana, 1896); insight (Runco, 2006; Sternberg & Davidson, 1995); intuition (Barron, 1968a, 1968b, 1995; Myers & McCaulley, 1985; Piirto & Johnson, 2004); introversion (Cross, Speirs Neumeister, & Cassady, 2007; Myers & McCaulley, 1985; Piirto & Johnson, 2004; Simonton, 1999); naiveté, or openness to experience (Cattell, 1971, 1990; Ghiselin, 1952); overexcitabilities (Dabrowski, 1965; Piechowski, 2006, Piirto, Montgomery, &

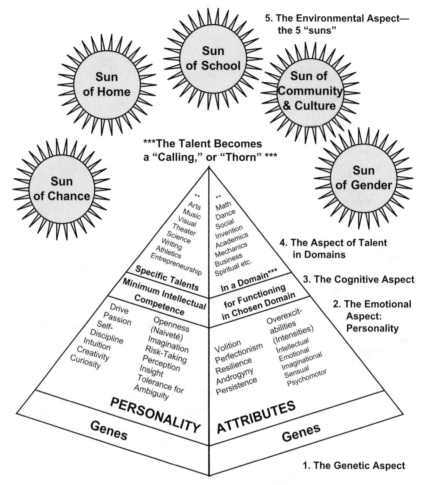

Figure 1.1. The Piirto Piiramid of Talent Development. ©Jane Piirto, 1993. All rights reserved.

May, 2008); motivation, or passion for work in a domain (Barron, 1968a, 1995; Bloom, 1985); perceptiveness (Myers & McCaulley 1985); persistence (Rayneri, Gerber, & Wiley, 2003; Renzulli, 1978); preference for complexity (Barron, 1995); resilience (Block & Kremen, 1996; Jenkins-Friedman, 1992; Renzulli 1978); risk taking (MacKinnon, 1978; Torrance, 1987); self-discipline (Piirto, 2004); self-efficacy (Sternberg & Lubart, 1992; Zimmerman, Bandura, & Martinez-Pons 1992); tolerance for ambiguity (Barron, 1968a, 1995); and volition, or will (Corno & Kanfer, 1993; Simonton, 1999).

This list is by no means discrete or complete, but shows that creative adults achieve effectiveness partially by force of personality. Talented adults who achieve success possess many of these attributes.

Personality is an area in which there are many competing theories. Personality theory can be psychoanalytic (ego psychology, object relations, transpersonalism); behavioral or cognitive (quantitative studies using factor analysis such as those of Cattell [1990] and Eysenck [1993]); or humanistic (using phenomenology, existentialism, Gestalt, humanistic, and transpersonal theories). Personality is sometimes equated with character and seen as directing how one lives one's life. The personality attributes mentioned here have been determined by empirical studies of creative producers, mostly adults, but in some cases, adolescents in special schools and programs were studied. Some research has indicated an evolutionary cause of personality preferences (Feist, 2007). Many studies of personality attributes have used the Myers-Briggs Type Indicator, based on the Jungian theory of personality. The Cattell 16 Personality Factors, the Eysenck Inventory, the Gough Creative Personality Inventory, the California Psychological Inventory, the Minnesota Multiphasic Psychological Inventory, and others have also been used in studies cited here.

The consolidation of personality traits into the Big Five through factor analysis (Costa & McCrae, 1992; McCrae & Costa, 1999) is noted here, but earlier work on creative people has noted these other traits listed earlier, and so I include the others as well. These were analyzed through what is called the "lexical tradition" (Costa & McCrae, 1992, p. 14) by researchers such as Cattell (1971). The Revised NEO Personality Inventory (NEO-PI-R) combines factors into facets and then into five domains: Neuroticism (N), Extraversion (E), Openness (O), Agreeableness (A), and Conscientiousness (C). It seems that the domain of openness to experience (O) includes creative attributes: Fantasy (O1), Aesthetics (O2), Feelings (O3), Actions (O4), Ideas (O5), and Values (O6). "Open individuals are unconventional, willing to question authority, and prepared to entertain new ethical, social, and political ideas" (Costa & McCrae, 1992, p. 15). However, other personality attributes on this instrument may also apply to writers; for example, Tender-Mindedness (A6), and, in the case of writers, Depression (N3). This is just speculation, and no known data exist on writers who have been assessed with this instrument; that is research yet to be conducted.

The creative writer can be considered to have these generic personality attributes found in creators, as well as others. This chapter discusses the personality attributes that writers seem to show. Those attributes on the base of the Piirto Piiramid of Talent Development referred to earlier, those that are generic, and those that also seem to appear in creative writers have been discussed in Chapter 2 of Piirto (2002) and are not discussed further here.

Numerous studies have come from the Institute for Personality Assessment and Research (IPAR), which was established after World War II at the University of California in Berkeley. MacKinnon (1978) directed IPAR, after serving on the assessment staff of the Office of Special Services, the forerunner of the CIA. In 1949 the Rockefeller Foundation, Carnegie Corporation, and Ford Foundation granted funds to start IPAR for the purpose of determining which people were most highly effective and what made them that way (Barron, 1963). Among the people studied were writers, architects, engineering

students, women mathematicians, inventors, and research scientists. The people studied were chosen by peer nomination; that is, the nominators were
college professors, professionals in the field, and respected experts or connoisseurs knowledgeable about the field. Among the researchers there were
Frank Barron, Donald MacKinnon, Harrison Gough, Ravenna Helson, Donald
Crutchfield, and Erik Erikson (Helson, 1999).

At IPAR, Frank Barron and his colleagues asked literature and drama professors at the University of California for the names of the most creative among
outstanding creative writers then writing (Barron, 1968a, 1968b, 1969, 1972,
1995). They came up with a list of 56 writers, who were invited to come to the
University of California to participate in extensive testing and interviewing.
These studies pioneered some of the tests and interview techniques still used
in studying human personality attributes and characteristics; for example, the
Q-sort method of interviewing and the Barron-Welsh Art Scale for evaluating
works of art. Some of the writers who came to campus were Truman Capote,
Frank O'Connor, Muriel Rukeyser, William Carlos Williams, MacKinlay
Kantor, Jessamyn West, A. B. Guthrie Jr., Andrew Lytle, Robert Duncan, Bill
Mauldin, and Kenneth Rexroth. Tests and interviews were conducted off campus with such writers as Norman Mailer, W. H. Auden, Marianne Moore,
Michael McClure, Arthur Koestler, and Sean O'Faolain. Also among these
writers who came to be tested was Saul Bellow, who told George Garrett about
being paid $10,000 to go to Berkeley and take psychological tests. Bellow said,
"They had Capote there, too – and what they ended up with was the feeling that
writers had more willpower.... And if that's all, it doesn't tell you anything,
except maybe that discipline helps" (quoted in Neubauer, 1994, p. 120).

Barron (1995), in describing this testing, wrote, "It was a painful and
taxing responsibility to ask these writers, many of whom had suffered much
in their own creative lives, to probe deeply into themselves and to answer the
questions... seemingly irrelevant and unworthy questions" (p. 183). The IPAR
studies were seminal in the research on writers.

WHAT PERSONALITY TESTS SHOW

There also exists information on the personalities of creative writers from personality tests developed by psychologists and psychoanalysts. Two of my own
small studies using the Myers-Briggs Type Indicator (MBTI) and the Overexcitabilities Questionnaire (OEQ) are discussed here (Piirto, 1978, 1995, 1998b).

The Myers-Briggs Type Indicator

The Myers-Briggs Type Indicator (MBTI) has been used to determine the
Jungian-based type preferences of many occupational groups, including scientists, artists, laborers, writers, and counselors. Creativity studies done using

the MBTI were done in conjunction with the other studies done at IPAR. Many writers preferred the N (Intuitive) and the P (Perceptive).

I administered the MBTI to a group of 15 successful women writers and to a comparison group of 15 female elementary school teachers. Two strong patterns emerged. In agreement with the IPAR data, most of the writers preferred Intuition (N) and Perception (P). As Myers and McCaulley said, "Data from the world is received in ways that go beyond the senses and that they preferred to see patterns, relationships, and meaning in all they perceive" (1985, p. 135). Seventy-five percent of the women writers preferred the NF (Intuition Feeling or NT (Intuition Thinking) combination, in contrast to only 20% of the comparison group of elementary school teachers. Instead, like most elementary teachers, the comparison group of teachers preferred the SF combination (Sensing and Feeling; Piirto, 1998c). Women in the general population are more likely to prefer Feeling than Thinking, and that is why the instrument itself has separate templates for males and females when scoring those preferences (also see Myers & McCaulley, 1985); this was true for the comparison group as well as for the women writers.

My research confirms what was found by Barron (1968a), who indicated that the writers he studied also preferred Feeling and Intuition: The writers were "distinctly more introverted than extraverted, more feeling than thinking, and more intuitive than oriented to sense experience" (pp. 237, 245). Since the IPAR study included more men than women writers, the results here show that there seem to be no great gender differences in personality type preferences, indicating that the "sun" of gender may be environmental, as postulated in my Piiramid of Talent Development (see Figure 1.1).

Overexcitability Questionnaire (OEQ)

I also published (Piirto, 2002; Piirto, in press) the transcripts of the OEQ for three male writers: a poet, a prose writer, and a playwright. The scores on these questionnaires indicated they had the highest levels of imaginational, intellectual, and emotional overexcitability.

PERSONALITY ATTRIBUTES OF WRITERS

This section discusses the following personality attributes of writers that may or may not be present in other creative people who practice their creativity in other fields or domains: (1) ambition/envy, (2) concern with philosophical matters, (3) frankness often expressed in political or social activism, (4) psychopathology, (5) depression, (6) empathy, and (7) a sense of humor. Examples are taken from anecdotes from the lives of writers. The methodology was qualitative, and the material comes from published interviews, memoirs, and biographies. Much of this was first published in Piirto (2002). The criterion for a writer being included as an example was that he or she would or does qualify for listing in the *Directory of American Poets and Writers* (www.pw .org/directory/), which has a very high standard for inclusion. A writer needs to earn 12 points to be listed, with the points given as follows: each book of poetry, fiction, or creative nonfiction (personal essays or memoirs) = 12 points; each chapbook = 6 points; each work of fiction or creative nonfiction (personal essays or memoirs) published in a literary journal, anthology, or edited Web publication = 3 points; and each poem published in a literary journal, anthology, or edited Web publication = 2 points. Currently, only about 7,355 writers are listed, of whom about 4,000 are poets, 1,900 are fiction writers, 100 are performance writers, and the remainder (about 1,100) are listed as both poets and writers. Many studies of creative writers have not used such a standard, but may use self-description rather than peer review and literary publication record. I am a participant-observer in this regard, as I am listed as both a poet and a writer (e.g., see Piirto, 1985, 1995) in this *Directory*.

Ambition/Envy

Ambition and its doppelganger, envy, are not unknown among writers. For example, the writer T. Coraghessan Boyle said he wanted to be "the most famous writer alive and the greatest writer ever" (Friend, 1990, pp. 60–68). Other writers who, like Boyle, have studied at the famous Iowa Writers' Workshop have also asserted this ambition. The writer Jane Smiley, then a recent graduate of the University of Iowa with a PhD in medieval literature, told me the same thing late one August night in a darkened van on our way to the Bread Loaf Writers' Conference in 1977 when we were confessing our dreams and hopes. She has since gone on to win both the National Book Award and the Pulitzer Prize, steadily increasing her fame and writing with extreme discipline and passion.

Writers need ambition, as do other creative producers, but that ambition often produces horrible feelings of inadequacy and anxiety. This may be because of the intimate subject matter of the creative writer – the self or the self, coded. The high rate of rejection that creative writers experience when they try to publish their work may also contribute to the intense feelings of envy paired with intense ambition. Poet Molly Peacock made no apology for her ambition:

> From when I was a little girl I wanted to be an artist, and I said to myself, "Somehow I'm getting out of Buffalo, New York." I had a drive to get out of that house and that town. That takes ambition, and my ambition is located in that very early desire to succeed. Of course, you can't be published in *The New Yorker* without a drive to succeed. But also you can't be published in issue one, volume one, of a brand new, teeny-tiny

literary enterprise without a similar hunger for success. . . . Ambition is a fact of anyone's life who aspires to anything. (Friman & Templin, 1994, p. 41)

Coleridge, in the 19th century, also experienced the envy of other writers, indicating that this is not a new phenomenon. In describing the reception of his poem, "Christabel," he said, "Three years ago I did not know or believe that I had no enemy in the world: and now even my strongest sensations of gratitude are mingled with fear, and I . . . ask – Have I one friend?" (Coleridge, 1872, p. 680). He described that he was begged to recite the work at many social gatherings and urged to publish it. "Since then, with very few exceptions, I have heard nothing but abuse, and this too in a spirit of bitterness."

The shadow side of the drive and resilience it takes to continue in the creative writing profession is the envy that one feels at the success of others. Envy can paralyze, but it can also serve to motivate. Friedman (1994) called envy "the writer's disease" (p. 5). She wrote, "It's desire that causes envy. Isn't desire the villain here? Yet how to be an artist without desire." Writers project that other writers are happy, successful, famous, and admired, and in so doing they give part of themselves away to the power of the extrinsic. How much praise and adulation is enough? Louis Simpson (1972) noted that friendships between writers do not seem to have longevity: "They become resentful of criticism and think that the other person is trying to do them in, or they become jealous of his success" (p. 175). Cynthia Ozick in her *Paris Review* interview described how she thought she would be Henry James by the age of 25, and then when that did not happen, she began to take note of those who were getting famous. Envy began to cut into her soul (Teicholz, 1989). She even wrote a short story called "Envy" (Ozick, 1971) in which a Yiddish writer is consumed by envy of the achievements of other writers who are able to write in English.

Other causes for envy exist. Many well-known writers teach at universities. Poet Jean Valentine described being so envious of her talented students that she quit teaching: "My students would come in with these wonderful poems, and I was jealous. I wasn't writing anything" (Bland, 2004, p. 51). Another cause of envy comes from wondering about one's legacy as a writer. Hemingway was famous for his jealousy of his contemporaries, but he also had a need to triumph over his predecessors: In Lynn's biography (1988), he is quoted as saying, "I started out very quiet and I beat Mr. Turgenev. Then I trained hard and I beat Mr. de Maupassant. I've fought two draws with Mr. Stendahl. . . . But nobody's going to get me in any ring with Mr. Tolstoy unless I'm crazy or I keep getting better" (p. 549). The rivalry and off-again, on-again friendship between poets James Dickey and Robert Bly during the 1960s led to a series of public statements about each other's patriotism during the protests about the

Vietnam War, but their friendship had always been fraught with envy as one and then the other ascended on the college reading circuit of the 1960s and 1970s (Hart, 2000). Both went on to popular success, Dickey with *Deliverance*, Bly with *Iron John*, but their differences remained.

Concern with Philosophical Issues: Aesthetics and Ethics

Ethically and morally, many writers seem to be concerned with the meaning of life and with the search for truth and beauty. They seem particularly concerned about behaving in an ethically consistent fashion. Supposedly this is the lofty purpose of literature, and that writers search for truth and beauty is not surprising. From Shelley's assertion of "beauty is truth, truth beauty," the purpose of literature has been put forth as a way to morally explicate and uphold human values.

Three examples follow. Poet Octavio Paz said, "Ever since I was an adolescent I've been intrigued with the mystery of freedom" (MacAdam, 1991, p. 103). This search for truth begins young. Yeats described himself at art school in London this way: "I was constantly troubled about philosophic questions" (Yeats, 1953, p. 53). He would tell his friends that the purpose of poetry and sculpture was to "keep our passions alive," and his friends would say that people would be better off without passions. He spent a week worrying about this problem: "Do the arts make us happier, or more sensitive and therefore more unhappy?" When he talked about these concerns to his friends, they would treat him with wry and paternalistic irony. Writer Joan Didion said, "I can recall disapproving of the golden mean, always thinking there was more to be learned from the dark journey. The dark journey engages me more" (Kuehl, 1978, p. 335).

In creative writing, the philosophical concern with the meaning of life is melded with the psychological concern with what makes human beings tick, and the two are explicated through dramatis personae in story or through the metaphors and images in verse. Material displaying the writer's concern with ethical, moral, and aesthetic matters is abundant. These were but a few examples.

Frankness that Is Often Expressed in Political or Social Activism

Writers attract the interest of others, probably because of their ability to say what they think. The Barron study (1968a, 1995) found through psychological testing and interviews that the writers were frank and needed to communicate their political views and were likely to take risks in doing so. Throughout history, the politics of writers seems to have been tended toward the pacifist, liberal, or left wing, no matter what era's issues they were reacting to. For example, 1991 National Book Award winner Norman Rush, a war resister to the Korean War, spent time in jail in the early 1950s where he wrote a novel that he hoped would be the beginning of a new genre, the "nonviolent thriller" (Rush, 1995, p. 219).

The writer may value freedom of expression more than the feelings of others. Writers throughout the world have often been the first to be thrown into jail or sent into exile for what they have written and said. The Russian writers Alexander Solzhenitsyn and Joseph Brodsky were sent to Siberia for what they wrote. The British writer Salman Rushdie was sentenced to death by the Ayatollah of Iran for his novel *Satanic Verses* and had to go into hiding in 1989, not emerging until 1998 when the political situation in Iran changed. The writers' organization, PEN, has a Freedom to Write Committee, which has a subcommittee called Writers in Prison, a watchdog group concerned about writers throughout the world who are persecuted for expressing themselves. Many of the "prisoners of conscience" throughout the world are writers. Writers Lillian Hellman and Dashiell Hammett, who were among those writers called before the House Un-American Activities Committee as suspected communist activists in the early 1950s, established grants administered through Human Rights Watch "to assist writers throughout the world who have been victims of political persecution." The organization publishes Action Alerts about writers who are detained. For example, the alert for June 2007 concerned the Russian journalist Vladimir Chugunov, who was captured by police and put into a psychiatric institution.

Most writers seem to be leftist or liberal. Nobel Prize winning Chilean poet and politician Pablo Neruda is an example of a writer exiled for his socialist convictions expressed in poems and essays. The award-winning movie *Il Postino* (1994) was a dramatic explication of the impact Neruda's poems and political beliefs had on a simple island man who delivered Neruda's mail while he was in exile in the early 1950s. Poets Robert Bly, Allen Ginsberg, Denise Levertov, Ted Berrigan, and others were leaders of the Vietnam antiwar movement in the United States, and Ginsberg tried to levitate the Pentagon at one notable protest meeting. At a less lofty level, young creative writers often publish frank underground newspapers that are the bane of their teachers and school administrators. "I was just telling the truth," they often say, surprised at the reactions of the authorities to their writing.

There is, though, a little diversity among writers in political and class beliefs. For example, the National Book Award nominee Mark Helprin is a senior fellow at the conservative Hudson Institute and was a speechwriter for Bob Dole in the 1996 presidential campaign. Helprin suggested that his minority status among writers (as a conservative Republican) has led to some censorship by bookstores and reading groups: "I've heard reports of bookstores that won't sell my books" (Schapiro, 1999). Writer John Irving and poet James Dickey were also rumored to be conservatives. Poet Howard McCord is a card-carrying member of the National Rifle Association.

Environmental activism expressed in frank remonstrance to polluters is also common among writers. The environmental concerns of such poets as Gary Snyder (2007), and Wendell Berry (2005) have gained much attention. Writer and poet Julia Butterfly Hill climbed a 1,000-year-old redwood tree in Humboldt, California, lived in its branches for 2 years, and wrote a memoir (Hill, 2001). She agreed to write the memoir only if the paper used was recycled and processed without bleach. She and other writers founded the Green Press Initiative, which advocates environmentally friendly printing and publishing practices.

In looking at published interviews, memoirs, and the like of contemporary writers, one often sees the frankness and social activism in the writers' assertions. Novelist Russell Banks stated that a writer must deal truthfully with what he sees: "One of the things I believe is that if you are a member of a society or culture that is racist and sexist – as ours is – and you don't offer an ongoing critique of that as part of your daily life, then you're inevitably going to end up participating in it" (Joyce, 1998). Norman Dubie, who grew up the son of a minister and a nurse, tried not to write political poems, but poems of witness. A Buddhist, he stopped writing in order to sit and meditate for 10 years, but he had to return to speaking. In 2004, he voiced this fear:

> I'm completely dismayed with the Bush administration and all the complicated ways in which the lives of real people are being ruined now and clearly, deep into the future.... God save us, he may get four more years, but I fear that terribly. If they get four more years, I think they'll try to reverse *Roe v. Wade*, and then all of our daughters are going to [take to] the streets. And all of a sudden, all those ungodly provisions of the Patriot Act are going to be used on our own children. (Gannon, 2004, p. 38)

Psychopathology

Some creative writers may be mad as well as angry. The personality tests that Barron (1963, 1968a, 1995) gave to the writers indicated that they showed many of the characteristics of manic-depressives and schizophrenics, but that their ego strength and intelligence were higher than the manic-depressives and schizophrenics. Creative writers were "markedly deviant" from the regular population, and the distinguished writers seemed to have tendencies to be schizoid, depressive, hysterical, or psychopathic and not to have rigid sex role expectations. Barron reported, "The writers appear to be both sicker and healthier psychologically than people in general.... The face they turn to the world is sometimes one of pain, often of protest, sometimes of distance and withdrawal, and certainly they are emotional" (Barron, 1968a, p. 244).

Jamison (1989), in a study of 39 British writers and 8 artists, found that 38% had been treated for affective illness, which is defined in the *Oxford English Dictionary* as "a condition (e.g., depression, mania) that affects the mood," whereas in the normal population less than 5% of people are treated for affective illness. The writers and artists also reported mental problems, including hospitalization, in their first-degree relatives to a greater extent than in the normal population Jamison said that psychiatrists should be cautious in their diagnoses and prescriptions of drugs as states of creativity are similar to those reported by people with mood disorders. The side effects of commonly prescribed drugs may damage the creative process. Several of the writers (17%) stopped taking lithium because of its deadening effects on their creative thinking.

Andreason (1987; Andreason & Canter, 1974) studied 27 male and 3 female faculty at the University of Iowa Writers' Workshop over a period of 15 years. She compared them with a group of hospital administrators, lawyers, social workers, and the like. The average age of both groups was 37 years. Bipolar manic-depressive affective disorder was found in 80% of the writers and in 30% of the comparison group, which itself had a higher than usual incidence of affective disorder. Two-thirds of the writers had sought psychiatric help. Two of the 30 writers committed suicide during the 15 years of the study. The verbal intelligence of the faculty members was no higher than that of the comparison group, about 125.

Andreason (1987) also studied the first-degree relatives of the writers and found that almost half also had occupations that emphasized creativity, such as teaching music or dance, though they may not have been in the writing field. This finding indicates that there may be a general creativity factor that is genetically transmitted.

Andreason had expected to find a higher incidence of schizophrenia among the writers, but instead she found manic-depression. The writers said they wrote during the long periods between episodes, rather than during the highs and lows characteristic of bipolar disorder. She noted, "Affective disorder may be both a 'hereditary taint' and a hereditary gift" (1987, p. 1292).

As an example, the poet Allen Ginsberg and his mother both experienced mental disorder. Early in his career, Ginsberg, suffering extreme self-doubt and almost arrested for burglary, checked himself into the New York Psychiatric Institute. (Incidentally, tests given at this time showed Ginsberg's IQ to be "near genius level," according to Miles, 1989.) Ginsberg's childhood in New Jersey had been odd, to say the least. His mother was a paranoid schizophrenic who was often institutionalized; Allen himself had to take her to the institution once. At home, she liked to be "natural," often striding around the house in the nude. Ginsberg's father was the well-known poet Louis Ginsberg, a teacher who tried to keep life somewhat normal for Allen and his brother. Ginsberg's moving 1961 poem "Kaddish" is an artistic revelation of his family's trials, an anguished expression of regret that when his mother died, insane in a mental hospital, they were not able to summon 10 Jewish men needed to say the Jewish prayer for the dead, the Kaddish (Ginsberg, 1984).

Psychoanalysts and psychologists have often stated that writers write because of deep-seated pathologies. From Sigmund Freud (1908/1976), who said that writers use their personal childhood fantasies; to E. Kris (1976) who said that writers write because of "regression in service of the ego"; to Albert Rothenberg (1990), who spoke of a Janusian two-faced process of creativity (in which he used case material from his psychiatric patients who were writers); to Jamison (1993), who detailed the family history of bipolar illness in writers; to Kaufman and Baer (2002), who noted that female poets were the most at risk for mental illness because of their inability to ignore the results of rejection and because writing poetry may exacerbate rather than heal mental problems, psychologists and psychiatrists have analyzed writers, searching for the "key" that will unlock the mystery of their creativity. Kaufman (2001) called it the "Sylvia Plath effect," evoking the tragic suicide of poet and novelist Sylvia Plath, wife of poet Ted Hughes, who later became British Poet Laureate. Hughes also suffered from depression, but did not attempt suicide, although the next woman in his life, Assia Wevill, also a writer, committed suicide and also killed their (probable) daughter (Feinstein, 2001).

The psychologist Leo Schneiderman (1988) suggested that William Faulkner wrote because of ego defects, including low self-esteem caused by an overprotective mother and a rejecting father; Lillian Hellman wrote out of narcissistic "chronic rage" that resulted from "material deprivation" (p. 42); Tennessee Williams wrote to compensate for his incestuous feelings toward his mother and sister; Flannery O'Connor wrote out of guilt for getting ill with lupus in her late twenties and being dependent on her mother during adulthood; John Cheever wrote because of the "early withdrawal of parental empathy" (p. 124); Vladimir Nabokov wrote out of a longing for his presexual days; Jorge Luis Borges wrote because of oncoming blindness and his shame after a series of crises in his family's fortunes in Buenos Aires; Samuel Beckett wrote out of a "character disorder marked by extreme rigidity and self-centeredness" (p. 163); and the playwright Harold Pinter wrote out of "regression to a past that was as emotionally deprived as is the present" (p. 205). Schneiderman concluded, "Great literary art is a synthesis of technical skill with tremendous fear, rage, or other powerful emotions, and . . . the fundamental character of great writers reveals significant failure along developmental lines, that is, a basic lack of maturity" (Schneiderman, 1988, p. 207).

Jamison (1993) made a diagram of the genealogies and documented manic-depressive illness in the first-degree relatives of these writers: Alfred Lord Tennyson; Henry, Alice, and William James; Herman Melville; Samuel Taylor Coleridge; Virginia Woolf; Ernest Hemingway; and Mary Wollstonecraft and her daughter Mary Shelley. Hans Christian Andersen, Honoré de Balzac, James Barrie, James Boswell, John Bunyan, Mark Twain, Joseph Conrad, Charles Dickens, Isak Dinesen, Ralph Waldo Emerson, William Faulkner, F. Scott Fitzerald, Nikolai Gogol, Maxim Gorky, Kenneth Grahame, Ernest Hemingway, Hermann Hesse, Henrik Ibsen, William Inge, Henry James,

William James, Charles Lamb, Malcolm Lowry, Antonin Artaud, Charles Baudelaire, John Berryman, William Blake, Louise Bogan, Rupert Brooke, Robert Burns, George Gordon, Lord Byron, Paul Celan, Thomas Chatterton, Samuel Taylor Coleridge, William Collins, William Cowper, Hart Crane, Emily Dickinson, T. S. Eliot, Anne Finch, Oliver Goldsmith, Thomas Gray, Gerard Manley Hopkins, Randall Jarrell, and many others. Poets were especially struck with such illness. She found family illness in many of these writers and poets, but not all of them. And, of course, given the times, the diagnoses could not have been made for all of them.

Depression

Forget full-blown psychopathology. How about good, old-fashioned depression that is perhaps not of the bipolar type? Examples of depression in creative writers abound, as witness the myriads of memoirs now being written that detail depression's effects. Burroughs (2002, 2003) traced his poet mother's depressions and, in further works, his own, along with his struggles with alcoholism. A 2006 movie based on his first memoir, *Running with Scissors*, featured Annette Bening uncannily channeling the poet mother. Evocative titles such as *Where the Roots Reach the Water* (Smith, 1999) and *In the Jaws of the Black Dog* (Mays, 1995) speak to the eloquence with which depressed writers try to describe their pain. I took a workshop from Smith in 1999, in which he described his attempts, while getting an MFA at the University of Montana, to function as a social caseworker. Writing creatively was impossible.

An anthology on the topic of depression among writers has been published (Casey, 2002) that features excerpts from creative writers' works on the topic. One was from the book by Styron (1990), *Darkness Visible*. Styron recalled that he had fallen into deep depression after stopping drinking in his early sixties: "The depression that engulfed me was not of the manic type – the one accompanied by euphoric highs. . . . I was sixty when the illness struck for the first time, in the 'unipolar' form." He said that the alcohol had served as a "shield against anxiety" and without it, "the shadows of nightfall seemed more somber, my mornings were less buoyant, walks in the woods became less zestful," and he experienced "visceral queasiness" while writing during the late afternoons (pp. 38, 62). He sought psychiatric help and was hospitalized and subsequently overmedicated.

Noting that other writers and artists had suffered from debilitating depression, including Albert Camus, Romain Gary, Jean Seberg, Randall Jarrell, Hart Crane, van Gogh, Virginia Woolf, Mark Rothko, Diane Arbus, William Inge, and the humorist Art Buchwald, Styron (1990) commented that depression yields no faith in ultimate rescue: "The pain is unrelenting, and what makes the condition intolerable is the foreknowledge that no remedy will come – not in a day, an hour, a month, or a minute" (p. 36). Styron called those artists and writers "doomed and splendidly creative men and women" who had childhood experiences where the depression took root. "Could any of them have had a hint, then, of the psyche's perishability, its exquisite fragility? And why were they destroyed, while others – similarly stricken – struggled through?" (p. 36).

Novelist Amy Tan spoke of the depression she suffered and the suicides in her family. She said in a 1995 interview, "Some of it is probably biochemical, but I think it's also in my family tree. I mean, my grandmother killed herself; she certainly had depression in her life." This became one of the themes of Tan's novel, *The Joy Luck Club*. Tan said, "And anyone, like my mother, who witnessed her own mother killing herself, is going to be prone to the same disease." Tan's father and brother both died of brain tumors, her father when she was 14 years old. Yet Tan said, "I didn't do anything about it for a long time, because, like many people, I worried about altering my psyche with drugs. As a writer, I was especially concerned with that. A lot of writers believe that the trauma and the angst that you feel is an essential part of the craft" ("The Spirit Within," 1995).

John Cheever (1991) struggled with alcohol and depression also and wrote in his diaries (published posthumously) that he had to continually try to tell himself that, for a person with his temperament, writing was not "a self-destructive vocation." Although writing had given him "money and renown," he thought that his drinking might have something to do with his writing: "The excitement of alcohol and the excitement of fantasy are very similar" (p. 52). In fact, the presence of alcohol and depression is so commonplace in the biographical information about prominent creative writers that it is odd to find an account where these two are not linked and present (Piirto, 2002; Waldron, 1989). The association is not new; teetotaler Upton Sinclair wrote an account of this phenomenon in 1956.

The sad end of suicide resulting from depression or psychopathology is a reality for many writers. Who can understand another's suicide? A person may have seemed to be on top of the world and then friends and relations make a grisly discovery of the corpse, and the people are left behind to ask why. Highly verbal, highly conceptual, highly opinionated, often nonconforming, frank, and highly driven, writers are prone to self-abusive and self-destructive behavior even as they are enriching the lives of their readers. But this is not always the case, and there are writers whose lives are not lived so tragically or who have, as Styron said, "struggled through." The high incidence of depression would seem to be an indication of the intense sensitivity with which creative people apprehend the world. It is as if the senses were tuned louder, stronger, and higher, and so the task becomes to communicate the experience of both pain and joy.

Empathy

The diaries of Dutch writer Etta Hillesum from 1941 to 1942 (published in English in 1985) are illustrative of the empathy that writers, indeed any artists, seem to feel for others' struggles; perhaps this deep empathy contributes to the deep depressions. She said that writers often feel for the rest of the world; they take on the troubles of the rest of the world. Hillsesum said she thought she understood why creative artists and writers become lost in drink, for one must have a strong sense of self not to go under morally, not to lose a sense of direction: "All my tenderness, all my emotions, this whole swirling soul-lake, soul-sea, soul-ocean . . . wants to pour out then, to be allowed to flow forth into just one short poem." At times like these she felt like "flinging myself headlong into an abyss, losing myself in drink" (Hillesum, 1985, p. 94). Each time she wrote something, she felt empty and apt to fall: "I sense it inside me; even in my most fruitful and most creative inner moments, there are raging demons and self-destructive forces."

Novelist Allan Gurganus spent much time nursing sick friends during the height of the AIDS epidemic. He was later asked to give many eulogies at their funerals. Using his sense of empathy, he reconstructed the good times of their lives for their living friends and relatives. He said, "What I found, in getting up in these little churches and fellowship halls, some in the South and Midwest, was that the more honest I was about the faults of the dead person, and the peccadilloes and the outrageous things, and the extreme opinionatedness of these people, the more laughs I got." People at the services began to feel better as they remembered their dead friends or relatives. "And the more laughs I got, the better people felt and the more present the missing person became in the spirit dimension and hovering over our heads. And the greater service I had done to them in terms of portraiture and to the people who gathered to remember them" (Garner, 1997). Gurganus later wrote a novel in which he tried to show the devastation of the AIDS epidemic so clearly that both gay and straight people could empathize.

A Sense of Humor

The intelligence to see what is incongruous, the wit to convey it, the presence of mind to not overdo punning, the irony to set aside tragedy by seeing its funny side, the farcical rolling of eyes and the tongue-biting snatching away of the perfect *bon mots* in mixed company – all bespeak the sense of humor present in writers. The ever-aware writer sees the humor in melodrama, the humor in making sly titles, the humor in sentimentality, and all keenly. Discrepant events draw the sharp mind and a humorist is born. For example, several writers, including John Ciardi, Isaac Asimov, and a few others, had a group that exchanged off-color limericks in the mail for years (John Ciardi, personal communication, July 1976). These intellectually gifted and creative people shared a love of humor – but a certain type of humor, primarily verbal. Sly humor, wry humor, off-color humor, colorful humor, team-written humor, satire, parody, and comedy are often made up by writers, written down by writers, and transmitted verbally in speech.

Humorist Calvin Trillin said, "I actually think of being funny as an odd turn of mind, like a mild disability, some weird way of looking at the world that you can't get rid of" (Plimpton, 1995b, p. 164). Humorist Woody Allen said, "I think if you have a comic perspective, almost anything that happens you tend to put through a comic filter" (Kakutani, 1995, p. 203). According to Garrison Keillor, humor makes a serious point: "Humor has to take up absolutely everything in your life and deal with it. . . . It's about our lives in America today, the ends of our lives, and everything that happened before and after (Plimpton, 1995a, p. 127). These three writers known for their humor display a serious purpose in their work and demonstrate that humor is used by writers to make points about the follies and foibles of all of us.

A case could be made that most writers, whether or not they are humorists, possess verbal wit. Perhaps they hide behind it and become class clowns or persons whose introversion is overcome by punning in public or by slipping into sarcasm, parody, or irony to be accepted in a crowd. Punning, in my experience, seems to be mostly a habit of speech practiced by bright male introverts. The image of the writer as humorist must take into account that many humorists are not known as sweet, nice, easygoing people, but are often rude, crotchety, and acidic.

Wallace Stevens, in trying to overcome his introversion and wanting to be accepted through people's laughter, turned to writing drawing-room comedies in his early twenties. He never finished these plays, and his biographer commented that Stevens transformed "his youthful proclivity for parody into its more hardened form of irony. . . . As a comedian he was in control" (Richardson, 1986, p. 164).

In summary, creative writers show personality attributes that are similar to creators in other domains, but they also may have other attributes that are more evident than in other creators. The recent emphasis on creativity in domains, as evidenced by Kaufman and Baer's (2005) recent anthology, should further explicate the difference among creators. My own work has featured these differences, in my textbooks and in my research (Piirto, 1992, 1994, 1998a, 1999b, 2006). And I am glad to have these comrades in this endeavor.

REFERENCES

Andreason, N. (1987). Creativity and mental illness: Prevalence rates in writers and their first-degree relatives. *American Journal of Psychiatry, 144,* 1288–1292.
Andreason, N., & Canter, A. (1974). The creative writer: Psychiatric symptoms and family history. *Comprehensive Psychiatry, 15,* 123–131.
Barron, F. (1958). The psychology of imagination. *Scientific American, 50,* 156–165.
Barron, F. (1963). *Creativity and psychological health: Origins of personal vitality and creative freedom.* Princeton, NJ: D. Van Nostrand.
Barron, F. (1968a). *Creativity and personal freedom.* Princeton, NJ: D. Van Nostrand.
Barron, F. (1968b). The dream of art and poetry. *Psychology Today, 2,* 18–23, 66.

Barron, F. (1969). The psychology of the creative writer. *Explorations in Creativity, 43*(12), 69–74.

Barron, F. (1972). The creative personality: Akin to madness. *Psychology Today, 6*, 42–44, 84–85.

Barron, F. (1995). *No rootless flower: An ecology of creativity.* Cresskill, NJ: Hampton Press.

Berry, W. (2005). *A way of ignorance: Essays.* Emeryville, CA: Avalon Publishing.

Bland, C. (2004). The world as her own: A profile of Jean Valentine. *Poets & Writers Magazine, 32*(6), 48–53.

Block, J., & Kremen, A. M. (1996). IQ and ego resiliency. *Journal of Personality and Social Psychology, 70*(2), 346–361.

Bloom, B. (Ed.) (1985). *Developing talent in young people.* New York: Ballantine.

Burroughs, A. (2002*). Running with scissors.* New York: Picador.

Burroughs, A. (2003). *Dry.* New York: Picador.

Casey, N. (Ed.). (2002). *An unholy quiet: Writers on depression.* New York: Harper-Collins.

Cattell, R. B. (1971). The process of creative thought. In R. Cattell (Ed.), *Abilities: Their structure, growth, and action* (pp. 407–417). Boston: Houghton Mifflin.

Cattell, R. B. (1990). Advances in Cattellian personality psychology. In H. Pervin (Ed.), *Handbook of personality: Theory and research* (pp. 101–111). New York: Guilford.

Cheever, J. (1991). *The journals of John Cheever.* New York: Knopf.

Coleridge, S. T. (1872). *Biographica literaria: or Biographical sketches of my literary live and opinions* (Vol. II). New York: Holt and Williams.

Corno, L., & Kanfer, R. (1993). The role of volition in learning and performance. In L. Darling-Hammond (Ed.), *Review of research in education, 19* (pp. 301–342). Washington, DC: American Educational Research Association.

Costa, P. T., & McCrae, R. R. (1992). *NEO PI-R professional manual.* Lutz, FL: Psychological Assessment Resources.

Cross, T. L., Speirs Neumeister, K. L., & Cassady, J. C. (2007). Psychological types of academically gifted adolescents. *Gifted Child Quarterly, 51*(3), 285–293.

Csikszentmihalyi, M., Rathunde, K., & Whalen, S. (1993). *Talented teenagers: The roots of success and failure.* New York: Cambridge University Press.

Dabrowski, K. (1965). *Personality shaping through positive disintegration.* Boston: Little, Brown.

Dewey, J. (1934). *Art and experience.* New York: Putnam.

Eysenck, H. J. (1993). Creativity and personality: Suggestions for a theory. *Psychological Inquiry, 4*(3), 147–178.

Feinstein, E. (2001). *Ted Hughes: The life of a poet.* London: Weidenfeld & Nicolson.

Feist, G. J. (1999). The influence of personality on artistic and scientific creativity. In R. J. Sternberg (Ed.), *Handbook of creativity* (pp. 273–296). New York: Cambridge University Press.

Feist, G. J. (2007). An evolutionary model of artistic and musical creativity. In C. Martindale & P. Locher (Eds.), *Evolutionary and neurocognitive approaches to aesthetics, creativity and the arts* (pp. 15–30). Amityville, NY: Baywood Publishing.

Freud, S. (1976). Creative writers and daydreaming. In A. Rothenberg & C. Hausman (Eds.), *The creativity question* (pp. 48–52). Durham, NC: Duke University Press. (Original work published 1908)

Friedman, B. (1994). *Writing past dark.* New York: HarperPerennial.

Friend, T. (1990, Dec. 9). Rolling Boyle. *New York Times Magazine,* pp. 50, 60–68.

Friman, A., & Templin, C. (1994). An interview with Molly Peacock. *Poets & Writers Magazine, 22*(1), 23–31.

Gannon, M. (2004). Return from silence: An interview with Norman Dubie. *Poets & Writers Magazine, 32*(6), 34–43.

Garner, D. (1997, Dec. 8). Interview with Allan Gurganus. *Salon Magazine.* Retrieved from www.salon.com/books/int/1997/12/cov_si_08gurganus.html.

Ghiselin, B. (1952). *The creative process.* New York: Bantam.

Ginsberg, A. (1984). *Collected poems, 1947–1980.* New York: Harper & Row.

Hart, H. (2000). *The world as a lie: James Dickey.* New York: Picador.

Helson, R. (1999). Institute of Personality Assessment and Research. In M. Runco & S. Pritzker (Eds.), *Encyclopedia of creativity* (Vol. 2, pp. 71–79). San Diego: Academic Press.

Hill, J. (2001). *Legacy of Luna.* New York: HarperCollins.

Hillesum, E. (1985). *An interrupted life: The diaries of Etta Hillesum, 1941–1943.* New York: Washington Square Press.

Jamison, K. R. (1989). Mood disorders and patterns of creativity in British writers and artists. *Psychiatry, 52,* 125–134.

Jamison, K. R. (1993). *Touched with fire: Manic-depressive illness and the artistic temperament.* New York: Free Press.

Jenkins-Friedman, R. (1992). Zorba's conundrum: Evaluative aspect of self-concept in talented individuals. *Quest, 3*(1), 1–7.

Joyce, C. (1998). Interview with Russell Banks. *Salon Magazine.* Retrieved from www. salon.com/books/int/1998/01/cov_si_05int3.html.

Kakutani, M. (1995). The art of humor, I: Interview with Woody Allen. *Paris Review, 136,* 200–222.

Kaufman, J. C. (2001). The Sylvia Plath effect: Mental illness in eminent creative writers. *Journal of Creative Behavior, 35,* 37–50.

Kaufman, J. C., & Baer, J. (2002). I bask in dreams of suicide: Mental illness, poetry, and women. *Review of General Psychology, 6*(3), 271–286.

Kaufman, J. C., & Baer, J. (Eds.). (2005). *Creativity in domains: Faces of the muse.* Mahwah, NJ: Lawrence Erlbaum.

Kris, E. (1976). On preconscious mental processes. In A. Rothenberg & C. Hausman (Eds.), *The creativity question* (pp. 135–142). Durham, NC: Duke University Press.

Kuehl, L. (1978). Interview with Joan Didion. In G. Plimpton (Ed.), *Women writers at work: The* Paris *Review interviews* (pp. 319–336). New York: Penguin Books.

Langer, S. (1957). *Problems of art.* New York: Charles Scribner's Sons.

Lynn, K. S. (1988). *Hemingway.* New York: Fawcett Columbine.

MacAdam, A. (1991). Interview with Octavio Paz. *Paris Review, 119,* 82–123.

MacKinnon, D. (1978). *In search of human effectiveness: Identifying and developing creativity.* Buffalo, NY: Bearly Limited.

Mays, J. (1995). *In the jaws of the black dog.* New York: HarperCollins.

McCrae, R. R., & Costa, P. T. (1999). A five-factor theory of personality. In L. A. Pervin & O. P. John (Eds.), *Handbook of personality theory and research* (2nd ed., pp. 139–153). New York: Guilford Press.

Miles, B. (1989). *Ginsberg.* New York: Simon & Schuster.

Myers, I. B., & McCaulley, M. H. (1985). *Manual: A guide to the development and use of the Myers-Briggs Type Indicator.* Palo Alto, CA: Consulting Psychologists Press.

Neubauer, A. (Ed.). (1994). *Conversations on writing fiction: Interviews with 13 distinguished teachers of fiction writing in America.* New York: HarperPerennial.

Ozick, C. (1971). *The pagan rabbi and other stories.* New York: Knopf.

Piechowski, M. M. (2006). *Mellow out, they say: If only I could.* Madison, WI: Yunasa Press.

Piirto, J. (1978). *The creative process and schooling of creative writers.* Paper presented at the National Association for Gifted Children Conference, Houston.

Piirto, J. (1985). *The three-week trance diet.* Columbus, OH: Carpenter Press.

Piirto, J. (1992). *Understanding those who create.* Dayton, OH: Ohio Psychology Press.

Piirto, J. (1994). *Talented children and adults: Their development and education.* New York: Macmillan.

Piirto, J. (1995). *A location in the Upper Peninsula: Essays, stories, poems.* New Brighton, MN: Sampo Publishing.

Piirto, J. (1998a). *Understanding those who create* (2nd ed.). Scottsdale, AZ: Gifted Psychology Press.

Piirto, J. (1998b). Themes in the lives of successful contemporary U.S. women creative writers. *Roeper Review, 21*(1), 60–70.

Piirto, J. (1998c). *Feeling boys, thinking girls, and judging teachers: Talented students and the MBTI.* Proceedings of the 1998 Conference of the Center for the Application of Personality Types (CAPT), Orlando, March 8.

Piirto, J. (1999). *Talented children and adults: Their development and education* (2nd ed.). Columbus, OH: Prentice Hall.

Piirto, J. (2002). *"My teeming brain": Understanding creative writers.* Cresskill, NJ: Hampton Press.

Piirto, J. (2004). *Understanding creativity.* Tempe, AZ: Great Potential Press.

Piirto, J. (2006, September). *The Piirto Piiramid and creativity in the domain of visual arts.* Keynote speech at European Council for High Ability Conference, Lahti, Finland.

Piirto, J. (in press). 20 years with the Dabrowski theory: An autoethnography. *Advanced Development.*

Piirto, J., & Fraas, J. (1995). Androgyny in the personalities of talented adolescents. *Journal for Secondary Gifted Education, I,* 93–102.

Piirto, J., & Johnson, G. (2004, May). *Personality attributes of talented teenagers: The HSPQ and the MBTI.* Paper presented at Wallace Symposium, Iowa City.

Piirto, J., Montgomery, D., & May, J. (2008). A comparison of Dabrowski's overexcitabilities by gender for American and Korean high school gifted students. *High Ability Studies, 19*(2), 141–153.

Plato. (1952). Dialogues: The ion. In R. Hutchins (Ed.), *The great books of the Western world* (Vol. 7). Chicago: Encyclopedia Britannica.

Plimpton, G. (1995a). The art of humor, II: Interview with Garrison Keillor. *Paris Review, 136,* 108–127.

Plimpton, G. (1995b). The art of humor, III. Interview with Calvin Trillin. *Paris Review, 136,* 16–175.

Prescott, F. C. (1920). *The poetic mind.* Ithaca, NY: Great Seal Books.

Rayneri, L. J., Gerber, B. L., & Wiley, L. P. (2003). Gifted achievers and gifted underachievers: The impact of learning style preferences in the classroom. *Journal of Secondary Gifted Education, 14*(4), 197–204.

Renzulli, J. (1978). What makes giftedness? Reexamining a definition. *Phi Delta Kappan, 60,* 180–184, 261.

Richardson, J. (1986). *Wallace Stevens: The early years, 1879–1923.* New York: William Morrow.

Rothenberg, A. (1990). *Creativity and madness.* Baltimore: Johns Hopkins University Press.

Runco, M. A. (2006). Reasoning and personal creativity. In J. C. Kaufman & J. Baer (Eds.), *Creativity and reason in cognitive development* (pp. 99–116). New York: Cambridge University Press.

Rush, N. (1995). Healthy subversions. In N. Baldwin & D. Osen (Eds.), *The writing life: A collection of essays and interviews with National Book Award winners* (pp. 215–228). New York: Random House.

Santayana, G. (1896). *The sense of beauty: Being the outline of aesthetic theory.* New York: Dover.

Schapiro, M. (1999). Rewriting Bob Dole: Interview with Mark Helprin. *Salon Magazine.* Retrieved from www.salon1999.com/weekly/interview 960714.html.

Schneiderman, L. (1988). *The literary mind: Portraits in pain and creativity.* New York: Insight.

Simonton, D. K. (1994). *Greatness: What makes history and why?* New York: Guilford.

Simonton, D. K. (1999). *The origins of genius: Darwinian perspectives on creativity.* New York: Oxford University Press.

Simpson, L. (1972). *North of Jamaica.* New York: Harper & Row.

Sinclair, U. (1956). *The cup of fury.* Great Neck, NY: Channel Press.

Smith, J. (1999). *Where the roots reach for the water.* New York: North Point Press.

Snyder, G. (2007). *Back on the fire: Essays.* Emeryville, CA: Avalon Publishing.

Sternberg, R., & Davidson, J. (1995). *The nature of insight.* Cambridge, MA: MIT Press.

Sternberg, R., & Lubart, T. I. (1991). An investment theory of creativity and its development. *Human Development, 34,* 1–31.

Styron, W. (1990). *Darkness visible: A memoir of madness.* New York: Random House.

Tannenbaum, A. (1983). *Gifted children.* New York: Macmillan.

Teicholz, T. (1989). Interview with Cynthia Ozick. In G. Plimpton (Ed.), *Women writers at work* (pp. 291–317). New York: Penguin.

The spirit within. (1995). Interview with Amy Tan. *Salon Magazine.* Retrieved from www.salon.com/12nov1995/feature/tan.html.

Waldron, A. (1989, March 14). Writers and alcohol. *Washington Post,* pp. 13–15.

Yeats, W. B. (1953). *The autobiography of William Butler Yeats: Consisting of reveries over childhood and youth, the trembling of the veil, and dramatis personae.* New York: Macmillan.

Zimmerman, B. J., Bandura, A., & Martinez-Pons, M. (1992). Self-motivation for academic attainment: The role of self-efficacy beliefs and personal goal setting. *American Educational Research Journal, 19*(3), 663–676.

2

The Creative Writer, Dysphoric Rumination, and Locus of Control

SAMANEH POURJALALI, E. M. SKRZYNECKY,
AND JAMES C. KAUFMAN

Throughout the course of writing this chapter, we have been struck with writer's block, mild anxiety as the deadline approached and passed, and sporadic depression about it remaining unwritten. However, we are still among the lucky. Academic writers have a structure to follow and basic rules that prevent the writing process from becoming too overwhelming. The fear of a blank page can be overcome by the creation of the title page, insertion of the author's contact information, and the importation of references. Academics regularly collaborate, use past research to guide present efforts, and seek input and feedback from colleagues.

Conversely, creative writers are often unable to partake of these benefits. Their reputation as artists may depend primarily on their imagination. In academic writing, gathering sources and reflecting other people's ideas constitute research; in poetry, these actions can be called plagiarism. When creative writers experience a roadblock, they do not have the luxury of the scientific manuals and databases with which to buffer their ideas. Most ideas and inspirations need to arise internally. Indeed, see Chapter 14 for more information about writer's block.

Historiometric and experimental data indicate several points of interest regarding creative writers and, specifically, poets. When compared to other creative professions, writers have a higher mortality rate (Cassandro, 1998; Kaufman, 2003; Kaun, 1991; Ludwig, 1995; Simonton, 1975). Both poets and fiction writers have higher suicide rates in comparison to other writers (Preti & Miotto, 1999). Writers also have a shorter lifespan than people in other occupations, including other artistic-related occupations (Cassandro, 1998; Kaun, 1991; Ludwig, 1995; Simonton, 1975). A large-scale study of almost 2,000 American, Chinese, Turkish, and Eastern European writers found that on average, poets died younger than fiction writers and non-fiction writers across all four cultures (Kaufman, 2003). Earlier studies (e.g., Ludwig, 1995; Simonton, 1975) also found poets to die the youngest of all writers. It is important to note, however, that general creativity (as associated with openness to experience) is *not* associated with earlier mortality (see Roberts, Kuncel, Shiner, Caspi, & Goldberg, 2007).

Why does creative writing bear this dark side? Dysphoric rumination, the concept of locus of control, existing stereotypes of the mad genius, and the creative artist's mood may offer insight into the psychology of the artist with regard to mental health, specifically depression and suicide ideation (which are the focus of this chapter).

THE CREATIVE ARTIST AND MENTAL ILLNESS

Before we delve into the research it is important to review some facts: Approximately 1 in 5 people in America (18 years or older) suffers from mental illness. Depressive disorders occur in approximately 10% of the population, and approximately 1.2% of Americans have bipolar disorder, or manic depression (National Institute of Mental Health [NIMH], 2001). Without knowing these rates, it is hard to make meaningful comparisons.

In one of most well known empirical studies, often used as a cornerstone for demonstrating a connection between creative writing and mental illness, structured interview were used to analyze 30 creative writers, 30 matched controls, and 1st-degree relatives of each group (Andreasen, 1987). Results revealed that the writers had a higher rate of mental illness, with a particular tendency toward bipolar and other affective disorders. Furthermore, the writers' 1st-degree relatives were more likely to both be creative and have affective disorders. It is worth pointing out, however, that there have been several critiques of the methodology – such as issues with the sample and the interviewing process (Lindauer, 1994; Rothenberg, 1990, 1995; Schlesinger, 2003).

In another study on eminent people, Jamison (1989) interviewed 47 British artists and writers and found that a significantly higher percentage of them suffered from some form of mental illness, particularly from affective disorders, than would be expected from population rates. Ludwig (1994) studied 59 female writers and 59 matched controls, and found that the writers were more likely to have mental illness, including mood disorders and general anxieties.

Several studies have used personality measures, such as the Minnesota Multiphasic Personality Inventory (MMPI) or the Eysenck Personality Questionnaire (EPQ), which also measure mental illness. The best-known line of research in this vein is by legendary researcher Frank Barron (1969), who tested many prominent and creative individuals throughout his work with the Institute for Personality Assessment and Research. Most creators scored higher on the pathology-related scales of the MMPI.

Typical creativity tests (such as those used in this study) reward anti-social or unusual behavior as much as they reward specifically creative behavior. It may not be that bizarre, then, that people who score high on creativity tests also demonstrate anti-social or unusual behavior. Such a finding could be more a statement on the creativity test used than any deeper insights into anti-social behavior and real creativity.

Historiometric research has also been utilized to assess the link between creativity and mental illness. Traditional historiometric research involves reading biographies of eminent people and noting life events (marriages, winning prizes, battling sea monsters). A typical historiometric study might analyze the word content of a president's inaugural address or categorize the themes present in Shakespearean sonnets (Simonton, 1990). Perhaps the most impressive historiometric study was conducted by Ludwig (1995), who investigated over 1,000 eminent individuals who were the subjects of major biographies written between 1960 and 1990. Among many other discoveries, he found a higher incidence of mental illness among people in artistic professions (e.g., writing, art, and theater) than in non-artistic professions (e.g., business, politics, and science), similar to Nettle's (2006) work. In another study, Ludwig (1998) found that visual artists with a more emotive style were more likely to suffer from depression and other disorders than artists with more formal styles.

THE CREATIVE POET

Poets seem to be among the least lucky of creative writers. Studies (e.g., Ludwig, 1995; Simonton, 1975) have found poets to die the youngest of all writers. Staltaro (2003) looked at 43 published poets and found that approximately one-third had a history of at least one psychiatric condition and more than half had been in therapy (this is notably higher than population rates). However, poets did *not* score significantly higher than the norm on a measure of current depression. Nettle (2006) examined poets, mathematicians, visual artists, and average folks, finding higher levels of schizotypy in poets and visual artists and lower levels in mathematicians. Kaufman (2005) studied 826 writers from Eastern Europe from the 4th century to the present day. He found that poets were significantly more likely to suffer from mental illness than any other type of writer (fiction writer, playwright, non-fiction writer). Similarly, Thomas and Duke (2007) found that eminent poets showed significantly more cognitive distortion than fiction writers; they hypothesized that poets were more apt to accept depressive thinking. Stirman and Pennebaker (2001) found that suicidal poets were likely to use words associated with the self (as opposed to the collective) in their poetry, as opposed to non-suicidal poets. The authors of the study suggested that this tendency revealed an inward focus and lack of social integration. Ludwig's (1995) large-scale study found poets to have among the highest rates of psychosis and depression of all of the many different professionals studied (ranging from business people to artists), as well as the highest number of suicides. Post (1996) found mixed results for poets: They were more likely to have bipolar disorders, but *less* likely to have affective and personality disorders than fiction writers and playwrights.

DYSPHORIC RUMINATION BY REVISION

Dysphoric rumination is marked by repetitive thoughts focused on questions of why, how, what if, and what now related to one's depressed mood and depressive symptoms (Lyubomirsky, Kasri, & Zehm, 2003). Ruminative thoughts like these are often absorbing, compelling, and self-perpetuating (Lyubomirsky & Nolen-Hoeksema, 1993). Therefore, they may tax one's cognitive capacities and thus hinder the writer's creative writing process. This especially concerns writers whose stories and poetry are inspired by and written as an expression of their tormented lives.

Two distinct dimensions of rumination are self- and symptom-focused rumination (McBride & Bagby, 2006). Self-focused rumination is defined by repetitive thoughts and behaviors on the self and the effects of depression (e.g., "Why do I act this way?"). Symptom-focused rumination is defined by rumination on the symptoms of depression (Bagby & Parker, 2001; Bagby, Rector, Bacchiochi, & McBride, 2004). Self-focused rumination appears to be a personality trait associated with neuroticism and, as such, is stable even in the absence of depression (Bagby et al., 2004). Depending on the writer's work, the dysphoric rumination in which the author engages may be of the self-focused or symptom-focused variety.

The process of revision requires rumination of phrases, word choices, events, and emotions associated with the piece. Even though rumination may help in organizing one's thoughts and emotions into compartmentalized cognitions, there appear to be various negative consequences to dysphoric rumination. Dysphoric rumination regarding one's self are related to decreased problem-solving abilities and increased depression (Lyubomirsky, Kasri, & Zehm, 2003; Nolen-Hoeksema, 1991, 1996), as well as poor goal achievement (Lyubomirsky et al., 2003; Ward, Lyubomirsky, Sousa, & Nolen-Hoeksema, 2003). If the writer's thoughts are a reflection of his/her inner turmoil, inspired by a troubled self, or the result of anguish or despair, then revision, for this artist, is in essence rumination of his/her distress. For such writers revision becomes deliberate dysphoric rumination (i.e., passively focusing on symptoms, causes, and consequences of personal distress; McCullough et al., 2007; Nolen-Hoeksema & Jackson, 2001). While ruminating about a past traumatic experience, which may be the basis for poetic inspiration, the individual may re-experience the "cognitive, affective, motivational, and physiological consequences of the transgression as if they were occurring once again" (McCullough et al., 2007, p. 491).

Depression may also occur or be prolonged if individuals ruminate about their anger or depressive symptoms (Kuehner & Weber, 1999; McCullough et al., 2007; Mor & Winquist, 2002; Nolen-Hoeksema et al., 1999; Rusting & Nolen-Hoeksema, 1998; Lyubomirsky et al., 1998; Lyubomirsky & Nolen-Hoeksema, 1995; Nolen-Hoeksema, 1991, 2001). Additional adverse effects of rumination include an increase in negative self-evaluations, external locus of control, and hopelessness (Lyubomirsky & Nolen-Hoeksema, 1995).

Studies have also indicated a positive correlation between rumination and revenge and a negative correlation between rumination and forgiveness; in addition, negative rumination may be a catalyst for displaced aggression (McCullough, Bellah, Kilpatrick, & Johnson, 2001).

The negative consequences of rumination arise as a result of dysphoric responses to rumination. Therefore, future studies and historiometric evaluations should assess the link between a writer's health, death, and work. Given the aforementioned studies on dysphoric rumination, it seems that the type of writing produced by the author is of great importance when drawing a relation between rumination and health. Perhaps a writer who produces a work that is reflective of hardships, sorrows, and hopelessness is more prone to illness and more likely to free himself of the pain of living. Perhaps writers whose stories are inspired by and reflective of the positive aspects of life are themselves less susceptible to mental health problems relative to other writers. Perhaps the reason the writer's cure does not work for the creative writer as a journal writer is due to revision extensive revision by the former. A creative writer whose story reflects his/her troubled life ruminates every time he/she revises his or her work. Such writers are, likely, undermining the health benefits of writing due to their constant involvement in the negative ideas that marks their tormented lives and makes up an interesting story.

FEMALE POETS AND WRITERS

Female poets were significantly more likely to suffer from mental illness (as measured by suicide attempts, hospitalizations, or specific periods of depression that warranted discussion in a brief biography) than other types of women writers (fiction writers, playwrights, and non-fiction writers) and male writers (fiction writers, poets, playwrights, and non-fiction writers; Kaufman, 2001a). A study comparing female poets with female journalists, politicians, actresses, novelists, and visual artists revealed that poets were significantly more likely to have mental illness than any other group (Kaufman, 2001a). This finding was dubbed the "Sylvia Plath Effect."

Why should poets, especially female poets, be at a greater disadvantage in terms of mental health when compared to other writers? One possibility is that females are more prone to ruminate about their emotions (Garnefski, Teerds, Kraaji, Legerstee, & van den Kommer, 2004). Rumination regarding a depressive mood is more prevalent among females (McBride & Bagby, 2006; Nolen-Hoeksema, Larson, & Grayson, 1999). The result of such reflection can be seen in the works of many female writers; male writing tends to exhibit less personal and more abstract concepts (Colley & Todd, 2002).

Previous studies have indicated that depressive affect among females may be indicative of elevated levels of interpersonal entanglement; in essence, the social expectation for females to be "affable" may in fact produce stress (Gore, Aseltine, & Colten, 1993). Females are generally more astute about external influences such as familial discord, the amount of royalties received, and critiques of their work (Kaufman & Baer, 2002). Historically, writing has been considered a masculine activity, requiring the female author to make the decision to be an artist or a woman but not both (Wallace, 2002). Despite this stereotype, female authors such as Anne Sexton, Edith Wharton, and Virginia Woolf have triumphed in attaining a notable place in literature.

THE WRITER AND SUICIDE

An early historiometric study of creativity and mental illness was done by Juda (1949), who embarked on a 17-year study of 409 German people. These included 113 creative individuals in the arts, 181 scientists, and 115 designated as control. Juda found more evidence of mental illness and more suicide in the artist group and their families. Jamison (1993) examined 36 major British and Irish poets born between 1705 and 1805. She found that, compared to general population, they were more than five times as likely to commit suicide. Several studies have examined suicide rates – with a variety of results, although writers tend to have higher rates. Lester (1994) studied writers from the United Kingdom, Russia, Japan, and the United States and found higher rates of suicide than in the general population. Stack (1997) examined suicide rates among Americans in the arts and found that artists were three times more likely to commit suicide than nonartists. Preti and Miotto (1999) examined suicide rates in architects, painters, sculptors, writers, poets, and playwrights, going back to the 1800s. They found that writers and poets had the highest rates of suicide and architects and painters had the lowest rates. A further investigation (Preti, De Biasi, & Miotto, 2001) found that musicians had a lower suicide rate than both literary and visual artists. Schneider (2002) looked at suicide rates in Swiss writers, artists, philosophers, composers, and mathematicians compared to the general population. Writers, artists, and philosophers had higher rates in the Swiss population; the other three groups had lower rates. Stack's (2001) investigation into suicide across many different occupations found that people in the arts did, indeed, have a higher-than-average suicide rate – but it is worth pointing out that he also found that dentists have (by far) the highest suicide rate.

The act of suicide can be thought of as a form of aggression both to one's self and to those left behind. This is not to lessen the fact that those who choose to end their lives suffer from, at the very least, mental turmoil and/or illness. However, planning and deliberation seem to be characteristic of the acts of suicide (as with Sylvia Plath, Anne Sexton, Ernest Hemingway). Artists who commit suicide may be regarded as poor problem solvers – in line with the research on dysphoric rumination revealing dysphoric ruminators as poor problem solvers (Lyubomirsky, Tucker, Cadwell, & Berg, 1999). However, the preparations taken to commit suicide suggests that these artists were intellectually intact enough to successfully plan and execute their deaths – as well as, in some instances, write a final note and/or poem (e.g., Robert E. Howard, Vladimir Mayorovsky). As such, it can be argued that the artist, through a cycle of depression and rumination, may be taking aggressive action against his or her persecutors (e.g., a spouse, publishers, one's self).

REVISION: "WHITE-HOT" VARIETY

"First thought, best thought."
– Allen Ginsberg (Timpane & Watts, 2001, p. 152)

Creative and eminent works are frequently believed to have materialized from sudden inspiration, an unconscious stroke of "genius." This myth, which shrouds great writings and specifically poetry, has its origins in the Romantic era (Sawyer, 2006; Sternberg & Lubart, 1999; see Chapter 10). Such a romanticized view of pure, untrained, unconscious inspiration and brilliance is not rooted in reality. Indeed, great works of writing are typically a result of laborious draft writing and countless revision (Sawyer, 2006; Weisberg, 1986). As poet Dylan Thomas once said, "Almost any poem is fifty to a hundred revisions – and that's after it's well along" (quoted in Hayes, 1989, p. 142).

Nonetheless, the biographies of many eminent poets, it is interesting to note that the publication dates or the writing of their best known works shares a relatively close timeline with their suicide. For example, John Berryman's *His Toy, His Dream, His Rest* (1968) was his final published work before jumping to his death in 1972. Sylvia Plath's final collection of poems, *Ariel*, was written in the last 6 months of her life (Ames, 1996). Anne Sexton's *An Awful Rowing toward God* was published posthumously in 1975, a year after her suicide. American poet Hart Crane's *The Bridge* was published in 1930, 2 years before his suicide.[1] Historians are left to speculate whether these writings were created with the intention of being the author's final work given that for many writers their sense of identity is integral to their craft (eminent writers are signified by their writings).

"White hot" poetry – poetry with few, if any, revisions – is a common element of work written by eminent poets who shortly thereafter committed

---

[1] It is important to note that there are many other possible reasons for such a connection, including the recency effect, i.e., the tendency to remember and enjoy the most recently produced work. This phenomenon has been found in creative work (Kaufman, Christopher, & Kaufman, 2008).

suicide. Well-known poetic giants such as Plath and Sexton did very little revision on their last great works. *Ariel* was written during Plath's last 6 months of life; this time frame suggests little chance for extensive revision (Timpane & Watts, 2001).[2] Plath had earned a reputation as a skilled and purposeful poet, poring over the thesaurus for the flawless word, yet she forfeited her regular writing tempo for a more urgent, speedy style near the end of her life (Ames, 1996). This lack of extensive revision was uncharacteristic, and as her personal complications mounted (funds were low, she was ill, and her husband, Ted Hughes, was expecting a child with his lover), she continued to write in this atypical style. What would have resulted had such poets continued to revise their final works? Perhaps the result may not have been their *final* work. Some authors' last works (e.g., Plath's *Ariel*) are considered among an author's finest. Yet these works were written close to their deaths, so that poets such as Anne Sexton, Hart Crane, Sergei Yesenin, and Randall Jarrell likely had little time for revision.

An intriguing question that remains to be answered is why the writer's cure does not help creative writers. As we will soon discuss, Kaufman and Sexton (2006) argue that "the formation of a narrative is a necessary precondition for expressive writing to have salutary effects" (p. 268). It may be likely that if poets like Plath or Sexton revised their poems more, thereby casting their traumatic/emotional events or inspirations in more of a narrative form with a beginning, middle, and end, their emotions/mental disturbances may have become more manageable. This begs the question: Does writing of a "white-hot" variety bring about and foster impulsiveness and mental instability, or is the lack of revision a consequence of the mental illness/depression?

RUMINATION AND THE STEREOTYPE

As previous studies have shown (see Chapter 16), poetry that is expressive or fragmented (i.e., frequent use of first-person pronouns) is less conducive to psychological health and may even be harmful to it (Lepore & Smyth, 2002). Conversely, poems following a concise narrative (i.e., frequent use of third-person pronouns) may provide more psychological benefits (Pennebaker & Seagal, 1999). Interestingly, linguistic analysis indicates that suicidal poets were more prone to use first-person pronouns (Stirman & Pennebaker, 2001). Kaufman and Sexton (2006) argue that the formation of a narrative is a necessary precondition for expressive writing to have salutary effects. In contrast, writing that is fragmented may not only fail to improve health, but may actually be harmful. The key elements are the degree to which the writing is expressive

---

[2]   The authors acknowledge the scholarly concern for authenticity regarding Sylvia Plath's final poems within the *Ariel* collection with regard to any possible editorial influence from Ted Hughes. Nonetheless, *Ariel* in its current published form is still largely considered to be the relatively undoctored work of the credited author.

and the degree to which a narrative is present. It is the interaction of these variables that creates the seemingly opposite findings present in the literature.

A feature of depression is the frequent and unintentional cognition of negative memories and ideas (Joorman et al., 2005). In turn, depression leads to rumination in an attempt to "figure out where it all went wrong" and remedy the negative situation; this results in prolonging and/or increasing depression (Nolen-Hoeksema, 2000; Nolen-Hoeksema et al., 1999; Roberts, Gilboa, & Gotlib, 1998). As stated earlier, studies have shown poets to have among the highest rates of psychosis and depression of all of the many different professionals studied (ranging from business people to artists), as well as the highest number of suicides. Thus, if poets engage in dysphoric rumination while composing or revising their poems, they may access negative memories faster, which may then act as negative reinforcement, causing depression or lowered affect (Joorman et al., 2005; Lyubomirsky, Caldwell, & Nolen-Hoeksema, 1998).

When imagining the likes of Poe or Plath, one cannot think about their "romanticism" without thinking of their addictions, neuroses, and assorted personal demons. Some argue that the correlation between creativity and mental disturbance is merely the result of the researcher's perspective (Schlesinger, 2002). There is a great deal of truth to this view; it is easy to get carried away by spurious correlations and see links where none exist. Others argue that, to some degree, artists may view depression and mood disorders positively. In a recent study of various artists, the participants responded that depression assisted them by fostering their creativity (Yarhouse & Kreeft Turcic, 2003). Romo and Alfonso (2003) studied Spanish painters and found that one of the implicit theories that they held about creativity involved the role of psychological disorders. This theory stated that isolation and personal conflicts were at the heart of art. These associations do not necessarily mean that artists *desire* such a connection. Indeed, others have suggested that creators use their art as a form of self-therapy, trying to heal themselves as they express their feelings (e.g., Spaniol, 2001). Kaufman, Bromley, and Cole (2006) studied how people's opinions about the "mad genius" stereotype were associated with their own creativity. They found that people who did better on the Remote Associates Test, a measure of creativity, tended to endorse the "mad genius" stereotype. People who rated themselves as being more creative tended to feel strongly about the stereotype – either agreeing or disagreeing with it – but were less likely to be neutral. It makes sense that people who are creative might think more about a connection between creativity and mental illness, regardless of the truth behind such a connection.

WOMEN AND RUMINATION

As we have noted earlier, research has found several interesting tendencies among female creative writers, namely the "Sylvia Plath effect" in which female poets have a higher probability of being mentally ill and of dying younger than other types of writers (Kaufman, 2001). Female creative writers may also have higher stress levels (Kaufman, 2001). Additionally, women are twice as likely as men to suffer from a major depressive episode (Kessler, McGonagle, Swartz, Blazer, & Nelson, 1993; Nolen-Hoeksema, 1990; Weissman & Klerman, 1977) and are more likely to ruminate or brood when depressed than men (Nolen-Hoeksema et al., 1999). Depressed females tend to analyze any potential causes, significance, and repercussion of their negative affect to a greater extent than males (Butler & Nolen-Hoeksema, 1994; Nolen-Hoeksema, 1987, 1991, 2001; Nolen-Hoeksema & Davis, 1999). This style of thinking seems to be present during the revision process of poems. The process of rumination, an external locus of control (i.e., "low sense of mastery"), and chronic strain (due to societal and/or personal expectations) negatively reinforce each other and prolong or bring about depressive symptoms (Kuehner & Weber, 1999; Nolen-Hoeksema et al., 1999; Piirto, 1998). This cycle of depression, strain, and rumination may all contribute to writing moving poetry, but at what cost?

CREATIVITY AND MOOD

There is more to the "dark side of creativity" literature than the question of mental illness. Another debate is whether being in a bad mood (officially known as "negative affect") will get you to be more creative (also see Chapter 7). Some studies have found results that support this connection. A few studies have found that positive mood inhibits creative performance (e.g., Kaufmann & Vosburg, 1997; see Kaufmann, 2003, for a review), while other studies have found that negative mood either has no effect (e.g., Grawitch, Munz, & Kramer, 2003) on creativity or can enhance creative performance. Kaufmann and Vosburg (2002) looked at positive and negative mood in creative problem solving. Interesting, they found that a positive mood led to better scores in early idea production (similar to past findings, most recently Gasper, 2004). But a negative mood led to better scores in later idea production. George and Zhou (2002) found that negative moods were related to higher levels of creativity (as measured by supervisor ratings) when rewards and recognition for creative work were salient.

An equally large body of research, however, has found that positive emotions and a good mood can have beneficial influences on creative performance. Several studies, many led by Alice Isen (Estrada, Isen, & Young, 1994; Isen, Daubman, & Nowicki, 1987; Isen, Johnson, Mertz, & Robinson, 1985; Isen, Labroo, Durlach, 2004; Montgomery, Hodges, & J. S. Kaufman, 2004), found that participants who were induced into a good mood showed higher creativity than those induced into neutral or negative moods. Similarly, Lynton and Salovey (1997) found that students in a good mood wrote better-constructed fiction and non-fiction than students in a bad mood, though reliable ratings for the creativity of the pieces were not obtained. Schere (1998) found that both writers and artists showed improved mood after being creative within their own domain (there was no effect when writers created art or artists wrote). Locher, Frens, and Overbeeke (2007) found that students in a good mood (induced by giving candy) rated a digital camera as having strong visual appeal. Still, there are studies that have found no relationship. Verhaeghen, Joormann, and Khan (2005) found that being in a current depressed mood was not associated with creativity. One criticism of this research could be that in nearly all studies, mood was induced. In other words, the moods were triggered by being asked to remember a happy or sad memory or being shown a funny or upsetting scene from a movie. Yet typically, people experience moods based on their own thoughts, emotions, or spontaneously occurring life events. Amabile, Barsade, Mueller, and Staw (2005) studied the relationship of creativity and mood in organizational employees working on potentially creative products. The researchers found significant results across their multiple measures. Creative performance (self and peer evaluated) was positively related to being in a good mood; however, there was no relationship between creative performance and being in a bad mood.

Flow, proposed by Csikszentmihalyi (1990), argues that participating in a creative event can be seen as an optimal experience. Perry's (1999) interviews with well-known writers found that creative writers consistently described writing in flow as being exhilarating, extraordinary, an out-of-body experience, and at times almost orgasmic. Most of the writers she interviewed saw their creative process as a markedly good thing.

A DETRIMENT: AN EXTERNAL LOCUS OF CONTROL

Julian Rotter's concept of locus of control (LOC) has its roots in sociobehaviorism. This theory, which incorporates social reinforcement, describes individuals' perception of the influences over their lives. An individual with a high internal locus of control believes that he/she is primarily responsible for the occurrences in his/her life, whereas an individual with a high external locus of control believes that other forces (such as fate or chance), external influences, and people are primarily responsible for the happenings in his/her life. Their LOC reflects one's self-efficacy and consequently one's self-esteem. In simplistic terms, Rotter's theory claims that behavior is determined by both external stimuli and the reinforcement of such stimuli (Shultz, Shultz, & Hergenhahm, 2006). The pivotal aspect of LOC is that it is the cognitive processing of such stimuli that determines individuals' perception of their ability to master their destiny (internal LOC) or succumb to the influences of external forces, such as luck or fate (external LOC).

The relation between creative writing and mental illness may be further explained using Rotter's LOC. We act on the world in relation to our perception of the world. Our sense of reality guides and dictates our responsive behavior. The working environment of a writer is bohemian in comparison to more conventional occupations. For writers with an internal LOC, this creative working environment may serve as a vault, impenetrable to outside influences or changes. In contrast, writers with an external LOC are like white rats in a "Skinner box." Due to an exaggerated perception of the environment influences, they believe they maintain very little *control.* The internals are confident in their abilities and resolute; they maintain personal responsibility for both their successes and failures. Conversely, writers in the mental Skinner box do not express the same cognitions regarding the environment as the internals. The externals are faced with anxiety, not knowing when the use of their services will expire or whether the subsequent reinforcement will be a food pellet (publication and success) or an electric shock (professional and personal failure). The poet and creative writer may be viewed as "an instrument played by the muses as they subject 'him' to their wiles" (Lavis, 2005, p. 154).

Let us now consider specific instances of the influence of LOC on the writer. The writing profession is rife with the stresses of deadlines, publication, and public acceptance. Additionally, there is little security within the profession. The manner in which writers combat these stresses can reflect their LOC. When compared to those with an external LOC, writers with an internal LOC are more adept at dealing with stress in a positive way. Specifically, internals encounter lower levels of stress and behave in ways that diminish negative reinforcements and help them execute their objectives (O'Brien, 1984). The internals recognize environmental stressors and appropriately manage their time so as not to negatively influence their mental or physical health. In comparison, externals typically exhibit behaviors incompatible with achieving their objectives, thereby increasing their stress levels (O'Brien, 1984).

In a study of gender and occupational status, external locus of control was correlated with lower achievement and socioeconomic status as well as lowered opportunity for social advancement (Smith, Dugan, & Trompenaars, 1997). In the corporate world men have traditionally held position of power, whereas women have traditionally held clerical and secretarial positions (Silverstone & Towler, 1983; Truss, Goffee, & Jones, 1995). This idea could be extended to the artistic world. To be a known and appreciated writer, one's work must be purchased and circulated to the public. Female writers, in comparison to male writers, have historically had to contend with societal pressures. Such traditional Western social expectations of females as caretakers (e.g., motherhood, wife, household management) may contribute to the conflict professional female creative writers experience (Kaufman & Baer, 2002; Piirto, 1998).

As described earlier, females also tend to be ruminators (Garnefski, Teerds, Kraaji, Legerstee, & van den Kommer, 2004; Nolen-Hoeksema et al., 1999) and are socialized early to be oriented toward the collective whereas males are socialized to be independent (Jack, 1991; Kirsch & Kuiper, 2002; Miller, 1976).

Social reinforcement of emotionality in females may contribute to ruminative tendencies; that is, girls, as opposed to boys, are *not* discouraged from
crying because that emotionality is considered a unique "feminine" characteristic (Nolen-Hoeksema, 1990). This social expectation of females to exhibit
nurturing, noncompetitive, passive qualities is not conducive to the fierce,
pressure-ridden world of art. As noted earlier, having one's work published
can be a harrowing, painful process. Tenacity and a stalwart constitution are
necessities. Males are typically socialized to have such qualities of determi-
nation. It is understandable then that female poets would have internalized
thoughts and behaviours resulting from an external locus of control as part of
their upbringing.

Men and women who engaged in dysphoric rumination have reported
feeling less control over their lives and less hopeful about their future (i.e.,
having an external locus of control; Lyubomirsky & Nolen-Hoeksema, 1995;
McBride & Bagby, 2006; Nolen-Hoeksema & Jackson, 2001). In particular,
females feel that negative emotions are not under their control, indicating an
external locus of control, in addition to feeling responsible for the emotional
energy in relationships (Nolen-Hoeksema & Jackson, 2001).

CONCLUSION

We have discussed the phenomenological relationship between mental illness
and eminent creative writers. Studies have found that eminent creative writers
(and especially eminent female poets) are more likely than other eminent
artists to suffer from mental illness, die young, and commit suicide (Cassandro,
1998; Kaufman, 2001, 2003; Kaun, 1991; Ludwig, 1994, 1995; Preti & Miotto,
1999; Simonton, 1975). We have also presented various theories as to why
creative writers are prone to these afflictions. Among such theories included
the concepts of dysphoric rumination, mood, and locus of control.

It is important to avoid flippancy when discussing creative writing and
mental illness. Yet neither should one refuse to examine and question this
topic for fear of causing offense. Rather, those within academia and the mental
health field should strive to explore and determine circumstances under which
the positive and healthy aspects of creativity are outweighed by the negative.

Despite existing data on creative writers and poets, there are more questions to be answered. The maintenance and promotion of both creativity and
mental health by artists (and all individuals) are viable psychological issues.
The idea that creativity may result in tragedy can be hard to comprehend. What
would have become of Plath, Crane, Howard, and Hemingway had they not
met their untimely demise? What gems would the literary world hold today?
What pains would their families and loved ones be spared? Such questions will
remain unanswered. Yet through increased attention to mental balance and
better understanding of the elements of creativity as they pertain to writers,

the psychological community can continue to strive for an encompassing understanding of the concept of creativity. The creative writer must evolve into a being able to both pragmatically solve his or her problems and maintain a state of mental health while influencing society's collective mind via art. The objective, then, of researching eminent writers is expressed through Dylan Thomas' eloquent words: "Do not go gently into that good night. Rage, rage against the dying of the light" (Thomas, 1937). A more thorough understanding of these phenomena will aid writers in combating their inner demons and thus not succumb to a stereotypically tragic end.

REFERENCES

Amabile, T. M. (1996). *Creativity in context: Update to The Social Psychology of Creativity.* Boulder, CO: Westview Press.

American Psychiatric Association (1994). *Diagnostic and statistical manual of mental disorders* (4th ed.). Washington, DC: American Psychiatric Association.

Ames, L. (1996). Sylvia Plath: A biographical note. In S. Plath, *The bell jar* (25th anniversary ed., pp. 277–296). New York: HarperCollins.

Andreasen, N. C. (1987). Creativity and mental illness: Prevalence rates in writers and their first-degree relatives. *American Journal of Psychiatry, 144,* 1288–1292.

Bagby, R. M., & Parker, J. D. A. (2001). Relation of rumination and distraction with neuroticism and extraversion in a sample of patients with major depression. *Cognitive Theory and Research, 25,* 91–102.

Bagby, R. M., Rector, N. A., Bacchiochi, J., & McBride, C. (2004). The stability of the Response Styles Rumination Scale in a sample of patients with major depression. *Cognitive Theory and Research, 28,* 527–538.

Barron, F. (1969). *Creative person and creative process.* New York: Holt, Rinehart & Winston.

Butler, L. D., & Nolen-Hoeksema, S. (1994). Gender differences in responses to depressed mood in a college sample. *Sex Roles, 30,* 331–346.

Cassandro, V. J. (1998). Explaining premature mortality across fields of creative endeavor. *Journal of Personality, 66,* 805–833.

Colley, A., & Todd, Z. (2002). Gender-linked differences in the style and content of e-mails to friends. *Journal of Language and Social Psychology, 21,* 380–392.

Csikszentmihalyi, M. (1990). *Flow: The psychology of optimal experience.* New York: HarperCollins.

Donaldson, C., & Lam, D. (2004). Rumination, mood and social problem-solving in major depression. *Psychological Medicine, 34,* 1309–1318.

Erikson, E. H. (1959). *Identity and the life cycle.* New York: International Universities Press.

Garnefski, N., Teerds, J., Kraaji, V., Legerstee, J., & Van Den Kommer, T. (2004). Cognitive emotion regulation strategies and depressive symptoms: Differences between males and females. *Personality and Individual Differences, 35,* 267–276.

Gore, S., Aseltine, R. H. Jr., & Colten, M. E. (1993). Gender, social-relational involvement, and depression. *Journal of Research on Adolescents, 3,* 101–125.

Haigh, E. A. P., Armey, M., Fresco, D. M., Auerbach, R., & Abela, J. R. Z. (2004, November). *Brooding and pondering: Isolating the active ingredients of depressive rumination with confirmatory factor analysis in an adult clinical sample.* Poster presented at the annual convention of the Association for Advancement of Behavior Therapy, New Orleans.

Hayes, J. R. (1989). Cognitive processes in creativity. In J. A. Glover, R. R. Ronning, & C. R. Reynolds (Eds.), *Handbook of creativity* (pp. 135–145). New York: Plenum Press.

Jack, D. C. (1991). *Silencing the self: Women and depression.* Cambridge, MA: Harvard University Press.

Jamison, K. R. (1989). Mood disorders and patterns of creativity in British writers and artists. *Psychiatry, 52,* 125–134.

Jamison, K. R. (1993). *Touched with fire.* New York: Free Press.

Joormann, J., Hertel, P. T., Brozovich, F., & Gotlib, I. H. (2005). Remembering the good, forgetting the bad: Intentional forgetting of emotional material in depression. *Journal of Abnormal Psychology, 114*(4), 640–648.

Juda, A. (1949). The relationship between highest mental capacity and psychic abnormalities. *American Journal of Psychiatry, 106,* 296–307.

Kaufman, J. C. (2001). The Sylvia Plath effect: Mental illness in eminent creative writers. *Journal of Creative Behavior, 35,* 37–50.

Kaufman, J. C. (2003). The cost of the muse: Poets die young. *Death Studies, 27,* 813–821.

Kaufman, J. C., & Baer, J. (2002). I bask in dreams of suicide: Mental illness and poetry. *Review of General Psychology, 6,* 271–286.

Kaufman, J. C., & Baer, J. (2005). *Creativity across domains: Faces of the muse.* Mahwah, NJ: Erlbaum.

Kaufman, J. C., Bromley, M. L., & Cole, J. C. (2006). Insane, poetic, lovable: Creativity and endorsement of the "Mad Genius" stereotype. *Imagination, Cognition, and Personality, 26,* 149–161.

Kaufman, J. C., & Sexton, J. D. (2006). Why doesn't the writing cure help poets? *Review of General Psychology, 10,* 268–282.

Kaufman, J. C., & Sternberg, R. J. (2007). Resource review: Creativity. *Change, 39,* 55–58.

Kaufman, S. B., Christopher, E. M., & Kaufman, J. C. (2008). The genius portfolio: How do poets earn their creative reputations from multiple products?" *Empirical Studies of the Arts, 26,* 181–196.

Kaun, D. E. (1991). Writers die young: The impact of work and leisure on longevity. *Journal of Economic Psychology, 12,* 381–399.

Kessler, R. C., McGonagle, K. A., Swartz, M., Blazer, D. G., & Nelson, C. B. (1993). Sex and depression in the National Comorbidity Survey 1: Lifetime prevalence, chronicity and recurrence. *Journal of Affective Disorders, 29,* 85–96.

King, S. (2000). *On writing.* New York: Scribner.

Kirsch, G. A., & Kuiper, N. (2002). Individualism and relatedness themes in the context of depression, gender, and a self-schema model of emotion. *Canadian Psychology, 43,* 76–90.

Kuehner, C., & Weber, I. (1999). Responses to depression in unipolar depressed patients: An investigation of Nolen-Hoeksema's response styles theory. *Psychological Medicine, 29,* 1323–1333.

Lavis, A. (2005). 'La muse malade,' 'The fool's perceptions' & 'Il furore dell'arte': An examination of the socio-cultural construction of genius through madness. *Anthropology & Medicine, 12,* 151–163.

Lefcourt, H. M. (1966). Internal versus external control of reinforcement: A review. *Psychological Bulletin, 65,* 206–220.

Leikin, J. B., & Lipsky, M.S. (Eds.). (2003). *American Medical Association complete medical encyclopedia*. New York: Random House Reference.

Lepore, S. J., & Smyth, J. M. (2002). *The writing cure: How expressive writing promotes health and emotional well-being*. Washington, DC: APA Books.

Lester, D. (1994). Suicide in writers. *Perceptual and Motor Skills, 78*, 698.

Lindauer, M. S. (1994). Are creative writers mad? An empirical perspective. In B. M. Rieger (Ed.), *Dionysus in literature: Essays on literary madness*. Bowling Green, OH: Bowling Green State University Popular Press.

Lovallo, W. R., & Thomas, T. L. (2000). Stress hormones in psychophysiological research: Emotional, behavioral, and cognitive implications. In J. T. Cacioppo, L. G. Tassinary, & G. G. Berntson (Eds.), *Handbook of psychophysiology* (2nd ed., pp. 342–367). New York: Cambridge University Press.

Ludwig, A. M. (1994). Mental illness and creative activity in women writers. *American Journal of Psychiatry, 151*, 1650–1656.

Ludwig, A. M. (1998). Method and madness in the arts and sciences. *Creativity Research Journal, 11*, 93–101.

Ludwig, A. M. (1995). *The price of greatness*. New York: Guilford.

Lyubomirsky, S., Caldwell, N. D., & Nolen-Hoeksema, S. (1998). Effects of ruminative and distracting responses to depressed mood on retrieval of autobiographical memories. *Journal of Personality and Social Psychology, 75*, 166–177.

Lyubomirsky, S., Kasri, F., & Zehm, K. (2003). Dysphoric rumination impairs concentration on academic tasks. *Cognitive Therapy and Research, 27*(3), 309–330.

Lyubomirsky, S., & Nolen-Hoeksema, S. (1995). Effects of self-focused rumination on negative thinking and interpersonal problem solving. *Journal of Personality and Social Psychology, 69*, 176–190.

Lyubomirsky, S., Tucker, L. T, Cadwell, N. D., & Berg, K. (1999). Why ruminators are poor problem solvers: Clues from the phenomenology of dysphoric rumination. *Journal of Personality and Social Psychology, 77*, 1041–1060.

Mamlin, N., Harris, K. R., & Case, L. P. (2001). A methodological analysis of research on locus of control and learning disabilities: Rethinking a common assumption. *Journal of Special Education, 34*, 214–225.

Martindale, C. (1972). Father absence, psychopathology, and poetic eminence. *Psychological Reports, 31*, 843–847.

McBride, C., & Bagby, R. M. (2006). Rumination and interpersonal dependency: Explaining women's vulnerability to depression. *Canadian Psychology, 47*, 184–194.

McCullough, M. E., Bellah, C. G., Kilpatrick, S. D., & Johnson, J. L. (2001). Vengefulness: Relationships with forgiveness, rumination, well-being, and the Big Five. *Personality and Social Psychology Bulletin, 27*, 601–610.

McCullough, M. E., Bono, G., & Root, L. M. (2007). Rumination, emotion, and forgiveness: Three longitudinal studies. *Journal of Personality and Social Psychology, 92*, 490–505.

McCullough, M. E., Orsulak, P., Brandon, A., & Akers, L. (2007). Rumination, fear, and cortisol: An in vivo study of interpersonal transgressions. *Health Psychology, 26*, 126–132.

Middlebrook, D. (1991). *Anne Sexton: A biography*. Boston: Houghton Mifflin.

Miller, J. B. (1976). *Towards a new psychology of women*. Boston: Beacon Press.

Mor, N., & Winquist, J. (2002). Self-focused attention and negative affect: A meta-analysis. *Psychology Bulletin, 128*, 638–662.

National Institute of Mental Health (NIMH) (2001). *The numbers count: Mental disorders in America*. Washington, DC: Author.

Nolen-Hoeksema, S. (1987). Sex differences in unipolar depression: Evidence and theory. *Psychological Bulletin, 101*, 259–282.

Nolen-Hoeksema, S. (1990). *Sex differences in depression.* Stanford, CA: Stanford University Press.

Nolen-Hoeksema, S. (1991). Responses to depression and their effects on the duration of depressive episodes. *Journal of Abnormal Psychology, 100*, 569–582.

Nolen-Hoeksema, S. (1996). Chewing the cud and other ruminations. In R. S. Wyer Jr. (Ed.), *Ruminative thoughts* (pp. 135–144). Mahwah, NJ: Erlbaum.

Nolen-Hoeksema, S. (2000). The role of rumination in depressive disorders and mixed anxiety/depressive symptoms. *Journal of Abnormal Psychology, 109*, 504–511.

Nolen-Hoeksema, S. (2001). Gender differences in depression. *Current Directions in Psychological Science, 10*, 173–176.

Nolen-Hoeksema, S., & Davis, C. G. (1999). "Thanks for sharing that": Ruminators and their social support networks. *Journal of Personality and Social Psychology, 77*, 801–814.

Nolen-Hoeksema, S., & Jackson, B. (2001). Mediators of the gender difference in rumination. *Psychology of Women Quarterly, 25*, 37–47.

Nolen-Hoeksema, S., Larson, J., & Grayson, C. (1999). Explaining the gender difference in depressive symptoms. *Journal of Personality and Social Psychology, 77*, 1061–1072.

Nettle, D., & Clegg, H. (2006). Schizotypy, creativity and mating success in humans. *Procedures of Biological Science, 273*, 611–615.

Nowicki, S. Jr., & Duke, M. P. (1983). The Nowicki-Strickland life-span locus of control scales: Construct validation. In H. M. Lefcourt (Ed.), *Research with the locus of control construct, vol. 2* (pp. 9–52). New York: Academic Press.

O' Brien, G. E. (1984). Locus of control, work, and retirement. In H. M. Lefcourt (Ed.), *Research with the locus of control construct, vol. 1* (pp. 7–72). Orlando, FL: Academic Press, Inc.

Peeters, F., Wessel, I., Merchelbach, H., & Boon-Vermeeren, M. (2002). Autobiographical memory specificity and the course of major depressive disorder. *Comprehensive Psychiatry, 43*, 344–350.

Pennebaker, J. W., Francis, M. E., Booth, R. J. (2001). *Linguistic Inquiry and Word Count (LIWC): LIWC 2001.* Mahwah, NJ: Erlbaum.

Pennebaker, J. W., & Seagal, J. D. (1999). Forming a story: The health benefits of narrative. *Journal of Clinical Psychology, 55*, 1243–1254.

Piirto, J. (1998). Themes in the lives of contemporary U.S. women creative writers at midlife. *Roeper Review, 21*, 60–70.

Post, F. (1994). Creativity and psychopathology: A study of 291 world-famous men. *British Journal of Psychiatry, 165*, 22–34.

Post, F. (1996). Verbal creativity, depression and alcoholism: An investigation of one hundred American and British writers. *British Journal of Psychiatry, 168*, 545–555.

Preti, A., & Miotto, P. (1999). Suicide among eminent artists. *Psychological Reports, 84*, 291–301.

Raskin, E. A. (1936). Comparison of scientific and literary ability: A biographical study of eminent scientists and men of letters in the nineteenth century. *Journal of Abnormal and Social Psychology, 31*, 20–35.

Roberts, J. E., Gilboa, E., & Gotlib, I. H. (1998). Ruminative response style and vulnerability to episodes of dysphoria: Gender, neuroticism, and episode duration. *Cognitive Therapy and Research, 22*, 401–423.

Romo, M., & Alfonso, V. (2003). Implicit theories of Spanish painters. *Creativity Research Journal, 15*, 409–415.

Rothenberg, A. (1990). *Creativity and madness: New findings and old stereotypes.* Baltimore: Johns Hopkins University Press.

Rothenberg, A. (1995). Creativity and mental illness. *American Journal of Psychiatry, 152,* 815–816.

Rotter, J. (1966). Generalized expectancies for internal versus external control of reinforcements. *Psychological Monographs, 80,* 1–28.

Rusting, C. L., & Nolen-Hoeksema, S. (1998). Regulating responses to anger: Effects of rumination and distraction on angry mood. *Journal of Personality and Social Psychology, 74,* 790–803.

Sawyer, R. K. (2006). *Explaining creativity: The science of human innovation.* New York: Oxford University Press.

Schlesinger, J. (2002). Issues in creativity and madness, part one: Ancient questions, modern answers. *Ethical Human Sciences & Services, 4,* 73–76.

Schlesinger, J. (2003). Issues in creativity and madness, part three: Who cares? *Ethical Human Sciences & Services, 5,* 149–152.

Schneider, P. B. (2002). Les ecrivains et le suicide [Writers and suicide]. *Schweizer-Archiv-fuer-Neurologie-und-Psychiatrie, 153,* 221–231.

Silverstone, R., & Towler, R. (1983). Progression and tradition in the job of the secretary. *Personnel Management, 15*(5), 30–33.

Simonton, D. K. (1975). Age and literary creativity: A cross-cultural and transhistorical survey. *Journal of Cross-Cultural Psychology, 6,* 259–277.

Simonton, D. K. (1990). *Psychology, science, and history: An introduction to historiometry.* New Haven, CT: Yale University Press.

Smith, P. B., Dugan, S., & Trompenaars, F. (1997). Locus of control and affectivity by gender and occupational status: A 14 nation study. *Sex Roles, 36,* 51–77.

Spaniol, S. (2001). Art and mental illness: Where is the link? *Arts in Psychotherapy, 28,* 221–231.

Stack, S. (1997). Suicide among artists. *Journal of Social Psychology, 137,* 129–130.

Stack, S. (2001). Occupation and suicide. *Social Science Quarterly, 82,* 384–396.

Sternberg, R. J., & Lubart, T. I. (1995). *Defying the crowd.* New York: Free Press.

Sternberg, R. J., & Lubart, T. I. (1999). The concept of creativity: Prospects and paradigms. In R. J. Sternberg. (Ed.), *Handbook of creativity* (pp. 3–15). New York: Cambridge University Press.

Stirman, S. W., & Pennebaker, J. W. (2001). Word use in the poetry of suicidal and non-suicidal poets. *Psychosomatic Medicine, 63,* 517–523.

Thomas, D. (1937). Do not go gently into that good night. In *Dylan Thomas: The poems.* London: J. M. Dent & Sons.

Timpane, J., & Watts, M. (2001). *Poetry for dummies.* New York: Wiley.

Truss, C., Goffee, R., & Jones, G. (1995). Segregated occupations and gender stereotyping: A study of secretarial work in Europe. *Human Relations, 48,* 1331–1354.

Wallace, D. (2002). Ventriloquizing the male: Two portraits of the artist as a young man by May Sinclair and Edith Wharton. *Men and Masculinities, 4,* 322–333.

Ward, A. H., Lyubomirsky, S., Sousa, L., & Nolen-Hoeksema, S. (2003). Can't quite commit: Rumination and uncertainty. *Personality and Social Psychology Bulletin, 29,* 96–107.

Weisberg, R. (1986). *Creativity: Genius and other myths.* New York: W. H. Freeman.

Weissman, M. M., & Klerman, G. L. (1977). Sex differences and the epidemiology of depression. *Archives of General Psychiatry, 34,* 98–111.

Yarhouse, M. A., & Kreeft Turcic, E. (2003). Depression, creativity, and religion: A pilot study of Christians in the visual arts. *Journal of Psychological Theology, 31,* 348–355.

3

"The more I write, the better I write, and the better I feel about myself": Mood Variability and Mood Regulation in Student Journalists and Creative Writers

ADÈLE KOHANYI

In the movie *The Hours*, the writer Virginia Woolf is depicted as odd and volatile. In one scene she is prostrate, incapable of leaving her bed, and in the next she explodes in a flow of fiery and meaningless utterances. When Woolf announces to her husband that she has at last found the opening sentence to her novel *Mrs. Dalloway*, he hopes that writing will be what it has always been for her, a respite from her suffering. Unfortunately, this moment of peace is not to last, because manic-depression will eventually drive Woolf to suicide. This movie is one of many that crystallizes the view that there is a relationship between bipolar mood disorder and creative writing. This relationship does not only exist in the popular imagination but has also been demonstrated by numerous systematic studies. The purpose of this chapter is to explore this association by studying mood variability, rather than bipolar mood disorder, and by studying student writers rather than eminent ones. A second goal is to determine whether the act of writing improves mood in writers.

In this chapter, I first briefly outline the relationship between mood disorders and creative writing. I then review evidence for a relationship between subclinical mood variability and bipolar disorder, thus making it reasonable to explore a link between mood variability and creative writing. Finally, I review the effects of mood on creativity before focusing on the effects of writing on mood.

MOOD DISORDERS AND CREATIVE WRITING

A growing body of research relying on biographies and autobiographies (Jamison, 1993; Kaufman, 2001, 2005; Kaufman & Sexton, 2006; Ludwig, 1992; Post, 1994, 1996; Walker, Koestner, & Hum, 1995) and on direct interviews with creative writers and other creators (Andreasen, 1987; Andreasen & Canter, 1974; Jamison, 1989; Ludwig, 1994; Piirto, 1998, 2002) suggests that creative writers have a higher rate of mood disorders than the general population (see

Chapters 2 and 16 for a review). Indeed, these studies consistently found that from 50% to 80% of creative writers studied suffered from a mood disorder (in particular, bipolar disorder), as compared with around 1.5% (bipolar) and 10% (unipolar) of the general population (Goodwin & Jamison, 2007).

IS THERE A RELATIONSHIP BETWEEN SUBCLINICAL MOOD VARIABILITY AND WRITING?

To the extent that there is a relationship between mood disorders and creative writing, it is reasonable to suppose that a relation exists between normal, subclinical mood variability and writing. This supposition relies on the assumption that bipolar disorder and normal mood variability exist on a continuum. Indeed, it has been claimed that bipolar illness spans a wide spectrum ranging from bipolar I at its most extreme, to bipolar II, cyclothymia, and temperamental instability (moody, agitated, and angry personality) at the lower extremes (Akiskal, 2003; Akiskal, Bourgeois, Angst, Post, Moller, & Hirschfeld, 2000; Angst & Marneros, 2001; Judd & Akiskal, 2003; Kelsoe, 2003). In other words, the contention is that subclinical mood variability exists on the lower end of a continuum with mood disorders at the upper end. Other researchers argue further that, at the end of the mild spectrum, there is considerable overlap between temperamental instability and normality (Akiskal et al., 2000; Goodwin & Jamison, 2007; Kraepelin, 1921).

There is some support for the existence of such a dimensional model. Clinicians anecdotally report the case of patients who exhibit symptoms of mood disorders and other mental illnesses, but in subsyndromal forms that do not meet *Diagnostic and Statistical Manual of Mental Disorders Fourth Revision* (DSM–IV) (American Psychiatric Association, 1994) criteria. These particular patterns of behavior have been called shadow syndromes (Ratey & Johnson, 1998).

More systematic studies also support the claim that normal mood and mood disorders span a continuum. For example, one study found that, within a population of normal teenagers, a subgroup exhibited depressive and cyclothymic temperaments, meaning that they showed characteristics of mood disorders but within the normal range (Akiskal et al., 1998). Another study revealed that relatives of individuals with bipolar disorder had a higher incidence of affective temperaments (cyclothymic or hyperthymic) than control groups (Lauer, Bronisch, Kainz, Schreiber, Holsboer, & Krieg, 1997). In addition, individuals who did not meet DSM–IV (1994) criteria for bipolar disorder responded to mood stabilizers (Akiskal et al., 2000). These claims have been disputed by some (i.e., Baldessarini, 2000; Meyer & Keller, 2003; Patten, 2006), but make tenable the hypothesis that there could be subclinical versions of mood disorders and that mood disorders exist on the same spectrum as normal mood variability.

Given that research has proposed a relationship between bipolar disorder and subclinical mood variability, it is possible that individuals who exhibit high mood variability are more likely to be involved in creative writing than individuals with more stable moods. This question was examined by investigating the parallels between participants' EEG patterns and their profiles on personality tests. Student poets not diagnosed with a mental illness were found to score higher than a nonwriting control group on the manic subscale of the MMPI (Makarec & Persinger, 1985). To my knowledge, no other study has investigated this hypothesis. However, there is an established relationship between mood and writing such that writing improves mood. I first examine the relationship between mood and creativity to place the discussion within a larger context and then focus on mood and writing.

RELATIONSHIP BETWEEN MOOD AND CREATIVITY

Research suggests that positive mood can either facilitate or inhibit creativity contingent on task requirements (i.e., Kaufmann, 2003; Vosburg, 1998a, 1998b). There is a solid body of research supporting the position that positive mood promotes superior performance on tasks such as word associations, word categorization, and creative problem solving. Indeed, participants in whom positive affect had been induced tended to generate more unusual responses on word association tasks than negative and neutral mood participants (Isen, Johnson, Mertz, & Robinson, 1985). For example, positive mood participants were more likely to respond "lush" as opposed to "rug" when prompted with the word "carpet." Positive mood participants also perceived more interrelatedness between seemingly disparate material and categorized stimuli into broader and more inclusive categories in sorting and rating tasks (Isen & Daubman, 1984). Such participants were more likely to rate atypical examplars such as "camel," "feet," and "elevator" as belonging to the category "vehicle" than other participants.

In addition, participants in positive affective states performed better on creative problem solving tasks (Isen, Daubman, & Nowicki, 1987). A typical creative problem is the candle task (Duncker, 1945). Participants are handed a box of tacks, a candle, and a box of matches and are challenged to attach the candle to a corkboard wall without wax dripping on the floor. These studies are generally believed to measure processes related to aspects of creativity, such as flexibility, originality, and the ability to identify unexpected relations between stimuli (Isen, Daubman, & Nowicki, 1987; Kaufmann, 2003; Kaufmann & Vosburg, 2002; Vosburg, 1998a, 1998b).

Various theories have been offered to explain the beneficial effects of positive mood on creative problem solving tasks. It has been suggested that positive mood "cues" a wide variety of material and subsequently affects how it is organized in working memory (Isen, 1984, 1987, 1993; Isen & Daubman,

1984; Isen et al., 1985). Material is then better connected and integrated in memory (Isen, 1984, 1987). The likelihood of making novel connections and of recombining stimuli in original ways increases in such a cognitive context (i.e., Isen & Daubman, 1984). Another perspective is that positive mood participants are more likely to regard the environment as safe, which fosters a more relaxed and exploratory approach to the task (Clore, Schwarz, & Conway, 1994). An additional possibility is that material encoded by positive mood participants is colored by their mood, meaning that metaphoric dimensions of words can become more salient (Isen & Daubman, 1984).

Although a large number of studies support the view that positive affect promotes aspects of creativity, there are studies supporting the opposite position as well. One such study on analogical problem solving (Jaušovec, 1989) observed whether participants previously exposed to a problem and its solution could transfer this knowledge to solve a similar problem. Positive mood participants showed an advantage over other moods in one task. However, positive affect was detrimental to performance on another task very similar to the one used by Isen and colleagues (1987) in a study supporting the facilitative effects of positive mood. Likewise, positive affect did not promote a superior performance on syllogism tasks or on problem-solving tests (Melton, 1995). Another study examined the effects of positive, negative, and neutral moods on creative problem solving and found that negative mood participants outperformed neutral, control, and positive mood participants, in that order (Kaufmann & Vosburg, 1997).

To reconcile these findings, it is important to consider that in the study by Isen and colleagues (1987), participants were manipulating physical objects (such as a box of tacks, a candle, and a box of matches) and could therefore easily monitor their own progress (Vosburg, 1998a). In contrast, in the Kaufmann and Vosburg study (1997), participants worked on a paper-and-pencil task (problem finding and problem solving) so that their progress could not be monitored as easily (Vosburg, 1998a). Likewise, in yet another study, positive mood participants generated more ideas than other participants in problem solving, problem finding, and creativity tasks (Vosburg, 1998b). However, their ideas were not deemed original or useful, whereas negative mood participants did not generate many ideas but theirs were of a better quality (Vosburg, 1998b). It seems that positive mood promotes creative problem solving under high satisficing conditions (generating a high number of solutions), whereas negative mood may facilitate task performance for more restrictive and optimizing requirements (generating fewer and yet superior ideas in terms of quality; Kaufmann & Vosburg, 1997; Vosburg, 1998b). In support of this contention, Weisberg (1994) examined the career of composer Robert Schumann to determine whether the work that he composed during highly productive hypomanic periods were of a higher quality than music composed during nonmanic phases. He found productivity to be unrelated to the quality of the music composed. It seems then that an abundance of ideas does not necessarily mean that these ideas are going to be good (Vosburg, 1998b).

An additional position is that negative mood is likely to prompt reactions such as rejection of conventional approaches and solutions (Kaufmann & Vosburg, 2002). These very processes are central to creative problem solving (Kaufmann, 1993). In addition, negative affect appears to facilitate problem finding, a necessary prerequisite to problem solving (Runco, 1994) and a central component of creativity itself (i.e., Getzels & Csikszentmihalyi, 1976). Indeed, suicidal thoughts, a clear marker of negative mood, were found to be strongly related to the ability to invent original and interesting problems to solve (Mraz & Runco, 1994).

EFFECT OF WRITING ON MOOD

As reviewed earlier in the chapter, both positive and negative mood may enhance performance on creative problem-solving tasks. Creativity also affects mood and, in the case of writing, mostly positively. Indeed, a wide variety of participants writing about a wide variety of topics have demonstrated that writing has a positive effect on mood. One set of studies examined writers' change of mood from before to after writing. College student participants were asked to write emotional essays (Brand & Powell, 1986), emotionally neutral papers, and research drafts (Brand & House, 1987), whereas professional writers were instructed to complete mood inventories when writing for their work (Brand & Leckie, 1988). All the participants' mood improved overall: Positive emotions were intensified and negative emotions blunted, regardless of the type of writing task. However, college students reported more positive attitudes toward writing when engaged in class assignments than when writing for themselves, except when writing research papers. In addition, students who considered themselves skilled writers and those who usually wrote on their own reported the least intensity and frequency of emotions. The overall mood of professional writers remained stable; there was no significant change in their mood from before to after writing. However, they did report overall positive affect when writing.

Other researchers examined participants' responses to written self-disclosure about trauma (see Chapter 16). In the typical study, participants were instructed to write about their "thoughts and feelings" about an emotional experience for as little as 15 minutes a day for 3 days. Their responses were then compared to those of individuals writing about a neutral topic (Pennebaker & Beall, 1986). Participants writing about trauma felt worse than controls immediately after writing (i.e., Pennebaker & Beall, 1986; Pennebaker, Colder, & Sharp, 1990; Pennebaker & Francis, 1996). However, this effect was temporary and typically dissipated rapidly (Pennebaker, 1997). Indeed, a meta-analysis of almost 150 randomized experiments (Frattaroli, 2006) revealed that, in the vast majority of cases, participants demonstrated physical and mental improvements on both objective and subjective (self-report-based) markers. For example, there was a reduction in the number of visits to health centers (Pennebaker & Beall, 1986), higher immune functioning (Petrie, Booth, Pennebaker, Davison, & Thomas, 1995), decreased absenteeism (Francis & Pennebaker, 1992), and improved grade point average (Cameron & Nicholls, 1998). These findings seem to apply to a wide range of participants regardless of gender (Pennebaker & Beall, 1986), culture (Dominguez et al., 1995; Rimé, 1995), social class (Bradley & Follingstad, 2003; Spera, Buhrfeind, & Pennebaker, 1994), and personality type (Cameron & Nicholls, 1998). In addition, age groups ranging from adolescents (O'Heeron, 1993) to nursing home residents (Caplan, 2000), health status ranging from healthy college students (Pennebaker et al., 1990) to cancer survivors (Low, Stanton, & Danoff-Burg, 2006), as well as prisoners in psychiatric hospitals (Richards, Beal, & Seagal, 2000) and rape victims (Brown & Heimberg, 2001) all benefited from the writing paradigm.

To benefit from writing, participants do not need to write about their own experiences nor do they have to write about traumas: Participants instructed to write about an imaginary trauma (Greenberg, Wortman, & Stone, 1996), positive aspects of a trauma (King & Miner, 2000), thoughts and feelings about entering college (Cameron & Nicholls, 1998), being laid off (Spera, Buhrfeind, & Pennebaker, 1994), positive experiences (Burton & King, 2004), life goals (King, 2001), and one's best possible future self (King, 2001; King & Miner, 2000) all showed beneficiary outcomes comparable to those experienced by participants writing about traumatic events.

It thus appears that it is the exploration of thoughts and feelings associated with an experience (Pennebaker & Beall, 1986) and writing about topics that could potentially enhance self-regulation (including affective regulation) (Greenberg et al., 1996; King & Miner, 2000) that result in mood and health improvements. Indeed, affective regulation involves facing a negative emotion and successfully surmounting it (Greenberg et al., 1996). Writing allows participants the opportunity to improve their ability to distance themselves from such emotions and eventually master their emotional reactions, regardless of how the reactions were triggered. By gaining such a sense of control, participants ultimately learn about themselves (King & Miner, 2000).

This is not to say that any type of writing is beneficial, because participants instructed to write about neutral topics do not experience the positive effects of writing (Pennebaker & Beall, 1986). What appears to be important is that the topic triggers an emotional reaction, positive or negative (Greenberg et al., 1996). In fact, participants instructed to avoid emotional content altogether or to provide strictly factual descriptions do not experience the positive effects of writing (Pennebaker & Beall, 1986).

In addition, participants need to be able to structure their thoughts into a coherent story. Merely listing traumatic events is not enough (Smyth, True, & Souto, 2001). Indeed, people whose writing evolved from a disorganized description to a coherent story benefited from the writing experience (Pennebaker, 1993). Conversely, those whose stories were coherent from the beginning did not experience the positive effects of writing (Meichenbaum & Fong, 1993). Furthermore, the formation of a narrative is believed to be pivotal for writing to be beneficial (Pennebaker & Seagal, 1999). An analysis of the words used in participants' writing about trauma revealed that when emotional expressions are controlled for, an increase in the use of insight words (e.g., understand, realize, thought, knew), causal words (e.g., because, reason, why), and more positive emotion words as compared to negative ones resulted in better health (Pennebaker, Mayne, & Francis, 1997).

What it is exactly about a narrative that is beneficial is not clearly understood, but there are many possible explanations (i.e., Kaufman & Sexton, 2006; Pennebaker, 2004; Pennebaker & Graybael, 2001; Sloan & Marx, 2004). Repressing a traumatic event has been linked to stress-related disorders, whereas disclosing a trauma in writing seems beneficial (Pennebaker, 1994). Furthermore, writing narratives seems to foster self-knowledge and provides insight (Cameron & Nicholls, 1998) so that participants are able to assimilate and give meaning to their experience (Pennebaker & Beall, 1986). The transformation of a text into a story is often marked by a perspective shift: Indeed, participants who wrote from the first-person perspective and then switched to the third person reported feeling better than those who continued to use the first person (Stirman & Pennebaker, 2001). It is also possible that once an experience is transformed into a story, it becomes simpler and more manageable and can be assimilated more readily, thus allowing the individual to move beyond the traumatic experience (Pennebaker & Seagal, 1999; Spera et al., 1994). In addition, when events are visited and revisited time and time again in writing, the emotional response to the events becomes dulled (Pennebaker & Seagal, 1999).

Participants who benefited the most from writing are those who wrote the most intensely, for the longest amount of time (Páez, Velasco, & González, 1999), and over the longest time span (Smyth, 1998). Although writing introspectively can be beneficial to mood, it is also plausible that very intense introspection can be harmful. It is possible that poetry writing, because it presumably calls for greater introspection, can leave a poet feeling worse after the act of writing (Kaufman, 2002; Kaufman & Sexton, 2006; see Chapter 2).

THE STUDY

Up to this point, I have contended that there is a relationship between bipolar disorder and creative writing. I then argued that mood disorders and normal mood variations exist on a continuum, which makes tenable the idea of a link between higher than average mood variability and creative writing. There is very little research linking subclinical mood variability and creative writing. Because of this dearth of research, I first reviewed the effect of mood on creativity and then reviewed the effect of writing (not necessarily creative) on mood. From this review, two hypotheses emerged. I expected creative writers (writers of fiction, plays, screenplays, and poetry) to exhibit more mood variability when compared to nonfiction writers (in the present case, journalists) because the research linking manic depression and writing concerns exclusively creative writers (variability hypothesis). In addition, both groups should exhibit greater mood variability than individuals who do not write (nonwriters). Further, I hypothesized that the act of writing would affect writers positively, heightening their experience of valence (experience of pleasure/displeasure) and lowering arousal (feeling of activation/deactivation). Creative writers should exhibit these changes more markedly than journalists because creative writing can potentially elicit the type of writing that Pennebaker and colleagues (1986–2008) have associated with an improved sense of well-being.

The participants were all college students; among them were 20 creative writers, 20 journalists, and 20 nonwriters (controls), with an equal number of males and females. Six creative writers wrote exclusively prose (novels, short stories, screenplays, plays), three wrote exclusively poetry, and the rest wrote a combination of prose and poetry. Among the journalists were five reporters, three editors, six sportswriters, three columnists, two who wrote about the economy, and one who wrote about the arts and entertainment. The demographics of the study reflected that of the college the students were attending.

To test the variability and regulation hypotheses, I used the method of experience sampling. Experience sampling provides a mean of investigating subjective experience (Reis & Gable, 2000). Typically, participants are asked to fill out a predetermined number of mood scales as they go about their days for specific periods of time (i.e., Kernis, Cornell, Sun, Berry, & Harlow, 1993). Such mood reports permit the calculation of mood variability (i.e., Penner, Shiffman, Paty, & Fritzsche, 1994). Experience sampling can also be used to study how particular events affect participants' mood (i.e., Knee, Patrick, Vietor, & Neighbors, 2004). The change in the pre- and postwriting mood scales can then be examined to determine how writing affects mood (i.e., Brand & Powell, 1986).

To capture mood variability, participants were asked to record their emotions at the moment of rating on an 8-point Likert type scale for 26 mood adjectives three times a day for 14 days. To see the effect of writing on their mood, they were asked to fill out the mood scales immediately before and immediately after writing for 10 times that they wrote.

People's representations of their emotional experiences can be depicted in the shape of a circle composed of two main dimensions, valence and arousal (Feldman Barrett & Fossum, 2001). I chose 16 mood adjectives because they captured the full spectrum of this affective circumplex: enthusiastic, peppy, happy, satisfied, calm, relaxed, quiet, still, sleepy, sluggish, sad, disappointed, nervous, afraid, surprised, and aroused (Feldman, 1995). I took the other adjectives from the Positive Affect Negative Affect Schedule-Expanded Form (PANAS-X; Watson & Clark, 1994). These adjectives measure Happiness (happy, delighted, joyful, cheerful) and Sadness (sad, blue, downhearted, alone, lonely). Four more adjectives were used because they measure Enthusiasm (enthusiastic, excited, lively, and energetic; Feldman Barrett, 1998).

The variability hypothesis stated that creative writers would exhibit more mood variability than either journalists or controls. After statistical analyses, creative writers as well as journalists were found to have lower mood variability than nonwriters. In addition, there was no significant difference between creative writers and journalists. This finding suggests that, for these student writers, there is no association between regularly engaging in creative writing and higher mood variability. One possible explanation is that the regulation hypothesis invalidated the variability hypothesis, meaning that for the creative writers and journalists, writing may have acted as a mood regulator, leveling mood variability. Further, it could have acted as a protective factor. Perhaps when mood variability is within the normal range, it can be assuaged by writing. Further, it has been suggested that creativity is central to mental health (i.e., Csikszentmihalyi, 1990; Maslow, 1968; Richards, 1990; Rogers, 1959). It is possible that the relationship between creativity and mental health is mediated by the "level of expertise of the writer" so that professional (eminent) writers may very well have "habituated" to writing and it is no longer beneficial to them (Runco, 1998, p. 644). On the other hand, apprentice writers fully enjoy the benefits of writing (Runco, 1998).

The absence of a difference between creative writers and journalists is possibly because journalism also elicits self-disclosure. Runco (1994) contended that creative writing facilitates self-disclosure because the writer is incited to find a problem, propose a solution, and then examine the consequences of implementing such a solution. This reasoning can very well be applied to journalistic writing: Instead of a personal or emotional problem, the apprentice journalist is more likely to tackle society's problem. In addition, journalists are often linking their thoughts about the events to their feelings and reactions to it, a practice very similar to the one attributed to Pennebaker's participants. Pennebaker also mentioned the importance of the writing moving from a disorganized state to an organized state in enabling the writer to feel better. Editing is a process through which the writing undergoes such a process, especially for those who write for an audience.

The regulation hypothesis was partly supported: The act of writing increased positive valence (writers reported feeling happier, more satisfied, more delighted, more joyful) and lowered arousal (participants reported feeling calmer, less nervous, more relaxed and enthusiastic). These findings add to the body of work delineating the benefits of writing outlined earlier and described by Pennebaker and colleagues (1986–2008). In addition, given that participants' writing was not collected and that they were not asked to indicate the genre and topic of their writing when filling out the writing forms, it seems that, for this group of writers, it is the mere act of writing that is beneficial. Indeed, many student writers ultimately want to go on and become "real" journalists and "real" writers. As one participant explained, "I want to become a journalist, so the more I write, the better I write, and the better I feel about myself." It is plausible that for these participants, writing is beneficial regardless of the topic because all writing can be seen as contributing to their professional development. They are exercising their chosen craft. Moreover, by writing, participants are exercising self-regulation in that they have set goals and are actively pursuing them, thus moving closer to their desired outcome, which overall contributes to an improved mood and sense of well-being (King, 2002).

Interestingly, journalists reported more satisfaction after writing than did creative writers. Perhaps creative writers are harder on themselves, and because journalists work on a deadline, it is possible that they feel relieved to have finished on time. Their projects are also clearly defined, and they get immediate feedback from other journalists and readers. Further, all the pieces that they work on are commissioned, published, and have an audience. Creative writers' pieces are not all published; in fact, only a few are. Additionally, journalists probably have a stronger sense of agency in that they are reacting to events by telling their readers what they think about those occurrences. Indeed, for one journalist, writing is about "responding to the world and contributing to the community." Perhaps creative writers are somehow frustrated by their lack of immediate gratification and by having fewer opportunities to receive feedback (Kaun, 1991).

In addition to completing mood scales, participants were also asked to write their thoughts about the effect of writing on mood (does writing influence your mood?[1]) and the effect of mood on writing (what mood are you typically in when you write?). I was interested in the subjective experience of participants, in the meaning that they made out of their experience (Bruner, 1990; Denzin & Lincoln, 2000) as budding writers.

Overall, participants' theories expressed in response to the question, "how does writing affect your mood," are reflected by the mood change captured by the mood scales. Indeed, almost all journalists and all creative writers reported

---

[1] The questions between parentheses were the actual questions presented to the participants.

that writing elevated their mood, and more than half reported a decrease in arousal on both scales and stated theory (feeling calmer, serene, peaceful). As one journalist explained, "It's just something about the creative process of being able to put words to paper that makes me feel good." Writers reported that writing made them feel creative, inspired, and imaginative. Participants also reported that writing helped them understand their thoughts and emotions. It helped them gain "insight." Journalists reflected that writing helped them structure and organize their ideas so that their thoughts could be fully developed and explored and could reach their "natural conclusion." They were able to focus on a specific topic in a methodical way, which made the events they described more manageable. Thus, writing "clarified [their] thinking."

However, no journalist reported the therapeutic and cathartic effect of writing, which creative writers did. One poet described writing as the "only time when I am completely honest with myself." In addition, creative writers reported being completely immersed by their writing; at such times they were in what Csikszentmihalyi (1990) called "flow," which has been described as the suspension of time, transcendence of self, and oblivion to the surroundings. One creative writer reflected, "[One gets] completely absorbed [in it] and enters another world."

For the next question, "what mood are you typically in when you write," participants reported almost opposite moods. Some creative writers and journalists reported feeling pensive and absorbed, a state that one described as "almost like meditation." Others described high energy and excitement because they regard writing as highly enjoyable, and "can't wait to get started." Creative writers as well as journalists reflected that their mood very much depended on how satisfied they were with their writing.

These apprentice writers seem to know themselves well and to be very attuned to the role and the effect of writing in their lives. It is possibly by writing that they reached this high level of self-knowledge. An alternative explanation would be that writers' theories about the effect of writing on mood drove their answers on the scales. For example, writers who believed that writing made them happy might automatically report positive emotions without introspecting at all. Conversely, those who held the belief that writing made them feel worse might fill out the scales according to these beliefs.

Thus, it seems that the relationship between manic depression and creative writing as it applies to distinguished novelists such as Woolf, Hemingway, Plath, and others does not extrapolate to a relationship between mood variability and writing in student writers. It is perhaps precisely because they are writing that participants' mood is more stable than that of controls. These findings do concur with earlier research that concluded that, after writing, participants overall feel better, less negative, and more positive (i.e., Brand & House, 1987; Pennebaker & Beall, 1986). Moreover, the study also suggests that, for these aspiring writers, it is the act of writing itself that seems to be beneficial and not the topic of the writing. This is perhaps because by writing they are moving closer to their aspiration of becoming "real" writers.

REFERENCES

Akiskal, H. S. (2003). Validating "hard" and "soft" phenotypes within the bipolar spectrum: Continuity or discontinuity? *Journal of Affective Disorders, 73*, 1–5.

Akiskal, H. S., Bourgeois, M. L., Angst, J., Post, R., Moller, H. J., & Hirschfeld, R. (2000). Re-evaluating the prevalence of and diagnostic composition within the broad clinical spectrum of bipolar disorders. *Journal of Affective Disorders, 59*(1), 5–30.

Akiskal, H. S., Placidi, G. F., Maremmani, I., Signoretta, S., Liguori, A., Gervasi, R., et al. (1998). TEMPS-I: Delineating the most discriminant traits of the cyclothymic, depressive, hyperthymic and irritable temperaments in a nonpatient population. *Journal of Affective Disorder, 51*(1), 7–19.

American Psychiatric Association. (1980–2000). *Diagnostic and statistical manual of mental disorders.* Washington, DC: Author.

Andreasen, N. C. (1987). Creativity and mental illness: Prevalence in writers and their first-degree relatives. *American Journal of Psychiatry, 144*(10), 1288–1292.

Andreasen, N. C., & Canter, A. (1974). The creative writer: Psychiatric symptoms and family history. *Comprehensive Psychiatry, 15*(2), 123–131.

Angst J., & Marneros A. (2001). Bipolarity from ancient to modern times: Conception, birth and rebirth. *Journal of Affective Disorders, 67*, 3–19.

Baldessarini, R. J. (2000). A plea for integrity of the bipolar disorder concept. *Bipolar Disorders, 2*, 3–7.

Bradley, R. G., & Follingstad, D. R. (2003). Group therapy for incarcerated women who experienced interpersonal violence: A pilot study. *Journal of Traumatic Stress, 16*(4), 337–340.

Brand, A. G., & House, G. (1987). Relationships between types of assignments, writer variables, and emotions of college composition students. *Alberta Journal of Educational Research, 33*(1), 21–32.

Brand, A. G., & Leckie, P. A. (1988). The emotions of professional writers. *Journal of Psychology, 122*(5), 421–439.

Brand, A. G., & Powell, J. P. (1986). Emotions and the writing process: A description of apprentice writers. *Journal of Educational Research, 79*(5), 280–285.

Brown, E. J., & Heimberg, R. G. (2001). Effects of writing about rape: Evaluating Pennebaker's paradigm with a severe trauma. *Journal of Traumatic Stress, 14*(4), 781–790.

Bruner, J. (1990). *Acts of meaning.* Cambridge, MA: Harvard University Press.

Burton, C. M., & King, L. A. (2004). The health benefits of writing about intensely positive experiences. *Journal of Research in Personality, 38*(2), 150–163.

Cameron, L. D., & Nicholls, G. (1998). Expression of stressful experiences through writing: Effects of a self-regulation manipulation for pessimists and optimists. *Health Psychology, 17*, 84–92.

Caplan, A. L. (2000). The morality of the mundane: Ethical issues arising in the daily lives of nursing home residents. In R. A. Kane & A. L. Caplan (Eds.), *Everyday ethics: Resolving dilemmas in nursing home life* (pp. 37–50). New York: Springer.

Clore, G. L., Schwartz, N., & Conway, M. (1994). Affective causes and consequences of social information processing. In R. S. Wyer & T. K. Srull (Eds.), *Handbook of social cognition: Vol. 1. Basic processes* (2nd ed., pp. 323–417). Hillsdale, NJ: Erlbaum.

Csikszentmihalyi, M. (1990). *Flow: The psychology of optimal experience.* New York: Harper & Row.

Denzin, N. K., & Lincoln, Y. S. (2000). Introduction: The discipline and practice of qualitative research. In N. K. Denzin, & Y. S. Lincoln (Eds.), *Handbook of qualitative research* (pp. 1–29). Thousand Oaks, CA: Sage.

Dominguez, B, Valderrama, P., Meza, M. A., Perez, S. L., Silva, A., Martinez, G., et al. (1995). The roles of emotional reversal and disclosure in clinical practice. In J. W. Pennebaker (Ed.), *Emotional disclosure and health* (pp. 255–270). Washington, DC: American Psychological Association.

Duncker, K. (1945). On problem solving. *Psychological Monographs, 58*(5, Whole No. 270).

Feldman, L. A. (1995). Variations in the circumplex structure of emotion. *Personality and Social Psychology Bulletin, 21,* 806–817.

Feldman Barrett, L. A. (1997). The relationships among momentary emotion experiences, personality descriptions, and retrospective ratings of emotion. *Personality and Social Psychology Bulletin, 23*(10), 1100–1110.

Feldman Barrett, L. A. (1998). Discrete emotions or dimensions? The role of valence focus and arousal focus. *Cognition and Emotion, 12*(4), 579–599.

Feldman Barrett, L. A., & Fossum, T. (2001). Mental representation of affect knowledge. *Cognition & Emotion, 15*(3), 333–363.

Francis, M. E., & Pennebaker, J. W. (1992). Putting stress into words: The impact of writing on physiological, absentee, and self-reported well-being measures. *American Journal of Health Promotion, 6,* 280–286.

Frattaroli, J. (2006). Experimental disclosure and its moderators: A meta-analysis. *Psychological Bulletin, 132*(6), 823–865.

Getzels, J. W., & Csikszentmihalyi, M. (1976). *The creative vision.* New York: Wiley.

Goodwin, F. K., & Jamison, K. R. (2007). *Manic-depressive illness: Bipolar disorder and recurrent depression* (2nd ed.) New York: Oxford University Press.

Greenberg, M. A., Wortman, C. B., & Stone, A. A. (1996). Emotional expression and physical health: Revising traumatic memories or fostering self-regulation. *Journal of Personality and Social Psychology, 71,* 588–602.

Isen, A. M. (1984). Toward understanding the role of affect in cognition. In R. S. Wyer & T. K. Srull (Eds.), *Handbook of social cognition* (Vol. 3, pp. 179–236). Hillsdale, NJ: Erlbaum.

Isen, A. M. (1987). Positive affect, cognitive processes, and social behavior. In L. Berkowitz (Ed.), *Advances in experimental social psychology* (Vol. 20, pp. 203–253). New York: Academic.

Isen, A. M. (1993). Positive affect and decision making. In M. Lewis & K. Haviland (Eds.), *Handbook of emotions* (pp. 261–277). New York: Guilford.

Isen, A. M., & Daubman, K. A. (1984). The influence of affect on categorization. *Journal of Personality and Social Psychology, 47*(6), 1206–1217.

Isen, A. M., Daubman, K. A., & Nowicki, G. P. (1987). Positive affect facilitates creative problem solving. *Journal of Personality and Social Psychology, 52*(6), 1122–1131.

Isen, A. M., Johnson, M. M., Mertz, E., & Robinson, G. F. (1985). The influence of positive affect on the unusualness of word associations. *Journal of Personality and Social Psychology, 48,* 1413–1426.

Jamison, K. R. (1989). Mood disorders and pattern of creativity in British writers and artists. *Psychiatry, 52,* 125–134.

Jamison, K. R. (1993). *Touched with fire: Manic-depressive illness and the artistic temperament.* New York: Free Press.

Jaušovec, N. (1989). Affect in analogical transfer. *Creativity Research Journal, 2,* 255–266.

Judd, L. L., & Akiskal, H. S. (2003). The prevalence and disability of bipolar spectrum disorders in the US population: Re-analysis of the ECA database taking into account subthreshold cases. *Journal of Affective Disorders, 73*, 123–131.

Kaufman, J. C. (2001). The Sylvia Plath effect: Mental illness in eminent creative writers. *Journal of Creative Behavior, 35*(1), 37–50.

Kaufman, J. C. (2002). I bask in dreams of suicide: Mental illness, poetry, and women. *Review of General Psychology, 6*(3), 271–286.

Kaufman, J. C. (2005). The door that leads into madness: Eastern European poets and mental illness. *Creativity Research Journal, 17*(1), 2005, 99–103.

Kaufman, J. C., & Sexton, J. D. (2006). Why doesn't the writing cure help poets? *Review of General Psychology, 10*(3), 268–282.

Kaufmann, G. (1993). The content and logical structure of creativity concepts: An inquiry into the conceptual foundations of creativity research. In S. G. Isaksen, M. C. Murdock, R. L. Firestien, & D. J. Treffinger (Eds.), *Understanding and recognizing creativity: The emergence of a discipline* (pp. 114–157). Norwood, NJ: Ablex.

Kaufmann, G. (2003). Expanding the mood-creativity equation. *Creativity Research Journal, 15*(2–3), 131–135.

Kaufmann, G., & Vosburg, S. K. (1997). "Paradoxical" mood effects of creative problem solving. *Cognition and Emotion, 11*, 151–170.

Kaufmann, G., & Vosburg, S. K. (2002). The effects of mood on early and late idea production. *Creativity Research Journal, 14*(3–4), 317–330.

Kaun, D. E. (1991). Writers die young: The impact of work and leisure on longevity. *Journal of Economic Psychology, 12*(2), 381–399.

Kelsoe, J. R. (2003). Arguments for the genetic basis of the bipolar spectrum [Special issue]. *Journal of Affective Disorders, 73*(1–2), 183–197.

Kernis, M. H., Cornell, D. P., Sun, C. R., Berry, A., & Harlow, T. (1993). There's more to self-esteem than whether it is high or low: The importance of stability of self-esteem. *Journal of Personality and Social Psychology, 65*(6), 1190–1204.

King, L. A. (2001). The health benefits of writing about life goals. *Personality and Social Psychology Bulletin, 27*(7), 798–807.

King, L. A. (2002). Gain without pain? Expressive writing and self-regulation. In S. J. Lepore & J. M. Smyth (Eds.), *The writing cure: How expressive writing promotes health and emotional well-being* (pp. 110–134). Washington, DC: American Psychological Association.

King, L. A., & Miner, K. N. (2000). Writing about the perceived benefits of traumatic events: Implications for physical health. *Personality and Social Psychology Bulletin, 26*, 220–230.

Knee, C. R., Patrick, H., Vietor, N. A., & Neighbors, C. (2004). Implicit theories of relationships: Moderators of the link between conflict and commitment. *Personality and Social Psychology Bulletin, 30*(5), 617–628.

Kraepelin, E. (1921). *Manic-depressive insanity and paranoia.* R. M. Barclay (Ed.) & G. M. Robertson (Trans.). Edinburgh: E & S Livingstone.

Lauer, C. J., Bronisch, T., Kainz, M., Schreiber, W., Holsboer, F., & Krieg, J. C. (1997). Pre-morbid psychometric profile of subjects at high familial risk for affective disorder. *Psychological Medicine, 27*, 355–362.

Low, C. A., Stanton, A. L., & Danoff-Burg, S. (2006). Expressive disclosure and benefit finding among breast cancer patients: Mechanisms for positive health effects. *Health Psychology, 25*(2), 181–189.

Ludwig, A. M. (1992). Creative achievement and psychopathology: Comparison among professions. *American Journal of Psychotherapy, 46*, 330–357.

Ludwig, A. M. (1994). Mental illness and creative activity in female writers. *American Journal of Psychiatry, 151*(11), 1650–1656.

Makarec, K., & Persinger, M. A. (1985). Temporal lobe signs: Electroencephalographic validity and enhanced scores in special populations. *Perceptual and Motor Skills, 60*(3), 831–842.

Maslow, A. H. (1968). *Toward a psychology of being.* New York: Van Nostrand.

Meichenbaum, D., & Fong, G. T. (1993). How individuals control their own minds: A constructive narrative perspective. In D. M. Wagner & J. W. Pennebaker (Eds.), *Handbook of mental control* (pp. 473–490). Englewood, NJ: Prentice Hall.

Melton, R. J. (1995). The role of positive affect in syllogism performance. *Personality and Social Psychology Bulletin, 21*(8), 788–794.

Meyer, T. D., & Keller, F. (2003). Is there evidence for a latent class called "hypomanic temperament"? *Journal of Affective Disorders, 75*(3), 259–267.

Mraz, W., & Runco, M. (1994). Suicide ideation and creative problem solving. *Suicide and Life-Threatening Behavior, 24,* 38–47.

O'Heeron, R. C. (1993). Confronting life events: Inner-city adolescents write about personal traumas. Unpublished doctoral dissertation, California School of Professional Psychology.

Páez, D., Velasco, C., & Gonzáles, J. L. (1999). Expressive writing and the role of alexythimia as a dispositional deficit in self-disclosure and psychological health. *Journal of Personality and Social Psychology, 77*(3), 630–641.

Patten, S. B. (2006). Does almost everybody suffer from a bipolar disorder? *Canadian Journal of Psychiatry, 51*(1), 6–8.

Pennebaker, J. W. (1993). Putting stress into words: Health, linguistic, and therapeutic implications. *Behavior Research and Therapy, 31,* 539–548.

Pennebaker, J. W. (1997). Writing about emotional experiences as a therapeutic process. *Psychological Science, 8*(3), 162–166.

Pennebaker, J. W. (2004). Theories, therapies, and taxpayers: On the complexities of the expressive writing paradigm. *Clinical Psychology: Science and Practice, 11*(2), 138–142.

Pennebaker, J. W., & Beall, S. (1986). Confronting a traumatic event: Toward an understanding of inhibition and disease. *Journal of Abnormal Psychology, 95,* 274–281.

Pennebaker, J. W., Colder, M., & Sharp, L. (1990). Accelerating the coping process. *Journal of Personality and Social Psychology, 58,* 528–537.

Pennebaker, J. W., & Francis, M. E. (1996). Cognitive emotional and language processes in disclosure. *Cognition and Emotion, 10,* 601–626.

Pennebaker, J. W., & Graybeal, A. (2001). Patterns of natural language use: Disclosure, personality, and social integration. *Current Directions, 10,* 90–93.

Pennebaker, J. W., Mayne, T. J., & Francis, M. (1997). Linguistic predictors of adaptive bereavement. *Journal of Personality and Social Psychology, 72,* 863–871.

Pennebaker, J. W., & Seagal, J. D. (1999). Forming a story: The health benefits of a narrative. *Journal of Clinical Psychology, 55,* 1243–1254.

Penner, L. A., Shiffman, S., Paty, J. A., & Fritzsche, B. A. (1994). Individual differences in intraperson variability in mood. *Journal of Personality and Social Psychology, 66*(4), 712–721.

Petrie, K. J., Booth, R. J., Pennebaker, J. W., Davison, K. P., & Thomas, M. G. (1995). Disclosure of trauma and immune response to hepatitis B vaccination program. *Journal of Consulting and Clinical Psychology, 63,* 787–792.

Piirto, J. (1998). Themes in the lives of successful contemporary U.S. women creative writers. *Roeper Review, 21*(1), 60–70.

Piirto, J. (2002). *"My teeming brain": Understanding creative writers.* Cresskill, NJ: Hampton Press.

Post, F. (1994). Creativity and psychopathology: A study of 291 world-famous men. *British Journal of Psychiatry, 165,* 22–34.

Post, F. (1996). Verbal creativity, depression, and alcoholism: An investigation of one hundred American and British writers. *British Journal of Psychiatry, 168*(5), 545–555.

Ratey, J. J., & Johnson, C. (1998). *Shadow syndromes: The mild forms of major mental disorders that sabotage us.* New York: Bantam.

Reis, H. T., & Gable, S. L. (2000). Event-sampling and other methods for studying everyday experience. In H. T. Reis & C. M. Judd (Eds.), *Handbook of research methods in social and personality psychology* (pp. 190–222). New York: Cambridge University Press.

Richards, J. M., Beal, W. E., & Seagal, J. D. (2000). Effects of disclosure of traumatic events on illness behavior among psychiatric prison inmates. *Journal of Abnormal Psychology, 109*(1), 156–160.

Richards, R. (1990). Everyday creativity, eminent creativity, and health: 'Afterview' for CRJ Issues on creativity and health. *Creativity Research Journal, 3*(4), 300–326.

Rimé, B. (1995). Mental rumination, social sharing and the recovery from emotional exposure. In J. W. Pennebaker (Ed.), *Emotional disclosure and health* (pp. 271–292). Washington, DC: American Psychological Association.

Rogers, C. (1959). Toward a theory of creativity. In H. Anderson (Ed.), *Creativity and its cultivation* (pp. 69–82). New York: Harper & Row.

Runco, M. (1994). Creativity and its discontent. In M. P. Shaw & M. A. Runco (Eds.), *Creativity and affect* (pp. 102–126). Norwood: NJ: Ablex.

Runco, M. (1998). Suicide and creativity: The case of Sylvia Plath [Special issue]. *Death Studies, 22*(7), 637–654.

Sloan, D. M., & Marx, B. P. (2004). Taking pen to hand: Evaluating theories underlying the written disclosure paradigm. *Clinical Psychology: Science and Practice, 11*(2), 121–137.

Smyth, J. M. (1998). Written emotional expression: Effect sizes, outcome types, and moderating variables. *Journal of Consulting and Clinical Psychology, 66,* 174–184.

Smyth, J., True, N., & Souto, J. (2001). Effects of writing about traumatic experiences: The necessity for narrative structuring. *Journal of Social & Clinical Psychology, 20*(2), 161–172.

Spera, S., Buhrfeind, E., & Pennebaker, J. W. (1994). Expressive writing and job loss. *Academy of Management Journal, 37,* 722–733.

Stirman, S. W., & Pennebaker, J. W. (2001). Word use in the poetry of suicidal and non-suicidal poets. *Psychosomatic Medicine, 63,* 517–523.

Vosburg, S. K. (1998a). The effects of positive and negative moods on divergent-thinking performance. *Creativity Research Journal, 11*(2), 165–172.

Vosburg, S. K. (1998b). Mood and the quantity and quality of ideas. *Creativity Research Journal, 11*(4), 315–324.

Walker, M. A., Koestner, R., & Hum, A. (1995). Personality correlates of depressive style in autobiographies of creative achievers. *Journal of Creative Behavior, 29*(2), 75–90.

Watson, D., & Clark, L. A. (1994). *Manual for the positive affect and negative affect schedule (expanded form).* Unpublished manuscript, University of Iowa, IA.

Weisberg, R. W. (1994). Genius and madness? A quasi experimental test of the hypothesis that manic-depression increases creativity. *Psychological Science, 5,* 361–367.

4

Characteristics of Eminent Screenwriters: Who *Are* Those Guys?

STEVEN R. PRITZKER AND DAVID JUNG MCGARVA

"Who *are* those guys?" was a line spoken repeatedly by Paul Newman in *Butch Cassidy and the Sundance Kid* (Goldman, 1969, p. 80) as a posse followed them. It is an apt description of the notoriety of screenwriters who have, for the most part, remained out of the limelight with no posses or paparazzi following them.

There is a considerable amount of research investigating the characteristics of eminent writers, including poets, fiction writers, and nonfiction writers. However, we were able to locate very little research employing a psychological perspective regarding the characteristics of screenwriters.

This chapter reviews information concerning Academy Award winning screenwriters from 1927–2007, from both a quantitative and qualitative approach. We compiled statistics on screenwriters regarding age of winning the award, longevity, gender, and nationality. By reviewing interviews with Oscar-writing screenwriters, we gathered information on qualitative themes, including experiences growing up, work experience before becoming screenwriters, motivation, work habits, writing, rewriting, collaboration, and experiences in the film business.

A BRIEF HISTORY OF SCREENWRITERS

It is important to look at screenwriters from a historical perspective because the film industry is a unique environment. A brief three-word description of the general attitude toward movie writers is provided by the title of an old movie: *They Were Expendable.*

This attitude dates to the early days of silent films when Mack Sennett gained fame by locking his writers in a room until they came up with acceptable stories. A few screenwriters earned substantial sums, but they were the exceptions. For example, Anita Loos started selling stories to D. W. Griffith for $25 each and ended up becoming a highly paid star writer when her scenarios helped turn Douglas Fairbanks into a star. Similarly, her friend Frances Marion parlayed her success writing Mary Pickford movies into a $50,000 a year contract with Paramount (Norman, 2007). Marion later earned two Oscars (*The Champ, The Big House*) in 4 years.

However, the majority of writers were warehoused in studios in places similar to what John Cromwell described at Paramount in 1930: "a barrack-like building – long halls, little cubby holes, typewriters clacking away behind doors" (Wilk, 2004, p. 27). Many writers punched time clocks. They worked on whatever scripts the studio assigned them and most of the time did not complete the story they were assigned. Most writers were considered inter-changeable:

> Milton Sperling said that many producers kept in their offices a goosing stick, which looked and functioned something like a cattle prod, and they found it amusing to use it on writers. "The cruelty," he remembered, "was intensified by the way people played along. The stakes were so big that many people submitted to humiliation." (Schwartz & Schwartz, 1982, p. 20)

Even if that story is apocryphal, it captures the essence of a relationship in which many writers were powerless. Jack L. Warner "enjoyed referring to his cadre of writers as 'schmucks with Underwoods'" (Wilk, 2004, p. XII). The producer Irving Thalberg used teams of writers on the same project because he saw himself as the driving creative force: "I, more than any single person in Hollywood, have my finger on the pulse of America. I know what people will do and what they won't do" (Dardis, 1976, p. 44). I. A. L. Diamond (*The Apartment*) recalled that "the major studios operated on the principle that the more writers on a script, the better it was going to be" (Froug, 1972, p. 149).

Who received writing credits on movies was determined by production companies. Carl Laemmle (who wanted to be called Uncle Carl) of Universal Studios gave his family members credit, leading Ogden Nash, a humorous poet, to write, "Uncle Carl Laemmle/has a very large faemmle" (Schwartz & Schwartz, 1982, p. 8).

However, Hollywood producers, beginning as early as Samuel Goldwyn in 1919, did go after big name literary and stage writers. Big name writers signed by the studios in Hollywood in the 1930s included Scott Fitzgerald, Dorothy Parker, S. J. Perelman, Aldous Huxley, Robert Benchley, Marc Connelly, John Dos Passos, Nathanael West, John O'Hara, Damon Runyon, Evelyn Waugh, and William Faulkner. "Even Sigmund Freud had been contacted by Samuel Goldwyn about coming to Hollywood to write a script about psychoanalysis" (Schwartz & Schwartz, 1982, p. 20). However, fame in other arenas did not necessarily translate into success in writing movies. Bitterness about Hollywood experiences was expressed in many novels including Scott Fitzgerald's *The Last Tycoon* and Nathanael West's *Day of the Locust*.

The shabby treatment of the majority of Hollywood writers and of many other workers in the film industry led to union organizing activity in the early

1930s. Studio heads founded the Academy of Motion Picture Arts and Sciences in 1928 to preempt unions from forming and to serve as a central organization with which they could control players in the industry. In 1933, a wage cut that the studio heads said was justified by the Depression led to a strike by union soundmen and the formation of the Screenwriters Guild, which eventually became the Writers Guild of America (Schwartz & Schwartz, 1982). Yet no minimum wage agreements were put in place until 1942 (Norman, 2007).

This history is important to understand because it highlights the thread of powerlessness that runs through much of the discussion with many Hollywood writers, even the ones at the top of the profession. For example, "Donald Ogden Stewart said that at formal dinners one was seated according to importance at the box office. Writers, if invited at all, sat at the bottom of the table, below the heads of publicity but above the hairdressers" (Schwartz & Schwartz, 1982, p. 19).

Writers under contract to the studios often had their own table in the commissary where they enjoyed each other's companionship. Julius Epstein (*Casablanca*) remembered, "It was a real club; that was the fun of it. There were 70 to 75 writers at Warners, 125 at Metro. . . . Only the writers could sit at the writers' table" (McGilligan, 1986, p. 178).

Over the years, the studio system has been weakened so that most writers today work on a project-to-project basis. A few writer-directors have gained the power to have their work produced with a minimum of interference. However, most screenwriters are still faced with the challenge of responding to a variety of other parties, including studio executives, company executives, directors, and actors. A script may go through a number of rewrites as the players change. Ted Tally (*Silence of The Lambs*) summed up the challenge:

> It's not fun unless it gets made. And unless it gets made, you're not going to feel legitimized. An unproduced script is not publishable. . . . A film script is only good for one thing. Otherwise it's dead. And in many cases you don't even own it. (Engel, 1995, p. 109)

John Briley (*Gandhi*) stated the situation bluntly:

> Writers are not the lowest of the low ("the aspiring starlet who was so dumb she screwed the writer") because people don't want good scripts. It's because they are, unlike all their other professional colleagues, utterly powerless. Powerless to protect their material, powerless even to really argue its merits. (Elbert, 1999, p. 134)

The perception in Hollywood of writers has not changed. Speaking about contract negotiations, Garrett (2007) reported in *Daily Variety*, "Film scribes are caught in a double whammy as strike deadlines approach: Collectively, they are generally less powerful than their actor and director counterparts" (p. 1). This lack of power was proven out in the resulting strike when the

Writers Guild was only able to make a settlement after the Directors Guild had made an agreement with production companies regarding payments for TV shows and movies distributed on the Internet. The 4 ½-month strike resulted in relatively small payments for writers whose work is written for the Internet or for shows and movies later distributed on the Internet. Because the Internet is viewed as a key future means of distribution, the deal was hailed as a triumph by the leaders of the Writers Guild with major financial benefits for the future.

The well-documented lack of respect for writers contrasts sharply with the findings of Simonton (2004), who analyzed award-winning movies in an attempt to measure the relative importance of different elements to film making. He concluded, "Screenwriting joins direction in constituting the two most critical predictors of a movie's success." He added, "Ultimately, a great film must tell a great story. This provides a link between filmmaking creativity and the creativity displayed in literature; especially in drama.... Many notable motion pictures are in fact adapted from successful novels and plays" (p. 170).

OUR STUDY

Our study focused on the 215 Academy Award winning screenwriters in any writing category from the first Academy Awards in 1927/28 through 2007. An example of the lack of general interest in screenwriters is the paucity of published biographical data about them. The only biographical item available for every writer who won an Oscar was his or her date of death. We accepted the dates listed in the Academy's own database as authoritative even when we found alternative dates.

The Academy does not publish dates of birth. We drew these from standard reference books, professionally edited Web sites, and obituaries. One date of birth came from a gravestone. For several writers it was difficult to find dates of birth, and it became clear that a few had made the choice to keep their ages private. We were successful in tracking down dates for 211 of the 215 writers.

Some of the data were provided through statistical calculations, including median age at which writers won the award and the median age of death. Other categories calculated include the percentage of women, minorities, and non-English-speaking writers who won. We also looked at how many individuals won more than one award and the number of winning writer-directors.

The use of Academy Award winners as the standard might be questioned because studios have been accused of manipulating the awards. However, Simonton (2002) found that the Academy Award provided the most reliable predictor of quality both in relation to other awards, especially those of the Writers Guild of America, and to future movie guide ratings.

Writers were selected for inclusion based on the availability of archival material including published interviews, biographies, and autobiographical books and articles. Because of the increased interest in screenwriters during the last 30 years, the majority of the writers who were included worked after 1950. A conscious effort was made to avoid choosing a preponderance of writer-directors. We reviewed the information and interviews of 101 writers (Appendix A), examining aspects such as early childhood experiences, education, number of marriages, and number of children.

Both authors read the written materials and coded themes of importance: experiences growing up, work experience before becoming screenwriters, motivation, work habits, writing, rewriting, collaboration, and reflections about the experience of being in the movie business.

EARLY LIFE HISTORY

The difficult early years of award-winning writer-director Preston Sturges (*The Great McGinty*) are illustrative of many writers' experiences. He was 8 years old when his mother decided to move to Paris with Preston while his father, a millionaire named Solomon Sturges, remained in Chicago. Preston wanted to stay with Solomon, but he told him, "I am not your father" (Spoto, 1990, p. 20). Preston grew up primarily raised by his mother, who was married at least four times in addition to cultivating a number of younger lovers. She was also a writer of sorts who managed to publish a poorly written book about her friendship with Isadora Duncan.

Preston's life as a young man involved moving from city to city without really developing any deep emotional ties or a profession. He finally landed a job as a stage manager and soon after, at age 29, he wrote his first play, *The Guinea Pig*, and then *Strictly Dishonorable*, which became a big hit that was eventually filmed. He then wrote three failed plays before moving to Hollywood where his script of *The Power and The Glory* made him a star writer. He eventually wrote and directed a number of films that became classics. Sturges illustrates Rothenberg's and Wyshak's (2004) thesis that exceptional creative talents are often completing the unfulfilled wishes of one of their parents who didn't have success in the same or a similar field.

Research on the lives of 160 exceptional creative fiction writers (Piirto, 2002) indicated an above-average difficulty in childhood including "orphanhood, parental disability, neglect, frequent moving, parental alcoholism, suicide of family members and other extraordinary childhood trauma" (p. 152). This may also be the case for eminent screenwriters. Examples of childhood difficulties experienced by screenwriters included early parental death or absence (Orson Welles, Billy Wilder, and John Huston), childhood illness (Francis Ford Coppola and Ronald Bass), parental divorce (Oliver Stone and Quentin Tarantino), family financial problems (Jane Campion, Billy Wilder, Richard Brooks, Dalton Trumbo, and Woody Allen), and becoming a refugee (Ruth

Prawer Jhabvala). In contrast, some writers such as Joel and Ethan Coen stated they had ordinary childhoods.

We did not have enough data to come to any conclusions regarding mental illness in family members or writers. However, some instances were reported; for example, Orson Welles' (*Citizen Kane*) brother waged a lifelong struggle with mental illness.

One interesting story related to three-time winner Sidney Aaron Chayefsky (*Marty, The Hospital, Network*), who, according to Considine (2000), developed an alter ego. Sidney pretended to have an Irish mother while he was in the Army because he wanted to avoid KP duty; his lieutenant gave him the nickname "Paddy." "Paddy" Chayefsky became a very different person from Sidney. He started eating bacon, which violated his Jewish tenets. Sidney Chayefsky would not have done such a thing. Sidney Chayefsky rarely swore, but for Paddy Chayefsky, "obscenity soon became a second language Paddy created to protect Sidney from his rage and just as he used his words, to protect him from other people" (p. 19). Paddy was the name Chayefsky used as a professional writer. In 1980, when Chayefsky wanted to disown the film of his script for *Altered States*, he used the name Sidney Aaron (Norman, 2007).

Education

Some writers such as William Goldman (*Butch Cassidy and the Sundance Kid, All the President's Men*) reported that they showed no particular talent for writing while younger. Tom Schulman (*Dead Poet's Society*) recalled, "As a kid I was a terrible writer. I was inarticulate and made C's on my writing papers, until I transferred schools in the tenth grade" (Engel, 2002, pp. 102–103). Robert Benton (*Kramer vs. Kramer, Places in The Heart*) was dyslexic so his father took him to a lot of movies. Notable high school dropouts include two-time winners Alvin Sargent (*Julia, Ordinary People*) and Quentin Tarantino (*Pulp Fiction*).

However, the majority of writers we reviewed (24 of 32 or 75%) had at least some college education. Oscar winners who attended film school include Alexander Payne (*Sideways*), Eric Roth (*Forrest Gump*), and Francis Ford Coppola (*Patton, The Godfather, The Godfather 2*). Jane Campion (*The Piano*) was an assistant to a director of commercials and documentaries before studying at Australian Film, Television and Radio School.

Marriage and Children

We found the mean number of marriages to be 2.1. In a random sample of 36, only one writer never married and he is openly gay. However, that result may be biased because it only includes writers whose interviewers and biographers mentioned spouses. The writer who won the award for the most marriages was Alan Jay Lerner (*An American in Paris, Gigi*) with eight wives. Edward Anhalt (*Panic in the Streets, Beckett*), John Huston (*The Treasure of the Sierra Madre*), and William A. Wellman (*A Star is Born*) were each married five times. Only two writers of a random sample of 34 were childless, with a mean of 2.9 children per writer.

THE CAREER PATHS TO BECOMING A SCREENWRITER

That any individual ever actually thinks he or she can make a living becoming a writer requires a tremendous act of faith. William Goldman wrote about how skeptical people would be when, after graduating from college, he told them he wanted to be a writer. He also had to fight his own self-doubt:

> We have hope but we also know the odds against us. Failure keeps us company. And that's the only company we have. Because nobody is going to do it for you. We have tunes in our head, but what if they stink? We have color and composition dancing behind our eyes, but what if no one cares? (1983, p. 84)

Billy Wilder (*The Lost Weekend, Sunset Boulevard, The Apartment*) summed up the challenge of becoming a successful screenwriter this way:

> If the truth be told, language barrier or not, refugees or not, very few people in general make it here, writing scripts. Whether you were born in Dresden or in Oklahoma – just look at the percentage of writers who have actually made it here as a screenwriter, against the percentage of those who've come out here and failed! Expert writers from the New York theatre . . . English authors and playwrights . . . novelists who wrote best sellers . . . guys who've had their stories published in magazines. Very few of them ever made it. . . .
>
> Motion picture writing is a profession in itself. It is a very difficult medium: you cannot just sit down and write a screenplay. . . . In order to write a successful screenplay, you have to have gone through some kind of engineering school. Most of those people . . . even the graduates of film schools, they were just writers. (Wilk, 2004, pp. 157–158)

We identified seven paths to becoming a screenwriter – journalism, play writing, novel writing, television writing, film school and screenwriting as the only profession, other show business occupations, and unrelated careers. The fact that screenwriters come to the field from so many different types of work is significant because, as Billy Wilder suggested, there may be a unique ability to construct a screenplay that is impossible to predict based on the ability to do other forms of writing. Some Oscar-winning writers did most of their work in other fields. Examples include novelist John Irving and playwright George Bernard Shaw.

Journalism

The pressure of deadlines inherent in journalism gave newspaper writers an advantage in the fast-paced world of early film-making. Ben Hecht (*Underworld, The Scoundrel*) and Charles MacArthur (*The Scoundrel*) were journalists, as were Herman J. Mankiewicz (*Citizen Kane*) and his brother Joseph Mankiewicz (*A Letter to Three Wives, All about Eve*). Additional journalists included Dalton Trumbo (*Roman Holiday, The Brave One*), Norman Krasna (*Princes O'Rourke*), S. J. Perelman (*Around the World in 80 Days*), Jeremy Larner (*The Candidate*), and Frank Pierson (*Dog Day Afternoon*).

The newspaperman as hero was a common theme in the 1930s, but its frequency lessened over time as journalism became a less common background for screenwriters. A contemporary example of a journalist-turned screenwriter is Cameron Crowe who won an award for *Almost Famous*, which was inspired by his experiences writing for *Rolling Stone* magazine when he was only 16.

Playwrights

As mentioned earlier, success in the theater often led to an opportunity to write screenplays. A number of playwrights ended up winning Academy Awards, including George Bernard Shaw (*Pygmalion*), Orson Welles (*Citizen Kane*), William Inge (*Splendor in the Grass*), Tom Stoppard (*Shakespeare in Love*), Steve Tesich (*Breaking Away*), John Patrick Shanley (*Moonstruck*), Alfred Uhry (*Driving Miss Daisy*), and double winners Alan Jay Lerner (*An American in Paris, My Fair Lady*) and Robert Bolt (*Dr. Zhivago, A Man for All Seasons*).

Television Writing

Television has provided training for writers since the 1950s. Paddy Chayefsky's award-winning original script for *Marty* was originally performed on TV. He went on to win additional awards for *The Hospital* and *Network*, a parody of the television business. Bo Goldman (*One Flew Over the Cuckoo's Nest, Melvin and Howard*) wrote and produced several shows on PBS in the 1970s.

Mel Brooks (*The Producers*) was a comic in the Catskills where he met Sid Caesar. He became a writer on *The Show of Shows* and continued working for Caesar on various TV shows for 10 years. After selling jokes since he was 16, Woody Allen (*Annie Hall, Hannah and Her Sisters*) became a junior writer on some Caesar TV specials (Parish, 2007). He then started doing his own stand-up comedy act. Marshall Brickman (*Annie Hall*) was a professional musician who then started writing for *Candid Camera* and *The Tonight Show*.

Situation comedy writing was the proving ground for James L. Brooks (*Terms of Endearment*), who created *Room 222* and co-created *The Mary Tyler Moore Show, Rhoda, Taxi,* and *The Simpsons.* Paul Haggis (*Crash, Million Dollar Baby*) worked on *The Facts of Life* and created *Walker, Texas Ranger,* and *EZ Streets.* Charlie Kaufman (*The Eternal Sunshine of the Spotless Mind*) wrote 30 episodes of situation comedies, including *Get a Life!*

Novelists

Writing a novel that was then optioned for a movie in Hollywood provided an opportunity for many screenwriters to start their careers. Charles Brackett (*The Lost Weekend, Sunset Boulevard, Titanic*) was a drama critic for *The New Yorker* and a novelist before he signed with Paramount. Frederic Raphael (*Darling*), William Goldman, Mario Puzo (*The Godfather, The Godfather, Part II*), Ruth Prawer Jhabvala (*A Room with a View, Howard's End*), John Irving (*The Cider House Rules*), and Neil Jordan (*The Crying Game*) all published novels before they wrote screenplays.

Film School and Screenwriting as a First Career

There is a growing trend in the film industry of students who attended film schools, such as University of California at Los Angeles, University of Southern California, and New York University, then becoming major writers, directors, and producers. Other screenwriters went right into the film business. Peter Jackson (*Lord of The Rings – Return of The King*) started making movies on his own. I. A. L. Diamond was offered a job as a junior screenwriter right out of college.

Other Show Business Occupations

Many screenwriters started as actors: for example, Horton Foote (*To Kill a Mockingbird, Tender Mercies*) and Sofia Coppola (*Lost in Translation*). Edward Anhalt and Stephan Zallian (*Schindler's List*) were film editors. Callie Khoury (*Thelma and Louise*) produced music videos. Sidney Buchman (*Here Comes Mr. Jordan*) started as an assistant stage director. Ronald Bass (*Rain Man*) was a Hollywood lawyer. Diablo Cody's (*Juno*) blog about her career as a stripper led to her discovery and ultimately winning the big prize with her first script.

Unrelated Fields

Clearly becoming a successful writer or working in show business is the most prevalent way of getting into the business, but some winners became writers after doing unrelated work. Michael Kanin (*Woman of the Year*) was a

Table 4.1. *Decade in which screenwriters won an Academy Award*

Number of award winners	Decade
66	30s
84	40s
30	50s
5	60s
1	80s

commercial and scenic artist. Quentin Tarantino (*Pulp Fiction*) worked in a video rental store, a job that gave him time to study a lot of films. Several lawyers became screenwriters, including Leo McCarey (*Going My Way*), Sonya Levien (*Interrupted Melody*), and Ronald Bass (*Rain Man*).

Summary

Of a sample of 142 winners for whom data were available, we counted 32 journalists/reporters (18 having their first wins in the 1930s and 1940s, 9 in the 1950s and 1960s, and 5 since then), 19 actors (6 of them since 1995), and 8 lawyers (7 of them from 1955 or earlier).

AGE AT WINNING AN AWARD

Among 198 winners, age at the time of an award ranged from 25 to 82, with a mean of 42.3 and median of 42 (Appendix B). This is in line with the peak years of creative productivity that Simonton (1994) calculated for the arts. Table 4.1 shows the age spread.

George Bernard Shaw is the exceptional individual who won at 82 for the 1938 adaptation of his play *Pygmalion*. Alan Jay Lerner later won in 1964 for the musical adaptation of *Pygmalion*, *My Fair Lady*.

Ageism is perceived to be very powerful in the film business. Prejudice in favor of younger writers is perceived to be so extreme that some screenwriters have actually pretended to be much younger than they are. Froug (1996) reported, "The fear of growing older is endemic in the Hollywood scene. Among some of its denizens, it reaches panic proportions and induces serious breakdowns and dangerous depressions" (p. 324). He stated that writers dye their hair and have facelifts and tummy tucks to look younger. Some have taken on younger partners to help their image in meetings with studio heads. A portion of a lawsuit for age discrimination by older writers against the major studios, networks, and agents was settled in 2008 by two agencies for 4.5 million dollars.

Given this bias, it is interesting to note that the age at which the award is first won, based on a moving average, went up in the last 10 years and is virtually at an all-time high of close to 50 after dipping to a low of under 40 in the 1990s.

LIFE EXPECTANCY

The mean lifespan of a winner was 72 (see Appendix C). This places eminent screenwriters at the top range of life expectancy in line with composers and painters. It also places them much higher on the scale than most writers, despite screenwriters' complaints about the difficulty of their work. Kaufman (2003) examined the lifespans of novelists, poets, playwrights, and nonfiction writers in the United States and elsewhere. The mean lifespan for American writers was 68.9 years, with only the novelists living longer at 72.7 years. The fact that screenwriters make a very good living is in keeping with the general trend of higher-earning people living longer. However, it is worth noting that the life expectancy of screenwriters is declining in contrast to the rise in the general population. From 1940 to 1950 the moving average was close to the mid-70s, whereas in the late 1970s it dipped below 70 and has remained there.

Winners who are still living at the time of this writing average 62 years old. Only one winner, with the exception of the blacklisted writers in the 1950s, received his award posthumously. In 1939, Sidney Howard (*Gone with the Wind*) died in an accident before receiving his Oscar. After winning their award, screenwriters have survived for periods of from less than 2 years – Joseph Farnham, the first-ever winner for Title Writing in 1927/28, Pierre Collings (*The Story of Louis Pasteur*), and Claudine West (*Mrs. Miniver*) – to almost 60 years: Cecil Lewis (*Pygmalion*) and Sidney Sheldon (*The Bachelor and the Bobby-Soxer*).

VARIOUS CATEGORIES OF WINNERS

Repeat Winners

Four individuals have won three Oscars each for writing. However, only one of them, Paddy Chayefsky, was a pure writer, not a writer-director or writer-producer. Billy Wilder was a writer-director on all of his awards, but co-wrote them with Charles Brackett and I. A. L. Diamond. Brackett won a third Oscar for *The Titanic* in 1956, which he wrote with two other writers. Francis Ford Coppola was a co-writer of one award-winning film and co-writer-director of both winning *Godfather* films.

A total of 30 writers won two or more awards. Many of them were screenwriters only: for example, Frances Marion, Robert Bolt, Horton Foote,

Bo Goldman, William Goldman, Ben Hecht, Ring Lardner Jr., Mario Puzo, Waldo Salt, Alvin Sargent, Dalton Trumbo, Michael Wilson, and Ruth Prawer Jhabvala. Writer-directors who won two awards included Woody Allen, Robert Benton, Joseph L. Mankiewicz, and the Coen brothers.

It may, as nominees say, be a thrill just to be nominated. Sixty percent of winners were never nominated again. The two writers with the most nominations are Woody Allen (14) and Billy Wilder (12).

Blacklisted Writers

An astonishing fact is that four of these double winners (Lardner Jr., Salt, Trumbo, and Wilson) were blacklisted after they appeared before the House Un-American Activities Committee hearings that began in 1947. Trumbo and Lardner went to jail after taking the First Amendment and refusing to name others who had allegedly attended meetings of the Communist Party or Communist front organizations. Trumbo (*Roman Holiday, The Brave One*) wrote these films under assumed names. He eventually received his Oscar for *The Brave One* in 1975; the award for *Roman Holiday* was presented to his widow in 1993. Wilson wrote *The Bridge on the River Kwai* with Carl Foreman, another blacklisted writer. They also received posthumous Oscars in 1984.

Women and Minority Writers

The chapter title, "Who *are* those guys?" reflects the high percentage of male award winners. Twenty women have won a total of 22 awards, less than 10% of the total. These include double winners Frances Marion in the 1920s and Ruth Prawer Jhabvala in the 1980s, who account for four of the ten solo writing credits. Muriel Box (*The Seventh Veil*) and Edna Anhalt (*Panic in the Streets*) shared story-writing credits with their husbands. Pamela Wallace (*Witness*) was credited with the story with her husband Earl and William Kelley. All the other women writers received credits on films along with male writers.

The percentage of female award winners has increased significantly over the past two decades. Since 1991, nine women won 19% of the awards, including Jane Campion and Sofia Coppola who also directed their movies. However, women now make up 24% of the membership of the Writers Guild so the percentage of female winners still is not proportional to the percentage in the guild, not to mention in the country. An increase in the number of female Hollywood production executives, including as heads of studios, may eventually help bring more women into key creative positions, but that is a slow process. In 2006, the percentage of women writers working in film was only 19%, the same figure as in 1999. The Writers Guild 2007 *Hollywood Writers Report* (Hunt, 2007) concluded, "Women writers have made no gains relative to male writers in recent years, and there is little evidence to suggest that this pattern is changing" (p. 21). Ironically, Robert Towne (*Chinatown*) commented;

> I think . . . that writers generally tend to identify with women, or even to identify themselves as women – particularly movie writers. I do. You are always the one at home sweating over the hot typewriter while the authority figure is out on the set, telling people what to do. (Brady, 1981, p. 370)

Minority and Non-English-Speaking Winners

The number of minorities winning awards is not calculated anywhere, but we can say it is very small. Although some African American actors, musicians, and sound engineers have won awards, we could not locate one African American writer. The same is true for American Latinos. Nobody born in Asia is represented, although Ruth Prawer Jhabvala moved from Germany to India when she was 12. Now she lives both in the United States and India.

Minority employment in film writing reported by the Writers Guild of America was only 6% in 2005 (Hunt, 2007). Minorities were proportionately underrepresented by 5 to 1. Latinos were underrepresented 9 to 1, Native Americans 5 to 1, African Americans 4 to 1, and Asians 3 to 1. Hunt summed up the loss caused by this lack of minority representation: "Industry diversity is not only about equal access to employment opportunities; it is also about opening spaces for the telling of stories that might not otherwise be told" (p. 51).

Because there is a best foreign film category, rarely does a film in a foreign language cross over and win in the writing category. Some foreign-language films that won Academy awards for writing were *The Red Balloon* (Albert Lamorisse), which contained no dialogue; *Divorce–Italian Style* (Ennio de Concini, Alfredo Giannetti, Pietro Germi), *A Man and a Woman* (Claude LeLouch, Pierre Uytterhoeven), *Missing* (Costa-Gravas), *Talk to Her* (Pedro Almodóvar), and *The Last Emperor* (Bernardo Bertolucci). All seven of these films were from Western European countries. Stellar writer-directors Ingmar Bergman (five nominations) and Federico Fellini (eight nominations) never won writing awards.

A number of awards have been received by writers from other English-speaking countries including the United Kingdom (Charlie Chaplin, George Bernard Shaw, Robert Bolt, John Briley, Peter Schaffer, Frederic Raphael, and Tom Stoppard), New Zealand (Peter Jackson), Ireland (Neil Jordan), and Australia (Jane Campion).

THE CREATIVE PROCESS

The interviews we reviewed focused primarily on film writers' professional experience. They highlighted aspects of the creative process, including work habits, the writing process, and surviving in the film business. Obviously more interviews were conducted with contemporary screenwriters, but we included perspectives from earlier eras as well.

Motivation to Write

Writers may be driven by a deep need to tell stories. Tom Schulman stated, "If you are a writer, you are never without a story to tell and never without a purpose in life" (Elbert, 1999, p. 29). There is also the power of motion pictures to reach a broad audience. John Briley (*Gandhi*) wrote,

> It had been my good fortune to fall into a profession where my work would be seen and responded to by all. . . . And if you wanted to make an impact, there was no better way for a writer to do so. And despite its egalitarian nature, I felt "the trade" gave me a certain sense of dignity, too. (Elbert, 1999, p. 136)

Deadlines create a pressure that can help get work completed. Walter Reisch (*Titanic*) recalled that at Fox,

> Zanuck would call you in to announce that he needed a picture in two weeks' time and not a day later. And you didn't have one day more. I worked to a deadline and I simply loved that way of working. It is very productive, you cannot stall, and if you are under pressure you always come up with something topical because you just don't have time to do a lot of research. (Greenberg, 1991, p. 223)

Bo Goldman found deep pride and purpose in his work: "The thing I've striven the most for in my life is to produce art. I'm an artist. Screenwriting just happens to be the way I express it." He added, "I approach writing the way Michelangelo approached a big block of marble or granite from which a statue was trying to fight its way out" (Engel, 2002, pp. 141–142).

Paddy Chayefsky recognized that individuals may be attracted to writing because "the need for fame and notoriety I think is part of the package that brings you into show business" (Brady, 1981, p. 223).

Money can also be a motivator. Walter Reisch said, "Nothing is more inspiring than to hear a man say, 'Here's a down payment!'" (Greenberg, 1991, p. 224).

Work Habits

Some writers treated screenwriting as a job in terms of maintaining regular work habits. Medford (1974) described James G. Webb's (*How The West Was Won*) work ethic: "Since writing was his trade, he believed that writers should get at it and he was as systematic at getting at it as any writer I ever knew, almost disheartening for one not so systematic" (p. 12). I. A. L. Diamond recalled that when he wrote "with Billy (Wilder), when we start on a script, it's ten to five, five days a week" (Froug, 1972, p. 152).

At the other extreme, Julius Epstein (*Casablanca*) only worked from 12 noon to 2 P.M. – "Never more than two hours a day" (McGilligan, 1986, p. 192). Yet he wrote three pages a day. You can imagine why it did not work out when Julius Epstein tried to team up with Billy Wilder.

The actual writing itself was joyful for some and agony for others. Ron Bass said, "The first draft is always a delight, the purest creative process" (Schanzer & Wright, 1993, p. 27). Woody Allen professed, "Nothing makes me happier than to tear open a big ream of yellow or white paper. And I can't wait to fill it! I love to do it" (Björkman, 1993, p. 8). Alan Ball (*America* Beauty) found it difficult to get into writing: "When I sit down in front of the computer, all of a sudden cleaning the refrigerator becomes incredibly attractive" (Engel, 2002, p. 176). Tom Schulman writes "so fast because I live in fear during the writing that my story is going to fall apart. So when I write I get anxious, terribly anxious. . . . It's a kind of all-night, trancelike torture" (Engel, 2002, p. 106).

Callie Khouri said,

> I haven't yet found a way to get up every day and go sit in my office for three hours. . . . I can't just sit down and write anywhere. I need a feeling of isolation. Even in my own office, which I thought looked like a great working environment because I was in my own house, I still find I really need to be where there are no people and there's simply nothing else to do but write. I can think of fifty ways to rearrange the top of my desk before I can write. (Schanzer & Wright, 1993, pp. 128–129)

Some writers recognize that they need to get into a flow state to write their best work. Bruce Jay Rubin (*Ghost*) stated, "If you are writing from the top of your head, that's something else altogether, that's just craft. I've had periods where that's all I could do because there was no flow" (Schanzer & Wright, 1993, p. 111).

Although the writers in the studios' heyday often had to write in an office, some writers today work on assignments in coffee houses, the park, and libraries. Woody Allen prefers to write on a bed (Moss, 1980). Rubin checks into a hotel and will not leave until he finishes the script (Engel, 2002). This "lock yourself in the room until you finish" mentality goes back to at the least the 1930s when Robert Riskin (*It Happened One Night*) would go to a resort in the desert with director Frank Capra when they were working on a project. Many directors such as Capra and Hitchcock worked extensively on script development without taking a writing credit.

Wherever they write, screenwriters need to find something that is intrinsically rewarding in the process. Marc Norman (*Shakespeare in Love*) stated that he

> kind of liked sitting in a pool of my own sweat: writing had begun to sneak up on me.... You better love the process of writing, because in the end that's all you're ever going to have. The praise and the blame you can't control. All you can really expect from the work is the satisfaction you get from it. (Engel, 2002, p. 156)

Developing Ideas for Original Scripts

Where does the inspiration for original films come from? Walter Reisch stated that when a producer "says he has a certain actor and wants you to write for this actor ... my mind immediately functions in that direction. Half the battle is won. It is all geared towards a personality" (Greenberg, 1991, p. 224).

Horton Foote described his process:

> I keep notebooks, and sometimes just a phrase in a notebook will start me off. I never know. I've also learned that you can't really predict the time for the consolidation of the idea. You can use your will, and you can say, "I know this is wonderful – I'm going to make it work" and it just won't do it. (Cincotti, 1997, p. 132)

Developing an idea into a story that really works is perhaps the greatest challenge of screenwriting. William Goldman stated, "The writing is never the problem, it's knowing what the structure is and what goes where and who the people are and how this scene relates to this.... I have to know all that before I start" (1981, pp. 12–13).

Writers pursue a variety of interesting methods to help realize their story. Robert Benton stated,

> When I'm writing a script, I tack up photos of the actors I have in mind, and I always have to be able to look up and see those pictures. I don't know how many of those people will end up in the film, but by looking at those pictures I hear the voice of the actor, I sense their presence. (Keathley, 2006, p. 32)

Ring Lardner Jr. used the interesting strategy of writing his screenplay as a first-person present-tense novella because he thought it would be an easier read: "I had found out that the great obstacle in getting attention paid to a piece of writing in the movies is that people have to read it – and most screenplays don't read very well, and treatments don't either" (Strugatz & McGilligan, 1997, p. 203).

Rewriting

Rewriting is an essential part of the process, Rubin stated, "As you write, you start to discover the deadwood around what you've written. You have to trim it back and find the living branches, the source that really works" (Schanzer & Wright, 1993, p. 112).

Working as a partner with a writer-director has its privileges. I. A. L. Diamond reported that, when he worked with Billy Wilder, "there is only one draft really, and a good part of the time, we don't even have a finished script when we start shooting" (Froug, 1991, p. 151).

Collaborating with Directors, Producers, Executives, and Actors

Stempel (1991) argued that screenwriters

> have to know how to use the collaborative process to their best advantage. They have to learn how to hustle. The more the process of screenwriting moves away from the family feeling of silent films or the organized procedures of the studio system, the more the screenwriters have had to learn how to manipulate the system or, increasingly, the systems of filmmaking. (p. 228)

Some writers developed successful long-term collaborative relationships. Ruth Prawter Jhabavala worked primarily with one director, James Ivory: "I write the screenplay and show it to him and he tells me mostly what he doesn't like . . . and then I redo it. And it might take over a period of two years or so" (Froug, 1996, p. 214).

Others have found the process to be hit and miss as they work with different individuals. Frederic Raphael (*Darling*) discussed both types of relationships. He recalled that Joseph Janni who produced *Darling* would tell him something was missing: "I'd say, 'Fine. What do you think it is?' And he'd say, 'I don't know.' But after a bit, you'd find he was right. It was the same with Stanley Kubrick. . . . [That's] the way the movies should be" (Baxter, 2006, p. 341). However, while working on *Darling* Raphael was instructed to meet people who might be familiar with the world of his amoral, promiscuous lead character "as if Shakespeare, before being allowed to write King Lear, would have been required to meet with a certain number of dethroned monarchs of a certain age in order to discover what they had in common" (Baxter, 2006, p. 326).

Because the often large numbers of producers and studio executives or individuals financing a movie may hold varying opinions, getting the green light to film becomes an obstacle course usually involving many rewrites. Julius Epstein commented, "Actors are ruining more scripts, I think. All the actors want to be known as improvisers, it seems – which I think is a terrible trend. . . . But most of them aren't; they just think they are. A lot of damage is done" (McGilligan, 1986, p. 180).

Auteurism, the notion that began in France that the director is the equivalent of an author of a film, makes many writers furious. I. A. L. Diamond voiced this view:

> Nobody goes around saying that architecture is a "contractor's medium." To say that the director is the "author" of a film is semantic nonsense. Unless he writes his own script, he's an interpreter. As Frederic Raphael . . . put it, "A director who can't originate a character or develop a situation is like a pastry cook who puts curlicues on somebody else's cake." (Froug, 1972, p. 166)

Walter Reisch argued that the studio system produced better movies because of the shared responsibility: "When the so-called *auteur* directors write everything, direct everything, cut and edit everything themselves, the end results turn out to be lopsided, cockeyed" (Greenberg, 1991, p. 224).

However many writers agree that writer-directors are able to protect their viewpoint and realize their vision. Joel Coen stated, "What makes us different from other directors is the way we work. When we've finished writing a scenario we always remain close to it. There are no big surprises. That's why our scenarios are so detailed" (Cahiers du Cinema, 2006, p. 116).

The Business of Writing

The happiest writers figure out a way to beat the system and make films they would like to do. Of course, directing is one way to achieve what is close to autonomy – at least as long as your films make money. Woody Allen has churned out a film a year for more than 30 years. Most of his films have not grossed a lot at the box office, but they have a relatively low budget so they usually make a profit.

Ron Bass set up his own organization: "my team – the people I employ as a sort of private development group" (Engel, 2002, p. 51). Bass said that he did not know of anybody else who used this method: "But in a way it's essentially what happens in the development process at a studio. . . . Legitimate criticisms and feedback . . . is (*sic*) what every writer needs" (pp. 61–62).

Edward Anhalt hired people to do research and handle all the details so he could focus on writing. In addition, many writers support a network of industry workers such as agents, managers, and lawyers who might help them get work, public relations firms who help them stay in the spotlight, and business managers to help manage their money.

Today's Tensions

The competition to sell screenplays is as intense as it has ever been. The Nicholl Award, a script-writing competition sponsored by the Academy of

Motion Picture Arts and Sciences, received more than 5,000 entries in 2006. New classes of students are graduating from film schools every year, and sometimes it seems that almost everybody in Los Angeles has a script to sell. Robin Williams told a story about a cop who stopped him and tried to peddle a treatment.

Big budget writers need to worry about how well their films do at the box office because the cost per film keeps going up, which makes the stakes higher. Sequels and threequels leave fewer openings for original scripts. Truly original scripts have difficulty getting sold because they are riskier.

CONCLUSION

This chapter provided an overview of the personal characteristics as well as statistical information concerning Oscar-winning screenwriters. There are many more questions beyond the scope of this chapter that we hope can be approached in future research. For example, how do nominees and nonwinners compare to award winners in terms of careers, family history, and longevity? Are there differences between comedy and drama winners? How do screenwriters compare to other writers such as novelists, nonfiction writers, and poets?

Eminent screenwriters register wide individual differences in their approaches to writing, their enjoyment of the writing process, and their philosophy about dealing with the pressures of the business. However, we suspect that screenwriters, for all their complaints, must be at least partially closet optimists. There is always hope that the next script will be the big one. Many writers as they struggle with script problems may take a moment to fantasize themselves at the podium clutching their Oscar and thanking all the people who helped them get there. After all, Hollywood is the land of dreams.

REFERENCES

Baxter, J. (2006). Frederic Raphael: Renaissance man. In P. McGilligan (Ed.), *Backstory 4: Interviews with screenwriters of the 1970s and 1980s* (pp. 317–343). Berkeley: University of California Press.

Björkman, S. (1993). *Woody Allen on Woody Allen: In conversation with Stig Björkman*. New York: Grove Press.

Brady, J. (1981). *The craft of the screenwriter*. New York: Simon & Schuster.

Cahiers du Cinema. (2006). *The Hollywood interviews*. Oxford: Berg.

Cincotti, J. A. (1997). Horton Foote: The trip from Wharton. In P. McGilligan (Ed.), *Backstory 3: Interviews with screenwriters of the 1960s* (pp. 114–134). Berkeley: University of California Press.

Considine, S. (2000). *Mad As hell: The life and work of Paddy Chayefsky*. Lincoln, NE: Iuniverse.com.

Dardis, T. (1976). *Some time in the sun*. New York: Scribners.

Elbert, L. T. (Ed.). (1999). *Why we write: Personal statements and photographic portraits of 25 top screenwriters*. Los Angeles: Silman-James Press.

Engel, J. (1995). *Screenwriters on screenwriting.* New York: Hyperion.

Engel, J. (2002). *Oscar-winning screenwriters on screenwriting.* New York: Hyperion.

Froug, W. (1972). *The screenwriter looks at the screenwriter.* New York: Macmillan.

Froug, W. (1991). *The new screenwriter looks at the new screenwriter.* Los Angeles: Silman-James Press.

Froug, W. (1996). *Zen and the art of screenwriting.* Beverly Hills: Silman-James Press.

Garrett. D. (2007, August 10). Writers scramble amid strike phobia: Scripters racing to line up multiple deals. *Variety.* Retrieved from http://www.variety.com/article/ VR1117970074.html?categoryid=1019&cs=1&query=writers+scramble.

Goldman, W. (1969). *Butch Cassidy and the Sundance Kid.* New York: Bantam.

Goldman, W. (1981). *Word into image: Portraits of American screenwriters.* Los Angeles: American Film Foundation.

Goldman, W. (1983). *Adventures in the screen trade.* New York: Warner Books.

Greenberg, J. (1991). Walter Reisch: The tailor. In P. McGilligan (Ed.), *Backstory 2: Interviews with screenwriters of the 1940s and 1950s* (pp. 201–245). Berkeley: University of California Press.

Hunt, D. M. (2007). *The 2007 Hollywood Writers Report: Whose stories are we telling?* Los Angeles: Writers Guild of America, West.

Katz, E. (Ed.). (2005). *The film encyclopedia* (5th ed.). New York: HarperCollins.

Kaufman, J. C. (2003). The cost of the muse: Poets die young. *Death Studies, 27,* 813–821.

Keathley, C. (2006). Robert Benton, the new traditionalist. In P. McGilligan (Ed.), *Backstory 4: Interviews with screenwriters of the 1970s and 1980s* (pp. 11–36). Berkeley: University of California Press.

Medford, H. (1974, November). James Ruffin Webb. *WGAw News,* p. 12.

Moss, R. F. (1980). Creators on creating: Woody Allen. *Saturday Review, 7,* 40–44.

Norman, M. (2007). *What happens next? A history of American screenwriting.* New York: Harmony Books.

Parish, R. J. (2007). *It's good to be the king: The seriously funny life of Mel Brooks.* Hoboken, NJ: Wiley.

Piirto, J. (2002). *My teeming brain: Understanding creative writers.* Cresskill, NJ: Hampton Press.

Rothenberg, A., & Wyshak, G. (2004). Family background and genius. *Canadian Journal of Psychiatry, 49*(3), 185–191.

Schanzer, K., & Wright, T. L. (1993). *American screenwriters.* New York: Avon Books.

Schwartz, N. L., & Schwartz, S. (1982). *The Hollywood writers' wars.* New York: Knopf.

Simonton, D. K. (1994). *Greatness: Who makes history and why.* New York: Guilford.

Simonton, D. K. (2002). Collaborative aesthetics in the feature film: Cinematic components predicting the differential impact of 2,323 Oscar-nominated movies. *Empirical Studies of the Arts, 20*(2), 115–125.

Simonton, D. K. (2004). Film awards as indicators of cinematic creativity and achievement: A quantitative comparison of the Oscars and six alternatives. *Creativity Research Journal, 16*(2/3), 163–172.

Spoto, D. (1990). *Madcap: The life of Preston Sturges.* Boston: Little, Brown.

Stempel, T. (1991). *Framework.* New York: Continuum.

Strugatz, B., & McGilligan, P. (1997). Ring Lardner Jr: American skeptic. In P. McGilligan (Ed.), *Backstory 3: Interviews with screenwriters of the 1960s* (pp. 193–229). Berkeley: University of California Press.

Walker, J. (Ed.). (2003). *Halliwell's Who's Who in the movies.* New York: HarperResource.

Wilk, M. (2004). *Schmucks with Underwoods.* New York: Applause.

APPENDIX A

Writers Whose Interviews and Information in Addition to Life Expectancy and
Age at Winning the Academy Award Were Included or Reviewed

Woody Allen	Paul Haggis	Bruce Joel Rubin
Pedro Almodóvar	Ben Hecht	Waldo Salt
Edward Anhalt	Sidney Howard	Alvin Sargent
Edna Anhalt	John Huston	Tom Schulman
Alan Ball	William Inge	Pierre Uytterhoeven
Ronald Bass	John Irving	John Patrick Shanley
Robert Benton	Peter Jackson	George Bernard Shaw
Bernardo Bertolucci	Ruth Prawer Jhabvala	Sidney Sheldon
Robert Bolt	Neil Jordan	Stirling Silliphant
Muriel Box	Michael Kanin	Donald Ogden Stewart
Sidney Box	Charlie Kaufman	Oliver Stone
John Briley	Michael Kelley	Tom Stoppard
Marshall Brickman	Callie Khoury	Preston Sturges
James L. Brooks	Norman Krasna	Ted Tally
Mel Brooks	Albert Lamorisse	Quentin Tarantino
Richard Brooks	Ring Lardner Jr.	Robert Towne
Charles Brackett	Jeremy Larner	Alfred Uhry
Sidney Buchman	Claude LeLouch	Earl Wallace
Jane Campion	Cecil Lewis	Pamela Wallace
Paddy Chayefsky	Michael Kanin	James R. Webb
Ethan Coen	Callie Khoury	Orson Welles
Joel Coen	Alan Jay Learner	William A. Wellman
Pierre Collings	Claude Lelouch	Claudine West
Ennio de Concini	Sonya Levien	Michael Wilson
Francis Ford Coppola	Herman J. Mankiewicz	Stephan Zallian
Sofia Coppola	Joseph L. Mankiewicz	
Cameron Crowe	Charles MacArthur	
Julius J. Epstein	Frances Marion	
Carl Foreman	Leo McCary	
Costa-Gavras	Marc Norman	
I A L Diamond	Alexander Payne	
Joseph Farnham	S. J. Perelman	
John Farrow	Frank Pierson	
Horton Foote	Mario Puzo	
Pietro Germi	Frederic Raphael	
Alfredo Giannetti	Walter Reisch	
Bo Goldman	Robert Riskin	
William Goldman	Eric Roth	

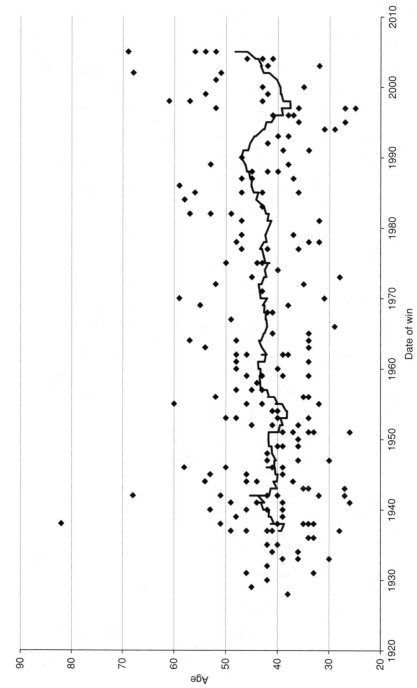

Age at first award, 1928–2006 ($n = 197$) with moving average (period = 20 winners).

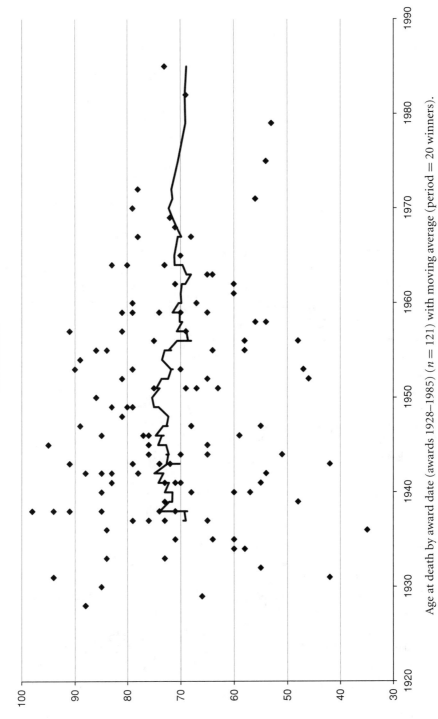

Age at death by award date (awards 1928–1985) ($n = 121$) with moving average (period = 20 winners).

5

The Tears of a Clown: Understanding Comedy Writers

SCOTT BARRY KAUFMAN AND AARON KOZBELT

Humor is an important part of the human condition. A world without laughter would be a world without a soul. Indeed, comedy serves many key purposes in life – reducing stress, defusing social tensions, revealing the absurdity of human behavior, and generally increasing the quality of life (Martin, 2007). One main vehicle by which funny thoughts are conveyed is through creative writing, which can blunt the edge of potentially controversial topics, evoke feelings of mirth in the reader, and contribute to increasing the audience's health through laughter.

Comedy writing takes many forms: stand-up comedy writing, sitcom writing, political satire writing as seen on *The Daily Show*, comedy screenwriting, comedy writing for Web sites like *Cracked* or *The Onion*, and literary fiction writing with a humorous bent. It varies from the attempts of a novice short story writer to the aesthetic achievements of Cervantes, Rabelais, and Shakespeare. Indeed, nearly any form of creative writing can be enhanced by humor.

But behind every punch line is a person generating that line. What do we know about *comedy writers*? What are they like? Humor has been the subject of a great deal of speculation and, more recently, a rather impressive array of empirical research (Martin, 2007) on a variety of humor-related topics. For instance, research has examined the link between humor and psychological well-being (Kuiper & Martin, 1998; Martin & Lefcourt, 1983; Ruch, 1997), the link between humor and physical well-being (Cogan, Cogan, Waltz, & McCue, 1987; Lefcourt, Davidson-Katz, & Kueneman, 1990; Martin & Dobbin, 1988; McClelland & Cheriff, 1997), defining characteristics of funny jokes (Attardo, 1997; Koestler, 1964; Raskin, 1985; Wyer & Collins, 1992), social aspects of humor (Apter, 1982; Long & Graesser, 1988; Mulkay, 1988; Robinson & Smith-Lovin, 2001), the psychobiology of humor and laughter (Bachorowski, Smoski, & Owen, 2001; Coulson & Kutas, 2001; Goel & Dolan, 2001; Provine & Yong, 1991), the development of humor in children (Barnett, 1990; Johnson & Mervis, 1997; McGhee, 1980), the evolutionary emergence of the human capacity for humor (Kaufman, Kozbelt, Bromley, & Miller, 2007; Storey, 2002), and the cognitive processes involved in humor appreciation or comprehension (Eysenck, 1942; Suls, 1972; Vaid, Hull, Heredia, Gerkens, & Martinez, 2003).

Considerably less research has investigated cognitive processes underlying humor *production* and the psychological correlates of individuals who are capable of consistently generating high-quality humor. Such persons range from the class clown in school to internationally famed humor writers and stand-up comedians. How can we understand the nature of humor, particularly its production, as manifested in creative writing and elsewhere? In cognitive and personality terms, how can we characterize humorous individuals – including creative writers? To what extent do findings about funny people in general inform the humorous side of creative writing and creative writers? To address these questions, we characterize different styles of humor production and review the correlates of humor production ability in the general population. We finish with a look at the psychology of the professional comedian as a possible means of understanding humor in creative writing.

FLAVORS OF HUMOR AND THEIR RELATION TO PERSONALITY

There is more than one "sense" of humor. Some distinctions about humor are content-based: Some people are always joking about sex, some are always joking about ethnic minorities, and some are always making puns. Alternatively, one can distinguish stylistic aspects of humor, ranging from bitter sarcasm to good-natured earthiness to hyper-cerebral dry wit to frivolous levity, and so on. Naturally, such distinctions apply to creative writing and writers as well.

People clearly appear to differ in the type and style of humor that they produce, but what exactly are these different styles of humor? To what extent do individuals agree about them? Are there relations between flavors of humor and other personality characteristics? One could imagine, for instance, that comedy writers who are introverted may use milder language and display more intellectually laden verbal wit, whereas more extraverted individuals may use sexual innuendoes and include more social satire and coarse language in their material.

To determine the correlates of different humor varieties, one must first empirically investigate these flavors in the general population. This task was undertaken by Craik and colleagues, who developed a list of 100 descriptive statements intended to capture the important facets of the domain of everyday humorous conduct (Craik & Ware, 1998): for instance, "Has difficulty controlling the urge to laugh in solemn situations" and "Chuckles appreciatively to flatter others." Each statement was printed on a separate card, forming the Humorous Behavior Q-sort Deck (HBQD). In a typical study, participants sort the cards into piles along a dimension ranging from most to least characteristic of a target person.

In one study, participants sorted the cards to describe a hypothetical person with a good sense of humor, generally speaking (Craik & Ware, 1998). High correlations among participants' card sorts were obtained. Averaging across all sorts for all participants, researchers could identify aspects of humor that were generally perceived to be positively or negatively associated with the concept of sense of humor, as well as those that were seen as irrelevant. Items having to do with skillful humor ability such as timing and quick wit were positively related to general humor. Items involving scorn, smiling inappropriately, and misinterpreting the intent of others' good-natured kidding were negatively associated with general humor. Finally, items capturing enjoyment of intellectual wit and word play, ethnic jokes, and chuckling appreciatively to flatter others were not associated with the humor concept. These results suggest that the Q-sort method captures how people generally conceptualize a sense of humor.

As a further exploration of the major dimensions underlying different styles of humor, several hundred university students were asked to describe their own humor styles using the HBQD, and the card sorts were then factor analyzed (Craik, Lampert, & Nelson, 1996). Analyses revealed five bipolar factors, corresponding to five humor styles. These were labeled as (1) *socially warm versus cold* ("reflects a tendency to use humor to promote good will and social interaction, in the positive pole, and an avoidance or aloofness regarding mirthful behavior at the negative pole" [Craik & Ware, 1998, p. 73); (2) *reflective versus boorish* ("describes a knack for discerning the spontaneous humor found in the doings of oneself and other persons and in everyday occurrences, at the positive pole, and an uninsightful, insensitive, and competitive use of humor, at the negative pole" [p. 75]); (3) *competent versus inept* ("suggests an active wit and capacity to convey humorous anecdotes effectively, at its positive pole, and a lack of skill and confidence in dealing with humor, at the negative pole" [p. 75]); (4) *earthy versus repressed* ("captures a raucous delight in joking about taboo topics, at the positive pole, and an inhibition regarding macabre, sexual, and scatological modes of humor, at the negative pole" [p. 75]); and (5) *benign versus mean-spirited* ("at its positive pole, points to pleasure in humor-related activities that are mentally stimulating and innocuous and, at its negative pole, focuses on the dark side of humor, in its use to attack and belittle others" [p. 75]). These five factors appear to represent the major implicit dimensions by which people characterize one another's sense of humor.

How do senses of humor relate to personality? Ware (1996) examined the correlations between the five factor scores on the HBQD and the big-five factor model of personality in university students. The results were consistent with expected relations between various personality variables and humor styles. For instance, greater extraversion was associated with more socially warm humor styles, but not with any of the other four humor style factors. Agreeableness was significantly correlated with a socially warm, competent, and benign humorous style. Conscientiousness was positively correlated with a benign humorous style. Neuroticism was negatively linked to the competent (versus inept) humorous style, and Openness was correlated with a reflective humorous style.

These results inform the relations between personality and humor styles in the general population; to what extent do they inform the sense(s) of humor in individuals who are professional humorists, such as writers or comedians? Some insight into this issue can be gleaned from another study in which university students were asked to sort the HBQD cards to describe the styles of humor of the following famous comedians: Woody Allen, Lucille Ball, Bill Cosby, Whoopi Goldberg, Arsenio Hall, and David Letterman (Craik & Ware, 1998). The researchers then looked at the correlations among the humor styles of the different comedians. For instance, according to the researchers, David Letterman's humorous conduct was judged as similar to that of both Woody Allen and Arsenio Hall, whereas Bill Cosby's humor profile was similar to that of Arsenio Hall. Each of these comedians was also judged to have a distinctive set of characteristics that described his or her humor. As an example, compare the characterizations of Lucille Ball versus Woody Allen, which showed only a rather mild correlation of $+.31$. Whereas Lucille Ball was characterized as enhancing humor impact by employing animated facial expressions, playing the clown, and delighting in the implicit buffoonery of the over-pompous, Woody Allen was characterized as engaging in self-deprecating humor, enjoying intellectually challenging witticism, enjoying word play, and manifesting his humor in the form of clever retorts to others' remarks.

In sum, the Q-sort method shows promise for quantifying the degree of similarity in humor styles between pairs of individuals, such as professional creative writers. In particular, this method could help differentiate the different humor styles of comedy writers across domains and even within domains. Across domains, one could compare the different humor styles of those who, say, write humor blogs versus screenplays. Within domains, one could more finely differentiate the humor style differences among stand-up comedians (for instance, Seinfeld-style humor versus the Sinbad variety) or between screenwriters (such as the Woody Allen type versus the Harold and Kumar type).

To further an understanding of potentially beneficial and detrimental humor styles, Rod Martin and his colleagues (Martin, Puhlik-Doris, Larsen, Gray, & Weir, 2003) developed the Humor Style Questionnaire (HSQ). Its focus is on the function of humor in everyday life. Based on a review of the literature, Martin et al. identified two healthy dimensions (affiliative and self-enhancing humor) and two potentially detrimental dimensions (aggressive and self-defeating humor) that likely characterized everyday humor functions. *Affiliative humor* is frequently displayed by individuals who "tend to say funny things, to tell jokes, and to engage in spontaneous witty banter to amuse others, to facilitate relationships, and to reduce interpersonal tensions" (p. 53). Thus, affiliative humor is used to enhance one's relationship with others. *Self-enhancing* humor "involves a generally humorous outlook on life, a tendency to be frequently amused by the incongruities of life, and to maintain a humorous perspective even in the face of stress or adversity" (p. 53). As its name suggests, it is used to enhance oneself. *Aggressive humor* "relates to the use of sarcasm, teasing, ridicule, derision, 'put-down,' or disparagement humor" (p. 54). It is used to enhance the self at the expense of others. Finally, *self-defeating* humor "involves excessively self-disparaging humor, attempts to amuse others by doing or saying funny things at one's own expense as a means of ingratiating oneself or gaining approval, allowing oneself to be the 'butt' of others' humor, and laughing along with others when being ridiculed or disparaged" (p. 54). It is used to enhance relationships at the expense of the self.

Martin and colleagues then created a questionnaire to assess all four dimensions, with eight items pertaining to each dimension. Validating their scale on a sample of 1,195 participants, the researchers factor analyzed the data and found that the four dimensions showed high internal consistencies, ranging from .77 to .81. Interestingly, even though the four dimensions were statistically separable, the two healthy dimensions (affiliative and self-enhancing humor) were significantly correlated with each other, as were the two detrimental dimensions (aggressive and self-defeating humor). They also found a reliable correlation between the self-report data and the same ratings by an individual's dating partner, suggesting that, even though the scale is a self-report measure, it is reasonably valid and in accordance with others' perceptions.

Other studies reported by Martin et al. (2003) have investigated the relations between the HSQ and measures of mood, psychological well-being, and social relationships. Results show that the two healthy humor dimensions (affiliative and self-enhancing) were positively related to measures of self-esteem, psychological well-being, and intimacy. Furthermore, self-enhancing humor was positively correlated with social support and optimism, suggesting that an optimistic outlook on life is closely linked to using humor for coping, perspective-taking, and emotion regulation. Both healthy humor dimensions were negatively correlated with anxiety and depression.

On the flip side, aggressive humor was positively correlated with self-report measures of hostility and aggression. Self-defeating humor was positively related to measures of depression, anxiety, hostility, aggression, and optimism and negatively related to self-esteem, psychological well-being, intimacy, and social support. Thus, different flavors of humor appear to be correlated with different aspects of psychological well-being.

These four dimensions have also been investigated in the context of the big-five factor model of personality. As reported by Martin et al. (2003), *extraverted* individuals tend to use more affiliative and self-enhancing humor, whereas those who score high in *neuroticism* show no relationship to affiliative humor, tend to use self-enhancing humor less, and tend to use aggressive and self-defeating humor more. Those who are more *agreeable* tend to use more self-enhancing humor and less aggressive and self-defeating humor, and those who are *conscientious* also use less aggressive and self-defeating humor. Those who score high in *openness to experience* tend to use affiliative and self-enhancing humor. Some sex differences have been also been noted. For example, Crawford and Gressley (1991) found that males tended to score higher on both detrimental humor styles dimensions (aggressive and self-defeating) of the HSQ.

Thus, the seemingly complex and elusive topic of flavors or styles of humor appears to be empirically tractable. This gives some cause for optimism in ultimately understanding something of the psychology of humor and the different manifestations of humor in creative writing and elsewhere.

HUMOR PRODUCTION AND CREATIVITY

In the previous section, we saw that individuals clearly differ in their styles of humor and that people largely agree on the dimensions of the differences. However, many of these data were self-report in nature, which is a limitation; moreover, these data have relatively little to say about the quality of humor that is produced. To what extent does the ability to produce high-quality humor – regardless of style – relate to other cognitive characteristics, such as creative ability, intelligence, or a propensity to self-monitor? In the next three sections, we take up these issues, one at a time.

Conceptually, humor production and creativity share many features, such as playfulness, risk taking, and exploiting loose but meaningful associations between concepts (Murdock & Ganim, 1993; Treadwell, 1970; Wicker, 1985; Ziv, 1980). For instance, Murdock and Ganim's (1993) content analysis of definitions and theories of humor suggested that humor and creativity are closely related and that humor production is essentially a subset of creativity. Both humor production and creativity, generally speaking, require novelty combined with value or quality; these are standard aspects of most definitions of creativity (Sternberg & O'Hara, 2000). Applying this notion to humor, it is easy to see that a familiar, tired joke will likely not be seen as funny; however, neither will a new joke that is so bizarre that it fails to communicate or be understood by the audience.

This conceptual relationship between humor and creativity is supported by empirical research using a variety of methodologies. These include creating humorous captions for cartoons or photographs (e.g., Feingold & Mazzella, 1993; Koppel & Sechrest, 1970; Kozbelt & Nishioka, in press; Masten, 1986; Ziv, 1980), TAT (Thematic Apperception Test) cards (Day & Langevin, 1969), generating witty word associations (Hauck & Thomas, 1972) or repartee statements (Feingold & Mazzella, 1993), and making up funny presidential campaign slogans (Clabby, 1980). In general, such studies have found positive but moderate correlations between these funniness ratings and a variety of putative measures of creativity, including the Remote Associations Test (Mednick, 1962) and divergent thinking tests in which participants are asked to come up with unusual uses of a common object, such as a brick.

Several representative studies in this vein serve to illustrate the typical sorts of results that have been found. For instance, Treadwell (1970) found positive correlations between the quality of humor production and three paper-and-pencil measures of creativity. Smith and White (1965), studying U.S. Air Force personnel, observed a positive association between wit and creativity. Townsend (1982) found that the quantity of humor positively predicted creative thinking in high school students. Fabrizi and Pollio (1987) found correlations between teacher and peer ratings of the humor of 11th graders and these students' originality and elaboration scores on the Torrance Test of Creative Thinking (Torrance, 1974). Finally, Ziv (1988) described studies showing that humor training is effective at enhancing creativity in adolescents. Overall, a meta-analysis of such studies has found an average correlation of .34 between humor production ability and creativity (O'Quin & Derks, 1997). These authors concluded that, although creativity and humor production do involve similar mental processes, they are nonetheless distinct, because the shared variance was only about 10%. Thus, whereas funny people are typically creative, individuals can be creative without being funny.

HUMOR PRODUCTION AND INTELLIGENCE

Are funny people also more intelligent than other individuals? Research on the link between IQ and divergent thinking in general is mixed. Some researchers have found support for a "threshold effect," in which divergent thinking ability and psychometric intelligence are positively correlated up until an IQ of approximately 120, after which the two constructs are no longer related (Fuchs-Beauchamp, Karnes, & Johnson, 1993; Getzels & Jackson, 1962; Sternberg & O'Hara, 2000). Others have found small to modest correlations across all levels of intellectual abilities (Kim, 2005; Precket, Holling, & Weise, 2006), and others still have found that crystallized intelligence shows a positive and moderate relationship to the generation of creative inventions, whereas fluid intelligence is only significantly correlated with the generation of creative inventions in the high end of the IQ spectrum, but not for those with average IQs (Sligh, Conners, & Roskos-Ewoldsen, 2005).

Although there is still some doubt on the relationship between IQ and creative potential generally, what is the relationship between IQ and humor production specifically? In an early effort to investigate the relation between intelligence and humor, Feingold (1983) developed tests of humor perceptiveness and humor achievement comprising questions about joke knowledge, in which participants were required to complete famous jokes (e.g., "Take my wife, _____"; Answer: "please") and identify the names of comedians associated with particular jokes (e.g., "I get no respect" linked with Rodney Dangerfield). Performance on the humor tasks was positively correlated with the WAIS short form measure of IQ (both information and vocabulary subtests were administered). Moreover, individuals with higher IQ scores self-reported greater interest in the films of Mel Brooks and Woody Allen – admittedly, more cerebral humorists than most. In another study, Masten (1986) administered the Vocabulary and Block Design subtests of the WISC-R and found substantial positive correlations between the subjects' combined score on the two subtests and academic achievement and humor production, measured by ratings given by two judges to cartoon captions.

The measurement of intelligence as a unitary IQ score may, however, be misleading (Horn & Cattell, 1966). A particularly important facet of intelligence for the production of humor in many contexts is verbal intelligence. The relation between humor and this aspect of intelligence has also been investigated. For instance, Feingold and Mazella (1991) developed tests to assess what they referred to as "verbal wittiness": (1) memory for humor, an aspect of crystallized intelligence, and (2) humor cognition, thought to be comparable to fluid intelligence. They assessed memory by tests of humor information and joke knowledge, whereas they measured humor cognition with tests of humor reasoning and joke comprehension. They found significant correlations between traditional measures of verbal intelligence and tests of humor cognition, whereas memory for humor was not strongly related to intelligence. Humor reasoning was also correlated with performance on the Remote Associates Test, putatively a measure of creative thinking, but one that is apparently more closely related to intelligence than creativity (Andrews, 1975; Mednick & Andrews, 1967). Feingold and Mazzella (1993) suggested that "verbal wittiness" may be viewed as a multidimensional construct consisting of mental ability and social and temperamental factors influencing humor motivation and communication. However, their conceptualization of humor ability was fairly narrow, relating mainly to individuals' familiarity with well-known jokes and popular comedians.

Even so, studies that have assessed humor using a more open-ended task like cartoon or photo caption creation have also found a relation between humor production ability and verbal intelligence. Feingold and Mazzella (1993) also observed a reliable positive correlation between verbal ability, measured by a multiple-choice test of word knowledge, and the quality of humor production, measured by ratings given by two judges to cartoon captions and repartee statements. Similarly, Koppel and Sechrest (1970), in a study of college fraternity brothers, found a small but reliable correlation between SAT scores and humor production ability, measured by peer ratings of newly devised cartoon captions.

In sum, although the relation between intelligence and humor production ability remains understudied, empirical research to date suggests that people who have knowledge of popular instances of humor, reason well using humor, and can produce funny captions tend to have higher intelligence, especially verbal intelligence. This suggests that professional comedy writers should also possess greater verbal intelligence – a hypothesis that awaits empirical testing.

HUMOR PRODUCTION AND SELF-MONITORING

An important aspect of comedy writing is the ability to write jokes appropriate to one's audience. For instance, it would be very poor taste if you were American and told Irish jokes in a bar in Dublin. Thus, it is reasonable to think that funny people may be better at self monitoring – that is, the degree to which one is sensitive to environmental cues of social appropriateness and regulates behavior accordingly (Turner, 1980).

Are funny people really higher self-monitors? Turner (1980) examined the association between humor production ability and self-monitoring. Turner administered the Self-Monitoring scale (Snyder, 1974), a measure of self-control of expressive behavior, self-presentation, and nonverbal affective display guided by situational cues. Humor ability was assessed three ways: (1) Participants were asked to rate the extent to which they considered themselves to be witty and the extent to which their close friends considered them to be witty; (2) participants were given 5 minutes to make up witty captions to go with a series of cartoons in which the original captions had been removed; and (3) participants were seated at a table with 18 miscellaneous objects, like a tennis shoe, a wristwatch, and a bread basket. The participants were instructed to create a 3-minute comedy monologue, describing these objects in a funny way, after being given only 30 seconds to collect their thoughts. In both the second and third methods, judges rated the participants' humorous productions for humorousness.

The results revealed that, as predicted, individuals with higher scores on the Self-Monitoring scale rated themselves as more humorous and produced responses that were rated as significantly more witty on both humor production tests. In a second study, Turner found that high self-monitors were also more likely to offer humorous comments during a group discussion, even without explicit instructions to be funny.

Turner suggested that the effective expression of witty statements may be attributable to the interest of self-monitors in initiating and maintaining social interaction in the early stages of friendship and their ability to control their affective displays – a skill that is essential for the appropriate execution of humor. According to Turner, "in attempting to meet these situational opportunities, the self-monitor, aided by control of his affective display, should develop an ability to be humorous" (p. 169). Research has indeed found a positive correlation between self-monitoring and a self-report measure of the tendency to initiate humor in social interactions (Bell, McGhee, & Duffey, 1986). Thus, the tendency to self-monitor may be an important contributor to the development of the ability to produce humor. In this view, high-quality humor production may be viewed as a type of social skill (Dewitte & Verguts, 2001). Although research has not directly examined the relation between self-monitoring and humor in the context of professional comedy writers, it is reasonable to assume that the ability to anticipate reactions to the written (or, in stand-up comedy, spoken) word would be a useful skill in the development of humor production ability.

THE PSYCHOLOGY OF THE PROFESSIONAL HUMORIST

The aforementioned studies on different styles of humor and their relation to personality, creativity, verbal intelligence, and self-monitoring mainly deal with individual differences in aspects of humor in the general population. Although these investigations suggest potential characterizations of professional humorists and humor writers, they have not typically targeted such individuals directly. If professional comedians represent the pinnacle of humor ability, insights into the mind of the comic writer may be gleaned by looking at this specific population. What are professional humorists like? To what extent do professional comedians have particular personality traits, preoccupations, and backgrounds that differ from those of the general population? How and to what extent do they differ from amateur or less effective humor producers?

Two sets of researchers have investigated the psychology of professional comedians. Adopting a psychoanalytic approach, Janus (1975; Janus, Bess, & Janus, 1978) studied the intelligence, educational level, family background, and personality of 69 comedians, all of whom were said to be famous and successful. They collected data using a variety of methods: clinical interviews, accounts of early memories, dreams, handwriting analyses, projective tests, and the Weschsler Adult Intelligence Scale (WAIS). After analyzing these sources of data, Janus concluded that comedians tended to be superior in intelligence, but also angry, suspicious, and depressed. In addition, their early lives were frequently characterized by suffering, isolation, and feelings of deprivation; in many cases, the comedians learned to use humor as a defense against anxiety, converting their feelings of suppressed rage from physical to verbal aggression. However, many comedians were also shy, sensitive, and empathic individuals whose comedic success was apparently due partly to an ability to accurately perceive the fears and needs of their audiences (cf. Turner, 1980). However, the rather dubious assessment methods – especially from the point of view of a more scientifically grounded psychology – and the lack of a control group make it difficult to know whether these characteristics are unique to comedians, are shared by noncomic entertainers, or extend to creative writers more generally.

Fisher and Fisher (1981) conducted a somewhat better controlled interview study of professional humor producers. They assessed the personality, motivations, and childhood recollections of 43 professional comedians (including 15 circus clowns) and scoured published biographical and autobiographical accounts of 40 comedians and clowns, from Woody Allen and Jackie Gleason to Jerry Lewis and Beatrice Lillie. They also administered the Rorschach inkblot test and the Thematic Apperception Test (TAT) to identify themes and preoccupations in the thoughts of the comedians. As a control, they included a sample of 41 professional actors. They also interviewed amateur humor producers, consisting of nonprofessional individuals who indicated on a questionnaire that they initiate humor frequently, along with children who were brought to them for treatment for behavior problems but who were frequently described by teachers and parents as demonstrating class clown qualities.

Fisher and Fisher found that professional comedians did not differ from actors in depression or overall psychological health, but did uncover several differences between the groups. The majority of the comics came from lower socioeconomic strata. Quite early, they displayed a talent for being funny, often acting as the class clown in school. Many in the sample entered comedy professionally through their interest in music. Compared to the actors, the professional comedians had to take on considerably more responsibility at an early age. They were also more likely than the actors to describe their fathers in highly positive terms and were more inclined to refer to their mothers as disciplinarians, aggressive critics, non-nurturing, and non-maternal. This finding was also discovered in a sample of amateur humor producers: The more that college students considered themselves to be comics, the more they saw their mothers as controlling and the fathers as softer in their child-rearing practices.

To corroborate these patterns, Fisher and Fisher also administered the Rorschach inkblot test to the parents of children who displayed class clown attributes in school. They found that the mothers of such children had significantly less symbiosis imagery, indicating that they displayed less of an interest and inclination in forming close attachments to other people. Additionally, they found that the fathers displayed more of a preoccupation with passive images or fantasies than a control group of fathers, suggesting that the fathers of these children were drawn to a passive stance.

Fisher and Fisher related these findings to those of Heilbrun (1973), who found that people who are raised by controlling, non-nurturing mothers tend to develop schizophrenia. Heilbrun found two types of men (Heilbrun's sample consisted only of men) who are raised by a non-nurturing mother. The "closed style" type was characterized by defenses such as isolation from social interactions and depression, whereas the "open style" type was characterized as extraverted and alert to ways of winning social approval. Also of note,

Heilbrun's open-adapters were considered to be "broad scanners" of the environment, looking for cues of what people expect of them, again in line with Turner (1980). Fisher and Fisher related this open style personality to the comics in their sample and argued that the comic's style of relating to people may partly mirror their early adventures with their mothers. They become experts in "reading" their mothers and then later learn how to "scan the world in a very sensitive way, looking for contradictions to decode and reconcile, hunting out cues as to how to win approval and support" (p. 207).

Fisher and Fisher also noticed that the professional comics displayed significantly more themes of contrasts and opposites. Among these contrasts, professional comics displayed a fascination with themes of good versus evil in inkblot fantasies. Fisher and Fisher linked this fascination to the comics' early life of having to maneuver between their fathers' call to goodness and their mothers' accusations of wrongdoing. They hypothesize that this situation may catalyze comics' obsession with themes of good versus evil and motivate much of their comedy.

What are some of the other motivations of the professional comedian? Fisher and Fisher hypothesized that comedians learn, through early life experiences, that life is absurd. They then spend their lives telling jokes to help them understand the absurdity of their own position. They note that much of humor involves spotting and giving meaning to ambiguities and that comedians are obsessed with instability, perhaps because of experiences with their mothers. They hypothesized that this focus on inconstancy may represent an effort at mastery and that comedians seek to adapt to a threat that was of painful intensity in their early childhood.

The researchers also noted that professional comics frequently seemed to put up a screen by retreating behind a barrage of jokes, as suggested in interviews and inkblot responses, in which they conjured up images about concealment. Compared to actors, they were more likely to refer to people wearing masks, creatures hiding, and objects that cannot be distinguished properly because they are obscured by darkness.

Fisher and Fisher also found that the majority of professional comedians in their sample conjured up imagery of smallness. The comics tended to have lower self-esteem and to say bad things about themselves, which the researchers linked to concerns of social relativism. They argue that the comedians' focus on their smallness may be a result of the reduced significance they felt as children and that much comic behavior is aimed at reducing the discrepancy of smallness between themselves and others. A main motivation may be to defend their basic goodness. Rorschach inkblot responses showed that many professional comedians would first depict a threatening creature as bad or ugly and then deny that the creature had negative qualities and portray it as good. "There is no question but that size strategies pervade the comic's codes and metaphors. . . . He is forever reducing or magnifying. He never reports things in their immediate proportions" (p. 216). According to Fisher and Fisher, declaring that badness is a meaningless concept may be an important form of self-defense for the comic. They also note that the low self-esteem and feeling of smallness existent among the professional comics may actually set the comic on a unique path: "We would emphasize ... the possibility that in some paradoxical way these negative self-feelings provide a durable base for shaping one's identity and going off on an independent trajectory" (p. 200).

How do comics view themselves? Fisher and Fisher found that they viewed themselves as healers. Many of the professional comedians expressed a dedication to being altruistic. They see their central duty as that of making people feel that events are funny. At the same time, the professional comics also viewed humor as a technique for controlling and dominating the audience. Indeed, Fisher and Fisher were impressed at how this view of the comic as a fool-priest is consistent with scholarly reviews of the history of the clown, the court jester, and the fool. They also noted how the contemporary comic serves a similar function as the court jester in earlier times. On the one hand, the comic presents him- or herself as the silly fellow who jokes, amuses, and entertains. On the other hand, the comic initiates opposing currents, uncovering truths that many people usually try to banish from awareness.

Overall, Fisher and Fisher found that this array of common patterns displayed among the professional comedians held across age, sex, national prominence, and ethnicity. They also found their patterns to hold across stage of career – professional humorists just starting out displayed the same patterns as those who had been in the business for years. However, Fisher and Fisher did find a significant difference between professional and amateur comics. College students who described themselves as funny did not produce the same pattern of inkblot fantasies as the professional comedians. The amateur comic scores (that is, the extent to which they initiated humor) were not significantly correlated with the number of good-bad images, "not bad" themes, descriptions depicting objects as small, themes of concealment, and images of hostility. In contrast, amateur producers (regardless of the extent to which they produced humor) were typified not by frequent references to things being small, but instead focused on bigness. Also, the amateur comics described themselves as not inclined to submit to working under pressure and were found to not push themselves to make deadlines. They also were found to score high on impulsivity and invested a great deal in observing others and anticipating their actions. This suggests that it might be particularly useful to study professional humor producers independent of college students, as "there is a unique pattern of qualities in the professional comic, who has dedicated his whole life to being the funny one, that we have yet to see duplicated" (p. 203).

Taken together, this research suggests that humor in professional comedians serves as a defense or coping mechanism in dealing with their early family experiences and the burden of having to take care of themselves. Comics may be motivated to make people laugh in order to gain acceptance and to reveal the absurdity of life to make sense of their own lives.

There is reason to believe that these results can also apply to comedy writers. As Runco (see Chapter 11) notes, writing is often a form of problem solving. Many writers are motivated to write to solve problems in their lives. Comedy writers may use comedy in their writing to help them understand themselves and the world and to do so in a fashion that controls the reader's emotions.

CONCLUSION

So what are comedy writers like? Stylistically, professional humorists and other funny individuals span a variety of flavors of humor. There is some evidence that they are more creative and verbally intelligent and adept at self-monitoring. Those who tell jokes for money tend to have had to overcome adversities in life and seem to use humor as a coping mechanism.

Although this short review has covered a few basic issues on the nature of humor and its relation to comedy writers, much research remains to be done. Indeed, even in the areas we have discussed and offered some tentative conclusions, there is a dearth of sound empirical studies and solid theoretical models – and for other issues in the study of humor, not even that. For instance, one ambitious objective would be to relate what is known about the psychology of humor to understanding the literary giants who have historically expanded our collective sense of what is funny – or somewhat less ambitiously, just to understand how domain-specific expert knowledge on writing enters into the process of humor. How do professional humorists differ from others in more cognitive aspects (rather than factors of personal background, motivation, coping, and so forth, which have been studied to date)? What is the time scale of generating humorous ideas and then developing them, in the context of creative humor writing? How accurately can professional humorists gauge the likely impact of their jokes? What theoretical models make the most sense of humor writing? Finally, in focusing here on the comedy *writer*, we have neglected the comedy *reader* and the processes by which he or she makes sense (and nonsense) of humorous writing. Researchers in general have only just started to study how humor emerges in creative writing, but with the use of new methodologies and an appreciation of the different styles of humor, we hope that the scientific study of humor production will not be a laughing matter.

REFERENCES

Andrews, F. M. (1975). Social and psychological factors which influence the creative process. In I. A. Taylor & J. W. Getzels (Eds.), *Perspectives in creativity* (pp. 117–145). Chicago: Aldine.

Apter, M. J. (1982). *The experience of motivation: The theory of psychological reversals.* London: Academic Press.

Attardo, S. (1997). The semantic foundations of cognitive theories of humor. *Humor: International Journal of Humor Research, 10,* 395–420.

Bachorowski, J.-A., Smoski, M. J., & Owen, M. J. (2001). The acoustic features of human laughter. *Journal of the Acoustical Society of America, 110,* 1581–1597.

Barnett, L. A. (1990). Playfulness: Definition, design, and measurement. *Play & Culture, 3,* 319–336.

Bell, N. J., McGhee, P. E., & Duffey, N. S. (1986). Interpersonal competence, social assertiveness and the development of humour. *British Journal of Developmental Psychology, 4,* 51–55.

Clabby, J. F. (1980). The wit: A personality analysis. *Journal of Personality Assessment, 44,* 307–310.

Cogan, R., Cogan, D., Waltz, W., & McCrue, M. (1987). Effects of laughter and relaxation on discomfort thresholds. *Journal of Behavioral Medicine, 10,* 139–144.

Coulson, S., & Kutas, M. (2001). Getting it: Human event-related brain response to jokes in good and poor comprehenders. *Neuroscience Letters, 316,* 71–74.

Craik, K. H., Lampert, M. D., & Nelson, A. J. (1996). Sense of humor and styles of everyday humorous conduct. *Humor: International Journal of Humor Research, 9,* 273–302.

Craik, K. H., & Ware, A. P. (1998). Humor and personality in everyday life. In W. Ruch (Ed.), *The sense of humor: Explorations of a personality characteristic* (pp. 63–94). Berlin: Walter de Gruyter.

Crawford, M., & Gressley, D. (1991). Creativity, caring, and context: Women's and men's accounts of humor preferences and practices. *Psychology of Women Quarterly, 15,* 217–231.

Day, H. I., & Langevin, R. (1969). Curiosity and intelligence: Two necessary conditions for a high level of creativity. *Journal of Special Education, 3,* 263–268.

Dewitte, S., & Verguts, T. (2001). Being funny: A selectionist account of humor production. *Humor: International Journal of Humor Research, 14,* 37–53.

Eysenck, H. (1942). Appreciation of humor: An experimental and theoretical study. *British Journal of Psychology, 32,* 295–309.

Fabrizi, M. S., & Pollio, H. R. (1987). Are funny teenagers creative? *Psychological Reports, 61,* 757–761.

Feingold, A. (1983). Measuring humor ability: Revision and construct validation of the Humor Perceptiveness Test. *Perceptual and Motor Skills, 56,* 159–166.

Feingold, A. (1992). Gender differences in mate selection preferences: A test of the parental investment model. *Psychological Bulletin, 112,* 125–139.

Feingold, A., & Mazzella, R. (1991). Psychometric intelligence and verbal humor ability. *Personality & Individual Differences, 12,* 427–435.

Feingold, A., & Mazzella, R. (1993). Preliminary validation of a multidimensional model of wittiness. *Journal of Personality, 61,* 439–456.

Fisher, S., & Fisher, R. L. (1981). *Pretend the world is funny and forever: A psychological analysis of comedians, clowns, and actors.* Hillsdale, NJ: Erlbaum.

Fuchs-Beauchamp, K. D., Karnes, M. B., & Johnson, L. J. (1993). Creativity and intelligence in preschoolers. *Gifted Child Quarterly, 37,* 113–117.

Getzels, J. W., & Jackson, P. W. (1962). *Creativity and intelligence.* New York: Wiley.

Goel, V., & Dolan, R. J. (2001). The functional anatomy of humor: Segregating cognitive and affective components. *Nature Neuroscience, 4,* 237–238.

Hauck, W. E., & Thomas, J. W. (1972). The relationship of humor to intelligence, creativity, and intentional and incidental learning. *Journal of Experimental Education, 40*, 52–55.

Heilbrum, A. B. (1973). *Aversive maternal control: A theory of schizophrenic development.* New York: Wiley.

Horn, J. L., & Cattell, R. B. (1966). Refinement and test of the theory of fluid and crystallized general intelligences. *Journal of Educational Psychology, 57*, 253–270.

Janus, S. S. (1975). The great comedians: Personality and other factors. *American Journal of Psychoanalysis, 35*, 169–174.

Janus, S. S., Bess, B. E., & Janus, B. R. (1978). The great comediennes: Personality and other factors. *American Journal of Psychoanalysis, 38*, 367–372.

Johnson, K. E., & Mervis, C. B. (1997). First steps in the emergence of verbal humor: A case study. *Infant Behavior & Development, 20*, 187–196.

Kaufman, S. B., Kozbelt, A., Bromley, M. L., & Miller, G. F. (2007). The role of creativity and humor in mate selection. In G. Geher & G. F. Miller (Eds.), *Mating intelligence: Sex, relationships, and the mind's reproductive system* (pp. 227–262). Mahwah, NJ: Erlbaum.

Kim, K. H. (2005). Can only intelligent people be creative? A meta-analysis. *Journal of Secondary Gifted Education, 16*, 57–66.

Koestler, A. (1964). *The act of creation.* London: Hutchinson.

Koppel, M. A., & Sechrest, L. (1970). A multitrait-multimethod matrix analysis of sense of humor. *Educational & Psychological Measurement, 30*, 77–85.

Kozbelt, A., & Nishioka, K. (in press). Humor comprehension, humor production, and insight. *Humor: International Journal of Humor Research.*

Kuiper, N. A., & Martin, R. A. (1998). Laughter and stress in daily life: Relation to positive and negative affect. *Motivation & Emotion, 22*, 133–153.

Lefcourt, H. M., Davidson-Katz, K., & Kueneman, K. (1990). Humor and immune-system functioning. *Humor: International Journal of Humor Research, 3*, 305–321.

Long, D. L., & Graesser, A. C. (1988). Wit and humor in discourse processing. *Discourse Processes, 11*, 35–60.

Martin, R. A. (2007). *The psychology of humor: An integrative approach.* Burlington, MA: Elsevier.

Martin, R. A., & Dobbin, J. P. (1988). Sense of humor, hassles, and immunoglobulin A: Evidence for a stress-moderating effect of humor. *International Journal of Psychiatry in Medicine, 18*, 93–105.

Martin, R. A., & Lefcourt, H. M. (1983). Sense of humor as a moderator of the relation between stressors and moods. *Journal of Personality and Social Psychology, 45*, 1313–1324.

Martin, R. A., Puhlik-Doris, P., Larsen, G., Gray, J., & Weir, K. (2003). Individual differences in uses of humor and their relation to psychological well-being: Development of the Humor Style Questionnaire. *Journal of Research in Personality, 37*, 48–75.

Masten, A. S. (1986). Humor and competence in school-aged children. *Child Development, 57*, 461–473.

McClelland, D. C., & Cheriff, A. D. (1997). The immunoenhancing effects of humor on secretory IgA and resistance to respiratory infections. *Psychology & Health, 12*, 329–344.

McGhee, P. E. (1980). Development of the sense of humour in childhood: A longitudinal study. In P. E. McGhee & A. J. Chapman (Eds.), *Children's humour* (pp. 213–236). Chichester: Wiley.

Mednick, M. T., & Andrews, F. M. (1967). Creative thinking and level of intelligence. *Journal of Creative Behavior, 1,* 428–431.

Mednick, S. A. (1962). The associative basis of the creative process. *Psychological Review, 69,* 220–232.

Mulkay, M. (1988). *On humor: Its nature and its place in modern society.* New York: Basil Blackwell.

Murdock, M., & Ganim, R. (1993). Creativity and humor: Integration and incongruity. *Journal of Creative Behavior, 27,* 57–70.

O'Quin, K., & Derks, P. (1997). Humor and creativity: A review of the empirical literature. In M. Runco (Ed.), *Creativity research handbook* (Vol. 1; pp. 227–256). Cresskill, NJ: Hampton Press.

Preckel, F., Holling, H., & Weise, M. (2006). Relationship of intelligence and creativity in gifted and non-gifted students: An investigation of threshold theory. *Personality and Individual Differences, 40,* 159–170.

Provine, R. R., & Yong, Y. L. (1991). Laughter: A stereotyped human vocalization. *Ethology, 89,* 115–124.

Raskin, V. (1985). *Semantic mechanisms of humor.* Dordrecht: D. Reidel.

Robinson, D. T., & Smith-Lovin, L. (2001). Getting a laugh: Gender, status, and humor in task discussions. *Social Forces, 80,* 123–158.

Ruch, W. (1997). State and trait cheerfulness and the induction of exhilaration: A FACS study. *European Psychologist, 2,* 328–341.

Sligh, A. C., Conners, F. A., & Roskos-Ewoldsen, B. (2005). Relation of creativity to fluid and crystallized intelligence. *Journal of Creative Behavior, 39,* 123–136.

Smith, E. E., & White, H. L. (1965). Wit, creativity, and sarcasm. *Journal of Applied Psychology, 49,* 131–134.

Snyder, M. (1974). The self-monitoring of expressive behavior. *Journal of Personality and Social Psychology, 30,* 526–537.

Sternberg, R. J., & O'Hara, L. A. (2000). Creativity and intelligence. In R. J. Sternberg (Ed.), *Handbook of creativity* (pp. 251–272). New York: Cambridge University Press.

Storey, R. (2002). Humor and sexual selection. *Human Nature, 14,* 319–336.

Suls, J. M. (1972). A two-stage model for the appreciation of jokes and cartoons: An information processing analysis. In J. Goldstein & P. McGhee (Eds.), *Psychology of Humor* (pp. 41–45). New York: Academic Press.

Torrance, E. P. (1974). *Torrance Tests of Creative Thinking.* Lexington, MA: Personnel Press.

Townsend, J. (1982). *Relationships among humor creative thinking abilities, race, sex, and socioeconomic factors of advantagedness and disadvantagedness of a selected sample of high school students.* Unpublished doctoral dissertation, University of Georgia.

Treadwell, Y. (1970). Humor and creativity. *Psychological Reports, 26,* 55–58.

Turner, R. G. (1980). Self-monitoring and humor production. *Journal of Personality, 48,* 163–172.

Vaid, J., Hull, R., Heredia, R., Gerkens, D., & Martinez, F. (2003). Getting a joke: The time course of meaning activation in verbal humor. *Journal of Pragmatics, 35,* 1431–1449.

Ware, A. P. (1996). *Humorousness and the Big Five: Links beyond extraversion.* Paper presented at the American Psychology Society Conference, San Francisco, June 28–July 2.

Wicker, F. W. (1985). A rhetorical look at humor as creativity. *Journal of Creative Behavior, 19*, 175–184.

Wyer, R. S., & Collins, J. E. (1992). A theory of humor elicitation. *Psychological Review, 99*, 663–688.

Ziv, A. (1980). Humor and creativity. *Creative Child & Adult Quarterly, 5*, 159–170.

Ziv, A. (1988). Using humor to develop creative thinking. *Journal of Children in Contemporary Society, 20*, 99–116.

PART II

THE TEXT

6

The Evolution of Creative Writing

DANIEL NETTLE

This chapter asks the big question; namely why, from the evolutionary history of our species, should the behavior of creative writing have emerged. Asking this big question – the evolutionary *why* – has become a more popular preoccupation in psychology in the last 2 years or so, as evidenced by the development of the paradigm known as evolutionary psychology (Buss, 2005). However, many remain skeptical about using the evolutionary *why* question for the behaviors of modern humans, and this skepticism might seem particularly apt for the case of creative writing, since creative writing is obviously a cultural activity and, moreover, one that developed only very recently. The first section justifies taking an evolutionary perspective nonetheless and explains what that perspective entails. The second section considers the evolution of creative writing from the point of view of the reader: Why should people want to attend to imaginary narrative? The next section considers the complementary problem: Why should some people (but not others) want to devote their time and energies to the creation of such narratives? The final section offers some tentative conclusions.

EVOLUTION AND CULTURE

Though various proto-writing activities are found earlier, it is generally agreed that true writing began to develop in Sumeria and in Egypt from about the fourth millennium B.C.E. This development is not a genetic change. Rather, writing is a cultural innovation that gradually took foot in a few societies, but remained absent from the vast majority until very much more recently. Even today, a sizable fraction of the world's population has no access to literacy. Thus, reading and writing are clearly cultural inventions, and because evolution shapes nature, not culture, they lie outside the explanatory scope of evolutionary thinking. Right?

Wrong. It is a common misconception that evolutionary explanations can only apply to behaviors or tendencies that require no cultural input to develop, but more careful consideration shows that this cannot be the case. Natural selection has shaped the kinds of minds we have. When a cultural invention like creative writing comes along, it will flourish if it is successful at capturing the attention and motivation of a significant number of people, and it will wither if it does not. Thus, though there are no evolutionary changes in the human genome that are there *for* reading and writing, reading and writing are there because they are able to flourish on the substrate formed by the evolved human mind. No matter that reading and writing do not exist in all cultures; where they do develop and there are the resources and population size to support them, they become widespread. It is quite legitimate to ask *why*, given the capacities and evolutionary history of the human mind, this would be the case.

Doubters may still want to object that we already have perfectly good explanations already for why people read and write creatively. Readers enjoy imaginative narrative because they enjoy empathizing with the characters, because reading transports them from their current circumstances and allows them to experience situations that they are unable to access in life, and so on. Writers write from ambition, because of their personality dispositions, as self-medication, to provide themselves with a sense of agency, and so on. These are all sensible explanations, and thus there is no need to invoke some evolutionary scenario.

This too is a misunderstanding and stems from a failure to make the evolutionary biologists' standard distinction between *proximate* and *ultimate* causation. The proximate explanation for why people read fiction may indeed be that they like to empathize with the characters. But why should human beings have such a nature that empathizing, even with nonexistent individuals, should be rewarding to them? Here, we are forced back again onto the need for an ultimate explanation, and only the evolutionary perspective can provide the kind of explanation we need. The same point could be made about writers. If writers write for fame and ambition, or for therapy, why should the creation of nonveridical worlds be effective at delivering these goods? Proximate explanations only take us so far. To terminate the explanatory search, we need, as Ludwig Wittgenstein famously pointed out, "remarks on the natural history of human beings" (Wittgenstein, 1953, §415).

Thus, though there are no evolutionary adaptations for reading and writing, there are evolutionary preconditions for these activities to have flourished. Biologists call these *pre-adaptations*. The evolved architecture of the mind continues to shape the cultural practices of production and consumption of creative writing. Thus, investigating the evolutionary background to creative writing is not just a historical exercise. Indeed, the point of evolutionary inquiry in general is rarely to find out about the past. It is to explain the present, albeit in terms of the past. The evolutionary perspective thus allows us to frame ideas about why creative reading and writing are the way they are today.

We can approach this question from two directions. First, what are the facts about the natural history of human beings that make us susceptible to consuming imaginative literature? In others words, how did the creative *reader* evolve? Second, what are the facts about the natural history of human beings that make some of us specialize in the production of such representations? In other words, how did the creative *writer* evolve? I address these two issues in turn in the second and third sections, respectively. Throughout this chapter, I take creative writing to mean the production of nonveridical (fictional) representations and narratives, and creative writers to mean people who produce such representations and narratives. By this definition, science writers and historians would not be creative writers. By this I mean no judgment about the relative merits of these different types of writing, and indeed, some of the points I make here would apply to factual writing, too. However, my primary interest is in imaginative literature and its authors.

THE EVOLUTION OF THE CREATIVE READER

Consuming nonveridical representations is a major activity in developed nations. For example, I recently calculated that the average Briton spends around 369 hours a year watching some kind of drama, with television being the biggest contributor (Nettle, 2005, p. 56). Add to this 100 hours a year for fiction reading (which seems a reasonable estimate; see Verboord, 2005, p. 320), and we have around 469 hours per year, or about 8% of all waking life immersed in the output of creative writing. Of course, the amount varies enormously among individuals, but the point is that a significant fraction of time and effort in societies that have developed fictional representations is devoted to their consumption. Because consumers of fiction receive no obvious economic, practical, or reputational benefit from it, this time allocation surely demands explanation. To say that people enjoy this activity or, as the economists would have it, derive utility from it, is fine, but is only a proximate explanation. We want to know why people would be so constituted that this activity would be rewarding for them.

A preliminary answer to this question must introduce three interlinked facts about the human way of life: our sociality, our theory of mind, and our capacity for language. These three and their ramifications are sufficient to ensure that nonveridical representations with certain attributes will be effective at sequestering our attention and emotion. Each of the three areas is the subject of a large evolutionary literature, but in the interests of brevity I give only a very brief treatment here.

Human beings are intensely social. In fact, primates, the order to which we belong, tend to be social, and humans are simply the most extreme case. Primate sociality is more than simply dwelling in large aggregations. Bison and bees do that. Rather, primate sociality appears to consist of living in aggregations in which pairwise relationships between individuals are variable and dynamic and must be kept track of mentally in order to behave in a strategically appropriate manner. For example, monkeys and apes are sensitive to whether individuals have groomed them or otherwise provided them with a benefit recently, who the allies and kin of others in the group are, and what the status of others is and how it has changed (Cheney & Seyfarth 1990, 2007; Seyfarth & Cheney 1984). This means that a successful group member has to attend to, gather, and recall a great deal of *social information*; what King Lear described as "Court news – Who loses and who wins, who's in, who's out" (Act V, scene iii).

Primates tend to have relatively large brains, a fact for which the leading explanation is what is known as the *social brain hypothesis* (see Dunbar, 1998, for a review). The dynamic complexity of primate social groups requires a lot of computing power. In particular, within the primates, the more complex the social world, the more social brain is needed to keep track of it. There is good evidence for this idea. The correlation across species of monkeys and apes between the relative size of the brain and the average size of the social group in which the animal lives is positive and strong (Dunbar, 1993). Humans have the largest relative brain size of all and, of course, the most complex and largest social aggregations. The social brain hypothesis, by attributing the historical enlargement of our brains to the need to handle more and more social information, predicts that modern humans will be both highly interested in and highly adept at handling information about other individuals and especially the relationships among them.

Related to the social brain hypothesis is the phenomenon of *theory of mind*. Theory of mind refers to the ability of human beings to compute and reason about the mental states of others (Premack & Woodruff, 1978). For example, because I can distinguish what I believe from what someone else believes and what I feel from what someone else feels, I can put myself into someone else's shoes in a simulated manner. I can even reckon about what Person A believes Person B believes. This is a sophisticated mental adaptation surely designed to cope with the strategic complexity of living in close-knit groups of socially smart others who may not share our interests (Baron-Cohen, 1994). Despite considerable research effort and debate, there is no universally accepted evidence of full theory of mind in any species other than humans (though some component abilities may be present; see Hare, Call, & Tomasello, 2001, and Povinelli, Nelson, & Boysen 1990; on chimpanzees). It may be that the extra complexity of human groups demanded, and the enlarged neocortex of the brain provided, this additional simulation mechanism to move human social cognition to a level beyond that of our near cousins.

The third human capacity relevant here is that of language. Debates continue about exactly why and through what stages language evolved, but a recent approach emphasizes social cognition as key. As groups get larger and larger, it becomes more and more difficult for any one individual to gather all the observations he or she needs to keep track of Lear's "court news." The risk of behaving inappropriately or naively for want of the right information increases, and thus there would be a big fitness payoff for individuals who can get their information on the cheap. Language, by transforming mental propositions about the relationships or intentions of others into an efficiently acoustically transmissible form, greatly reduces the cost of keeping up to date. This leads to the so-called gossip hypothesis of language: that language's primordial function is to exchange information about other social group members (Dunbar 1993, 1996). There is considerable face plausibility to the gossip hypothesis. Though language as it now exists clearly can be used for many other purposes, studies of spontaneous conversations show that social concerns predominate (Dunbar, Duncan, & Marriott, 1997).

Using language to gossip in turn produces a further problem (Nettle 2006a): Why should one believe the assertions of other language users? After all, they could be pouring poison in our ears for their own purposes. There is no simple solution to this dilemma, except to verify information from multiple sources and to develop preferred gossip partners with a proven track record. Both of these principles are relevant to the functioning of fictional worlds.

Summarizing the argument to this point, our evolutionary history as primates with exceptionally large and complex social groups has driven an expansion of the human brain and provided it with the capacity to simulate the mental states of others; a linguistic system for trading information, especially about the social world; and a deep interest in and adeptness at handling social information. These are the building blocks for a theory of the evolution of creative reading.

Most societies, for most of human history, did not use writing. Presumably this is because their spatial scale was such that face-to-face conversation was sufficient to serve the functions of language in distributing social and other information. Note, though, that fiction still existed. All societies have traditions of myth, folktales, and so on. We must assume that these innovations simply exploited the evolved motivation to consume social information by providing particularly vivid information about agents who did not actually exist. As the spatial scale of society increased, writing systems began to evolve. A standard argument is that their functions are initially economic and administrative. That is, an increased scale of society and of movement of goods creates the need for permanent accounting practices. However, given the strong bias of the human mind toward social information, it was inevitable that writing systems would be used to record social tales, both veridical (history and biography) and nonveridical (fiction).

What picture of imaginative literature arises from this account? There is a range of possibilities. At one end of the spectrum, we can argue that consuming imaginative representations is directly beneficial to the individual.

For example, imagined scenarios could allow the honing of useful mind-reading skills, aid development of sophisticated locally appropriate moral and social behavior, and allow mutually beneficial social norms to be transmitted (for arguments for such benefits and others, see Nussbaum, 1995; Wilson, 2002). At the other end of the spectrum, we could view imaginative literature as completely parasitic, like a virus of the mind (for discussions of this "meme" approach, see Dennett, 1990, in the context of aesthetics in particular and Aunger, 2000, more generally).

Let us unpack this position a little further. The metabolic machinery of human cells is designed by evolution to reproduce our own tissues. Viruses get into cells and exploit that machinery for their own ends – to make more viruses. This is wholly contrary to the host's interests, but this arms race of exploitation and defense ends up with very ingenious viruses and occasional infections.

For the imaginative literature case, the parallels are as follows. Our brains are designed for vital social cognition about the real agents with whom we live. Imaginative representations get in and exploit this machinery, by making us attend to and think about social worlds that in fact do not exist and therefore are of no use to us. To overcome the resistance of the host, imaginative representations have to be exceptionally attention grabbing. Both in content and in style, they have to be intrinsically much more interesting than veridical narrative would have to be. In fact, there is an arms race between literature and its audience in which it constantly has to find ways of being new and more attention grabbing than earlier versions (see Martindale, 1990, on some consequences of this arms race for stylistics).

The debate between a beneficial and a parasitic account of literature is very similar to a current debate in evolutionary genetics. The human genome contains many copies of sequences that proliferate despite not actually coding for any gene product. Some have viewed these transposable elements as having a subtle function and therefore being beneficial to the host genome, whereas others view them as persisting and proliferating essentially parasitically. An emerging compromise is that they are best viewed as independent replicators with interests distinct from those of their hosts, but sometimes they enhance their own reproductive success by being pressed into serving functions in the host's physiology (Burt & Trivers, 2006).

I have proposed a similar account for imaginary narrative (Nettle, 2005). Essentially, such representations persist because they are good at grabbing the audience's attention, whether or not there is any actual fitness benefit to the audience in having their attention so grabbed. However, this does not preclude imaginary narratives coming to serve certain social and psychological functions, which they clearly do for many people. Indeed, perhaps a key determinant in the "fitness" of any particular work of literature is its ability to come to serve such functions for the people of its time.

This view leads directly to predictions about imaginative literature. First, consuming it should engage the same psychological machinery as social life in general does. There is evidence that this is the case. Individuals skilled in theory of mind and empathy also have more exposure to imaginative literature than individuals less skilled (Mar, Oatley, Hirsch, de la Paz, & Peterson, 2006). The most plausible explanation for this increased exposure is that the same abilities are involved in both domains, and so those with strong empathetic skills seek out fiction (for an approach to novels from the perspective of theory of mind abilities, see Zunshine, 2006). A second prediction concerns the content. Essentially, most literature should deal with the social interactions of small groups of characters in domains that are important to our biology, such as love, sex, death, status, alliances, and kinship. In particular, imaginary narrative should be expected to explore the different perspectives of different individuals on the same event, as well as the effects of private knowledge on behavioral outcomes. This is because, according to the account sketched earlier, we have evolved to use our brains and especially our theory of mind for precisely such purposes. We should thus find it intrinsically rewarding to attend to such issues, in a way that attending to, say, the physical configurations of inanimate objects is not. Fiction and drama can be very fruitfully read from this perspective (see, e.g., Carroll, 1999; Nettle, 2005).

However, the argument so far implies that the only type of literature that could be successful is naturalistic in form, when this is clearly not so. Atran (2002) has presented evidence that narrative can enhance its memorability by containing a small amount of what he calls counterintuitive material; essentially, events that cannot be explained within the normal functioning of things or, in other words, magic. Too much magic, and the narrative becomes incredible and hard to retain. However, a small amount of magic in experimental stories actually enhances recall, probably because the reader is forced to process them more deeply in the search for an explanation. It is important that the rest of the story follows the logic of real social interactions, though. This has important implications for religious narrative (perhaps the most successful form of narrative of all in the long term) and for genres such as science fiction and magical realism.

Successful literature can also persist because of its aesthetic and formal properties. Exactly how this works is beyond the scope of this chapter, but it is clear that striking, ambiguous, or polysemous use of language, like minimal counterintuitive content, can serve to heighten attention, deepen processing, and thus increase recall of imaginative narrative.

Earlier in the section, I touched on the idea that using language to exchange social information raises the problem of reliability. How are we to know who to trust, whose court news to take seriously, and whose to discount? I suggested that people mitigate this problem by incrementally developing preferred social exchange partners. This strategy has implications both within literary narrative and in terms of author preference. Readers develop favorite authors to whom they return and whose entire output they read, and this must partly reflect the discovery that that author is a rewarding voice to attend to. Within works of fiction, particular characters become preferred conduits of information and eyes with which to see, a phenomenon that can be exploited in multi-narrator works such as Faulkner's *As I Lay Dying* and Fowles' *The Collector*.

We have, then, established some basic reasons why our evolved psychology might make us prone to attend to nonveridical narratives about the world, provided that those narratives are of the right general form to engage our social cognition, and given that such narratives may make use of counterintuitive elements and unusual uses of language to maximize psychological impact. We now turn to the complementary question. Why should some people spend their lives producing such narrative?

THE EVOLUTION OF THE CREATIVE WRITER

The life of primates is marked by two interrelated dynamics: status and reciprocity. High-status individuals are looked at more and have greater access to mates and resources. Status is achieved through physical dominance, kin ties, and other alliances. As for reciprocity, one monkey grooms another and thereafter is more likely to receive aid if in distress (Seyfarth & Cheney, 1984), and many alliances are based on reciprocity.

In the previous section I argued that humans have, for reasons essentially to do with the complexity of social life, come to rely on symbolic representations of their social world in addition to their personal information gathering. This reliance immediately creates opportunities, both in the domain of status and that of reciprocity. To take reciprocity first, worthwhile social information becomes a benefit that an individual can provide, rather like grooming, that will lead to a sense of gratitude, indebtedness, and positive regard. This is presumably what is occurring when we are dying to tell others the news we have heard. In a way, the storyteller is exploiting this psychology of reciprocity. By furnishing social narratives that everyone wants to listen to, he or she achieves a kind of goodwill in the minds of others. The cultural evolution of writing merely allows the process to go on at a larger remove.

We can link this process more specifically to status. The human transition to the world of symbolic representations opens a new avenue to status, based not on physical prowess, but on the quality of symbolic representations one produces. In a world where there are many competing voices, to whom should one listen? Henrich and Gil-White (2002) suggest that this is a general problem for a species that learns its information socially. They suggest that humans have an evolved psychology of *prestige*. Prestige is a kind of high status accorded for cultural reasons. Prestigious individuals are granted all the usual advantages of high social status. In return, they are preferential learning sources; they are imitated and attended to, because they have a proven ability to produce high-quality representations or practices worthy of emulation. The psychology of prestige explains the cult of celebrity and the halo that surrounds successful artists and intellectuals.

Thus, an obvious explanation for why people write creatively is that they can achieve prestige and good regard by doing so. Evolutionary psychologist Geoffrey Miller has taken this idea further in an influential book and a series of papers (Miller 1999, 2000, 2001). In a species in which fitness is strongly dependent on having a good social and symbolic brain, it is very important to choose a mate who is of high quality in this regard, because it is after all that mate's genotype that will go into one's offspring. Thus, individuals who could display that they have good social insight, and moreover good capacities to use verbal representations to express it, would thereby be signaling that they are the kind of individuals who would be good to mate with. Thus, behaviors such as creative writing could be considered to originate as mate-attraction signals.

A number of empirical predictions follow from this hypothesis. First, people should find verbal creativity and intelligence attractive. Surveys of the desirability of characteristics in a potential mate confirm that both sexes do indeed find those qualities attractive (Buss, 1989). In particular, women find a hypothetical individual who is artistically creative especially attractive for a short-term mating when they are in the fertile phase of their menstrual cycles, when the probability of conception after intercourse is at its highest (Haselton & Miller, 2006). Preferences in the fertile phase are thought to reflect preferences for individuals with the highest genetic quality, so this evidence is particularly suggestive for the mate-signaling approach to artistic behaviors. However, it also raises the question of why there would be different preferences at different points in the menstrual cycles, or different preferences for a long rather than a short-term relationship; In other words, why is not artistic creativity universally preferred? I return to this question later.

Is there any evidence in actual behavior (as opposed to hypothetical preferences) that artistically creative individuals have elevated mating success? Nettle and Clegg (2006) found, in a sample of poets and visual artists, that those who had achieved some measure of creative success (being published or exhibited) had significantly greater numbers of sexual partners than those who produced as a hobby or than control adults who did not produce at all. Clegg (2006) replicated this pattern in a separate sample of visual artists. These results are supportive of the mate-attraction hypothesis as long as we make some ancillary assumptions. The first is that the published or exhibited individuals were producing work thought to be of high quality. The researchers had no access to the work and thus could not verify its quality in any way, but the mate-attraction hypothesis demands that it is not merely producing, but producing well, that will lead to mating success. The second is that the number of partners is a good proxy of success in attracting mates. It is not axiomatic that this is true, because finding a single mate of high quality might entail greater mating success than finding a higher number of inferior mates. However, if we assume that the number of partners is some kind of reflection of partner availability, it may on average reflect overall mate availability.

Second, the output of creative writing should be at its highest when mate-finding effort is at its peak. This hypothesis can be framed on the micro- and macro- timescales. At the micro-level, Griskevicius, Cialdini, and Kenrick (2006) found that informing college students that a piece they were writing would be read by an eligible member of the opposite sex made them write in ways that were judged more imaginative and creative than when no cue of mating relevance was giving. On the macro-level, Miller (1999) showed for a sample of writers (as well as for musicians and visual artists) that peak production tends to be in young adulthood, when reproductive competition is at its height, and it gradually declines thereafter. We might also predict that output would be diminished by marriage, because the need to attract a new mate is diminished at this point. However, many artistic individuals are promiscuous or continue to switch partners through life, a phenomenon to which I return later.

Taken together, the studies reviewed so far are supportive of the view that creative behaviors, when good, are attractive, and consequently, creative output leads to mating opportunities. Note, by the way, that this in no ways implies that writers *have in mind* to attract sexual partners when they are writing or deciding to write. That would be to conflate proximate and ultimate explanations. They may have all kinds of things in mind. The point is that the tendency to turn one's current preoccupations into imaginative writing have persisted because of sexual selection, not that mating is the preoccupation of people who write.

Overall, then, the view that artistic output is a form of mating effort is worth taking seriously. However, this raises another set of questions. The distribution of creative writing is very uneven across individuals, much more so than the distribution of creative reading. Some people never feel any urge to write creatively. Others experiment when young adults (the period of peak reproductive effort, note), but do not continue. Still others feel a strong urge to produce and keep this up throughout their lives. Why? The evolutionary account suggested so far has posited only benefits of creative writing. Surely, everyone would want to appear attractive and gain prestige. Surely, with the most artistically creative individuals gaining the most matings in each generation, after a few hundred years, everyone in the population would be equally motivated to create.

To see why this does not occur, we need to take on two further notions from evolutionary biology. The first is that of the trade-off. An individual spending resources on producing offspring cannot simultaneously be using them to grow larger. Thus, for a given energy budget, individuals face an allocation problem between reproduction and growth. Natural selection will gradually home in on ways of finding the optimum switch point between the two activities, but bear in mind that that switch point may be different for different individuals because of differences in ecology, because of differences in what others around are doing, or because of differences in the individual's attributes (see later). Thus, it will be quite normal to find populations in which there is variability between individuals in how they allocate energy to one function rather than another (Wolf, van Doorn, Leimar, &Weissing, 2007).

The second biological notion we have to take on board is that of heritable differences in quality. In every generation, there are many new genetic mutations, and the vast majority of these reduce the biological performance of the individual (for evidence on this point, see Vassilieva, Hook, & Lynch 2000). Because of the weight of genetic mutation, some individuals are better able than others to build any particular structure. Classic examples are the peacock's train or the coloring of guppies, in individuals in good condition, who are well nourished and relatively free of parasites, can create better signals than poorer quality individuals. Determining the upper limit on how good a signal the individual can produce leads to different optimal switch points for different individuals. For example, a poor-quality male may never be able to compete to hold a territory and may do better to remain small and hope for the odd sneak mating. His optimal point to stop growing is thus affected by his genetic quality.

In human life, trade-offs abound. For example, given that, unlike most mammals, we are species in which males may (but do not always) stay around and invest time and energy in their offspring, males face a trade-off between investing in their existing mates and offspring and doing things that would get them further mates. (This is known as the "dad versus cad" trade-off.) Another trade-off arises between achieving status through wealth and power and achieving it though the cultural prestige of producing in an artistic arena. Different individuals make different trade-offs among these various functions. The allocation may be determined genetically, as creative activity runs in many families, or by early life inputs, or by some combination of the two. In particular, there is a trade-off surrounding creative writing. To write successfully requires one to devote a huge amount of energy and time building up skill and a track record in an area. The chance of success is highly uncertain, and the activity itself excludes many alternative rewards – money, stability, family life – that might otherwise be pursued. Given all these trade-offs, different individuals invest in the activity to different extents. Can we conclude anything about what determines the level of investment?

Artistic production is what economists call a "winner take all" market. Robustly, throughout all human creative endeavors, there are a very small number of people who do extremely well and a large majority who fail. This has long been known empirically (see Simonton, 1999), but the evolutionary perspective allows us to understand why it must be so. If creative production is a competitive signaling system of individual quality, then only the best handful of individuals will have their signals attended to. The system only works because it is easy to use the signals to discriminate and because the best signals can only be produced by the best individuals. If these conditions are not met, then the system cannot function. Thus, not only will most people who attempt creative writing never receive an audience, but writing for being read is not even worth attempting for individuals without at least relatively excellent mental qualities. Thus, one reason why many people are not drawn to write for the consumption of others is a subconscious assessment that this is not an arena in which they will show to advantage. They may do well in other arenas – physical, financial, moral – and they would do better to specialize in them. Conversely, some people may write or be drawn to creative writing because they do not have the characteristics demanded by the other, perhaps more conventional, signaling systems of the society in which they live – they are not good hunters or office workers. Note again that this no way implies a conscious reasoning process in deciding whether to write or not. It merely says that there are mechanisms of some kind that guide us toward certain choices rather than others. These mechanisms are not at all well understood, but conscious reasoning as an adult probably plays little or no role in them.

In general, people will invest in creative writing to the extent that they have qualities that give them an edge in this field to a greater extent than they give them an edge in alternative activities. Such qualities are intelligence, though this does not discriminate between investment in, say, science or engineering versus the arts, and personality. In particular, the personality traits of openness to experience and neuroticism have often been found to be characteristic of creative writers (see Nettle, 2007). High scorers on the openness to experience dimension have an allusive, associational cognitive style that leads to an appreciation of the metaphorical and metaphysical. This appreciation makes high scorers adept at producing semantically unusual and arresting representations, and thus, it is unsurprising that they should be drawn to creative writing. Their openness gives them an edge. However, as with other personality dimensions, increasing levels of openness also have costs. High scorers have increased risk of hallucinations, delusions, and other psychotic-like experiences. Many empirical studies confirm that proneness to psychosis and artistic creativity go hand in hand (Nettle, 2006b; Schuldberg, 2000; see Chapter 2).

Neuroticism is a personality dimension associated with vigilance to harm, rumination, and anxiety. Increasing neuroticism increases the risk of mood disorders like depression, and epidemiological evidence confirms that such disorders are very common among writers and poets (Andreasen, 1987; Jamison, 1989). Why should high neuroticism provide an edge in creative writing? It is possible that the ability to ruminate and strive at high intensity for long periods, which is required for creative writing, comes more easily to those with a predisposition to worry. Certainly, a laid-back temperament that views the world as essentially benign and satisfactory seems unlikely to produce the effort of spirit necessary for great art.

Must we therefore conclude that all those who are high in intelligence, high in openness, and high in neuroticism will become creative artists of some kind, basically because they have the attributes to do well in this arena? There may be other motivational variables that are relevant too. If Miller's hypothesis is correct, then creative writing is something more specific than just one way to gain prestige. It is a way to gain access to mating more particularly. As I argued earlier, mating effort and parenting effort cannot be maximized simultaneously. Helen Clegg, using a sample of visual artists, showed that the more prolific and successful that artists were, the more short-term-oriented their mating strategy was (i.e., the more casual relationships they had without a long-term commitment; Clegg, 2006). Thus, those who choose the lifelong artistic strategy tend to be choosing mating effort over parenting effort or other activities.

This brings us back to the question of why artistic creativity is found to be attractive especially in short-term mates and especially (for women) during the fertile phase of the menstrual cycle (Haselton & Miller 2006). Women have to trade off the genetic quality of their mates against other attributes, such as their resource endowment and likelihood of staying around to invest in any offspring. In a short-term mate during the fertile period, the balance is tipped toward genetic quality. Inasmuch as creative output signals quality, then, the preference makes sense. At other points in the cycle or when the emphasis is on long-term mating, the balance may be shifted toward a different optimal mate. Thus, the creative writer is signaling not only mental qualities but also something about his or her life history strategy, something that is not necessarily desirable in a partner. Thus, writers are simultaneously seen as attractive and as "mad, bad and dangerous to know."

CONCLUSIONS

In this chapter, I have outlined some of the ideas arising from taking an evolutionary perspective on creative writing. Because creative writing is a recent cultural invention, there cannot rightly be said to be any genetic adaptations for it. However, production and consumption of creative writing are conditioned by the pre-adaptations of the human mind and human motivational structure.

I have argued what seem to me to be the merits of certain specific ideas, notably the social brain hypothesis and Miller's mate-attraction account of creative behaviors. Note, though, that the evolutionary perspective is a way of thinking rather than a commitment to these specific hypotheses. Completely different accounts of creative writing could be given that are equally Darwinian.

I have also given no account of creative writing that is done privately, with no intention of publication. Such writing is widespread, and its existence is perhaps easy to predict from the perspective of the social brain hypothesis because it would involve engaging and practicing social cognition skills. The evidence for the therapeutic value of writing is very strong (Pennebaker, 1997). The written medium may function as a cultural support for and extension for our naturally occurring processes of social reflection and thought, which are especially valuable for those high in neuroticism and thus prone to rumination on social dilemmas and the causes of behavior. In the third section I focused only on the ultimate reasons why people might want others to read what they have written, not the reasons that they might write per se. This is not to deny that many people who begin writing for intrapersonal reasons then go on and disseminate what they have written interpersonally.

The evolutionary perspective, here as in other cases, does not itself create any new knowledge and often points us to things we knew anyway. However, it is a powerful way of bringing together the big picture, in this case about why human beings attend to imaginative narratives and why some people but not others devote so much of their time and effort to producing them. It also allows us to go deeper in explanatory terms. Rather than just saying that creative writing exists because some people want to write it and a lot of people want to read it, it allows us to ask why we would be such creatures as to want to do these things, and in that regard, it is a worthwhile perspective to take.

REFERENCES

Andreasen, N. C. (1987). Creativity and mental illness: Prevalence rates in writers and their first-degree relatives. *American Journal of Psychiatry, 151*, 1650–1656.

Atran, S. (2002). *In gods we trust: The evolutionary landscape of religion.* New York: Oxford University Press.

Aunger, R. (2000). *Darwinizing culture: The status of memetics as a science.* Oxford: Oxford University Press.

Baron-Cohen, S. (1994). The Mindreading system: New directions for research. *Current Psychology of Cognition, 13*, 724–50.

Burt, A., & Trivers, R. (2006). *Genes in conflict: The biology of selfish genetic elements.* Cambridge, MA: Belknap.

Buss, D. M. (1989). Sex differences in human mate preferences: Evolutionary hypotheses tested in 37 different cultures. *Behavioral and Brain Sciences, 12*, 1–49.

Buss, D. M. (Ed.). (2005). *Handbook of evolutionary psychology.* New York: Wiley.

Carroll, J. (1999). The deep structure of literary representations. *Evolution and Human Behaviour, 20*, 159–173.

Cheney, D. L., & Seyfarth, R. M. (1990). *How monkeys see the world.* Chicago: University of Chicago Press.

Cheney, D. L., & Seyfarth, R. M. (2007). *Baboon metaphysics: The evolution of a social mind.* Chicago: University of Chicago Press.

Clegg, H. (2006). *Creativity: Psychological and evolutionary perspectives.* Unpublished doctoral dissertation, Open University, Milton Keynes, UK.

Dennett, D. C. (1990). Memes and the exploitation of the imagination. *Journal of Aesthetics and Art Criticism, 48,* 127–135.

Dunbar, R. I. M. (1993). Coevolution of neocortical size, group size and language in humans. *Behavioral and Brain Sciences, 16,* 681–735.

Dunbar, R. I. M. (1996). *Grooming, gossip and the evolution of language.* London: Faber.

Dunbar, R. I. M. (1998). The social brain hypothesis. *Evolutionary Anthropology, 6,* 178–190.

Dunbar, R. I. M., Duncan, N. D. C., & Marriott, A. (1997). Human conversational behavior. *Human Nature, 8,* 231–246.

Griskevicius, V., Cialdini R. B., & Kenrick, D. T. (2006). Peacocks, Picasso and parental investment: The effects of romantic motives on creativity. *Journal of Personality and Social Psychology, 91,* 63–76.

Hare, B., Call, J., & Tomasello, M. (2001). Do chimpanzees know what conspecifics do and do not know? *Animal Behaviour, 61,* 139–151.

Haselton, M. G., & Miller, G. F. (2006). Women's fertility across the menstrual cycle increases the short-term attractiveness of creative intelligence. *Human Nature, 17,* 50–73.

Henrich, J., & Gil-White, F. (2002). The evolution of prestige: Freely conferred deference as a mechanism for enhancing the benefits of cultural transmission. *Evolution and Human Behaviour, 22,* 165–196.

Jamison, K. R. (1989). Mood disorders and patterns of creativity in British writers and artists. *Psychiatry, 52,* 125–134.

Mar, R. A., Oatley, K., Hirsh, J., de la Paz, J., & Peterson, J. B. (2006). Bookworms versus nerds: Exposure to fiction versus non-fiction, divergent associations with social ability, and the simulation of fictional worlds. *Journal of Research in Personality, 40,* 694–712.

Martindale, C. (1990). *The clockwork muse: On the predictability of artistic change.* New York: Basic Books.

Miller, G. F. (1999). Sexual selection for cultural displays. In R. I. M. Dunbar, C. Knight, & C. Power (Eds.), *The evolution of culture* (pp. 71–91). Edinburgh: Edinburgh University Press.

Miller, G. F. (2000). *The mating mind: How sexual selection shaped human nature.* London: Heinemann.

Miller, G. F. (2001). Aesthetic fitness: How sexual selection shaped artistic virtuosity as a fitness indicator and aesthetic preferences as mate choice criteria. *Bulletin of Psychology and the Arts, 2,* 20–25.

Nettle, D. (2005). What happens in *Hamlet?* Exploring the psychological foundations of drama. In J. Gottschall & D. S. Wilson (Eds.), *The literary animal: Evolution and the nature of narrative* (pp. 56–75). Evanston: Northwestern University Press.

Nettle, D. (2006a). Language: Costs and benefits of a specialised system for social information transmission. In J. C. K. Wells, S. Strickland, & K. Laland (Eds.), *Social information transmission and evolutionary biology* (pp. 137–152). London: Taylor & Francis.

Nettle, D. (2006b). Schizotypy and mental health amongst poets, visual artists and mathematicans. *Journal of Research in Personality, 40,* 876–890.

Nettle, D. (2007). *Personality: What makes you the way you are.* Oxford: Oxford University Press.

Nettle, D., & Clegg, H. (2006). Creativity, schizotypy and mating success in humans. *Proceedings of the Royal Society of London B, 273,* 611–615.

Nussbaum, M. C. (1995). *Poetic justice: The literary imagination and public life.* Boston: Beacon.

Pennebaker, J. W. (1997). Writing about emotional experiences as a therapeutic experience. *Psychological Science, 8*, 162–166.

Povinelli, D. J., Nelson, K. E., & Boysen, S. T. (1990). Inferences about guessing and knowing by chimpanzees (Pan troglodytes). *Journal of Comparative Psychology, 104*, 203–210.

Premack, D. G., & Woodruff, G. (1978). Does the chimpanzee have a 'theory of mind'? *Behavioral and Brain Sciences, 1*, 515–526.

Schuldberg, D. (2000). Six subclinical spectrum traits in normal creativity. *Creativity Research Journal, 13*, 5–16.

Seyfarth, R. M., & Cheney, D. L. (1984). Grooming, alliances and reciprocal altruism in vervet monkeys. *Nature, 308*, 541–543.

Simonton, D. K. (1999). *Origins of genius: Darwinian approaches to creativity*. New York: Oxford University Press.

Vassilieva, L. L., Hook, A. M., & Lynch, M. (2000). The fitness effects of spontaneous mutations in *Caenorhabditis elegans*. *Evolution, 54*, 1234–1246.

Verboord, M. (2005). Long-term effects of literary education on book-reading frequency: An analysis of Dutch student cohorts 1975–1998. *Poetics, 33*, 320–342.

Wittgenstein, L. (1953). *Philosophical investigations*. Oxford: Blackwell.

Wilson, D. S. (2002). *Darwin's cathedral: Evolution, religion, and the nature of society*. Chicago: University of Chicago Press.

Wolf, M., van Doorn, G. S., Leimar, O., & Weissing, F. J. (2007) Life-history trade-offs favour the evolution of animal personalities. *Nature, 447*, 581–584.

Zunshine, L. (2006). *Why we read fiction: Theory of mind and the novel*. Columbus: Ohio State University Press.

7

Literary Creativity and Physiognomy: Expressiveness in Writers, Readers, and Literature

MARTIN S. LINDAUER

Psychology views the rather unusual phenomenon of physiognomy somewhat warily if not disparagingly (Lindauer, 1984a). To justify my coverage of this controversial (and misunderstood) topic and to validate its inclusion in a discussion of literary creativity, I digress at the outset to explain my focus on the creative literary work – the literary stimulus, "the word" – rather than, as is often the case, the creative author (Lindauer, 1984c). The stage is further set with examples that clarify the complex nature of physiognomy, followed by a brief coverage of related definitional matters, methods of study, history, and theory. After these preliminary yet important considerations, I turn to the main focus of this chapter, the role of physiognomy in literature, but not before setting it within its larger place in the arts generally. Following my argument that physiognomy not only bears on literary works but also on creative authors and receptive readers, I conclude with some suggested studies.

PRELIMINARY MATTERS: SETTING THE STAGE

The Creativity of the Work

The creativity of writers – or for that matter anyone who is creative – is not just about particular individuals and such personal matters as the role of childhood experiences, family relationships, and emotional conflicts. It also depends, in the specific case of authors, on the judgments of readers (experts, critics, reviewers, the public) and the nature of the literary work (imagery and metaphors, characterization and plot development, stylistic features, use of language). A close relationship therefore exists between creative authors, creative works, and readers. These interconnections are illustrated, for example, by imagery – the "sounds, pictures, and colors in one's head" (Lindauer, 1972, 1977, 1983). Authors translate their richly endowed capacity for imagery into evocative verbal passages to which readers respond with their own imagery. A consideration of the creative writer is therefore inseparable from readers'

117

reactions to their work and the work itself. Writers are therefore called creative because of what they write and how it is received by readers – not by who they are or how they developed; that analysis comes afterward.

Of the three major components of creativity noted in the previous paragraph, this chapter focuses on the creative work. Typically, however, the creative writer receives the major share of attention, at least in psychology, and understandably so. Personality, early childhood, the abnormal, the unconscious, and similar intrapsychic factors are more intriguing than, say, prose style or readers' preferences. Consider, too, how difficult it is to study the creative writer while at the same time taking into account the work and reader (not to speak of historical and cultural influences, the marketplace, critics and other institutional gatekeepers, as well as the role of luck, serendipity, and fashion). Psychologists have to make a choice, and characteristically, they opt for the more riveting aspect of creativity: the genius, the "mad artist," the creative writer.

When readers and works are featured, moreover, they are often treated as a roundabout means for disclosing something about authors. Readers' preferences and judgments are taken for granted (the "universal reader") and used as a "lens" through which authors are understood. Similarly, a literary work receives short shrift when it is treated as an indirect "filter" for revealing the personal characteristics of the author. Without slighting the importance of writers, it is their writing, in the final analysis, that defines them as creative. Without a novel, play, short story, poem, or other literary product, there is no author – or reader.

The question then becomes this: What is it about authors' writing that makes them creative? Or alternatively, What is it about a work that deserves our admiration? The list of possibilities is long, incomplete, and uncertain. Important roles are certainly played by the grace and forcefulness of language, the originality of imagination and the freshness of imagery, the unusualness and novelty of ideas, the arresting characters and complex characterizations, and the unexpected twists and turns of plot development. In this chapter, I propose to add a less well-known factor, physiognomy, to the list of phenomena that make a work creative.

Physiognomy Introduced

Physiognomy refers to the affective perception of persons, places, objects, and actions – and yes, even words (Lindauer, 1984a, 1987). Consider the meaningless and unfamiliar nonsense words "maluma" and "taketa," which correspond to irregularly round and sharply angular shapes, respectively. Maluma – the word or the shape – is "calm," "peaceful," and "restful," whereas taketa is "angry," "excited," and "threatening." The two also differ in size, spatiality (distance), and color (Lindauer, 1986, 1988b, 1990a, 1990b). These evocative meanings occur naturally, immediately, spontaneously, and universally.

Physiognomy, like imagery, is therefore a phenomenon that links together literary works, authors, and readers (Ahsen, 1982; Bilotta, Guare, & Lindauer, 1981; Dailey, Martindale, & Borkum, 1997). Thus, authors are talented at writing physiognomically endowed passages to which readers attribute physiognomic meanings.

Whether wrong, right, or partially correct, physiognomic attributes are perceived as inherent in the stimulus rather than constructed or inferred. Learning, associations, memories, and stereotypes play a role but only to supplement and build on an innate capacity for assigning affect to animate and inanimate objects. To minimize secondary factors, the strategy is to study physiognomic perception across cultures and among young children for whom conventional meanings are either absent or not yet learned. Accordingly, nonliterate and young people match apparently unrelated words, shapes, and colors to one another, to stick figures, and even to smells; these connections are neither random nor arbitrary (Greenauer & Lindauer, 1981). Physiognomic attributes have also been assigned to the well-known illusion of movement, the autokinetic effect, in which stationary meaningful shapes seem to move in directions and velocities that are congruent with their meanings (Comalli, 1960; Comalli, Werner, & Wapner 1952; Gostin & Lindauer, 1973). Thus, an airplane "moves" slower, and from left to right (or the reverse), compared to a rocket that "streaks" up or down, although both shapes are in fact stationary.

More familiar are physiognomic messages from the face, which attracts-repulses, invites-discourages, arouses-calms, welcomes–rejects, interests-bores. Among the top 10 quotations about body language with which undergraduate judges agreed, the eyes dominated (Lindauer, 1991a):

A silent look can still have voice and words.
The eyes can insult, or, they can make the heart dance with joy.
A person can be as cold as ice.
Love lights up eyes.
Eyes can be full of hate, or good or sinister looks.
A woman can wear a smile on her lips, and have a tear in her eye.
Eyes speak all languages.
Eyes ask, assert, and prowl.
Judge not according to appearance.
A person can be as gloomy as night.

Judgments of facial photographs, in the diagnostic context of the Szondi test, are used as a projective measure of personality. In more everyday settings, the power of physiognomy is demonstrated by the self-consciousness of presidential candidates, celebrities, and other public figures in controlling their facial expressions during debates, interviews, "photo-ops," and publicity shots. Frowns, smiles, shrugs, and eyes rolled up, down, or sideways can be more revealing than the words spoken. An unacknowledged belief in physiognomy may explain why college and job applications often require a photograph.

A Brief History and Theoretical Overview of Physiognomy

The physiognomy of the face, along with the body in general and its various parts, occupies a prominent place in the history of psychology. The extent to which people rely on physiognomic cues, the consistency with which they are communicated and understood, and their accuracy have been of interest since at least Aristotle's *Physiognomica* and reached a popular frenzy with the publication of *Von der Physiognomik* by the Swiss theologian and mystic Johann Caspar Lavater (1741–1801). The reliance on outward signs as indicators of inner psychological states is illustrated in a diversity of ways, including the masks worn in Greek theater and, in medieval times, the belief that the seven deadly sins revealed themselves in facial expressions. Closer to our time, Kretschmer (1888–1964) tied bodily features to personality, psychopathology, and criminality. The linkage between physique and temperament was updated by Sheldon's (1898–1977) visceratonic endomorph, somatonic mesomorph, and cerebrotonic ectomorph.

The centerpiece of the body language/physiognomic thesis is Darwin's classic work in 1872 on the evolution of emotions, *The Expression of the Emotions in Man and Animals*. The fox is a sly and cunning creature – and so too are people who appear fox-like (clever, shrewd). Consequently, the meanings assigned to the outward appearance of animals and humans are important considerations in evolutionary biology (Alley, 1988; Rhodes & Zebrowitz, 2002).

For Gestalt psychologists like Köhler (1947), physiognomic perception is "tertiary," following first, sensory reception, and, second, its organization into units. The latter is also called "geometric-technical" to contrast it with the expressiveness of perception, a third or tertiary (physiognomic) stage. The Gestalt position on physiognomy's development in children and in the larger context of comparative psychology underlies Werner's (1948) sensory-tonic theory of perception (see also Werner, 1952, 1955). Within a Gestalt framework, too, Arnheim extensively discussed physiognomy in the arts (Arnheim, 1966, 1969, 1974, 1984, see especially 1972), including literature (1948, 1970, 1984).

A major question that runs through these theoretical positions is whether physiognomic perception is inborn or learned. A related issue is the extent to which physiognomy can be artificially enhanced (through cosmetic surgery) or suppressed (by masking facial expressions). In common thought, though, it is an accepted truism that inner psychological traits are revealed by external physical characteristics. Thus, when people meet, especially for the first time, or when they appraise strangers, physiognomic cues are expected, looked for, taken seriously, interpreted, and applied with confidence.

In scientific circles, though, physiognomy is less well received. For some, it is a discredited, superficial, or exaggerated phenomenon. Perhaps as a response to this negative judgment, the term "physiognomy" has been replaced with more sophisticated concepts. Hormones take the place of the choleric, phlegmatic, melancholic, saturnine, mercurial, and sanguine humours of the body associated with different personalities; the localization of brain function replaced Gall's (1758–1828) phrenology and its claim that bumps on the skull were external signs of internal psychological traits. In a similar vein, the relationship between external stimuli and their psychological implications is categorized under labels that are more neutral than the term "physiognomy": face and person perception, self-image, personal attractiveness, gender studies, nonverbal behavior, interpersonal communication and distance, body and gestural language, proxemics (the spatial relationships between people), kinesics (the movements of and between people), and utterances (voices "insist" and scorn).

Other changes from earlier views of physiognomy have also occurred. Physiognomy has been broadened from its original emphasis on the face to other parts of the body (shoulders, posture), and extended from the perception of emotions to the perception of personality, intelligence, and social characteristics (shyness). In addition, physiognomy is no longer exclusively ascribed to people but is now also applied to objects, places, and events: Mountains are awesome, clouds are threatening, a room is inviting, rivers are wild (or tranquil), and crowds swell. "Still waters run deep" describes a strong and silent person (both people and rivers are "deep").

PHYSIOGNOMY IN THE ARTS AND LITERATURE

Physiognomy is a prominent feature of the arts (Gombrich, 1960, 1972; Lindauer, 1970a, 1970b, 1984b; see earlier references to Arnheim), where its presence is more dramatic than in everyday settings in which people present themselves fleetingly and guardedly and ordinary language is limited to the literal, physical, and concrete (Danow, 1984, p. 161). Artists, moreover, are gifted at translating the subtle but normally masked physiognomic properties of colors, forms, lines, shapes, arrangements, and movements into art. In abstract paintings, for example, colors, lines, and shapes communicate affect despite the absence of recognizable objects. Similarly, portraits, unfinished sketches, and the scanty lines of caricatures convey the essential character of a person. In music, conductors use their hands not only to mark the beat but also to communicate affective changes through the vigor and pattern of movements. In response, musicians sway, stiffen, rise on their toes and up from their chairs, and change positions to augment their playing. In atonal music, sounds and rhythms enhance if not initiate a mood (a flattened note is "sad"). Marble, bronze, and wood sculptures "insist" on being touched, an impulse anticipated (and discouraged) by warnings posted nearby. In theater, the gestures and bodily movements of actors, as well as dancers, convey resignation, impatience, joy, and other feelings (as does the stirrings or gasps of their audiences).

In literature, as elsewhere in the arts, physiognomy adds subtle nuances of meaning to augment and occasionally replace the straightforward exposition of characters, events, and places. A voice "insists"; a stance signals "nearness" or "distance," hostility or peacefulness. Dialogue, too, aside from specific words, reveals inner states and emotional undertones by its pace (number of words, abruptness). Physical descriptions of places, even the weather, carry affective-physiognomic nuances. "It was a dark and stormy night . . ." Physiognomically endowed words also foreshadow subsequent events, hinting at what is to come and raising expectations, as well as emphasizing actions without italics or exclamation points. One word in particular, and not another, fits into the "flow" of the narrative and seems "right" (Tytler, 1982, p. 127; see also Danow, 1984; Dufrenne, 1973/1953; Edel, 1955; Friedman, 1981). Creative writing instructors urge their students, "Show, don't tell."

Physiognomy is therefore an expressive part of language, what Magliola (1972, p. 83) calls "gestural," and which for Edel (1955) adds "atmosphere." Words on a page of literature, in other words, go beyond their dictionary definitions by transmitting a penumbra of feelings and moods. Thus, eyes are described in ways that suggest warmth or coldness, as in Homer's description of Athene as "bright-eyed." Similarly evocative are descriptions of the mouth and face generally. The treacherous Cassius in Shakespeare's tragic-historical play *Julius Caesar* has a "lean and hungry look," and his eyes are portrayed in ways that suggest furtiveness, sneakiness, and untrustworthiness. These images hint at his subsequent betrayal of Caesar. General appearance is crucial, too. The "good-hearted" women in the works of Bronte, Thackeray, and Trollope have a "homely, plain look," perhaps to support their firmness of character. Physical descriptions of people ("literary portraits") deepen their characterization and enrich the storyline. How would you, as a reader, react to a fictional character with "a thin mouth, small temple, high forehead, prominent chin, red hair"? Now add, "a dark countenance." What happens when "squared shoulders" are added?

Readers of literature, not necessarily consciously, are especially sensitive to the affective connotations of words, those meanings that exceed literal definitions. Strictly speaking, letters, words, phrases, and sentences are physical and sensory stimuli composed of straight, slanted, and curved lines of various shapes, forms, sizes, lengths, and spatialities. Like any text, literary material is attended to, perceived, and organized. But unlike ordinary prose, literary passages are also transformed into "good forms" with figural (salient) and holistic qualities; literature is "belles-lettres." Words do not lie inertly on a page, but resonate with a rhythm and flow that "sing," "pulsate," "shine," and reverberate like a song. A literary text is exciting-brooding, calm-agitated, lively-dead.

It also seems reasonable to suppose that readers vary in their sensitivity to literary language, with some partially or completely unaware of physiognomic undercurrents (Lindauer, 1988, 1991b). Other readers are more receptive to a work's physiognomic implications, just as are some viewers of art and listeners to music. Perhaps this is why, at least in part, interpretations of literature differ and readers disagree (as is true of any art).

The physiognomic implications of literary prose, for casual readers, may be hard to discern, obscured as they are by the direct, clear, and concrete meanings of words. Hence the difficulty of studying physiognomy in literature compared to nonverbal paintings and music. Nonetheless, readers are to some degree affected by the physical characteristics of letters, the spaces between lines, the density of paragraphs, the place where sentences start and end, and the overall shape and layout of a page.

These extraverbal properties are especially evident in poetry. The poems of e. e. cummings, without capitalization and with other unusual features (e.g., sentence structure), most likely taps into physiognomic effects. In modern poetry, where the meanings of words and their allusions are not easy to decipher, the shapes of words, sentence configuration, and line patterns evoke a mood, a vague sense of what the poem is about. Sensitive readers therefore pore carefully over each word, as well as consonants, vowels, and syllables, and read passages aloud to find clues to a poem's multiple shades of affect and layers of meaning.

Creative authors, talented at using language, choose physiognomically redolent words that best translate their ideas and feelings into fresh and expressive terms, phrases, and passages that arouse, they hope, a corresponding physiognomic resonance in readers. Authors may also manipulate the latent physiognomic meanings of a text in ironic or contradictory ways so as to create an impression that is the opposite of the words' dictionary meaning. When physiognomic and literal meanings play against each other, they arouse tensions in readers that encourage them to continue reading until the disparity is resolved. Whether physiognomic effects are complementary or contradictory, the reading experience is enriched and the understanding of a character, event, or place is deepened. Pleasure, enjoyment, and appreciation are enhanced, and perhaps an "ah-ha" moment of insight is provoked.

References to the writer's "voice," style, and what the French writer Flaubert called "le mot juste," the exact or appropriate word – not "red" or "pink" but "carmine" – touch on physiognomic effects. The right (physiognomic) word has a dramatic flair, an impact, a sparkle. Nineteenth-century authors like the Brontes, Dickens, Jane Austen, and Joseph Conrad, writing at a time when physiognomy was widely discussed, explicitly admitted that Lavater, its major exponent, influenced their work. So, too, at least implicitly, were Carlyle, Baudelaire, Goethe, Balzac, and George Sand. On the other hand, Thackeray, Trollope, George Eliot, and Stendhal specifically denied Lavater's influence on their work. Authors known for their physiognomic descriptions, whether or not they acknowledged their indebtedness to Lavater or mentioned physiognomy specifically, include Poe, Hawthorne, Dickens, Stendhal, D. H. Lawrence, and Blake.

PHYSIOGNOMY, SYNESTHESIA, AND THE LITERARY EXPERIENCE

Closely related to physiognomy, and likewise enhancing the literary experience by adding evocative meanings to prose, is synesthesia, an intersensory experience in which stimulation of one sense evokes another sense (Marks, 1975, 1978, 1982; McKellar, 1968, 1997). (Synesthesia is also called "verbal synesthesia" or "phonetic symbolism"; Lindauer, 1991b.) Words, vowels, consonants, and syllables (and their sounds) are flat-rough, cold-hot, gray-colorful. For Tennyson, flowers "speak": red roses cry, white roses weep, the lily whispers, the larkspur listens. Poe writes of "the sound of coming darkness" and "the murmur of the gray twilight." Well known is Kipling's, "Dawn comes up like thunder."

Synesthetic effects, like physiognomic ones, are abundant in the arts. A musical note is "bright" (a sound evokes a visual experience) or "scratchy" (a sound–touch connection). Similarly, yellows or blues in paintings are "warm" or "cold," "bright" or "distant," respectively. (The same can be said of actors.) "Picasso's paintings seem to roar and stamp, while Paul Klee's whisper a soliloquy" (McKellar, 1997, p. 47). In the classic Disney movie *Fantasia*, the music of Bach and Schubert accompany, in a fitting and convincing way, the visual patterns, shapes, and colors on the screen.

Synesthesia is present in verbal material too, especially in literary texts, and like physiognomy, it characterizes certain authors' works. It also describes the way they write. Thus, some writers can only work with a pencil of a certain sharpness, size, color, and thickness; require a particular kind of paper; and must sit in a specific place. A writer friend wrote his words over and over again until the paper nearly tore in order to get a "feel" for what he was trying to say. Some readers, tuned in to synesthesia, respond with a shiver, "pang," "click," an involuntary "Wow!" or a "Whoa!"

In many of these examples, the sight of a word or object evokes not only a sensory response (a sound, taste, smell, tactile experience, and the like) but also a physiognomic (affective) reaction. Thus, a color (a visual experience) is "loud" (synesthetic) as well as "soothing" (physiognomic); a willow tree is "weeping" (sensory) and "graceful" (affective). The joint effects of synesthesia and physiognomy are illustrated by the background music in films that precedes action and accompanies dialogue. The synesthetic impact of music heightens the physiognomic tone of the spoken words that are heard and the physical actions seen. In the movie *Fantasia*, referred to earlier, Mussorgsky's "Night on Bald Mountain" plays in the background to augment the physiognomic feeling of danger, of things out of control, of panic, of a struggle to overcome (McKellar, 1997, p. 42). In a similar vein, readers react differently to a poem or story read aloud (by themselves or others) compared to a silent reading, because of variations in the inflection of the voice, pauses, and the location and timing of breaths. Sound (synesthetically) prompts affect (physiognomy) – or perhaps the reverse.

Physiognomy and synesthesia work together in less dramatic ways, too. Take the word "mountain," which denotes, on a literal level, a specific object with a certain shape, size, mass, and other physical characteristics. But the word "mountain," embedded in a literary context, also calls to mind, in physiognomic terms, a sense of awe and wonder and a feeling of looming danger. At the same time, the word synesthetically triggers "coldness" and "roughness," mistiness and grayness.

These two features of language add to and amplify the definitional meanings of words by jointly setting a tone, generating a feeling, establishing a mood, and creating an atmosphere. Admittedly, though, it is difficult to distinguish between physiognomy and synesthesia. The "soft" and "yielding" qualities of a person are both physiognomic (affective) and synesthetic (sensory). Should physiognomy be considered a special case of synesthesia or the reverse, or are both dependent on something else, like imagery? I return to this question later.

LITERARY CREATIVITY, THE TEXT, AND PHYSIOGNOMY

What makes an author (or anyone) creative? Despite decades of research and numerous research articles, essays, special journal issues, books, handbooks, and collections of readings, a great deal remains unknown or only incompletely understood. Progress has been limited, in my view, because of an almost exclusive focus on the writer (or artist generally). The consequence has been the relative neglect of the reader (or any audience) and the work (or artistic product, broadly speaking). Yet it is the reader and work, as I have emphasized in the introduction, which identify an author as creative.

Contrast psychology's emphasis on the creative person with the professional literature addressed to writers, such as *The Writer's Chronicle*, published by the Association of Writers and Writing Programs; the acclaimed *Poets & Writers Magazine*; and the schedule of events posted at writers conferences and workshops. These contain few articles or presentations on the personal and psychological factors that contribute to authors' creativity. Instead, most pieces are about the *craft* of writing; that is, how to write better and more effectively, the way good writers write and what makes writing good, how to improve one's writing and avoid common mistakes, and similar matters that center on technique and the work rather than the author. (Discussions of writer's block are an exception.) When creativity is discussed, the focus is on the *activity* of writing and its eventual outcome, the *product*. Likewise, interviews of writers probe less into the nature of their creativity than on what they *do*; that is, how and what they write. It is assumed that what writers do is, by definition," creative." Writers themselves talk and write about who and what influenced their work in general or a particular piece, how they treated a theme or character, changes in their work over time, and the intended audience for their work, not to speak of the "business" of writing: tours, signings at book stores, marketing, and sales.

Creative writers, unlike psychologists who write about them and do research that culminates in published articles on creativity, focus primarily on the art of writing, or the nature of what they write – the word. This includes physiognomy, as I have emphasized in this chapter, along with the closely related phenomenon of synesthesia. The text, I have argued, is critical for understanding creativity, not only for its physiognomic character, along with associated synesthetic effects, but also because the work is the converging point for writers (who produce it) and readers (who react to it). To repeat an earlier point: Without a work there would be no creativity or, indeed, a writer or reader. Creative authors, among their many talents, are able to pen powerful words that trigger, in readers, affect (physiognomy), sensory undercurrents (synesthesia), pictures-in-the-head (images), and other evocative responses.

Not all creative authors though, are known for their physiognomic prowess. Some emphasize styles that are introspective, stream-of-consciousness, symbolic, realistic, allegorical, metaphorical, and fantastic. Accordingly, not all great works of literature (or art in general) are physiognomically endowed. Further, not every reader is attuned to physiognomic content, and for them, such writings are "flat," leaving them unmoved by subtle affective touches. Literature has many kinds of authors, readers, and genres; individual differences count here as they do elsewhere. The physiognomic endowment of passages may depend on the kind of creative writer (novelist, playwright, poet, memoirist) and type of literature (epic, poem, sonnet, western, thriller, avant-garde, experimental). Just as creativity is not applicable to every activity, every person, and at every age, a physiognomic quotient is not the same in all areas of art, for every artist and reader (or audience), or at different time periods. Physiognomy applies to some writers, some works, and some readers. The same variability applies to synesthesia and imagery.

That said, physiognomy is also found in some nonwriters, ordinary prose, and everyday reading; physiognomy is not limited to artists, creative people, works of art, and arts audiences. What people write (notes, letters, reports, diary entries), the way they present this material (word choice, handwriting, pen, pencil, or computer printout), and how their writing is received by others (with interest, inattention, rejection) are influenced by several factors. These include knowledge of the rules of grammar and composition – and physiognomy, among other subtle phenomena like synesthesia.

CONCLUSION

In psychology at least, physiognomy has not been heralded as a particularly important characteristic of creative writers, readers, or literary works (Lindauer, 1984c). But as I have argued, physiognomy has the virtue of relating creative authors, the prose they write, and the readers they address. Physiognomy has an additional advantage: It is found across the arts and in ordinary contexts as well.

However, the case for physiognomy, alas, is largely speculative. Little research has actually been done on the physiognomy of writers, readers, and literary texts, at least in recent years (Arcamore & Lindauer, 1974; Lindauer, 1975, 1988a). The reasons for this neglect are many. For one, several important issues remain unresolved, such as untangling innate and learned factors in its origins, development, and expression.

Other longstanding but unsettled questions include physiognomy's underlying perceptual-cognitive base; its relationship to symbols, language, and metaphors; its ties to empathy and intuition; and its dual role in both person and object perception. Perplexing, too, is whether physiognomy comes under the heading of synesthesia or the reverse, or whether it is dependent on something else, such as imagery.

Then there are the disguises under which physiognomy currently operates (e.g., nonverbal communication, gestural language) that need to be unpacked so that their expressive features can be recognized. Otherwise, physiognomy appears to have faded into obscurity. But to ignore the historical roots of such contemporary topics as, say, person or social perception, is to lose sight of the experiential richness and conceptual complexity of physiognomy-by-any-other-name, and yes, to make the same mistakes of the past that were made under its rubric.

The failure to give physiognomy its proper due is most likely to change if several relatively simple issues are addressed. A first suggested step is to correlate with one another the physiognomy of creative authors, the physiognomic sensitivity of readers, and the physiognomy of literary material. Indicators of the physiognomy of writers and readers could be obtained by testing them with the Physiognomic Cue Test (Stein, 1975), the only instrument I know of that measures physiognomy. As for the physiognomic properties of literary works, they could be established by polling experts, such as professors of English literature, to find a consensus on selections that are physiognomically rich. (The sample should also include materials, authors, and readers that are not physiognomically endowed.)

Another basic issue meriting immediate research attention is the relationship between physiognomy and synesthesia, and the two with imagery. Does one precede, accompany, or follow the other? An experimental approach might take the following general form. Participants would first be exposed to literary material that is amply endowed with imagery (or physiognomy or synesthesia). They would then be presented with a relatively neutral text (a list of nouns, let's say, or line drawings). The latter would be rated on a checklist of physiognomic descriptors (or synesthetic or imagistic, depending on which variable was presented first). What was the effect of pre-exposure to imagistic (or physiognomic or synesthetic) material on subsequent neutral stimuli? (For a study that examines the impact of paintings in a similar manner, see Lindauer [1983].) The outcomes of these rather basic but easily managed empirical studies can be built on to tackle some of the more perplexing and complex matters raised earlier, such as the underlying perceptual nature of physiognomy.

Physiognomy is an elusive phenomenon, perhaps more so in literature than paintings or music. (Reading takes more time than a glance at a canvas or listening to a chord so there are greater opportunities for non-physiognomic effects.) Nonetheless, authors follow certain ground rules, whether consciously or not, one of which undoubtedly revolves around ensuring that their prose is enriched with physiognomic treatments of settings, characters, and dialogue. Alert readers, moreover, implicitly expect, look for, and are affected by allusions to the physiognomic properties of a character, place, and discourse.

Physiognomy is an ideal topic for investigating creativity. It is simultaneously about the creative writer, the creative work, and the reader of creative texts. Physiognomy in a literary context is therefore a means for taking an integrative approach to the study of creativity. In addition, physiognomy has close ties to synesthesia and imagery, two other powerful ingredients of creative fiction. Furthermore, investigations of the role of physiognomy in literary creativity exemplify a rare interdisciplinary exchange between scientific inquiry and art. Surely it is time to recognize the importance of physiognomy as of more than quaint historical interest and to take it seriously as a major factor in perception, creativity, and literature.

REFERENCES

Ahsen, A. (1982). Principles of imagery in art and literature. *Journal of Mental Imagery*, 6, 213–250.
Alley, T. R. (Ed.). (1988). *Social and applied aspects of perceiving faces. Resources for ecological psychology*. Hillsdale, NJ: Erlbaum.
Arcamore, A., & Lindauer, M. S. (1974). Concept learning and the identification of poetic style. *Psychological Reports, 35*, 207–210.
Arnheim, R. (1948). Psychological notes on the poetical process. In R. Arnheim, W. H. Auden, & D. A. Stouffer (Eds.), *Poets at work* (pp. 125–162). New York: Harcourt Brace.
Arnheim, R. (1966). *Art and visual perception: A psychology of the creative eye*. Berkeley: University of California Press.
Arnheim, R. (1969). *Visual thinking*. Berkeley: University of California Press.
Arnheim, R. (1970). Words and their place. *Journal of Typographic Research, 4*, 199–212.

Arnheim, R. (1972). The Gestalt theory of expression. In R. Arnheim (Ed.), *Toward a psychology of art: Collected essays* (pp. 51–73). Berkeley: University of California Press.

Arnheim, R. (1974). *Art and visual perception: A psychology of the creative eye (the new version)*. Berkeley: University of California Press.

Arnheim, R. (1984). Visual aspects of concrete poetry. In J. O. Strelka (Ed.), *Literary criticism and psychology* (pp. 91–109). University Park: Pennsylvania State University Press.

Bilotta, J., Guare, J., & Lindauer, M. S. (1981). The relationship between field-independence/dependence, creativity, and physiognomy among men and women. *JSAS Selected Documents in Psychology, 1,* 2287.

Comalli, P. E. Jr. (1960). Studies in physiognomic perception. VI. Differential effects of directional dynamics of pictured objects on real and apparent motion in artists and chemist. *Journal of Psychology, 49,* 99–109.

Comalli, P. E. Jr., Werner, H., & Wapner, S. (1952). Studies in physiognomic perception: III. Effect of directional dynamics and meaning-induced sets on autokinetic motions. *Journal of Psychology, 43,* 2898–2899.

Dailey, A., Martindale, C., & Borkum, J. (1997). Creativity, synesthesia and physiognomic perception. *Creativity Research Journal, 10,* 1–8.

Danow, D. K. (1984). Physiognomy: The codeless science. *Semiotica, 50,* 15–171.

Dufrenne, M. (1973/1953). *The phenomenology of aesthetic experience*. Evanston: Northwestern University Press.

Edel, L. (1955). *The modern psychological novel*. New York: Grove Press.

Friedman, J. B. (1981). Another look at Chaucer and the physiognomists. *Studies in Philology, 78,* 138–152.

Gombrich, E. H. (1960, Winter). On physiognomic perception. *Daedalus,* 228–242.

Gombrich, E. H. (1972). The mask and the face: The perception of physiognomic likenesses in life and art. In E. H. Gombrich, J. Hochberg, & M. Bloch (Eds.), *Art, perception, and reality* (pp. 30–45). Baltimore: Johns Hopkins University Press.

Gostin, L. O., & Lindauer, M. S. (1973). Autokinesis for meaningful stimuli and the effect of set. *Perceptual and Motor Skills, 36,* 979–986.

Greenauer, M., & Lindauer, M. S. (1981). Physiognomic properties of positive and negative stimuli among five-year old children (Report No. PS102 417). East Lansing, MI: National Center for Research on Teacher Learning (ERIC Document Reproductive Service. No. ED206 416).

Köhler, W. (1947). *Gestalt psychology*. New York: Liveright.

Lindauer, M. S. (1970a). Physiognomic properties of abstract art and titles. *Proceedings of the 78th Annual Convention APA, 5,* 493–494.

Lindauer, M. S. (1970b). Psychological aspects of form perception in abstract art. *Science de l'Art, 7,* 19–24.

Lindauer, M. S. (1972). The sensory attributes and functions of imagery and imagery evoking stimuli. In P. W. Sheehan (Ed.), *The function and nature of imagery* (pp. 131–147). New York: Academic Press.

Lindauer, M. S. (1975). *The psychological study of literature*. Chicago: Nelson-Hall.

Lindauer, M. S. (1977). Imagery from the point of view of psychological aesthetics, the arts, and creativity. *Journal of Mental Imagery, 1,* 343–362.

Lindauer, M. S. (1983). Imagery and the arts. In A. A. Sheikh (Ed.), *Imagery: Current theory, research, and applications* (pp. 468–506). New York: Wiley.

Lindauer, M. S. (1984a). Physiognomic perception. In R. J. Corsini (Ed.), *Wiley encyclopedia of psychology* (Vol. 1., pp. 34–35). New York: Wiley.

Lindauer, M. S. (1984b). Physiognomy and art: Approaches from above, below, and sideways. *Visual Arts Research, 10*, 52–65.

Lindauer, M. S. (1984c). Psychology and literature. In M. H. Bornstein (Ed.), *Psychology and its allied disciplines* (pp. 113–154). Hillside, NJ: Erlbaum.

Lindauer, M. S. (1986). Perceiving, imaging, and preferring the colors of physiognomic stimuli. *American Journal of Psychology, 99*, 233–255.

Lindauer, M. S. (1987). Physiognomic perception. In R. J. Corsini (Ed.), *Wiley encyclopedia of psychology* (condensed version, pp. 398–399). New York: Wiley.

Lindauer, M. S. (1988a). Physiognomic meanings in the titles of short stories. In C. Martindale (Ed.), *Psychological approaches to the study of literary narratives* (pp. 74–95) Hamburg: Helmut Buske.

Lindauer, M. S. (1988b). Size and distance perception of the physiognomic stimulus "taketa." *Bulletin of the Psychonomic Society, 26*, 217–220.

Lindauer, M. S. (1990a). The effects of the physiognomic stimuli *taketa* and *maluma* on the meanings of neutral stimuli. *Bulletin of the Psychonomic Society, 28*, 151–154.

Lindauer, M. S. (1990b). The meanings of the physiognomic stimuli *taketa* and *maluma*. *Bulletin of the Psychonomic Society, 28*, 47–50.

Lindauer, M. S. (1991a). *Physiognomic expression in literary materials: Bridging the humanities and science*. Paper presented at the Society for Science and Literature Conference, Montreal, October.

Lindauer, M. S. (1991b). Physiognomy and verbal synesthesia: Affective and sensory descriptions of nouns with drawings and art. *Metaphor and Symbolic Activity, 6*, 183–202.

Magliola, R. R. (1972). The phenomenological approach to literature: Its theory and methodology. *Language and Style, 5*, 79–99.

Marks, L. E. (1975). On colored-hearing synesthesia: Cross-modal translations of sensory dimensions. *Psychological Bulletin, 82*, 303–331.

Marks, L. E. (1978). *The unity of the senses: Interrelations among the modalities*. New York: Academic Press.

Marks, L. E. (1982). Synesthetic and poetic metaphor. *Journal of Experimental Psychology: Perception and Performance, 8*, 15–23.

McKellar, P. (1968). *Experience and behavior*. Baltimore: Penguin.

McKellar, P. (1997). Synaesthesia and imagery: *Fantasia* revisited. *Journal of Mental Imagery, 21*, 41–54.

Rhodes, G., & Zebrowitz, L. A. (Eds.). (2002). *Facial attractiveness: Evolutionary, cognitive, and social perspectives. Advances in visual cognition* (Vol. 1). Westport, CT: Ablex.

Stein, M. I. (1975). *The Physiognomic Cue Test*. New York: Behavioral Publications.

Tytler, G. (1982). *Physiognomy in the European novel*. Princeton: Princeton University Press.

Werner, H. (1948). *Comparative psychology of mental development*. New York: International Universities Press. (Original work published 1926)

Werner, H. (1952). On physiognomic perception. In G. Kepes (Ed.), *The new landscape in art and science* (pp. 280–282). Chicago: Paul Theobald.

Werner, H. (Ed.). (1955). *On expressive behavior*. Worcester, MA: Clark University Press.

8

The Literary Genius of William Shakespeare: Empirical Studies of His Dramatic and Poetic Creativity

DEAN KEITH SIMONTON

The psychology of creative writing can be approached numerous ways, but among the most direct is to scrutinize the creativity of the single most outstanding exemplar of the phenomenon. In the case of English literature that exemplar's identity leaves little no room for doubt. The appropriate author is the person known as William Shakespeare, a writer long considered the greatest playwright and poet in the English language. So prominent and durable was his influence that modern English is very much a repository of the hundreds of words and expressions that the Bard himself devised (Macrone, 1990). For instance, he enlarged the lexicon with the verbs "blanket," "champion," "gossip," "misquote," "puke," "swagger," and "torture"; the nouns "eyeball," "mountaineer," and "pageantry"; and the adjectives "bloodstained," "domineering," "fashionable," "majestic," and "unreal." And Shakespeare coined such durable expressions as "in my mind's eye," "all the world's a stage," "full circle," "good riddance," "in my heart of hearts," "to thine own self be true," "heart on my sleeve," "hob nob," "an itching palm," "caviar to the general," "the dogs of war," "eaten me out of house and home," "a dish fit for the gods," "fair play," "for goodness' sake," "foregone conclusion," "household words," "a lean and hungry look," "the milk of human kindness," "one fell swoop," "to the manner born," "the primrose path," "short shrift," "too much of a good thing," "what the dickens," "neither rhyme nor reason," "neither a borrower nor a lender be," "more in sorrow than in anger," "brevity is the soul of wit," "brave new world," "bated breath," "uneasy lies the head that wears a crown," "what's past is prologue," "a tower of strength," "a spotless reputation," "laugh oneself into stitches," "knock, knock! Who's there?", "something wicked this way comes," "strange bedfellows," "such stuff as dreams are made of," "pomp and circumstance," "wild-goose chase," "the better part of valor is discretion," "method in the madness," "breathe one's last," "budge an inch," "the crack of doom," "we have seen better days," "the world's mine oyster," "vaulting ambition," "a pair of star-crossed lovers," and "to be, or not to be." No wonder that his contemporary Ben Jonson said that Shakespeare "was not of an age, but for all time."

Nor was Shakespeare's influence limited to English literature. His work has been translated into all of the world's major languages, and by that means he has managed to exert an impact on entirely distinct literary traditions. For example, the Chinese poet Liu Bo-duan, in his "Ode to Shakespeare," proclaimed, "Three hundred years have passed 'twixt then and now, / Yet all the world looks to that mountain's brow!" (translated in Giles, 1965, p. 418). Indeed, the impact of his pen even extends beyond literature. The repertoire of classical music is replete with Shakespeare-inspired operas, ballets, tone poems, and songs by such notable composers as Hector Berlioz, Ambroise Thomas, and Charles Gounod in France; Guiseppe Verdi in Italy; Felix Mendelssohn and Otto Nicolai in Germany; Franz Schubert in Austria; Peter Tchaikovsky, Serge Prokofiev, and Dmitri Shostakovich in Russia; and Benjamin Britten in Shakespeare's own England. Moreover, his plays have provided scripts for hundreds of motion pictures, including several dozen versions of *Hamlet*. And the number of paintings devoted to illustrating famous scenes and characters in those plays is virtually uncountable. It should come as no big surprise, then, that one scholar ranked Shakespeare as the most influential creative writer of any time or place (Hart, 1987; see also Cattell, 1903; Murray, 2003). Indeed, on a scale of historical impact the Bard was placed only slightly below the commanders Alexander the Great and Napoleon Bonaparte!

Given Shakespeare's exalted status as the premiere English-language writer, can we learn anything about the psychology of literary creativity from his life and works? I think the answer is affirmative. To make my case, I review the research on two of the most outstanding products of his creative mind: the 37 plays and the 154 sonnets.

THE 37 PLAYS

The best place to begin our inquiry is the corpus of plays attributed to Shakespeare. After all, when I discussed earlier his impact on world literature and civilization, it is this specific set of contributions that claim the lion's share of the influence. Accordingly, I focus on the 37 plays that make up the traditional canon (thus omitting the *Two Noble Kinsmen*). These plays can be used to examine three major aspects of dramatic creativity: style, content, and impact.

Style

Martindale (1990) has amply documented the ubiquity of stylistic change. The poetry of T. S. Eliot is not written in the same style as that of Samuel Taylor Coleridge, whose own poetic style differs from that of William Shakespeare. Although Martindale's research concentrates on stylistic change within artistic traditions, he has also scrutinized stylistic change within the careers of literary creators. In particular, he has content analyzed the poetry of John Dryden, William Wordsworth, and William Butler Yeats. What drives this stylistic change is the quest for originality. Rather than merely repeat what has already been done, creative writers seek out novel means of expression. The upshot is within-career stylistic change. But does this generalization apply to the specific case of Shakespeare's dramatic output?

The answer can be obtained by subjecting the 37 plays to various kinds of content analysis (see, e.g., Derks, 1994; Martindale, 1990; Simonton, 1986, 1997b). Table 8.1 lists the plays in approximate chronological order (Simonton, 1999). The composite dates assigned to the plays are averaged across 13 alternative date assignments. Despite some minor disagreements on some specific dates, the consensus is quite substantial (viz. coefficient alpha for the 13-item composite is .999; Simonton, 1986). In any case, when these dates are used as the basis for trend analyses, two major kinds of developmental changes can be distinguished.

On the one hand, some stylistic indicators exhibit positive monotonic trends (Elliott & Valenza, 2000; Simonton, 1986, 2004). As Shakespeare's career progressed, his plays display an increase in the incidence of colloquial words and expressions as well as in the occurrence of speech endings, double endings, and light or weak endings. Although the concept of colloquialism is self-explanatory, the other terms require definition. Speech endings occur when the playwright divides a line between two or more speakers. Double (or feminine) endings entail the addition of an extra unstressed syllable at the end of a line (i.e., 11 rather than the 10 syllables of iambic pentameter). Finally, light endings involve ending a line with either a pronoun or an auxiliary verb, whereas weak endings involve ending a line in a conjunction or preposition.

On the other hand, different stylistic indicators exhibit negative monotonic trends (Elliott & Valenza, 2000; Simonton, 1986, 2004). Specifically, as Shakespeare's creative career advanced, he was less inclined to use archaic words or expressions, and he became less likely to include 5-foot rhymes (especially rhymed couplets). The decline in archaisms closely parallels the ascent in colloquialisms, whereas the decline in rhymes corresponds closely to the increase in speech, double, and light or weak endings.

It should be evident that these trends illustrate an overall developmental tendency. As expressed by Shakespeare scholars, "Taken as a whole, they reveal a movement toward ever greater freedom in the use of both verse and prose.... By the end of his career, his style has virtually been transformed from one of formal and rhetorical regularity to one of vast flexibility and range" (Craig & Bevington, 1973, p. 39). I would also argue that this stylistic shift is a manifestation of the dramatist's drive toward increased originality, a drive that required that he leave behind the constraints in which he initially created his plays. It is important to observe that these trends are so consistent that it is

Table 8.1. *Date estimates and popularity measure for 37 Shakespeare plays*

Play	Date Composite	Stylistic	Popularity
1. Henry VI, Part 1	1591	1592	3
2. Henry VI, Part 2	1591	1592	6
3. Henry VI, Part 3	1591	1592	0
4. Comedy of Errors	1592	1592	33
5. Richard III	1593	1593	48
6. Titus Andronicus	1593	1592	13
9. Two Gentlemen of Verona	1593	1593	13
7. Love's Labour's Lost	1593	1595	21
8. Taming of the Shrew	1594	1593	58
10. Romeo and Juliet	1595	1596	78
11. Richard II	1595	1594	42
12. Midsummer Night's Dream	1595	1596	69
13. Merchant of Venice	1596	1598	68
14. King John	1596	1595	13
15. Henry IV, Part 1	1597	1596	50
16. Henry IV, Part 2	1598	1597	36
17. Much Ado about Nothing	1598	1599	50
18. Henry V	1599	1597	55
19. Julius Caesar	1599	1598	57
20. As You Like It	1599	1598	64
21. Merry Wives of Windsor	1600	1600	41
22. Twelfth Night	1601	1602	66
23. Hamlet	1601	1603	100
24. Troilus and Cressida	1602	1600	23
25. All's Well That Ends Well	1603	1604	25
26. Measure for Measure	1604	1603	51
27. Othello	1604	1602	74
28. Lear	1605	1604	78
29. Macbeth	1606	1606	83
30. Anthony and Cleopatra	1607	1609	50
31. Timon of Athens	1607	1605	3
32. Coriolanus	1608	1609	21
33. Pericles	1608	1608	8
34. Cymbaline	1610	1610	38
35. Winter's Tale	1610	1609	47
36. Tempest	1611	1609	69
37. Henry VIII	1613	1613	19

possible to predict a play's date using the stylistic indicators as predictors. Table 8.1 shows the outcome of one such prediction (Simonton, 1986). Except for some modest regression toward the mean at the upper and lower ends of the date distribution, the correspondence between observed and predicted dates is extremely high. If the predicted date is not in the exact same year, at least the prediction is within a year or two. This agreement underlines the inexorable nature of stylistic development within the Bard's career. He could not stay in one place, but rather had to move incessantly forward.

Content

Writers do not create in a bubble insulated from their personal lives or from the rest of the world. If anything, writers are actually more open than nonwriters to experiences and circumstances – events that often provide the content of their work (Simonton, 1983). This event–content relationship is amply demonstrated in the 37 plays attributed to William Shakespeare (Simonton, 1986, 2004). This demonstration begins by assessing the 37 plays on the prominence of nearly four dozen themes (Simonton, Taylor, & Cassandro, 1998) and then correlating the presence of those themes with two sets of factors: endogenous and exogenous.

Endogenous Factors

The first set of factors concerns Shakespeare's age at the time a given play was created. This set actually contains two variables: age linear and age quadratic (Simonton, 1999). The former gauges any general tendency for a theme's prominence to increase or decrease. The second determines whether the relationship is nonmonotonic, such as an inverted-U function. Analyses then revealed the following four thematic trends. First, Shakespeare's treatment of competition and rivalry in politics and commerce declined as a linear function of age. Second, his discussion of the conflicts in personal life first increased and then decreased, yielding an inverted-U curve with a peak in the period in which he produced his greatest tragedies. Third, his treatment of romantic, chivalric, and courtly love first increased and then dramatically decreased, producing an inverted-J age curve. Hence, love tended to be a more youthful preoccupation. Fourth and last, approximately the same age curve obtained for the theme of the individual as the object of ridicule or of laughter. So comedy and satire also appear to peak earlier in the career, with the latter part being relegated to more serious issues.

The main point of these four findings is that Shakespeare appeared to undergo some developmental changes in values and interests. These changes left an imprint on the plays that appeared over the course of his career.

Exogenous Factors

This set of variables concern major political events that might influence the thematic content of the plays. Data analyses indicated that the creativity of this literary genius was responsive to such external circumstances (Simonton, 1986). Three effects stand out. First, when his native country was under attack by a foreign power, he was more likely to discuss the topic of political expansion, conquest, and empire as military goals. Second, Irish rebellions against English rule were more likely to provoke interest in human conflicts caused by people with contrary modes of life. Third, and most interesting, was Shakespeare's reaction to conspiracies against the life and rule of the English monarch. Such dramatic events stimulated treatment of such themes as the burdens of the monarchy, the myth of the royal personage, natural and unnatural or monstrous acts, and patterns of love and friendship within the family. Given how hereditary monarchy is based on family relationships and the supposed natural order of the universe, this thematic concentration appears to be a reasonable response.

But the principal lesson of this analysis is that the Bard's creativity was responsive to political events that were likely to exert an impact on contemporary English society. He was not a disinterested bystander.

Impact

Although Shakespeare's dramatic genius cannot be denied, it remains true that he did not always create at the highest possible level. This conclusion is immediately apparent by scanning the plays listed in Table 8.1. At one extreme appears *Hamlet*, an unquestionable masterpiece, whereas at the other extreme is *Henry VI, Part 3*. To be sure, the Bard is not unusual in this respect. The output of most creators – even those acclaimed as geniuses – tends to be quite uneven (Simonton, 1997a). To appreciate better the magnitude of this feature, it is necessary to scrutinize quantitative measures of the relative impact of the 37 plays. Such popularity scores have been computed based on 19 distinct assessments, including performance frequencies in various venues, the number of complete recordings and single-play book editions, the number of film and opera adaptations, and so forth (Simonton, 1986). In addition to being highly reliable (coefficient alpha = .88), this 19-item composite correlates with alternative evaluations, such as how often the play is quoted and subjective ratings of the plays by Shakespeare scholars. The resulting popularity scores were then log-transformed and converted into a 0–100 rating scale. The scores are given in the last column of Table 8.1.

Not surprisingly, *Hamlet* comes out on top of the list and *Henry VI, Part 3* at the bottom. Moreover, it should be apparent that the popularity of the plays seems to be a curvilinear function of the author's age. The most popular plays were created around mid-career. Even so, it is also true that the post-peak plays, on the average, are slightly more popular than the pre-peak plays. In fact, when the popularity scores are regressed on linear and quadratic functions of age, we obtain an inverted-backward J curve with a peak at around age 38 (Simonton, 1999). This optimum is a bit ironic because at this age Shakespeare composed one of his less successful plays of this period, namely, *Troilus and Cressida*. This exception to the overall trend illustrates the important lesson that there are many positive and negative errors around any fitted curve. Indeed, *Hamlet* counts as a positive error, with its popularity actually exceeding what we would predict on the basis of the Bard's age at the time of its creation. Such prominent residuals emerge because the age function only explains 27% of the variation of popularity. That means that 73% of the variance is unaccounted for. So what else besides Shakespeare's age is involved?

This turns out to be a very difficult question to answer. Shakespeare wrote dramas in more than one genre – histories, comedies, tragedies, and romances, to be specific. It is likely that the predictors of impact are not identical across the genres. For instance, the introduction of intellectual puns has a positive consequence for tragedies but a negative consequence for comedies (Derks, 1989). In the first genre such puns may add comedy relief, whereas in the second such puns may detract from the somewhat coarser humor favored in his comic plays. Nevertheless, some thematic predictors appear to cut across these genre distinctions (Simonton, 1986). For example, his most popular plays are somewhat less likely to treat the history of the English monarchy, but are somewhat more likely to discuss parent–child relationships and to examine madness, frenzy, or emotional excess. *Hamlet* has all of these content attributes. It deals with a Danish monarchy, treats Hamlet's relationship with his mother and Polonius's relationship with his two children, and presents the feigned madness of Hamlet and the real madness of Ophelia. Finally, I should point out what perhaps should be obvious to any aficionado of Shakespeare's dramatic output: His tragedies are the most popular of his plays (Simonton, 1986). And *Hamlet* is the most popular of his tragedies.

It may seem disappointing to have unearthed so few correlates of dramatic impact. Yet this paucity of predictors also provides a valuable lesson. A literary masterwork, drama or otherwise, is an extremely complex creation that probably requires the confluence of a huge number of contributing factors. Even a mind as great as Shakespeare's could not discover a magic formula that would guarantee his success in the theater. As a consequence, his creative output could not help but be a little bit of a hit-or-miss affair.

THE 154 SONNETS

As just described, the 37 plays are too heterogeneous to expect a consistent set of impact predictors to transcend all of the variation. One solution to this problem of heterogeneity is to study the 154 sonnets attributed to the same writer. These poems are far more homogeneous. Nearly all consist of 14 lines of iambic pentameter grouped into three consecutive quatrains and a concluding couplet. Almost all use the exact same rhyme scheme as well (viz., abab cdcd efef gg). Furthermore, their subject matter is far more limited than Shakespeare's dramatic productions. Given these constraints, it may be easier to identify a specific set of variables that correlate with the differential success of the sonnets. For let there be no misconceptions: Although the sonnets as a collection are considered among the greatest achievements of English poetry, just like the plays these poems vary immensely in quality. As one scholar put it, although some sonnets "bear the unmistakable stamp of his genius," others "are no better than many a contemporary would have written" (Smith, 1974, p. 1747). Consequently, the relative impact of these sonnets also can be assessed in terms of a popularity index that records how often each sonnet is found in anthologies, how frequently it is quoted, and the extent to which it is discussed in literary digests. The outcome was a 27-item composite measure that spanned more than a century of critical judgment, from 1867 to 1974 (Simonton et al., 1998). This popularity indicator was then used as a dependent variable in two distinct investigations.

Study One

The first investigation was a preliminary inquiry into the content and style variables that predict sonnet popularity (Simonton, 1989). Potential predictors of popularity were identified from a variety of thematic and stylistic variables. After a series of data analyses, a sonnet's popularity was found to be a consistent function of four main variables.

First, the popularity rating is highest in those sonnets that treat a very distinctive theme: attitudes toward change, whether positive or negative. Connoisseurs of the sonnets will have some appreciation for this association. Many of the Bard's best poems deal with the effects of the passage of time, particularly the adverse effects of aging on one's love.

Second, the more popular sonnets are prone to score higher on a variety of indicators of linguistic complexity (cf. Kammann, 1966). For example, such sonnets are more likely to feature a large number of different words relative to the total number of words, and they are more likely to have a large number of adjectives relative to the number of verbs. In addition, they are more likely to contain words only used once in the entire collection of sonnets.

Third, sonnet popularity is positively related to the richness of issues that are touched on in the poem. That is, great sonnets grapple with a wide range of themes or questions rather than concentrating on a single topic.

Fourth and last, the popularity rating of a sonnet is positively associated with the amount of primary process imagery and negatively associated with the amount of secondary process imagery. These two measures come from Martindale's (1975) dictionary for computerized content analysis of literary text, albeit more recently he relabeled these measures primordial and conceptual to avoid the psychoanalytic associations (Martindale, 1990). Primary process or primordial imagery concerns concrete experiences, sensations, and desires, whereas secondary process or conceptual imagery concerns abstract ideas and concepts. Interestingly, primary process imagery in the speeches of

U.S. presidents also predicts their assessed charisma (Emrich, Brower, Feldman, & Garland, 2001). So, in a sense, sonnets high in primary process may be considered more charismatic.

It is noteworthy that these variables account for almost a quarter of the variation in the differential popularity of the 154 sonnets. We were justified in believing that it would be easier to identify predictors if the literary products belonged to a more homogeneous genre. Furthermore, many of the predictor variables seem to converge on a single suggestion: Great poems stimulate a wealth of semantic associations. Certainly this would be the case for those sonnets that (a) span a greater variety of themes, (b) use a diversity of words, and (c) favor a highly concrete lexicon over one much more abstract.

Study Two

One problem with the preceding investigation – and for that matter all of the studies of Shakespeare's plays – is that it treats each sonnet as a single static unit. Yet this treatment overlooks a very significant feature of poetry: It unfolds over time. A poem is comparable to a miniature musical composition. Read line by line, the words convey a series of images, metaphors, and meanings that change in a dynamic manner. This temporal structure is especially critical in the case of poetry written in the sonnet form. Usually each of the three quatrains evokes a distinctive idea, image, or mood, which then is somehow encapsulated by the concluding couplet. Therefore, rather than look at the whole sonnet, it may prove instructive to examine how these transformations take place within each sonnet. Such an investigation may divulge those within-poem transformations that are most likely to yield a highly effective composition.

The second inquiry into the 154 sonnets adopted this very strategy (Simonton, 1990). Using computerized content analysis, the study assessed the distribution of various kinds of words across the three quatrains and the one couplet, comparing the distributions between unpopular and popular sonnets, using the same 27-item composite measure devised in the first investigation. Two findings proved especially provocative.

The first finding concerned the introduction of unique words; that is, the use of words that appear only once in the entire set of sonnets. The more popular the sonnet, the less likely the Bard would insert a unique word in the third quatrain and couplet. In other words, in the more successful poems Shakespeare was more likely to use more commonplace words in the last two sonnet units. The contrast between the worst and best sonnets is equivalent to about two unique words for the third quatrain and almost four words for the couplet. Hence, these differences are not trivial. In addition, these differences must be contrasted against the earlier finding that the more popular sonnets tend to feature more unique words. Thus, the decline in such usage in the last two units of the sonnet becomes all the more striking.

SONNET POPULARITY

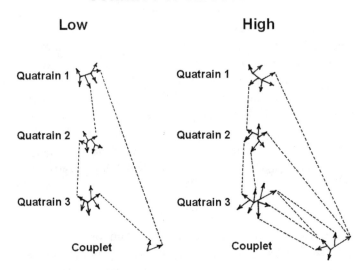

Figure 8.1. Graphic representation of the likely associative connections that distinguish unpopular from popular sonnets.

The second finding concerns the number of different words in each sonnet unit. As in the case of unique words, the more popular sonnets tend to contain a greater variety of words overall. Yet when we compare the more popular to the less popular sonnets, we learn that this variety is intensified. The association between total words and the number of distinct words is greater for the more renowned poems. Even more critically, this linguistic diversity is differentially distributed across the four units of the poem. In particular, whereas couplets in mediocre sonnets tend to show a decrease in the number of different words, the couplets in high-impact sonnets tend to display a conspicuous increase. It is as if the Bard is suddenly pulling out all the stops when he composes the last two lines of the sonnet.

I realize that these two sets of empirical results are less than easy to digest. To render the findings more intelligible, I would argue that Shakespeare is using the lexicon to enhance the semantic connections between the four units of the poem – and especially between the final quatrain and the concluding couplet. This associative contrast is illustrated in Figure 8.1. Here the arrows indicate associations elicited by various words in the unit, whereas the dotted lines represent associative connections established between words in different units. In unpopular sonnets the associations evoked are relatively small in number and the number of associative links between the units of the poem even smaller still. In popular sonnets, in contrast, the associations are noticeably greater in the final quatrain and concluding sonnet. These associations then enlarge the number of semantic connections between those two units and between both of those units and the previous two quatrains. The upshot is a more compact semantic vehicle for expressing an idea or mood.

We can never know whether the Bard knew what he was doing. Perhaps he was sometimes just lucky enough to chance on those words to produce an optimal aesthetic effect. In support of this conjecture is the fact that the truly popular sonnets represent only a small proportion of the total collection. It was not easy for even Shakespeare's genius to conceive of a reliable means to the creation of a literary masterpiece. Where expertise ends, inspiration or chance must begin.

CONCLUSION

In this chapter I have used the plays and sonnets of William Shakespeare to gather some insights into the psychology of literary creativity. Although I believe that these insights have intrinsic value, I am also aware that critics may raise objections to the approach adopted in this chapter. To be specific, critics might easily raise two somewhat paradoxical objections. On the one hand, the works that provide the basis for the conclusions might not be by William Shakespeare. On the other hand, these works are exclusively the creations of a single creator known as William Shakespeare. Let me look at each objection in turn.

Not Shakespeare!

A large number of knowledgeable and sober individuals have questioned whether the man who lived in Stratford-on-Avon was the bona fide author of the plays and poems attributed to William Shakespeare. The list of doubters includes creative writers like Charles Dickens, Ralph Waldo Emerson, Henry James, and Mark Twain; eminent actors like Charlie Chaplin, John Gielgud, Leslie Howard, Derek Jacobi, Orson Welles, and Walt Whitman; and even two notables in the history of psychology: Sigmund Freud and William James. Some anti-Stratfordians have even championed a specific rival claimant, such as Francis Bacon, Christopher Marlowe, or Edward De Vere, the 17th Earl of Oxford. Although the last claimant is perhaps the favored alternative author at present, other candidates surface from time to time, such as Sir Henry Neville. If the authorship of the plays and sonnets is in doubt, how can we put any faith in any of the reported empirical results?

The best place to begin my answer is to note that many of the studies reviewed in this chapter make no assumption whatsoever about who actually wrote the works. Certainly this innocence holds for all of the investigations conducted on the 154 sonnets. Absolutely none of the factors associated with a sonnet's popularity has anything to do with who actually wrote them. Further-more, many findings regarding the 37 plays are not contingent on resolving the authorship debate. For example, the correlation between thematic content and a play's popularity would remain the same no matter whether it was Oxford, Bacon, Marlowe, or Neville who created the works.

Other empirical results are only contingent on authorship if the author's identity has consequences for the variables investigated. For instance, we have discussed several longitudinal trends that seem to presume that we know the author's age at the time of composition. On closer examination, however, the assumption is usually much more limited; namely, that the composite dates shown in Table 8.1 have the plays placed approximately in the right temporal order. If so, then all of the conclusions regarding the stylistic trends are still valid no matter what the true dates may be. The same general argument also applies to the curvilinear relationship between age and popularity. The only qualification is that we cannot infer the age at which the peak takes place without knowing the actual age of the author at the time of composition. Yet even then we can draw the inference that the peak appears at some time in the middle of the career rather than near the beginning or toward the end.

When we come down to it, the only findings that require that we know the absolute rather than relative dates are those results concerning external political events and the thematic content of the plays. Yet this very contingency also suggests that these correlations might actually provide a means to determine the relative plausibility of the rival candidates. Indeed, one recent investigation adopted this strategy, testing alternative chronologies to determine whether some other dating of the plays might yield superior correspondences (Simonton, 2004). The results were telling. The chronology that produced the strongest agreement between political events and corresponding thematic content was identical with the composite dating shown in Table 8.1 except with the dates placed just 2 years earlier. In other words, there was about a 2-year lag between a given class of political event and its manifestation as a theme in a Shakespeare play. Such a short lag does not rule out the candidacy of the Stratford man nor that of any other near contemporary, such as Bacon and Neville. Yet it does raise some problems for those candidates who died much too early, such as Marlowe and Oxford.

To be sure, a Marlovian or Oxfordian might challenge the assumption that the composite dates given in Table 8.1 provide reasonable relative positions for the 37 plays. It is conceivable that the plays might be placed in a different order and shifted forward by a lot more than 2 years so that their thematic content would still conform to external events, but with a different match between an event and the play responding to that event. However, this solution introduces a problem even bigger than the one it was attempting to solve. If we tamper with the temporal order of the plays, then we will necessarily undermine the magnitude of the stylistic progression. Indeed, some alternative datings of the plays would imply, if true, that Shakespeare showed almost no stylistic change during the course of his career but rather jumped back and forth between "early" and "late" styles (Elliott & Valenza, 2000; Simonton, 2004). This lack of developmental growth would render the Bard more odd than typical as a literary creator.

At present I believe the best response is as follows: Whoever wrote the plays was very likely a contemporary of the man who was born and died in Stratford. It might actually be that man. If some scholar wishes to argue that it was someone who died much earlier, then it behooves that person to provide a play chronology that provides a comparable set of correspondences. Alternatively, the individual can simply argue that the playwright ignored what was transpiring all around him (or her).[1]

Just Shakespeare?

Apart from the authorship question is another issue. Can we really learn anything about the psychology of literary creativity from the life and work of a single creator, no matter how exemplary? Perhaps the author is too much of a genius to be comparable to any other literary creator. Or maybe his creativity is so unique, so absolutely sui generis, that it is impossible to generalize beyond these 37 plays and 154 sonnets. My answer to this challenge is more ambivalent.

On the one hand, I have no doubt that some of the reported findings may only apply to a subset of creative writers. For example, it could be that the factors responsible for the creation of a great sonnet are restricted to those creators who happen to have lived in England during the reigns of Queen Elizabeth I and King James I. It could even be the case that, say, the relationship between

---

[1] Keith Sawyer (see Chapter 10) suggests another way that the works *of* Shakespeare might not be *by* Shakespeare; namely, that these works or at least the plays actually constitute an instance of collaborative creativity. My response is threefold. First, the works of Shakespeare – the plays, sonnets, and narrative poems – exhibit a tremendous amount of stylistic homogeneity. For example, except for a few identifiable scenes and acts, the same person who wrote the highly personal and individualistic sonnets also wrote the plays (Elliott & Valenza, 2000). In fact, the style of early Shakespeare in any genre is closer to the style of late Shakespeare in any genre than are any of his styles to the styles of any of his collaborators (e.g., John Fletcher). Whatever suggestions might have been made by actors and others, the canon was written almost entirely by a single hand. Second, the greater the amount of collaboration seen in a given play, the more inferior is the product. *Two Noble Kinsmen* and *Pericles* were not even included in the First Folio, and those plays that were, such as *Timon of Athens*, *Henry VI, Part I*, and perhaps *Titus Andronicus,* are counted among his worst plays. In contrast, masterpieces like *Hamlet*, *King Lear*, and *Othello* show no stylistic heterogeneity, and *Macbeth* merely shows some minor postcompositional tampering (e.g., the inclusion of some songs by Thomas Middleton). Third, Sawyer's speculations regarding Shakespeare's creativity are predicated on the assumption that the Stratford man wrote the plays – the man who was also a minor actor and partner in the company. If the plays were actually written by someone more peripheral to those directly involved in the performances, then collaborative opportunities disappear. To be sure, once the author delivers a script to the players the latter are free to make all kinds of deletions, insertions, and modifications – changes that account for the discrepancies among various versions of the plays. Yet those unauthorized changes cannot count as collaborations.

a particular theme and the popularity of a sonnet or play is confined to just Shakespeare. Perhaps only the Bard was inspired to write exceptional dramas when dealing with madness and emotional excess. Yet even here there might be a lesson; namely, that creators do best when they write about favorite themes. So a general principle might still apply simply by raising the level of abstraction in which we discuss the results.

On the other hand, I also cannot question the conclusion that many of the findings derived from the analysis of Shakespeare's life and work have to apply to a larger group of literary creators. For instance, a large body of research has accumulated on the relation between age and creative achievement, including the production of literary products in various genres (e.g., Dennis, 1966; Lehman, 1953; Simonton, 1975, 2007). Indeed, the first such empirical study was conducted in 1835, making it the oldest scientific analysis of creativity, literary or otherwise (Quételet, 1835/1968). Better yet, this research has arrived at an inverted-backward J age curve just like that found for the popularity of the 37 plays, with a peak in the late 30s. As a result, it can be affirmed with minimal qualification that the career trajectory identified for Shakespeare's dramatic output is prototypical of what is generally found for other literary creators. He exemplifies the rule. The same conclusion probably applies to some other findings as well.

Ultimately, it is up to future research to decide the extent to which Shakespeare – or whoever it was who wrote the plays and sonnets – can provide insights into the psychology of literary creativity. But the more we know about the general phenomenon, the more that we may eventually learn about this very special phenomenon. It may even come to pass that continued research on his dramatic and poetic creativity will someday help solve the authorship problem. If so, then studying the creative products of the Bard may help us understand him as much as it helps us understand literary creativity.

REFERENCES

Cattell, J. M. (1903). A statistical study of eminent men. *Popular Science Monthly, 62,* 359–377.
Craig, H., & Bevington, D. (Eds.). (1973). *The complete works of Shakespeare* (rev. ed.). Glenview, IL: Scott, Foresman.
Dennis, W. (1966). Creative productivity between the ages of 20 and 80 years. *Journal of Gerontology, 21,* 1–8.
Derks, P. L. (1989). Pun frequency and popularity of Shakespeare's plays. *Empirical Studies of the Arts, 7,* 23–31.
Derks, P. L. (1994). Clockwork Shakespeare: The Bard meets the Regressive Imagery Dictionary. *Empirical Studies of the Arts, 12,* 131–139.
Elliott, W. E. Y., & Valenza, R. J. (2000). Can the Oxford candidacy be saved? A response to W. Ron Hess: "Shakespeare's dates: The effect on stylistic analysis." *The Oxfordian, 3,* 71–97.

Emrich, C. G., Brower, H. H., Feldman, J. M., & Garland, H. (2001). Images in words: Presidential rhetoric, charisma, and greatness. *Administrative Science Quarterly, 46,* 527–557.

Giles, H. A. (Ed.). (1965). *Gems of Chinese literature.* New York: Dover. (Original work published 1923)

Hart, M. H. (1987). *The 100: A ranking of the most influential persons in history.* Secaucus, NJ: Citadel Press.

Kammann, R. (1966). Verbal complexity and preferences in poetry. *Journal of Verbal Learning and Verbal Behavior, 5,* 536–540.

Lehman, H. C. (1953). *Age and achievement.* Princeton, NJ: Princeton University Press.

Macrone, M. (1990). *Brush up your Shakespeare!* New York: Harper & Row.

Martindale, C. (1975). *Romantic progression: The psychology of literary history.* Washington, DC: Hemisphere.

Martindale, C. (1990). *The clockwork muse: The predictability of artistic styles.* New York: Basic Books.

Murray, C. (2003). *Human accomplishment: The pursuit of excellence in the arts and sciences, 800 B.C. to 1950.* New York: HarperCollins.

Quételet, A. (1968). *A treatise on man and the development of his faculties.* New York: Franklin. (Reprint of 1842 Edinburgh translation of 1835 French original)

Simonton, D. K. (1975). Age and literary creativity: A cross-cultural and transhistorical survey. *Journal of Cross-Cultural Psychology, 6,* 259–277.

Simonton, D. K. (1983). Dramatic greatness and content: A quantitative study of eighty-one Athenian and Shakespearean plays. *Empirical Studies of the Arts, 1,* 109–123.

Simonton, D. K. (1986). Popularity, content, and context in 37 Shakespeare plays. *Poetics, 15,* 493–510.

Simonton, D. K. (1989). Shakespeare's sonnets: A case of and for single-case historiometry. *Journal of Personality, 57,* 695–721.

Simonton, D. K. (1990). Lexical choices and aesthetic success: A computer content analysis of 154 Shakespeare sonnets. *Computers and the Humanities, 24,* 251–264.

Simonton, D. K. (1997a). Creative productivity: A predictive and explanatory model of career trajectories and landmarks. *Psychological Review, 104,* 66–89.

Simonton, D. K. (1997b). Imagery, style, and content in 37 Shakespeare plays. *Empirical Studies of the Arts, 15,* 15–20.

Simonton, D. K. (1999). *William Shakespeare.* In M. A. Runco & S. Pritzker (Eds.), *Encyclopedia of creativity* (Vol. 2, pp. 559–563). San Diego: Academic Press.

Simonton, D. K. (2004). Thematic content and political context in Shakespeare's dramatic output, with implications for authorship and chronology controversies. *Empirical Studies of the Arts, 22,* 201–213.

Simonton, D. K. (2007). Creative life cycles in literature: Poets versus novelists or conceptualists versus experimentalists? *Psychology of Aesthetics, Creativity, and the Arts, 1*(3), 133–139.

Simonton, D. K., Taylor, K., & Cassandro, V. (1998). The creative genius of William Shakespeare: Historiometric analyses of his plays and sonnets. In A. Steptoe (Ed.), *Genius and the mind: Studies of creativity and temperament in the historical record* (pp. 167–192). New York: Oxford University Press.

Smith, H. (1974). *Sonnets.* In G. B. Evans (Ed.), *The Riverside Shakespeare* (pp. 1745–1748). Boston: Houghton Mifflin.

PART III

THE PROCESS

9

In Search of the Writer's Creative Process

TODD LUBART

Once upon a time there was a young child named Alice[1] who wanted to become a writer. Inspired by numerous children's books and the imaginative tales that these books told, Alice dreamed of a literary career. One day at school, Alice's teacher proposed an exciting task for a young author: Each student had to invent a short story, write the text, and then read it aloud to the class. Alice was delighted, but when she got home and started to work on the assignment she realized that the teacher had never indicated how to proceed. There were no clear instructions on how to write a story, how to generate ideas, or how to put them together. This assignment was quite different from most schoolwork, such as solving math problems, because normally the teacher showed students how to proceed by giving examples and working through a sample problem while specifying the method to use at each step. Schoolwork, in general, was similar to making a cake: The teacher provided the ingredients, there were instructions about how to put them together, and everyone was supposed to end up, more or less, with the same cake. Apparently writing a story was quite different. Students were supposed to find their own ingredients, decide how to put them together in their own way, and end up with something different from each other.

Alice decided to get started right away with her literary composition. She was very excited, but as she searched in her mind for an idea for her story she kept coming back to stories that she had read. It was not easy to find a new idea. After an hour she did not have anything written. "Was this normal?" she asked herself. Do all writers experience a phase of groping for an idea? Did she have "writer's block," which she had heard adults discuss in a hushed voice on a few occasions? Obviously she needed some help to get started on her writing assignment. However, it was getting late and dinner was going to be served. She left her desk and came to the table to eat dinner with her parents. That

---

[1] This name was chosen at random soon after reading the complete literary works of Lewis Carroll. The "Alice" mentioned in this chapter is not meant to refer to any living, dead, or to-be-born person. Alice does not even have an e-mail address.

149

night there was spaghetti with mushrooms. The mushrooms were particularly good, and after the meal she went promptly to bed. Then her mother came to read her a few pages of *The Time Machine* for her bedside story.

Alice fell asleep. As she slept it seemed that her mind did not want to stop thinking about her school assignment. She decided to borrow Mr. Wells' time machine and to visit a few authors that she had heard about to find out more about how to write a short story. She was familiar with Rudyard Kipling's *Jungle Books*, so she decided to start with him. When she arrived, he was having a cup of tea in his English cottage. He was happy to share his own experience as an author, which seemed to suggest that during his literary work he was temporarily possessed by a muse:

> My daemon was with me in the *Jungle Books, Kim* and both Puck books, and good care I took to walk delicately, lest he should withdraw. I know that he did not, because when those books were finished they said so themselves with, almost, the water-hammer click of a tap turned off.... When your Daemon is in charge, do not think consciously. Drift, wait, and obey. (Kipling, 1937/1985, p. 162)

This was a somewhat mysterious description suggesting an out-of-body experience. Alice wanted to know more, and Rudyard suggested that she contact Samuel Taylor Coleridge, who was living in a faraway place called Xanadu. On her arrival in Xanadu, she met a multicolored cat that claimed to be Samuel Taylor Coleridge. The cat was smoking a strange sort of pipe and talked in riddles. Apparently, the literary creative process, be it story writing or poetry, involved taking certain substances that were not available in one's local grocery store. Indeed Coleridge mentioned how opium was particularly stimulating in his own writing process, putting him in an altered state of mind that allowed his creative juices to flow. Unfortunately, opium was potentially harmful to one's health and was certainly not good for children. In any case, Coleridge's account seemed a bit dubious, and Alice asked for another contact with whom to explore further the writing process. Coleridge suggested seeing a poet and playwright named Shakespeare.

Shakespeare met Alice at the Globe theatre. When she asked how he got his ideas and developed them into literary works, he declared, "To be, or not to be, that is the question." Indeed, is one born an author with an innate knowledge of the creative process, or can one learn to be creative and become an author through practice? Is one creative in all kinds of literary activities such as poetry, playwriting, and inventing tales and novels? Was there some secret part of creative writing that was revealed to only a few, or was all this attention to creative writing, in fact, much to do about nothing because creative writing was like all kinds of problem solving?

Meeting creative writers was interesting, but Alice started to think that a scientific approach might be worth investigating to help her discover the keys to the writing process. Thus, she set her time machine for a modern library in the early 21st century and connected to the psychology database. As she went online, three little doors popped up. One was marked "writing process – keep out," a second was labeled "creative process – not for you," and finally there was a tiny door labeled "creative writing process – a mystery must remain mysterious." Being somewhat curious by nature, Alice could not resist the temptation to open each door.

THE WRITING PROCESS

Behind the "writing process" door, Alice discovered a number of people busy writing scientific articles about how people write. According to some early models of the writing process, such as proposed by Hayes and Flower (1980), there are three main cognitive activities: (1) planning what to write, (2) generating or drafting text, and (3) editing or revision.

During the planning process the writer sets goals for the content of the written text that will be generated and specifies how to reach those goals (Hayes & Nash, 1996). Planning may involve several procedures, such as defining the essential skeleton of a text, using analogies with existing works and then deviating from these works, or creating a brief thumbnail sketch of the future work. Planning draws on the writer's knowledge of the subject of the future text, as well as his or her strategic knowledge of how to translate a goal into an action plan. During planning, the author must decide which topics will receive more emphasis than others and make decisions about the content and format of the text.

The generation process is hypothesized to rely partially on associative processes that enable a text to develop as a conceptual chain, within the boundaries of the literary genre or the constraints of the specific task. There may be conscious, focused, purposeful idea generation or unconscious, loose thought that yields ideas for a literary production without any real intention. Emotional associations as well as cognitive-logical ones may be involved. These associations bring information into working memory. This information may be stored in long-term memory or accessed from outside sources such as books, magazines, images, or the Internet. A particularly important aspect of text generation, according to Sharples (1996), is the primary generator, or guiding idea from which the rest of the text will be developed. As William Faulkner put it, "With me a story usually begins with a single idea or memory or mental picture. The writing of the story is simply a matter of working up to that moment, to explain why it happened or what caused it to follow" (Plimpton, 1958, p. 121). The primary generator, the concept that serves as the starting point for idea generation and elaboration, is potentially idiosyncratic for each writer and can be more or less elaborate, which will influence the richness of associations resulting from a memory search. Torrance, Thomas, and Robinson

(1996) conducted an empirical analysis of idea generation during a prewriting phase and a compositional phase in an essay task with undergraduate students. They found that idea generation activities occurred both in prewriting and compositional phases, as expected, and that the ideas generated during composition, but not in prewriting planning, were somewhat more original (statistically rare) than those generated during the prewriting phase.

The revision process involves comparing an existing text to a writer's goals or ideal text, diagnosing the differences, and deciding how to reduce or remove these differences to bring to the text as close as possible to the desired status. Revision involves reading one's text to identify weaknesses and putting in place strategies to handle these weaknesses. It can concern the content of the ideas to be expressed as well as the nature of their linguistic expression. Revision can occur at the level of the whole text based on global goals, such as to render a story more interesting or more suspenseful. Alternatively, revision can occur at the sentence level in which individual words or phrases are modified. Revision can occur together with idea generation or in a postdraft phase. Thus, revision contributes to adjust and reshape a text.

These three main processes evolve as the writer gains expertise, such that experienced authors will accomplish planning, generation, and revision differently from novices, because they have a more developed goal structure in mind during their compositional activities. For example, experts revise more at the whole text level, and novice writers tend to focus locally on the sentence level. Furthermore, these writing processes occur, according to Bereiter and Scaramalia (1987) in two problem spaces: content and rhetorical ones. Knowledge and beliefs are treated in the content space, and intended or actual verbal representations are found in the rhetorical space. The writing process involves a constant movement between the two spaces.

It is also important to note that planning and evaluation occur naturally in tandem with text generation. Hayes and Flower (1986) give a clear example of this tendency to mix planning, production, and revision for a writer who is trying to describe the job of being a writer: "The best thing about it is – what ? Something about using my mind – it allow me the opportunity to – uh I want to write something about my ideas – to put ideas into action – or to develop my ideas into – what ? into a meaningful form ? Oh, bleh! – say it allows me – to use – Na – allows me – scratch that." Finally, the following sentence resulted: "The best thing about it is that it allows me to use my mind and ideas in a productive way."

Hayes (1996) proposed an updated model of the writing process in which the three main processes described previously (planning, generation, and revision) are placed in a more integrated perspective involving the cognitive functions of reflection, text production, and text interpretation. Reflection includes planning, problem solving, and decision making. Production involves the cognitive operations of turning mental representations of ideas into spoken or written text. For example, information is retrieved from long-term memory, placed in working memory, and elaborated into parts of a sentence, which are then placed into text. Text interpretation involves reading, listening, and creating internal representations from linguistic and graphic sources and revision-related actions. These cognitive processes interact with a person's motivation, affect, and memory and the task environment, which includes text under construction, the compositional situation (computer or paper, physical composing environment), and the social environment (audience, network of collaborators).

THE CREATIVE PROCESS

When Alice opened the "creative process" door, she entered into a multicolored room full of people. There were artists, writers, scientists, and mathematicians, and several psychologists in white coats were furiously taking notes about what all these creative people were saying. For example, Henri Poincaré (1908/1985), a French mathematician, described his discovery of Fuchsian mathematical functions. He began with days of conscious work, trying to prove that Fuchsian functions could not exist. He "tried a great number of combinations and reached no results" (p. 26). After drinking coffee one evening, he could not sleep. As he described, "Ideas rose in crowds; I felt them collide until pairs interlocked, so to speak, making a stable combination.... I had established the existence of a class of Fuchsian functions" (p. 26). Poincaré formalized his results in writing, elaborated on his initial idea, and, guided by an "analogy with elliptic functions," explored the mathematical properties of Fuchsian functions. Then he had to travel and "forgot" about his work. At one moment during his trip, he stepped on a bus and an idea came to him "without anything... seeming to have paved the way for it": The transformations involved in Fuchsian functions were the same as those in non-Euclidean geometry (p. 26). After returning from his trip, Poincaré verified his idea. Then he began work on some seemingly unrelated mathematical issues without much success. He decided to take a break for a few days near the sea. There during a walk, another idea concerning non-Euclidean geometry came with "brevity, suddenness and immediate certainty" (p. 26). On his return, he thought about this idea, exploring systematically its implications for Fuchsian functions. His work, however, led him to realize that there was one difficulty that remained. At this point he went away for his military service. Although his mind was "very occupied" by his duties, one day an idea of how to solve his mathematical problem "suddenly appeared." After returning from his military service he had "all the elements and had only to arrange them and put them together" (p. 26). He wrote his finalized ideas "in a single stroke." Poincaré went on in his essay to note that the creative process seems to start with conscious work on a problem. This is followed by unconscious work, which, if successful, results in a "sudden illumination." Then another phase of conscious work follows "to put in shape the results of this inspiration," to explore the consequences, to formalize and to verify the idea (p. 27).

Based on this kind of introspective evidence, Wallas (1926) formalized the four-stage model of the creative process. Preparation involves a preliminary analysis, definition, and setting up of a problem. It requires conscious work and draws on one's education, analytical skills, and problem-relevant knowledge. The incubation phase follows. During incubation, there is no conscious mental work on the problem. Unconsciously, however, the mind may continue to work on the problem, forming "trains of associations." Many associations or idea combinations are believed to occur during incubation. The unconscious mind rejects most of these combinations as useless, but finds occasionally a promising idea. Poincaré referred to aesthetic criteria that unconsciously allowed promising ideas to be selected and the vast majority of useless ideas to be rejected. A third phase, called illumination, occurs when the promising idea breaks through to conscious awareness. Illumination can be characterized by a "flash," a sudden enlightenment. Wallas suggested that illumination is often preceded by an intuitive feeling that an idea is coming. He called this "intimation" that occurs at the "fringe" of consciousness. The illumination phase is hypothesized to be somewhat delicate and easily disturbed by outside interruptions or by trying to rush the emerging idea. After the illumination phase, there is a phase of conscious work called verification, which involves evaluating, refining, and developing one's idea. Wallas (1926) noted that during creative problem solving a person could return to earlier phases in the process. For example, if an idea proves to be flawed during verification, one may incubate on how to resolve this difficulty. In addition, the phases could co-occur if a person was, for example, engaged in preparation for one aspect of a problem and incubation for another aspect of the problem.

For a number of researchers, the four-stage model or a variant of it has served and continues to serve as the basis for understanding the creative "problem-solving" process (Amabile, 1996; Busse & Mansfield, 1980; Ochse, 1990). The term "problem" is conceived broadly as any task that an individual seeks to accomplish. Thus, writers and artists who seek to express their feelings, scientists who seek to understand a complex phenomenon, and people who seek to solve conflicts in their everyday lives are all considered to be engaged in problem solving (see Runco & Dow, 1999). In terms of extending or enhancing the basic four-stage model, several authors have suggested that it is important to distinguish a problem-finding or problem-formulation phase from the preparatory phase during which relevant information is gathered and preliminary ideas are advanced (Amabile, 1996; Getzels & Csikszentmihalyi, 1976). Problem finding involves recognizing that a problem exists and finding gaps, inconsistencies, or flaws with the current state of the art. Einstein and

Infeld (1938) noted the importance of raising new questions, formulating a problem, and seeing old problems from new angles. In a related vein, Isaksen and Treffinger (1985) proposed that creative problem solving begins with a "mess-finding" stage from which problems are defined.

Some authors distinguish problem finding (noticing that something is not right, not good, or lacking) from problem posing (expressing the problem) and problem construction (developing a detailed representation of the problem; Mumford, Reiter-Palmon, & Redmond, 1994). Empirical studies of problem finding have operationalized this activity either in terms of the time spent manipulating or exploring problem elements before proposing an initial idea or in terms of question-asking behaviors (Getzels & Csikszentmihalyi, 1976; Glover, 1979; Jay & Perkins, 1997; Kay, 1991; Moore, 1985; Rostan, 1994).

With regard to other phases of the creative process, some authors have suggested that a phase of frustration occurs after the preparatory phase when the analytic mind reaches its limit on dealing with the problem; the subsequent frustration may provoke incubation (Goleman, Kaufman, & Ray, 1992; Hutchinson, 1949). Sapp (1992) proposed that between incubation and the moment of illumination there may often be a "point of creative frustration" (p. 24). A person may become blocked or fail to find creative ideas during incubation. At this point of frustration one can either start over and fall into the same traps, accept a less-than-optimal solution (perhaps rationalizing that it is creative), or push ahead, exploring further alternatives or moving in a new direction, perhaps reconceptualizing the problem. Thus, creative frustration involves making a decision on how to deal with difficulties encountered during problem solving.

The nature of incubation – a period during which a problem is "put aside" often because of an impasse in problem solving – has also been explored (Guilford, 1979; Smith & Dodds, 1999). Incubation may involve the automatic spreading of activation in memory, passive forgetting of problem details or entrenched ideas that do not work, broad attention and use of serendipitous cues from the environment, or associative thinking through a random or directed combination process (Ochse, 1990; Olton, 1979; Smith & Dodds, 1999). Concerning the final part of the creative process, some authors have proposed an implementation phase or communication phase in which the creative production is presented in a social environment (Amabile, 1996; Stein, 1974).

After analyzing descriptions of the creative process by contemporary novelists, Ghiselin (1952/1985, 1956, 1963) rejected "superficial" stage-based descriptions of the creative process, favoring an integrated approach instead. This more complex view of the creative process has been evoked by a number of other studies. Studies of the creative process in art though introspection, interviews, observations, and examinations of sketchbooks and finished works show that the creative process involves a series of brief interactions between productive and critical modes of thinking, as well as planning and compensatory actions (Eindhoven & Vinacke, 1952; Israeli, 1962, 1981). Based on interviews with artists, Calwelti, Rappaport, and Wood (1992) found evidence for the simultaneity of processes such as centering on a topic, working on new ideas, expanding ideas, evaluating, and taking distance from one's work. In Getzels and Csikszentmihalyi's (1976) study of art students making a still-life drawing, activities involved in formulating or defining the artistic problem were observed both in the predrawing phase and the drawing production phase. Getzels and Csikszentmihalyi (1976) noted, "In a creative process, stages of problem definition and problem solution need not be compartmentalized" (p. 90). Finally, through protocol analysis of the sketching process in architectural designers, an overall conception of an architectural design emerged in which new designs were formed in parts, with deletions, transformations, a "dialectic" movement between general design qualities and issues in the specific task, and moments of active sketching mixed with moments of contemplation (Goldschmidt, 1991).

Based on these kinds of observations, many current views of the creative process focus on the subprocesses that are involved in creative work, rather than describing the overall creative process. These processes may include problem finding, definition and redefinition, divergent thinking, synthesis (bisociation, Janusian thinking, homospatial thinking), analogy and metaphor, analysis and evaluation (Getzels & Csikszentmuhalyi, 1976; Guilford, 1950, 1967; Koestler, 1964; Lubart, 1994; Mumford, Supinski, Threlfall, & Baughman, 1996; Osborn, 1953; Perkins, 1981; Reiter-Palmon, Mumford, O'Connor Boes, & Runco, 1997; Rothenberg, 1979, 1996; Runco, 1991; Smilansky, 1984; Ward, Smith, & Vaid, 1997; Weisberg, 1993).

Some authors have proposed creative process models that organize the subprocesses. For example, Mumford, Mobley, Uhlman, Reiter-Palmon, and Doares (1991) specified a set of core processes for creativity that operate on information organized in categorical structures. These processes, which occur in the following loosely structured sequence, are problem construction, information encoding (and retrieval), category search (specifying relevant information schemas), specification of best fitting categories, combination and reorganization of category information to find new solutions, idea evaluation, implementation of ideas, and monitoring. The model allows for dynamic cycling between different processes as deemed necessary during problem solving. The core processes for creativity are themselves complex and involve more specific processes. For example, combination and reorganization involve reasoning, analogy use, and divergent thinking processes.

Focusing on two sets of creative processes, Finke, Ward, and Smith (1992) advanced the Geneplore model in which creativity involves generative processes and exploratory processes. The generative processes concern the construction of loosely formulated ideas called preinventive structures. Generative processes include knowledge retrieval, idea association, synthesis, transformation, and analogical transfer. The exploratory processes concern the examination, elaboration, and testing of the preinventive structures. Exploratory processes include interpretation of preinventive structures, hypothesis testing, and searching for limitations. These two sets of processes are combined together in cyclical sequences that lead to creative products, as can be illustrated in literary works. For example, Stephen Donaldson in his work on *The Chronicles of Thomas Covenant the Unbeliever* describes how he used the generative process of selectively combining the concepts of being an "unbeliever" and having leprosy, which Donaldson knew about from his experiences in India (Ward, 2001; see also Chapter 12 in this volume). It is proposed that the most creative people devote relatively more time and energy to exploratory processes, have a rich conceptual knowledge base, and have a heightened sensitivity to the features of ideas that make them more or less promising to pursue and develop.

Other, diverse proposals about the creative process have focused on the processes of idea generation and idea evaluation. Basadur (1995) characterized creative problem solving in terms of ideation–evaluation cycles that vary in their frequency according to the nature of the problem to be solved and the point in problem solving (e.g., at the beginning vs. in a final implementation phase). Runco and Chand (1995) proposed that ideation and evaluation together with problem finding are the "primary components" of the creative process; knowledge and motivation influence these processes. In the psychodynamic approach to the creative process, primary and secondary processes and their interaction are discussed (Kris, 1952; Kubie, 1958; Suler, 1980). The primary process operates on unstructured, illogical, subjective thoughts and yields ideational material that is then shaped by the reality-based, controlled, evaluative secondary process. The chance-based theories of the creative process involve a process of idea formation through "random" variations and combinations and a process of evaluation that leads to selective retention of the best ideas (Campbell, 1960; Simonton, 1988).

CREATIVE PROCESS IN WRITING

Finally, Alice opened the third door, wondering if there is a specific form of the creative process that can be identified in the domain of writing. Csikszentmihalyi (1996) replied that he had examined creative writers' processes through in-depth interviews with nine writers. Their mode of literary creation could be described in terms of a problem-solving process. In general, he proposed that the same basic phases – preparation, incubation, illumination, evaluation, and elaboration – characterize creative writing as they characterize creative work in other fields. Creative writers started often with a phrase or a small string of words or images and worked through elaboration and revision to achieve a larger idea. In fact there were many small creative moments rather than one big bang in which the plot or the main idea was revealed. Thus, there was an important place for generating small bits of ideas and then connecting or revising them. Creative writing, in this perspective, involves collecting fragments of dialogue, descriptions, scenes, or images (which are often stored in a writer's notebooks or diaries for future use), seeing the relevance of some stored information or personal experiences for a work in progress, combining fragments, elaborating on sequences of text, and revising the text. It is essentially an incremental process. Of course, these different subprocesses can occur in recursive, nonlinear sequences, at a conscious or unconscious level. In terms of subprocesses, it is interesting to note that Moore (1985) examined the problem-finding process in a writing task with middle school students, using a procedure inspired by Getzels and Csiksentmihalyi's (1976) previously mentioned research with artists. Students were given a set of objects and asked to create a literary composition based on the objects; similar to results in the artistic domain, creative writing was associated with the number of objects explored, the rarity of these objects, and the time spent in the prewriting phase.

Another key feature of creative work is the implication of a state of unusually productive mental flow. Several literary creators, as well as creative people in other fields, have described being in a temporary state of heightened awareness, complete engagement, and concentration. For example, the novelist Richard Stern described being at times in a pure state of engagement with respect to the act of writing, the characters, the situation, the words. The poet Mark Strand described in a similar way the moments when he would lose the notion of time, becoming completely involved in his work and being pushed beyond himself through the process of writing, in a state of total communication.

Once Csikszntmihalyi had finished, Doyle (1998) stepped forward and reported on her extensive interviews with five contemporary fiction writers concerning the steps involved in writing their literary pieces. In general, their descriptions indicated that the creative writing process started with a "seed incident," an event that was "touching, intriguing, puzzling, mysterious, haunting or overwhelming" (p. 30). These events did not fit in the regular narrative scripts that guide daily life and thus could be viewed as the start of a literary problem that deserved exploration. The next step was to capture the seed incident in a verbal or visual-verbal format, such as a sentence, a paragraph, or a picture with a caption. For example, based on an incident involving her landlady, the fiction writer Mary LaChapelle wrote the line, "I am a poodle." With this line she entered what Doyle calls the "fiction world" in which the author imaginatively explores the poodle's world and elaborates a story. Of course, the writer does not stay in the fiction world indefinitely. According to

LaChapelle's description, she quickly returned to reality with questions such as how she could develop the dog's point of view and make her story work. Doyle calls this the "writing realm," in which literary concerns are raised and decisions are made.

The writing process can thus be described as a constant movement between the fiction world and the writing world. The fiction world is characterized, according to the authors examined, by a passive attitude in which the story unfolds in front of their eyes; Kathleen Hill described the phase in terms of a voice that "took over," which echoes Rudyard Kipling's account. The fiction world seems to involve productive thinking, improvisation, and a lack of reflective, evaluative thought. This description echoes Piirto's (2004) description of the use by certain writers, such as William Butler Yeats, Octavio Paz, and James Merrill, of automatic writing to foster improvisation. In fact Merrill claimed that he would write down everything that came to his mind to allow himself to express his innermost ideas, his unconscious ones that existed on the "edge" of language. In contrast, the writer's world is active, critical, and directive. For example in the writer's world, the extent to which the story is on course or that characters are well developed may be examined; the writer is an artisan attempting to hone his or her composition. Doyle notes that the creative process in writing shares many features with a general problem-solving process. However, she suggests that narrative improvisation in the fiction world, often involving taking a character's viewpoint, is a feature specific to the creative writing process. Finally, Doyle highlights the cyclical nature of the creative process, which involves "navigating" between the fiction world and the writer's world.

Alice turned her head as she heard someone tapping away on a computer keyboard; Turner (1994) had written an artificial intelligence program called MINSTREL, which creates short stories about knights and ladies in King Arthur's court. The creativity is based on a set of procedures that transform an existing basic story into a new one by adapting its features based on examples of stories (case-based reasoning) within the same genre. The story-writing task is treated as a problem-solving process with a set of constraints to be satisfied. The computer program has encoded knowledge of literary goals to be reached, such as suspense or tragedy, and stylistic goals concerning how story elements should be presented and in what order. Thus, search and transformation are the basic keys for creativity within a well-defined kind of story realm. MINSTREL is able to generate reasonable, well-structured stories that have some intrigue and differ from previously existing stories that are part of the program's database. The same kind of programming procedures can also be used to create other products, such as mechanical inventions that are transformations of existing objects.

Finally, Alice noticed someone in the distance with a beret and a French bread under his arm, who was tallying up some columns of data and making graphs. Lubart was working on an empirical study in which he examined how different moments of evaluation in the process of writing a story affected the creativity of the production. Based on writers' accounts, he was testing several theories about the role of evaluative thinking in the creative process. For example, during an author's work, was there some ideal sequence of mental events in which evaluation was particularly useful for creative writing?

In fact there were three competing visions of the role of evaluation in the creative writing process. First, some arguments favored the use of evaluation very early in the creative writing process. This evaluation could prevent a writer from choosing and developing an idea that was not very original. Fledging ideas are easy to reorient, modify, or eventually drop. Thus, early evaluation would contribute to possible major changes in a literary work before the author got too attached to it. A second hypothesis postulated the contrary approach: Evaluation should be postponed during the early phases of the creative literary process in order to let ideas develop. Criticism too early would kill off original thinking, according to some writing guidebooks. Third, some accounts reported that a cyclic use of evaluation, in conjunction with idea generation, would be optimal because it would allow creative thinking to stay on track at each step in the literary composition process.

To test these competing views, Lubart (1994) asked undergraduate university students to write original short stories based on a given title or a set of character descriptions. The creativity of these stories was assessed by a set of graduate-school level teaching assistants who specialized in the field of literary composition. In a first study, undergraduate students were asked to generate stories, and as they worked they were interrupted at certain points and asked specifically to evaluate their story in progress. In one condition, students were interrupted very early in their work, after a few minutes into their 30-minute story composition task. Each student in this group evaluated his or her progress and then continued. In a second experimental condition, students were allowed to work uninterrupted and then were asked to evaluate their progress after completing more than half of their work. In a third experimental condition, students were interrupted once in the first part of their work and then later in the second half of their compositional exercise. This third group was modeled after the idea that some evaluation at each step of the writing process would be best. Finally, there was a control group in which participants did not evaluate their compositions according to any particular schedule. The results showed that the group that evaluated quite early in their work, after only a few minutes of writing activity, produced, on average, more creative stories than the other groups (later evaluation, evenly spaced evaluation, and control groups). This result was replicated in a second, more naturalistic study in which students were asked to note their evaluative thoughts as they worked and to concentrate on evaluation at certain moments in their writing. The extent to which participants followed the instructions was verified using their evaluation log, collected with the short story written composition. Interestingly, in a parallel study, in which evaluation was examined during an artistic task of making a still-life drawing, no particular moment of evaluation was associated with enhanced creativity scores. This result, which needs of course to be examined further in other research, suggests that the ideal sequencing of certain components of the creative process may differ according to the domain (such as literary vs. visual arts).

CONCLUSION

Suddenly Alice heard an alarm clock ringing. It was time to wake up and get ready for school. During breakfast, she thought about all the people she had met during the night. Things started to become clearer concerning the creative process in writing.

First, it seemed important to distinguish the process of writing, in general, from the process of creative writing, in particular. The writing process, in general, could be seen as a kind of linguistic problem solving. There were probably some specificities of creative writing that involve the use of certain kinds of thinking that are not necessarily involved much, if at all, in noncreative writing tasks. Of course, all writing may involve a small degree of creative work, unless the writing task involves simply copying an existing text. Second, it seemed useful to distinguish the creative process, in general, from a more specific creative process involved in creative writing. For example, the creative process in writing may differ somewhat from the creative process in art. In addition, within a domain, such as literary composition, there may be process differences in the ideal sequence of cognitive processes for different tasks, such as writing a short fictional story or writing a novel. The evidence remains limited for the moment, however, concerning the specificity of creative story composition once the cognitive processes involved in writing, in general, and in creative work, in general, are taken into account. Any specificity that may exist may concern particularly the sequencing of specific cognitive processes rather than the simple use or nonuse of specific processes. Third, there is probably no single "creative process" that one can follow like a recipe to be sure to produce a creative product. Indeed, probably a multitude of paths can lead to a creative story (and an even greater number of paths can lead to a noncreative production). It may be possible, however, to identify the optimal process for a specific person to generate creative work given that individual's background and cognitive and personality profile, and taking into account that person's environment. Finally, it was clear that there remains much to explore about the nature of the creative process in writing.

That morning as Alice stepped onto the school bus, an idea came to her for the story that she had to write. She could not write it down right away, but promised herself that once at her desk she would note the idea and develop it into a complete story. She thought again about her future career as an author. Perhaps she should explore other career options as well. Maybe she should study psychology and conduct research on creative writers.

REFERENCES

Amabile, T. M. (1996). *Creativity in context.* Boulder, CO: Westview Press.

Basadur, M. (1995). Optimal ideation-evaluation ratios. *Creativity Research Journal,* 8(1), 63–75.

Bereiter, C., & Scaramalia, M. (1987). *The psychology of written composition.* Hillsdale, NJ: Erlbaum.

Busse, T. V., & Mansfield, R. S. (1980). Theories of the creative process: A review and a perspective. *Journal of Creative Behavior, 14*(2), 91–103, 132.

Calwelti, S., Rappaport, A., & Wood, B. (1992). Modeling artistic creativity: An empirical study. *Journal of Creative Behavior, 26*(2), 83–94.

Campbell, D. T. (1960). Blind variation and selective retention in creative thought as in other knowledge processes. *Psychological Review, 67*(6), 380–400.

Csikszentmihalyi, M. (1996). *Creativity: Flow and the psychology of discovery and invention.* New York: HarperCollins.

Doyle, C. L. (1998). The writer tells: The creative process in the writing of literary fiction. *Creativity Research Journal, 11*(1), 29–37.

Eindhoven, J. E., & Vinacke, W. E. (1952). Creative processes in painting. *Journal of General Psychology, 47,* 165–179.

Einstein, A., & Infeld, L. (1938). *The evolution of physics.* New York: Simon & Schuster.

Finke, R. A., Ward, T. B., & Smith, S. M. (1992). *Creative cognition: Theory, research, and applications.* Cambridge, MA: MIT Press.

Getzels, J., & Csikszentmihalyi, M. (1976). *The creative vision: A longitudinal study of problem finding in art.* New York: Wiley.

Ghiselin, B. (1956). The creative process and its relation to the identification of creative talent. In C. W. Taylor (Ed.), *The 1955 University of Utah research conference on the identification of creative scientific talent* (pp. 195–203). Salt Lake City: University of Utah Press.

Ghiselin, B. (1963). Automatism, intention, and autonomy in the novelist's production. *Daedalus, 92*(2), 297–311.

Ghiselin, B. (Ed.). (1985). *The creative process: A symposium.* Berkeley: University of California Press. (Original work published in 1952)

Glover, J. A. (1979). Levels of questions asked in interview and reading sessions by creative and relatively non-creative college students. *Journal of Genetic Psychology, 135*(1), 103–108.

Goldschmidt, G. (1991). The dialectics of sketching. *Creativity Research Journal, 4*(2), 123–143.

Goleman, D., Kaufman, P., & Ray, M. (1992). *The creative spirit.* New York: Plume.

Guilford, J. P. (1950). Creativity. *American Psychologist, 5,* 444–454.

Guilford, J. P. (1967). *The nature of human intelligence.* New York: McGraw-Hill.

Guilford, J. P. (1979). Some incubated thoughts on incubation. *Journal of Creative Behavior, 13*(1), 1–8.

Hayes, J. R. (1996). A new framework for understanding cognition and affect in writing. In C. M. Levy & S. Ransdell (Eds.), *The science of writing: Theories, methods, individual differences, and applications* (pp. 1–27). Mahwah, NJ: Erlbaum.

Hayes, J. R., & Flower, L. S. (1980). Identifying the organization of writing processes. In L. Gregg & E. Steinberg (Eds.), *Cognitive processes in writing* (pp. 3–30). Hillsdale, NJ: Erlbaum.

Hayes, J. R. & Flower, L. S. (1986). Writing research and the writer. *American Psychologist, 4*(10), 1106–1113.

Hayes, J. R., & Nash, J. G. (1996). On the nature of planning in writing. In C. M. Levy & S. Ransdell (Eds.), *The science of writing: Theories, methods, individual differences, and applications* (pp. 29–55). Mahwah, NJ: Erlbaum.

Hutchinson, E. D. (1949). *How to think creatively.* New York: Abingdon-Cokesbury.

Isaksen, S. G., & Treffinger, D. J. (1985). *Creative problem solving: The basic course.* Buffalo, NY: Bearly Limited.

Israeli, N. (1962). Creative processes in painting. *Journal of General Psychology, 67,* 251–263.

Israeli, N. (1981). Decision in painting and sculpture. *Academic Psychology Bulletin, 3*(1), 61–74.

Jay, E. S., & Perkins, D. N. (1997). Problem finding: The search for mechanism. In M. A. Runco (Ed.), *The creativity research handbook* (Vol. 1, pp. 257–293). Cresskill, NJ: Hampton Press.

Kay, S. (1991). The figural problem solving and problem finding of professional and semiprofessional artists and nonartists. *Creativity Research Journal, 4*(3), 233–252.

Kipling, R. (1985). Working tools. In B. Ghiselin (Ed.), *The creative process: A symposium* (pp. 161–163). Berkeley, CA: University of California Press. (Original work published 1937)

Koestler, A. (1964). *The act of creation.* New York: Macmillan.

Kris, E. (1952). *Psychoanalytic exploration in art.* New York: International Universities Press.

Kubie, L. S. (1958). *Neurotic distortion of the creative process.* Lawrence: University of Kansas Press.

Lubart, T. I. (1994). *Product-centered self-evaluation and the creative process.* Unpublished doctoral dissertation, Yale University, New Haven, CT.

Moore, M. T. (1985). The relationship between the originality of essays and variables in the problem discovery process: A study of creative and noncreative middle school students. *Research in the Teaching of English, 19*(1), 84–95.

Mumford, M. D., Baughman, W. A., Threlfall, K. V., Supinski, E. P., & Costanza, D. P. (1996). Process-based measures of creative problem-solving skills: I. Problem construction. *Creativity Research Journal, 9*(1), 63–76.

Mumford, M. D., Mobley, M. I., Uhlman, C. E., Reiter-Palmon, R., & Doares, L. M. (1991). Process analytic models of creative capacities. *Creativity Research Journal, 4*(2), 91–122.

Mumford, M. D., Reiter-Palmon, R., & Redmond, M. R. (1994). Problem construction and cognition: Applying problem representations in ill-defined domains. In M. A. Runco (Ed.), *Problem finding, problem solving, and creativity* (pp. 3–39). Norwood, NJ: Ablex.

Mumford, M. D., Supinski, E. P., Threlfall, K. V., & Baughman, W. A. (1996). Process-based measures of creative problem-solving skills: III. Category selection. *Creativity Research Journal, 9*(4), 395–406.

Ochse, R. (1990). *Before the gates of excellence: The determinants of creative genius.* New York: Cambridge University Press.

Olton, R. M. (1979). Experimental studies of incubation: Searching for the elusive. *Journal of Creative Behavior, 13*(1), 9–22.

Osborn, A. F. (1953). *Applied imagination.* New York: Scribners.

Perkins, D. N. (1981). *The mind's best work.* Cambridge, MA: Harvard University Press.

Piirto, J. (2004). *Understanding creativity.* Little Rock, AK: Great Potential Press.

Plimpton, G. (Ed.) (1958). *Writers at work: The Paris Review interviews.* New York: Viking.

Poincaré, H. (1908/1985). Mathematical creation. In B. Ghiselin (Ed.), *The creative process: A symposium* (pp. 22–31). Berkeley: University of California Press.

Reiter-Palmon, R., Mumford, M. D., O'Connor Boes, J., & Runco, M. A. (1997). Problem construction and creativity: The role of ability, cue consistency, and active processing. *Creativity Research Journal, 10*(1), 9–23.

Rostan, S. M. (1994). Problem finding, problem solving, and cognitive controls: An empirical investigation of critically acclaimed productivity. *Creativity Research Journal, 7*(2), 97–110.

Rothenberg, A. (1979). *The emerging goddess: The creative process in art, science and other fields.* Chicago: University of Chicago Press.

Rothenberg, A. (1996). The Janusian process in scientific creativity. *Creativity Research Journal, 9*(2–3), 207–231.

Runco, M. A. (1991). *Divergent thinking.* Norwood, NJ: Ablex.

Runco, M. A. (Ed.). (1994). *Problem finding, problem solving, and creativity.* Norwood, NJ: Ablex.

Runco, M. A., & Chand, I. (1995). Cognition and creativity. *Educational Psychology Review, 7*(3), 243–267.

Runco, M. A. & Dow, G. T. (1999). Problem finding and creativity. In M. A. Runco & S. Pritzker (Eds.), *Encyclopedia of creativity* (pp. 367–371). San Diego, CA: Academic Press.

Sapp, D. D. (1992). The point of creative frustration and the creative process: A new look at an old model. *Journal of Creative Behavior, 26*(1), 21–28.

Sharples, M. (1996). An account of writing as creative design. In C. M. Levy & S. Ransdell (Eds.), *The science of writing: Theories, methods, individual differences, and applications* (pp. 127–148). Mahwah, NJ: Erlbaum.

Simonton, D. K. (1988). *Scientific genius: A psychology of science.* New York: Cambridge University Press.

Smilansky, J. (1984). Problem solving and the quality of invention: An empirical investigation. *Journal of Educational Psychology, 76*(3), 377–386.

Smith, S. M., & Dodds, R. A. (1999). *Incubation.* In M. A. Runco & S. R. Pritzker (Eds.), *Encyclopedia of creativity* (Vol. 2, pp. 39–43). San Diego: Academic Press.

Stein, M. I. (1974). *Stimulating creativity: Individual procedures.* New York: Academic Press.

Suler, J. R. (1980). Primary process thinking and creativity. *Psychological Bulletin, 88*(1), 144–165.

Torrance, M., Thomas, G., & Robinson, E. J. (1996). Finding something to write about: Strategic and automatic processes in idea generation. In C. M. Levy & S. Ransdell (Eds.), *The science of writing: Theories, methods, individual differences, and applications* (pp. 189–205). Mahwah, NJ: Erlbaum.

Turner, S. (1994). *The creative process: A computer model of storytelling and creativity.* Hillsdale, NJ: Erlbaum.

Wallas, G. (1926). *The art of thought.* New York: Harcourt Brace.

Ward, T. B. (2001). Creative cognition, conceptual combination, and the creative writing of Stephen R. Donaldson. *American Psychologist, 56*(4), 350–354.

Ward, T. B., Smith, S. M., & Vaid, J. (1997). *Creative thought: An investigation of conceptual structures and processes.* Washington, DC: American Psychological Association.

Weisberg, R. W. (1993). *Creativity: Beyond the myth of genius.* New York: W. H. Freeman.

10

Writing as a Collaborative Act

R. KEITH SAWYER

"APRIL is the cruellest month": this famous line introduces T. S. Eliot's five-part poem, *The Waste Land*. Published in 1922, the poem soon made the young poet famous (Eliot, 1971). *The Waste Land* is a loosely connected series of images that paint a bleak, fragmented view of modern urban life. How would the psychology of creativity explain the creative process that led to *The Waste Land*? One common psychological approach is to focus on the writer's personality – Eliot's childhood experiences or his personality profile. A second common psychological approach is to analyze the mental structures possessed by Eliot – such as the store of metaphors, analogies, and even vocabulary that he had amassed during his years of study. In this chapter, I argue for a third approach – one that extends beyond the writer and the typewriter to encompass the collaborative interactions from whence creative writing emerges.

The creation of *The Waste Land* cannot be fully explained without analyzing collaborative interactions (Badenhausen, 2004). The process began when Eliot gave his good friend Ezra Pound the initial typewritten manuscript of his 800-line poem, asking for his suggestions. Before returning this first manuscript to Eliot, Pound deleted entire pages of it, moved stanzas around, and rewrote many of the lines. By the time he was done, he had shortened Eliot's initial typed manuscript by half – the published poem came out at only 433 lines. Soon after Pound's editing, Eliot's wife Vivien also wrote in several revisions on the manuscript; several of her newly written lines made it into the final poem. These handwritten notes were no doubt followed by conversations between Eliot and his editors about their recommendations.

Writing seems to be the least collaborative of all creative acts and far removed from social and contextual influences. You do not need anyone's help to write poetry; you do not need to use complex tools or to collaborate in a system of cooperative work. Many of us think of writing as the private, personal expression of a person's very private inner vision. But these beliefs about writing are myths that are based in our culture's individualist assumptions about how creativity works. In this chapter I draw on several biographies of writers to support my claim that writing is a deeply collaborative activity.

Our culture's individualistic beliefs about creativity have influenced the types of writing that we psychologists choose to study. We tend to study those writers engaged in genres of writing that seem to be the least collaborative: literary poetry and prose. But the psychological processes of creative writing occur in a much broader range of activities, including the writing of advertising copy, promotional brochures, weekly magazine features, e-mails between professionals, sitcom and movie scripts, and popular genres such as romance novels and comic strips. Taken in this broader context of writing creativity, high art writing – poetry and novels – does not form a representative sample of the human potential for creative writing.

As the example of Eliot and *The Waste Land* shows, even apparently solitary forms of creative writing such as poetry and prose novels are more collaborative than is usually believed. The individualistic paradigm underlying psychological research leads us to focus on the inner mental processes of the solitary writer and to neglect the social and collaborative processes of creative writing. In this chapter, I begin by arguing that collaboration is at the core of all creativity, including writing creativity, and I present a theoretical framework that focuses on the collaborative dimension of all creativity. Then I discuss several examples of creative writing in which collaborative processes are central to the creative product that is ultimately generated.

FROM THE LONE GENIUS TO THE GROUP GENIUS

My approach to the study of creativity is based in a theoretical framework of *socioculturalism*, an interdisciplinary approach that explains creative products and processes in terms of their social and cultural contexts and the collaborative interactions that occur as those products are generated (Sawyer, 2006). The sociocultural approach brings together psychologists, sociologists of science and art, and anthropologists who study art, ritual performance, and verbal creativity in different cultures. Socioculturalists argue that explaining creativity requires understanding not only individual inspiration but also social factors like collaboration, networks of support, education, and cultural background.

Socioculturalists argue, along with many other psychologists who study creativity (e.g., Ward, Finke, & Smith, 1995; Weisberg, 1986), that several widely held beliefs about creativity are wrong. Cultural beliefs about creativity vary dramatically across cultures; people in the United States tend to hold extremely individualistic beliefs about creativity. They believe that creators work best when they are alone and unconstrained by convention or institutions. They believe that creations emerge, essentially fully formed, in a sudden flash of insight. They believe that too much education interferes with creativity and that the most significant insights come from outsiders because they have not been forced to master the received wisdom. But decades of research have shown that these beliefs are largely false – or, at best, misleading (Berkin, 2007; Sawyer, 2006; Weisberg, 1986).

Those who hold to these beliefs most strongly rarely have difficulty accepting that *economic* innovations might emerge from collaboration – the computer, software programs, the DVD player – or from new organizational forms that deliver services more effectively, as with Wal-Mart's distribution network or Southwest Airlines' boarding and seating procedures. But individualists are likely to hold to their beliefs more tightly when it comes to those creative activities that are considered to be "high art" in our culture – writing, musical composition, and fine art painting. For example, we think that writers largely work alone, that they are blessed with a special gift, that they have a valuable message to communicate, and that they feel compelled to communicate that message.

These U.S. beliefs about creativity are extremely recent; they can be dated historically to the Romantic period of the early 19th century (Sawyer, 2006). Before this time, for centuries of European history, writers – like visual artists – were essentially scribes who worked collaboratively, in studios characterized by apprenticeship structures. Writers were not thought of as individuals with a special message to communicate; rather, they were thought of as craftsmen, generating texts with specific social functions. In contrast to this tradition, the 19th-century Romantics were revolutionary; they valued the artist's imagination more than mastery of the traditions of the past. In the Romantic period, contemporary conceptions of creativity were born. At this time, people began to believe that the poet had a privileged spiritual status (Engell, 1981).

The Romantics believed that creativity required a regression to a state of consciousness characterized by emotion and instinct, a fusion between self and world, and freedom from rationality and convention. Our conceptions of creativity are inspired by these 19th-century images: the starving poet who cannot afford to leave his barely furnished apartment; the genius composer with the stub of a chewed pencil, working out a symphony in her head while she lies in bed, sick and alone; or the visionary painter, out of step with convention and his peers, whose work never leaves the studio until long after a miserable death.

But today more than ever, the most important forms of creativity in our culture – movies, television shows, big science experiments, music videos, compact disks, computer software, video games – are joint cooperative activities of complex networks of skilled individuals. It is ironic that the United States today has one of the most individualist conceptions of creativity in history, because perhaps more than any other society, creativity in the United States is a collective, institutional activity (Garber, 2002). The creative products that U.S. society is best known for today – including movies, music videos, and video games – are all made by organized groups of highly specialized individuals. To explain the creativity of complex collaborating groups, we need a sociocultural framework because it allows us to understand how groups of people work together and how the collective actions of many people result in a final created product.

In what I call *group genius*, a product is created by a group, a work team, or an ensemble. Some of the purest examples of group genius are the improvisations of jazz ensembles. To explain jazz creativity, one must focus on the musical interaction among members of the ensemble (Sawyer, 2003a). Of course, each musician is individually creative during the performance, but the creativity of the group as a whole can only be explained by examining social and interactional processes among the musicians. No one can generate a performance alone; the performers have to rely on the group and on the audience to collectively generate the emergent performance. In some improvised performance genres, the audience is consciously and actively involved; for example, in Chicago improv theater, the actors always ask the audience members to shout out suggestions before they begin to improvise a scene, and many groups stop in the middle of a scene to ask the audience to tell them what should happen next (Sawyer, 2003b).

Group genius involves *distributed cognition* – a process in which each member of the team contributes an essential piece of the solution and these individual components are all integrated together to form the collective product. Most of our culture's important creative products – including creatively generated texts – are too large and complex to be generated by a single individual; they require a team or an entire network of distributed individuals, with a division of labor and a careful integration of many specialized creative workers.

Although writing seems a uniquely solitary activity, much creative writing today is just as collaborative as other creative products. For example, the scripts of every movie and television show are created by teams of writers, each contributing throughout the process. Here is a transcript of the artists and writers working on the Cartoon Network's cartoon, *Samurai Jack*, in the meeting led by creator Genndy Tartakovsky. These collaborative writing sessions are so common in the television industry that they have their own name: the *story meeting*. Andy has come up with a new story idea. There are about 10 people in the room; except for Andy and Tartakovsky, whenever one of the others speaks up, I simply indicate "artist" (from Wilkinson, 2002):

> ANDY: We're looking to do the story we talked about, where Jack gets infected with a virus and it takes over his arm. Then it would slowly take over his whole body. Then half of him becomes evil, and he's going to fight himself.
>
> TARTAKOVSKY: How do we set it up?
>
> ARTIST: Could he have battled Aku, and Aku has a cold, and he sneezes on him?

TARTAKOVSKY (Nods): It's almost like we're at the end of another show with a great fight. Except this one starts with a battle. And he's fighting these robots, and Aku's commanding them. It's cold and drafty, and Aku starts sneezing, and says, "Oy, I've got to get some chicken soup."

ARTIST: Oy?

ARTIST: How do we get it out that he's infected?

ARTIST: We had talked about him showing a guy his face. And it's half in shadow.

ARTIST: He becomes Aku.

ARTIST: He becomes *Jaku*.

ARTIST: The more evil he becomes, the more erratic his body is.

ARTIST: Maybe somebody's getting robbed, he saves him, and the guy thanks him, and he's walking away, and in Jack's other hand is the guy's watch.

ARTIST: Do we need to find somebody to summon him? Is there a psychic battle with himself?

ARTIST: Or a fight in his head? I was thinking, he knows a place to cleanse himself – a monastery. And the monks help him.

ARTIST: The B story is no one's trusting Jack – they see him and they run.

TARTAKOVSKY: It's always stronger if Jack can help himself. I like the image of Jack as Aku with one eye. I like it half and half. The more I think about it, the body of the show is him fighting himself.

ARTIST: He realizes he'd better get out of the city before he hurts someone, so he travels to a village.

TARTAKOVSKY: I still want to keep it real simple, though.

ARTIST: At the monastery, they tie him up so he can't do any harm.

TARTAKOVSKY: Does Aku know that Jack has what he has?

ARTIST: No, he's too sick.

It is clear from this brief excerpt of this collaboration that no single person is in charge. Even though the discussion started with Andy's story idea, Andy says nothing after getting it started. Ideas are suggested by everyone present; those ideas are immediately elaborated and modified by others. Tartakovsky is the manager, but he does not dominate the group. The script emerges from the discussion and ends up being a collective creation of 10 people. It would be difficult to imagine that a psychological analysis of any one member of the group could provide a scientific explanation of the final script that results.

In recent years, more and more creative writing– even the writing of novels and children's books – is being done by collaboratives. In Italy, a four-man collective from Bologna has collaboratively written two successful novels. Their first, *Q*, sold more than 200,000 copies in Italy, received good reviews, and made the short list for several literary prizes. Their second, titled simply *54*, has also sold well. In Britain, several companies now specialize in collaboratively written fiction. A company named Hothouse won the 2007 Waterstone children's book prize with a collaboratively written teenage novel titled *Darkside* (Sidelsky, 2007). Although most novels today continue to be written by single authors, these examples of collaborative writing show that there is nothing inherently solitary about literary art.

MEDIEVAL WRITING

Earlier I claimed that before the Romantic period, writers worked collaboratively and were conceived of as craftsmen rather than artists. This is true even of the most highly valued texts in English that emerged in the medieval period: Shakespeare's plays (see Chapter 8) and the King James Bible.

The prose style of the King James Bible, even for many non-Christians, represents the pinnacle of the writing arts in the English language. It has a rhythmic nature that lends itself to oral presentation. It has both grace and power. But this translation was not the work of a single lone genius; it was created by a government committee of about 50 men, made up of scholars, ministers, politicians, and others. The revising committee never read from the written first drafts; instead, the drafts were read aloud and the editors revised based on how they sounded (Nicolson, 2006).

Shakespeare, considered one of the most talented writers ever to work in English, did not leave authoritative texts. He almost certainly did not write every word of his plays; several texts show signs of revision and collaboration. Following the convention of the Elizabethan period, a playwright was commissioned by actors to develop a play for their company, and the playwright worked collaboratively with the company from beginning to end (Thomson, 2003). (Shakespeare was somewhat unique in that he was a member of an acting company as well as a playwright.) The playwright took direction from the acting company on many things: What sort of topic would fit well into the current season? What roles can we create for our talented clown actor? And, be sure not to create more female roles than we have boys available to play them. Or, if we need to have one actor play two characters, make sure that there is time for him to change costumes. Plays were shortened or extended at the request of the actors.

On completion of the play, the company owned all intellectual rights to it; there was no conception of authorial ownership during this period (that emerged later, after the Romantic era shifted our conceptions of creativity). If the actors chose to speak different lines than were written, that was their prerogative. Writers were frequently paid to add new scenes to older plays written by others. In this system, many writers chose to work collaboratively with others; half of the plays produced between 1590 and 1642 were generated by more than one writer (Bentley, 1971, p. 199). As Thomson wrote, the author was "the virtually anonymous shaper of a commodity for playhouse use" (2003, p. 45).

For many of Shakespeare's plays, as with those of other playwrights during this time, multiple texts remain, and these have significant variations. In fact two versions of *King Lear* are so different that some scholars consider them to be completely different works. Some scholars explain these variations by suggesting that the texts were not written by Shakespeare himself, but were later written from memory by an actor in his company. Many actors would have learned their lines not from reading the script, but through verbal instruction. With the high degree of collaboration between the actors and the playwright, plays could easily change during rehearsal and evolve over the course of a production, such that the "final" version would no longer correspond to the original script. Was it the original script that was published, or was it the actual version as performed by the company? Which would we consider to be more authentic? That depends on our conceptions of authorship and creativity.

A. J. Minnis's classic book, *Medieval Theory of Authorship* (1984), documented a shift in the conception of the author that occurred between 1100 and 1400: a shift from the belief that the author's voice was direct from God to a belief that the author possessed his or her own status and a unique style associated only with that author. This opened up the space for the emergence of what Minnis called "vernacular writers" who wrote about everyday events in their lives (Minnis provides Chaucer as an example) rather than writing as the voice of God.

Before and during this period, writers did not create their own texts in the fashion we associate with authors today; instead, they translated existing religious texts. But these medieval texts were typically commented on or "glossed" extensively, with the comments sometimes written directly in the manuscript margins, other times printed directly in-line with commentary following each paragraph, and, most commonly, provided in extensive prefaces and academic prologues. At the time, reading practices were such that readers read the commentaries along with the original texts, so that the experience of the reader was an experience co-created by a historical series of writers. Today, we prefer to read the unadorned "original text," but this is a historically unique practice, again driven by our view of texts as generated by solitary individuals rather than as representing a collective enterprise.

These historical examples show that today's conception of writing creativity is historically unique. For many centuries of European history, texts were created using very different processes from those we expect to occur today. There was a high degree of collaboration, both among writers and between writers and those who commissioned their texts. Writers were thought of as craftsmen for hire, rather than uniquely inspired artists. In such a society, the explanations that a scientist might develop for how texts are created would naturally be different from today's psychological theories.

THE INKLINGS

I have argued that our culture's conception of writing creativity changed as a result of the Romanticism of the early 19th century. But although our conception of writing changed, the actual processes of writing have continued to be collaborative and deeply social. Some of today's most famous writers work very closely with others. For some writers, their closest collaborators are their editors – demonstrated by the earlier example of T. S. Eliot and Ezra Pound. A second example is the short story writer Raymond Carver; many of his stories were substantially changed by his editor, Gordon Lish, who in some cases deleted more than half of Carver's text and wrote entire new paragraphs to be inserted (Sawyer, 2006).

In addition to collaborating with editors, many writers also work closely with other writers. A classic example is the group of writers that formed at Oxford University in the 1920s and contained C. S. Lewis and J. R. R. Tolkien (Farrell, 2001). Both Lewis and Tolkien felt like outsiders; each of them liked to write mythical fiction and poetry, and they knew that these genres would not be taken seriously by their colleagues in the English department. Lewis and Tolkien formed a group with about four other local scholars, and Lewis came up with a name for the group: the Inklings. This name was a pun that described them as writers and also as people who were searching with "vague or half-formed intimations and ideas," as Tolkien wrote (1967, p. 387). Every week they would meet in someone's quarters, and some weeks again at the Eagle and Child pub in Oxford, to discuss Nordic myths and epics and read aloud from their own works in progress.

There was another characteristic that made Lewis and Tolkien different from their colleagues – they were both Christians at a time when most Oxford scholars were avowed atheists. Late on the night of September 19, 1931, Lewis and Tolkien walked around the quadrangles until three in the morning, talking about the fine points of the New Testament myth. Tolkien argued that although Christ's death and resurrection had the structure of a myth, it had nonetheless actually happened because God had intentionally caused real events to unfold in the form of a myth, to make the events easier for people to understand. After this conversation, Lewis became a Christian believer.

Before the Inklings formed, Lewis had written a few unremarkable poems; Tolkien had been privately writing stories about elves and wizards since he was 18. Gradually, as trust built within the group, both men began to share their secret writing hobby. Tolkien sent Lewis one of his early unfinished epic poems, and Lewis gave him detailed comments on the stories of Beren and his gnomish allies, the orcs and the Narog. Other members of the group began experimenting with similar mythical fiction. In Lewis's case, his deepening Christian beliefs led him to explore the mythical nature of Christianity.

The themes that would later appear in each writer's books first emerged during the weekly discussions of the Inklings, and each group member explored their shared vision in different ways. After a new idea emerged in discussion, the members would return home and draft a chapter capturing the idea; then they would take turns reading their drafts aloud at the next meeting and listen to critical suggestions from the others. Tolkien's own lens on the circle resulted in *The Hobbit* and the three-volume *The Lord of the Rings*, an epic tale of elves, wizards, dragons, and hobbits. Lewis's lens resulted in *The Chronicles of Narnia*. Without the creative circle, these works that today have been read by millions might not exist.

Our image of the writer is one of solitude and inner inspiration. But *The Lord of the Rings* and *The Chronicles of Narnia* were not solo works, authored by lone geniuses; they unfolded in a collaborative circle. Of course, each member of the group eventually had to return to his private study and prepare the next draft, and cognitive psychology has an important role to play in explaining the mental processes that take place there. But no explanation of the processes that resulted in these texts could be complete without a thorough analysis of the social and collaborative interactions that preceded and followed each of these private bouts of writing.

THE CREATIVE PROCESS

The myths that our culture holds about creativity tend to influence the ways that psychologists study creativity. These include the myth that creativity is primarily about a special moment of creative insight, one that emerges from the unconscious, and the myth that creativity is primarily a solitary activity. These myths partially explain why cognitive psychologists have dedicated substantial research to the moment of insight (Sawyer, 2007) and why personality psychologists study the traits associated with creativity (Sawyer, 2006; see Chapter 1 in this volume). When it comes to creative writing, many nonwriters believe that writers have a special ability to write excellent prose in their first draft, with only minor editing to follow.

This myth was perhaps first promulgated by Romantic poets like Coleridge. Coleridge wrote a preface to his famous poem, "Kubla Khan: Or, a Vision in a Dream," describing how the entire poem came to him in a dream during a medication-induced nap; after waking up, he wrote down the entire poem. As with most of these insight stories, on further examination it turns out to be false (Lowes, 1927; Schneider, 1953). Scholars who have examined Coleridge's notes have discovered that he read many different books that contributed material to the poem. In some cases, word-for-word phrases from these books appear unmodified in his poem. Early drafts of the poem that have been discovered among Coleridge's notes also include early drafts of the preface, with versions of his insight story that describe the insight in very different ways, making it obvious that Coleridge created the story for public consumption. Coleridge was known to be fascinated with dreams; he was famous among his friends for making up stories about how he created his poems. During the Romantic period, the general public expected poets to write in this fashion, so perhaps it is not surprising that a writer would create a public version of events that conformed to the public's expectations. In every culture, creativity myths are propagated, in part, by creators themselves – in many cases because they believe them too, but also because it is to their advantage to present public images that conform to the contemporary beliefs about how creativity works.

Creative writing is hard work; it involves a large amount of conscious editing and analysis, and it takes place over long periods of time with frequent revisions. Stories that make it seem otherwise, like Coleridge's, are almost always false. Csikszentmihalyi's extended interviews of five creative writers (1996) identified several important features of creative writing; these features also held true for Coleridge, despite the myths he created for public consumption. First, the five writers could only be significantly creative after first immersing themselves in the domain of literature; they knew more about literature and the history of writing than nonwriters. (Likewise, Coleridge read widely about Kubla Khan before writing his poem.)

Second, the five writers emphasized the constant dialogue between unconscious inspiration and conscious editing, between passionate inspiration and disciplined craft. They all agreed with the importance of listening to their unconscious. They kept notebooks nearby at all times, so that sudden snippets of text or dialogue could be quickly scribbled down for later evaluation. They constantly came up with small bits of text, little snippets of a scene or a character, that they wrote down in these notebooks, and they had no idea whether those ideas would ever be used in a finished published text. Poet Mark Strand starts writing this way: "I'll jot a few words down, and that's a beginning" (quoted in Csikszentmihalyi, 1996, p. 241). Novelist Anne Lamott is typical: She takes index cards everywhere, knowing that small bits and pieces of dialogue or character traits or events might come to her at any time. These cards are then stored in a folder or a notebook, are frequently read, and much later can be slipped into an ongoing story, one that was not even conceived when the original snippet was written. And like a photographer who ends up printing only a small percentage of all the photos she takes, Anne Lamott never uses most of her index cards. In this way, the process of creative writing is very much like the creative process in all fields – it involves a high degree of idea generation, followed by a period of selection (Ward, Finke, & Smith, 1995).

Although many writers talk about a dialogue with the unconscious, this process is very different from our culture's insight myths, as represented by Coleridge's false story. A creative text emerges from a long process of hard work, during which the conscious and unconscious minds are in constant dialogue and during which many small sparks of insight emerge from the unconscious. So although unconscious inspiration plays a critical role, its role can only be understood within the context of these periods of hard work, including the hard work that precedes each spark, the hard work to elaborate the implications of each spark, and the hard work of weaving these daily small sparks together into a unified work.

Many creative writers today use a *problem-finding* style; they don't know what they're doing until they've done it (Lamott, 1994, p. 22). They start a work with only a phrase or an image rather than a fully composed plot, and the work emerges from the improvisational act of writing and revising. Moore (1985) replicated with student writers the famous Getzels and Csikszentmihalyi (1976) study of problem finding in artists. Moore found that student writers resembled art students in their problem-finding behavior; the writers whose stories were rated the most original by experts were the ones who used a problem-finding style. In the problem-finding style, there is never a single big insight; instead, there are hundreds and thousands of small mini-insights. The real work starts when many mini-insights are analyzed, reworked, and connected to each other, and as with every other type of creativity, many ideas that sound good at first end up in the trash.

This view of creative writing – involving hard, conscious work, interspersed with constant small sparks of insight – is quite similar to the creative process in other domains. Psychologists now know that creativity is based in everyday thought processes (Sawyer, 2007; Ward, Finke, & Smith, 1995); the idea that creativity is associated with a sudden mysterious flash of insight that is somehow different from everyday, incremental cognition is a myth (Weisberg, 1993). Even when people have a sudden "Aha!" sensation, laboratory experiments have demonstrated that incremental thought processes can be identified that logically lead to the moment of insight (Sawyer, 2007). As with Coleridge's story, once you scratch beneath the surface of one of the famous historical insight stories, you always find the same thing: hard work, immersion in a domain, and a slow emergence of the work over a long period of time that is marked by constant small sparks of insight, never a single blinding flash. This vision of creative writing does more justice to writers themselves; working writers know that they are hard-working, skilled professionals, not simply lucky folks who were blessed by a muse. Our myths make writing seem easy, when in reality it is not.

CONCLUSION

Our culture has been characterized by mass literacy for several generations, which has led us to believe that the norm for linguistic creativity is written text. That is why the title of this book is *The Psychology of Creative Writing*, rather than *The Psychology of Linguistic Creativity*. But from the broader perspective of human cultural history, linguistic creativity has been overwhelmingly oral; the emergence of creative writing is relatively recent, and it is based on our evolved abilities with spoken language. Before the modern onset of mass literacy, even written texts were deeply influenced by their origins in orality; for example, medieval texts often contain shorthand that signifies their intended use as guides for spoken performance. The committee that wrote the King James Bible did their editing by first reading the text aloud.

More than any other genre of writing, poetry is influenced by its oral roots. Because poetry was transmitted orally in cultures that were not literate, the structure of the poem had to be easy to remember. Cognitive psychologists have discovered that techniques associated with poetry – like alliteration, meter, and rhyme – increase the memorability of a text (Rubin, 1995). Through most of human history, verbal creations had to be easy to remember; in oral cultures, all composed texts had features that we today associate with poetry, because otherwise they would not be remembered and would disappear from history.

Our culture's valuation of written language over spoken language tends to reinforce our beliefs in the solitary and private nature of creativity – because the spoken word is always more social and more interactive than the written word. Oral texts are always performed on certain occasions and always play a social function. Oral texts change over time, and their state at any moment reflects the creative contributions of uncountable creators, over many generations.

Our culture's romantic beliefs about how writing originates – from the inner spirit of a uniquely gifted individual – lead us to focus on the kinds of writing that align with that myth and to neglect other forms of creative writing that clash with that myth: the spoken word poems composed for poetry jams; successful romance novels, which some of the best writers can generate several times each year; the script of a successful situation comedy or movie, which is generated by a staff of writers, often in collaboration with the actors; wikis, online texts that are collaboratively generated; and "fan fiction," alternative versions of popular novels (often science fiction) that are written by fans. Theories of creative writing must be capable of accounting for all of these genres, and accounting for these genres requires a fundamentally collaborative theory of writing. I have provided several examples in which even poetry and prose involve a high degree of collaboration; in response to this research, a new form of literary criticism known as *genetic criticism* has begun to focus on the evolution of manuscripts from drafts to published form, examining the collaborative process that involves editors, colleagues, and publishers (Deppman, Ferrer, & Groden, 2004).

Most scientific studies of creativity have been limited to those expressions of creativity that are highly valued in Western cultures. In studies of writing creativity, this bias is reflected in a focus on high-culture forms – the kinds of novels and poetry that are taught in English literature courses, rather than science fiction, poetry slam texts, or cartoon bubbles. The bias in creativity research toward these fine arts is out of step with the creative world; the arts in postwar America have been characterized by a valorization of spontaneity, improvisation, and pop culture, not only in performance but even in writing and painting – Black Mountain and beat poets, bebop musicians, abstract expressionists, modern dance, and installation art (Sawyer, 2006). We need to take care to avoid developing explanations of writing creativity that are based on a mythical view of the solitary, inspired genius and instead develop explanations that capture the fundamentally collaborative nature of writing creativity.

Of course, individual psychological processes are a key component of writing creativity. Studies of creative writers extend back at least to Barron's study of 26 professional creative writers while at the Berkeley IPAR (Barron, 1972), which found that writers score high on traits such as verbal fluency, conceptual thinking, and flexibility. And studies of creative cognition (e.g., Ward, Finke, & Smith, 1995) provide us with many insights into how the mind processes literary techniques such as metaphor and analogy. But with creative writing, perhaps more than any other creative domain, cultural beliefs tend to interfere with a full and complete explanation of the phenomenon. In this chapter, I have attempted to balance the generally individualistic focus of psychology with attention to the collaborative dimensions of writing.

As Eliot's collaborator Ezra Pound wrote, "It is tremendously important that great poetry be written; it makes no jot of difference who writes it" (1954, p. 10).

REFERENCES

Barron, F. (1972). *Artists in the making.* New York: Seminar Press.

Bentley, G. E. (1971). *The profession of dramatist in Shakespeare's time, 1590–1642.* Princeton, NJ: Princeton University Press.

Berkin, S. (2007). *The myths of innovation.* Sebastopol, CA: O'Reilly Media.

Csikszentmihalyi, M. (1996). *Creativity: Flow and the psychology of discovery and invention.* New York: HarperCollins.

Deppman, J., Ferrer, D., & Groden, M. (Eds.). (2004). *Genetic criticism: Texts and avant-textes.* Philadelphia: University of Pennsylvania Press.

Eliot, T. S. (1971). *The Waste Land: A facsimile and transcript of the original drafts including the annotations of Ezra Pound.* New York: Harcourt Brace Jovanovich.

Engell, J. (1981). *The creative imagination: Enlightenment to romanticism.* Cambridge, MA: Harvard University Press.

Farrell, M. P. (2001). *Collaborative circles: Friendship dynamics and creative work.* Chicago: University of Chicago Press.

Garber, M. (2002, December). Our genius problem. *Atlantic Monthly,* 64–72.

Getzels, J. W., & Csikszentmihalyi, M. (1976). *The creative vision.* New York: Wiley.

Lamott, A. (1994). *Bird by bird: Some instructions on writing and life.* New York: Pantheon Books.

Lowes, J. L. (1927). *The road to Xanadu: A study in the ways of the imagination.* Boston: Houghton Mifflin.

Minnis, A. J. (1984). *Medieval theory of authorship.* London: Scolar Press.

Moore, M. (1985). The relationship between the originality of essays and variables in the problem-discovery process: A study of creative and non-creative middle school students. *Research in the Teaching of English, 19,* 84–95.

Nicolson, A. (2006, Sept. 30–Oct. 1). God's work via committee. *Wall Street Journal,* p. P14.

Pound, E. (1954). A retrospect. In T. S. Eliot (Ed.), *Literary essays of Ezra Pound* (pp. 3–14). London: Faber and Faber.

Rubin, D. C. (1995). *Memory in oral traditions: The cognitive psychology of epic, ballads, and counting-out rhymes.* New York: Oxford University Press.

Sawyer, R. K. (2003a). *Group creativity: Music, theater, collaboration.* Mahwah, NJ: Erlbaum.

Sawyer, R. K. (2003b). *Improvised dialogues: Emergence and creativity in conversation.* Westport, CT: Greenwood.

Sawyer, R. K. (2006). *Explaining creativity: The science of human innovation.* New York: Oxford University Press.

Sawyer, R. K. (2007). *Group genius: The creative power of collaboration.* New York: Basic Books.

Schneider, E. (1953). *Coleridge, opium, and Kubla Khan.* Chicago: University of Chicago Press.

Sidelsky, W. (2007, August). Strength in numbers. *Prospect,* 137.

Thomson, P. (2003). Conventions of playwriting. In S. Wells & L. Cowen (Eds.), *Shakespeare: An Oxford guide* (p. 49). New York: Oxford University Press.

Tolkien, J. R. R. (1967). Letter to William Luther White. In H. Carter & C. Tolkien (Eds.), *Letters of J. R. R. Tolkien* (p. 387). London: Allen and Unwin.

Ward, T. B., Finke, R. A., & Smith, S. M. (1995). *Creativity and the mind: Discovering the genius within.* New York: Perseus.

Weisberg, R. W. (1986). *Creativity: Genius and other myths.* New York: W. H. Freeman.

Wilkinson, A. (2002, May 27). Moody toons: The king of the cartoon network. *New Yorker,* 76–81.

11

Writing as an Interaction with Ideas

MARK A. RUNCO

Creative studies benefit in numerous ways from biographical and autobiographical accounts. The benefits may be especially obvious in studies of writers, given that the evidence is often quite explicit and well articulated. After all, writers are experts at self-expression. Assuming that the biographical or autobiographical account is itself written or is in some way linguistic, it is likely that the data provided by writers are more informative than, say, those provided by a dancer or painter who writes about his or her life. Rothenberg's (1990) account of the novelist John Cheever comes to mind, as does Albert (1996) on the Brontes; Ippolito and Tweney (2003) on Virginia Wolfe; Henrickson (2003) on Mark Twain; and my own modest work on Sylvia Plath (1998).

Certainly there are methodological concerns with all biographical studies. They do not provide the same kind of data as experimental and controlled studies and are open to various biases that can undermine internal validity. Still, they provide useful illustrations and suggest hypotheses that can later be tested in a more controlled fashion. Additionally, biographical studies retain a realistic level of analysis. There is little reductionism, for example, just to name one experimental problem that is largely avoided by biographical studies (Runco & Okuda, 1993). The level of analysis in biographical studies is the creative individual rather than one particular personality trait, one particular cognitive process, or one particular psychological or social need. Experimental studies provide reliable data, but their advantage – experimental control – is also their disadvantage. They sometimes distort the dynamics within the lives of creative persons and the creative process (Gruber, 1988).

Losing sight of the dynamic qualities of creative lives is especially troubling because it may be those same dynamic qualities that best distinguish them. Consider in this regard the tendency of creative persons to behave in contradictory ways. Barron (1963) put it exactly that way, describing creative individuals as manifesting a "contradictory personality," an idea echoed and reinforced more recently by the extensive research of Csikszentmihalyi (1996).

Such contradictions may be vital for some expressions of creativity, but are nearly impossible to uncover in highly controlled studies.

The eccentricities, foibles, and contradictions of creative individuals often draw attention. No wonder so many biographies and case studies are published each year. It is also no surprise that, when thinking about creativity, audiences tend to look at the novel, poem, or literary product, as well as the writer him- or herself, but writers themselves probably look to the process instead. In this chapter I argue that studies of creative persons should follow suit and also look more to process than product or personality. The rationale for a process view is outlined and the benefits of that process. I also present concerns with the product approach to creative work and explore several intriguing hypotheses.

The first intriguing hypothesis is that *writing provides more opportunities for self-expression and problem resolution than other domains of creative work.* A second and similarly provocative hypothesis is that, unless simply copying material in a mindless fashion, *every writer is creative, not just writers of fiction and fantasy.* These two ideas are discussed in the context of the creativity literature. The first is relevant to the debate over *domain specificity*, for it clearly implies an important difference among domains. The second idea, that every writer is creative, is relevant to the debate over the distribution of creative talents. It is contrary to definitions of creativity that require social judgment (Csikszentmihalyi, 1990). A third hypothesis offered here, and the one to which we turn first, is that *the contradictory personalities of creative persons are in fact a reflection of their flexibility and adaptability.*

CREATIVITY AND ADAPTATION

John Donne (1572–1631), probably best known for "Divine Poems," "For Whom the Bell Tolls," and "Death Be Not Proud," exemplifies the contradictory creative personality mentioned earlier. A recent biographer described Donne in the following manner:

> The scion of an adamantly Catholic family who became a conforming Protestant, . . . the military adventurer who raided Cadiz with the Earl of Essex, . . . the rising civil servant who wrecked his career for love, . . . the harassed father scrabbling to support an ever-increasing brood . . . Donne could be many people, and his admirers were sometimes uncomfortable with his contradictions. (Smith, 2007, p. R6)

This description not only explicitly identifies contradictions; it also suggests that the seemingly oxymoronic nature of creative individuals may reflect their adaptive capacity – and their complicated lives. Perhaps they behave one way as they adapt to one situation but then behave quite differently when they adapt to another of life's pressures. This behavior is consistent with the adaptability that is often included in descriptions of creative individuals (Cohen, 1989; Runco, 1994). In fact, creative individuals may actively seek out this kind of complicated life! After all, a *preference for complexity* is common among creative persons (Barron, 1995; Eisenman, 1992).

Many of our social roles reflect adaptations to various developmental stages. Here is another description of the author of "For Whom the Bell Tolls": "The various Donnes that posterity has inherited represent stages in the life and growth of a singular individual, the different forms one soul took on" (Stubbs, 2007, quoted by Smith, 2007, p. R6). Along the same lines, consider this description:

> In the 1620s, long after he had taken holy orders and become Dr. John Donne, the earthy, erotic poems written by rakish Jack Donne were still circulating in manuscript copies among the Jacobean elite. There surely were occasions when the dean of St. Paul's Cathedral found it embarrassing to know that somewhere someone was reading "The Flea," which urged a nervous mistress to surrender her virginity, or "The Sunne Rising," whose narrator lolled abed in his lover's arms and bid this "busie old foole" to go wake up someone else. Donne never allowed these poems to be published. In his youth, he wanted to be perceived as a "literary gentleman," not a plebeian professional. Later, while he was writing some of the most beautiful religious verse in English, the author of "Death Be Not Proud" deemed it wiser not to print early work that would remind his patrons of the promiscuous courtier he had once been. (Smith, 2007, p. R6)

Changes occurring through the lifespan no doubt influence the character of creative efforts. Middle adulthood apparently took Donne in a somewhat conventional direction, at least compared to that reflected in his earlier poems. Others may become increasingly radical and risqué as they age; conventions may mean less and less. This is apparent in the *androgeny shift* that occurs in middle and late adulthood, with men opening up to what are traditionally considered to be feminine behaviors and women doing the same for what are considered to be masculine behaviors (Sigelman & Rider, 2008). That by itself is intriguing, given the relationship of psychological androgeny and creative performance (Harrington & Anderson, 1981). Donne's shift was toward conventionality, but the important thing is not the direction of change but the fact that change is possible. It may even be necessary. After all, situations and capacities change as we age, so there are various pressures to adapt. Some highly creative persons adapt by intentionally experimenting throughout adulthood. Lindauer (1992) described a clear example of this in his studies of painters and their *old age style*.

Adaptations of this nature are tied to values as well as preferences. They are in fact tied to something more general, namely self-concept. In adulthood, creative persons are probably well aware of their talents, and as life throws new situations and challenges in the way, they probably realize that those talents can and should be used. Self-concept and the recognition of oneself as creative are somewhat stable, as are the values and goals that direct intentional adaptations. Consider in this regard Smith's (2007) reference to "Donne's decades-long search for his proper place in the world, for a community he could truly call home" (p. R6). This kind of search is not uncommon in self-reports of creative writers. In a recent memoir, Lisa Alther, author of the novel titled *Kinfolks* (and reviewed by Reynolds, 2007a, p. R9 in the article aptly titled "Kinfolks: Falling off the Family Tree"), noted, "Everything I've ever written has been an attempt to work out who I am."

This brings us to the benefit of writing and the idea introduced earlier that the process of writing offers something that other domains do not; namely, the opportunity for self-disclosure. It is of course not an all-or-nothing feature; very likely all creative domains offer some opportunities. Yet because it allows easy expression, writing may facilitate self-disclosure more than other domains.

WRITING AS SELF-DISCLOSURE

Henry David Thoreau (1817–1862) kept a journal and saw its virtues throughout his life. He started writing in it at age 20 in the year 1837. Twenty-five years later he had compiled more than two million words. A recent editor of that opus described it this way: "that by which his life could be defined, and the creation of which was central to his existence. . . . Thoreau seemed to think of it also as a place to argue with himself, to chew on things" (Cramer, 2007, quoted by Reynolds, 2007b).

In 1851 Thoreau himself wrote, "Of all strange and unaccountable things, this journalizing is the strangest. . . . 'Say's I to myself' should be the motto of my journal." Also compelling is the first entry, in 1837: "I avoid myself." That sounds very much like the reason he started the journal. In all probability he kept it up for those 25 years because he found how useful it was. He discovered the benefits of writing.

Something should be said about Cramer's (2007) observation: "Thoreau who was neither a naturalist, philosopher, environmentalist, social reformer, nor Transcendentalist, but all of these at all times." If this is accurate, Thoreau was not unlike Leonardo Da Vinci in that both exemplified a generality of creative talents. This is worth noting because of the debate over the specificity and generality of creativity and talent (e.g., Baer, 1998; Plucker, 1998). Then again, it is likely that there are both commonalities and differences among domains. They may all show some generality and some specificity. This chapter describes writing as different from other domains because the symbol system is so extensive and well known that self-disclosure is easier than in other domains. A commonality among domains is discussed later in this chapter.

Thoreau's journals suggest another difference among domains. In particular, Thoreau hints at his *naturistic* inclinations (cf. Solomon, Powell, & Gardner, 1999). Consider in this regard the 1859 entry from the journal: "Why, the roots of letters are things. Natural objects and phenomena are the original symbols or types which express our thoughts and feelings, and yet American scholars, having little or no root in the soil, commonly strive with all their might to confine themselves to the imported symbols alone." Apparently Thoreau himself gave some thought to symbol systems and a great deal of thought to the natural world.

Many other writers have kept journals and propounded the benefits of written self-disclosure. These autobiographical reports are subjective and, from the experimental/scientific point of view, unreliable, but they are interesting and in some ways consistent with controlled studies. The research of Pennebaker, Kiecolt-Glaser, and Glaser (1997) is especially impressive, given its experimental controls and the use of blood tests (i.e., T-cells) before and after experiences keeping journals. Pennebaker et al. reported that immune systems are much more effective when people have regular opportunities for written self-disclosure.

One hypothesis to explain the benefits of writing involves adaptation. The idea here is that, by writing, individuals adapt to their hassles and problems. The writing allows adaptation and in fact is the adaptation. You may think that adaptation should occur without the writing, but often hassles and so on are not fully articulated; they are hazy and thus difficult to grasp in a fashion that allows adaptation. But if they are written, they are put into a form that can then be addressed and perhaps resolved. This makes perfect sense in the context of the creativity literature and in particular in the context of research on *problem finding*. Using those terms, written self-disclosure would also allow careful and detailed *problem identification* and *problem generation*, and when those are done well, problem solving is much easier (Runco, 1994).

This hypothesis about adaptation would explain why Piaget and many other creative persons have used writing as a means of exploring new ideas (Gruber, 1996). Writing is, for them, not just a recording of ideas; it is a way of interacting with ideas. As such, the ideas and thinking in general may change as the individual writes – as a direct result of the writing. That may involve a change in how the individual thinks about life or particular problems. It can be seen as a kind of adaptation.

Whorf (1956) suggested that we can only think about things if we have the language to label them. His opinion is an extreme one, with a particular direction of effect, from language to thinking. In a sense language is a constraint on thinking. An alternative, implied by constructivist cognitive theories such as Piaget's (1970), is that language is dependent on thinking, rather than the other (Whorfian) way around. This would explain why you do not hear many young children talking about hypothetical and remote things. Children think about the immediate environment and concrete things (Piaget, 1970). Because they think only about concrete things, they can only talk about concrete things.

There may be no need to choose between these two extreme views. A bi-directional interplay between language and thinking is entirely consistent with the view outlined here, that written self-disclosure allows adaptation. Individuals might, then, develop new ideas while writing, as Piaget did (Gruber, 1996), or they might simply capture their thoughts in the writing. It is even possible that Piaget's definition of adaptation can be applied here in that writing puts the individual in control of experience. That is entirely consistent with what Piaget labeled assimilation and described as the first stage of adaptation. The second stage, accommodation, is also likely, at least if the individual's thinking does in fact change as a result of the writing.

These speculations and the larger literature on writing and health are especially intriguing because of the widely recognized association between psychopathology and creativity. Not surprisingly, many of the seminal studies on that topic involved writers (Andreasen, 1987; Barron, 1968; Jamison, 1989; Ludwig, 1998).

Writing may very well provide creators with something that is not provided by other domains. Alternatively, writing may provide more of the benefit than those other domains. One way to describe writing's unique advantage and benefit is in terms of the amount of detail and exploration allowed by writing. Surely a choreographer can read a great deal into a long dance, and an artist can read huge amounts into a painting. Both of these media, as well as all media that allow creative work, provide extensive information to those who look for and can interpret it. Some of it may be symbolic, and some of it presymbolic, affective, and aesthetic. But consider how long it takes to read a novel, how much ground is covered, how much information can be conveyed. It is quite possible that there is more information there than in, say, one painting or one dance, and therefore more potential for catharsis, exploration, and self-disclosure. Then again, although paintings are static, there is perspective, texture, shade, and so on in the medium, and the artist can use each element. There is also the content of the particular artwork.

Writing may have an advantage over the other domains and media used in creative efforts because it allows labeling, and thereby unambiguous problem identification. Surely dancers and choreographers and all other creative individuals feel their work, even if they are not using language. All domains have symbol systems. But with language, a problem, concern, or idea can have a clear-cut label. (For instance, "I have a problem; I call it 'mother in law.'") Other domains may allow creative people to feel their problems and even manipulate them, but none, save perhaps mathematics, allows such an unambiguous labeling. The assumption here is that labeling a problem is useful. At least the problem would no longer be free-floating. It can be categorized and processed more easily, once labeled. However, this is speculative, and contrasting writing with the other domains and media might be comparing apples and bananas, as one of my Norwegian students once put it.

WHO IS CREATIVE?

What about comparisons within the domain of writing? Who is a creative writer? The easy answer is that fiction is highly creative because it is less connected to reality than is, say, journalism or science writing. It might be best to use a continuum, however, with highly imaginary writings (fantasy, if you will) at one extreme and factual records at the other, and a range of variations between the two. After all, writers often write about what they know and often draw from experience; fiction can be an interpretation of and based on reality. Then there are the historical novels that take the basics from archives and similar records but fill in the blanks to make a good story.

This continuum might imply that writers of facts are the least creative and writers of fantasy are the most creative. Yet in one very important sense *every writer is creative*. Every writer interprets information in a constructive fashion. No writer simply finds sentences waiting to be transcribed onto his or her word processor, and individuals who merely copy something are not really writing – they are transcribing. If any composition is involved, any interpretation at all, there is room for creativity, and in fact a need for it. Chomsky (2006) was correct that language is necessarily creative, although he may have meant this primarily in the sense of generative grammar, which is a bit different from my proposal about the construction of meaning. The creative process sometimes works on a preverbal level (Tweney, 1996), so it is not just composition in the grammatical sense that allows creative thinking.

This perspective of writing is based on the notion of the theory of *personal creativity*, which is made up of (a) the original interpretation of experience, (b) ego strength, (c) discretion, and (d) intentions and interest (Runco, 1996). The last of these elements is the driving force behind creativity. This force is often intrinsic motivation, although extrinsic factors sometimes play a role as well (Eisenberger & Shanock, 2003), and sometimes creative interpretations are constructed because of a combination of intrinsic and extrinsic motivation. In any case, effort is not expended unless there is some drive. Discretion is also required because creative work requires both originality and effectiveness (Cropley, 1967; Runco & Charles, 1993), and the individual often needs to find the right balance of the two. Originality is absolutely necessary for creative thinking; it is always acknowledged in theories of creativity (Rothenberg & Hausman, 1976; Runco, 1988), but if it operates in isolation the result is more likely to be psychotic and entirely unrealistic instead of creative and meaningful. Creative persons have the potential to construct original interpretations of their experience, but they also have the discretion to know when to do so and when not to, as well as the discretion to find an effective balance of originality and fit.

This suggests yet another idiosyncratic feature and potentially unique benefit of writing: More than other symbol systems and domains, it may allow the creator to find the right balance between originality and fit. It may also offer opportunities to develop a rationale for the original insights offered in the creative product. This possibility assumes that written products contain more information than other creative products, which is debatable, and of course it may not be sheer quantities that are important. Indeed, the arts may so often be wonderful because of the kind of information they stimulate and capture rather than the amount of information.

Some creators are apparently not all that good at finding a balance of originality and realism. This explains why creative persons are often deemed highly eccentric (Weeks & Ward, 1999) and contrarian (Runco, 1999), and some of them even spend time in jail (Brower, 1999; Eisenman, 1992) – and many of them deserve it. Some of these eccentricities, social surprises, and crimes may result from poor judgment and excessive originality. More accurately, they may result from the nonconformity, autonomy, and independence that are frequently helpful for original thinking. When unguarded, those things throw off the balance of originality and effectiveness. In many social contexts it is not good to follow an entirely original interpretation of laws and regulations. It is useful or even vital to do that in one's creative efforts, but not when conventionality is most adaptive and appropriate.

Originality may be intentionally exaggerated, with similar off-balance and uncreative results. Eccentricity and outrageous behavior are often salient and tend to demand attention; they are thereby reinforced and the individual may behave in that fashion to an increased degree as time passes. They may even exaggerate their nonconformity and independence as part of *impression management* (Kasof, 1995) and to earn attributions and accolades of creative talent. Clearly they are not earning accolades because of true creativity but instead are just gaining attention because of their outrageous behavior, and any one labeling such behavior "creative" does not recognize the need for effectiveness and discretion.

Ego strength is involved in this process. This is a kind of self-confidence that allows personal originality to be expressed rather than inhibited. As noted earlier, originality is most likely when the individual is autonomous and unconventional, but pressure on that person is usually much greater to behave in a conventional fashion. Individuals may need to draw on their ego strength to resist social pressures to conform so they can think and act in an original and unconventional fashion. Balance and discretion are of course still involved, for otherwise the ego strength will lead to exaggerated and inappropriate originality.

The interesting thing here is that the cognitive aspect of personal creativity is the least important contribution to the process. The cognitive bases of creative thinking are, in this view, universal. We all have the potential to construct interpretations, and if we ourselves construct them, they are original. If they are effective and original, they are creative. This should not imply that all of our thinking is creative. Very frequently we draw on routine, assumption, and experience, in which case our thinking is not original or creative. We all have the potential to construct creative ideas, but very frequently we do not invest the time and effort but instead go through our days the same way we always have.

What is most important for the present purposes is that even writers of nonfiction are creative. Science writers – scientists simply writing up their ideas, theories, and empirical findings, for example – are creative in their writing (and often in their research as well) in the same manner as a writer of fiction. Both use interpretive and constructive processes. Only transcription, free of interpretation, is uncreative writing.

WRITING AS PRODUCT AND PROCESS

Creative studies are often divided into one of the following categories: person (or personality), product, place (or press), or process. Simonton (1995) added *persuasion*, the idea being that famous creators influence the way other people think, and Runco (2006) added *potential*, the rationale being that many of the contributions to creative achievement and productivity are overlooked without an examination of potential. I recently offered a modest update of the 4- and 5-P frameworks (Runco 2007, 2008). It puts the various perspectives into a hierarchy and recognized both creative potentials and performances.

Writing is best described as a process rather than a product, and it may be that very process that benefits the writer. The benefit may result from the self-discovery allowed by writing or the fact that writers must consider different options, find words, and think of various perspectives while writing. Recall here the hypothesis given earlier in this chapter about writing as *problem identification*. This does not mean that the product is unimportant. Writing may lead to an insight, for example, or a recognition of the source of anxiety. It may be that the writing leads to a nicely defined description of a problem, which can then be shared with others, for social support, or at least it can be better approached once it is clearly articulated.

As a matter of fact, there are several reasons to view the creative process and product as complementary. Most obvious here is that the process leads to products. These may be tangible products, such as inventions and publications and so on, each of which no doubt resulted from creative work and the use of some creative process. The process may also result in intangible products. Consider the process of divergent thinking (Runco, 1991). It is by no means synonymous with creative thinking; however, thinking divergently can lead to original ideas and as such may lead to creative insights and solutions. This process has a result – ideas and solutions. Those are products of the individual's thought.

Ideas may be personal, however, and not shared. Can they still be creative? They may be original and effective, so the answer is yes, they can be creative. The only thing that might keep them from being deemed creative is a social requirement. If creative things must change the way other people think or be judged by others to be creative, then personal ideas may not fit the bill. But that contention surely is just plain silly. In fact, it would confuse "creativity" with other things for which we already have names. If someone does something, creative or not, that other people notice, he or she will earn recognition and fame. Recognition and fame are, however, extricable from creative talent. Thus, if an idea is effective and original on a personal level, it is creative. If it also influences the way other people think, it has social impact.

There are several specific problems with any view of creative writing that emphasizes the product. Products are, for example, often misjudged. This is apparent in the *overestimation* of a literary work. Such overestimation occurs when an interpretation of a literary work "goes too far ... [and] an excess of wonder leads to overestimating the importance of coincidences which are explainable in other ways" (Eco, 1992, p. 50, quoted by Henrickson, 2003). It is similar to the problem that can be avoided by scientific parsimony. Sometimes authors do not mean much by particular expressions or passages, but readers and literary critics see a great deal in them. Eco (1992) claimed that eminent writers are often overestimated. He gave Shakespeare, Dante, Virgil, and Homer as examples.

Parker (1981, p. 182, quoted by Henrickson, 2003) also found overestimations in literature and felt they reflected "an overriding compulsion to make sense of the printed text at all costs." He also described how readers and critics frequently confused "non-meanings, partially authorial meanings, and inadvertent, intentionless meanings" with "genuine authorial meanings" (Parker, 1984, p. 10).

This issue is one part of a longstanding debate over "the text," the idea being that texts themselves may be meaningful independent of the intent of the author. The opposing view is that texts cannot be interpreted unless the author and his or her intent are taken into account. My feeling is that there is a parallel in studies of all creative products. Products often do not inform us about the process or the person, only about the product. There may be a large discrepancy, as is the case when critics see meaning in what was for the author meaningless or when an author makes a mistake but critics see it as intentional. In literary criticism this debate over the text is sometimes called the *intentionality fallacy.*

Overestimation may explain the *Matthew effect*. Henrickson (2003, p. 255) explained this very well:

> A second reason for the tendency to sacralize the works of canonical authors, regardless of their merit, may be the Matthew effect. First identified by Merton (1968), the Matthew effect is named for a passage from the Gospel According to St. Matthew: "For unto every one that hath shall be given, and he shall have abundance: but from him that hath not shall be taken away even that which he hath"... As Merton (1968) rephrased the passage, "the Matthew effect consists in the accruing of greater increments of recognition for particular scientific contributions to scientists of considerable repute and the withholding of such recognition from scientists who have not yet made their mark" (p. 3). If we replace "scientists" with "canonical authors" and "scientific contributions" with "literary works," we have, mutatis mutandis, a Matthew effect for literature.

Henrickson (2003) gave two useful examples. One involved Mark Twain and the aphorism, "It is better to be thought a fool than to open your mouth and prove it." Many people attribute that to Twain and others to Lincoln. Henrickson (2003) found it, with biblical phrasing, in Proverbs! The other example is the oft-cited expression, "If I have seen further, it is because I have stood on the shoulders of giants," which is almost always attributed to Isaac Newton. According to Henrickson (2003), this expression was "traced first to Didacu Stella, but finally attributed to Bernard of Chartres, who got it... from Priscian. Insofar as a common enough phrase was popularly attributed to Newton, this is another example of the Matthew effect, that is, if he said one thing well, he must have said every well-said thing."

Verbal products, be they novels or short aphorisms, are easily misjudged. Such misjudgment and misinterpretation may not be all that surprising because such highly subjective processes are involved. Additionally, judgments are often offered by experts, and experts have such large investments that certain biases are likely. The problem of most relevance to the present discussion is that aphorisms, phrases, and even full texts may not be indicative of the author's intent or meaning. In that light such products are not the best indicator of the author's creative talent.

CONCLUSION

Writers sometimes have, like other creative individuals, contradictory personalities. These may reflect their complicated lives and as such be a direct result of their preference for complexity. They like the complications and complexity and allow them or seek them out, perhaps thinking that they stimulate their thinking or benefit their writing. The complexities provide a kind of *eustress* (Skinner, 1983). Yet the appreciation of complexity may depend on the adaptability of writers and on the process of writing. That process may provide them with an outlet and an opportunity to explore issues and concerns. Using the concepts *problem identification* and *problem definition* from creative studies, it may provide them with opportunities to conceptualize and to clearly identify and define problems and concerns. (There is no doubt a clear benefit when ambiguous concerns and problems are conceptualized and articulated.)

Writing may have an advantage over simply thinking things through because it is easier to review one's ideas when they are in print. In fact, just getting it in print (which is, after all, the writing process) exercises one's thinking and creativity and requires that ideas be structured and communicable. Lyubomirsky, Sousa, and Dickerhoof (2006) reported that writing does indeed have a benefit over merely thinking things through. They also found that the benefits occur when individuals write about negative rather than positive experiences. Perhaps *catharsis* is, then, also a factor, at least some of the time. Catharsis occurs when psychic tension is relieved though self-expression. Csikszentmihalyi (1988) was specific about this in his definition of *cathartic originality* as apparent when artwork reflects current discomforts. The hypotheses presented earlier in this chapter about the benefits of articulating one's own thinking fits into this line of thought because artists may not be aware of what is troubling them (Jones, Runco, Dorinan, & Freeland, 1997). Csikszentmihalyi (1988) put it this way:

> The impressions artists work with come from many sources. One that is very prevalent among contemporary painters contains memories of childhood. Whether the viewer realizes it or not, and often also unbeknown to the artist, the images that form the core of a great number of modern works represent the rage or the ecstasy of childhood which the artist tries to recapture in order to integrate it into current experience.... Such works occasionally achieve a magical synthesis of past and present, an abolition of objective time, a healing through the reactivation of former pain which can now be tolerate by the mature person. We might call such an achievement "abreactive originality," borrowing a term from psychoanalysis to describe the successful release of psychic tension through the symbolic reordering of repressed traumatic experiences. (p. 219)

Cathartic originality is suggested by Lindauer's (1992) descriptions of the stylistic changes of aging artists. Lindauer described how these changes allow the artist to compensate for emotional, physical, and sensory disabilities that develop as one grows old. He gave several examples of artists who changed their style as a "result of personal conflicts in late life" and added,

> In literature... authors are said to change when they are able to accommodate to life's new demands.... Wordsworth, for example, was unable to shift from the spontaneousness of his youth... to philosophical and contemplative reactions more appropriate to later life.... Shakespeare, on the other hand, met aging's new requirements by shifting from works of history and comedy to tragedy. (p. 219)

Much of this is consistent with research on music therapy showing that the benefits of "making music" reflect the process of "conceptualizing one's symptoms into sounds" (McClary, 2007, p. 155). It is also consistent with another hypothesis given earlier in this chapter about adaptation. In fact, adaptation is very frequently tied to creative work (Cohen, 1989; Richards, 1990; Runco, 1994). Put simply, the hypothesis offered here is that writing allows a particular kind of adaptation.

Adaptation and creativity are not synonymous. An individual may adapt to a social pressure by conforming, for instance, in which case there is no creativity. Of course, writers tend to work alone. They need not, then, take into account social pressures, as they would if they were working in groups or a more social setting. This suggests yet another potential benefit to writing – there is great freedom from social expectations and pressures while exploring and articulating one's thinking – but there is also a downside. As Kaun (1991) noted, professional writers often experience long delays in gratification and in fact are eventually opening themselves up to literary criticism. If they have written about something that is truly and personally meaningful, which certainly describes self-disclosure, that criticism may hurt deeply. Kaun also described problems with working alone when writing.

Many empirical questions remain. Several of the claims made in this chapter were described as "hypotheses" for that reason. They are not entirely unjustified and speculative. This chapter shows their rationale and how they fit with previous research. Given the potential benefits of writing for our psychological and physical health, they are hypotheses that should indeed be tested with sound empirical research.

REFERENCES

Albert, R. S. (1996). What the study of eminence can teach us. *Creativity Research Journal, 9,* 307–315.

Andreasen, N. C. (1987). Creativity and mental illness: Prevalence rates in writers and their first-degree relatives. *American Journal of Psychiatry, 144,* 1288–1292.

Baer, J. (1998). The case for domain specificity of creativity. *Creativity Research Journal, 11,* 173–178.

Barron, F. (1963). The needs for order and for disorder as motives in creative activity. In C. W. Taylor & F. Barron (Eds.), *Scientific creativity: Its recognition and development* (pp. 153–160). New York: Wiley.

Barron, F. (1968). *Creativity and personal freedom.* New York: Van Nostrand.

Barron, F. (1995). *No rootless flower: An ecology of creativity.* Cresskill, NJ: Hampton Press.

Brower, R. (1999). Dangerous minds: Eminently creative people who spent time in jail. *Creativity Research Journal, 12,* 3–13.

Chomsky, N. (2006). *Language and mind* (3rd ed.). Cambridge, MA: Cambridge University Press.

Cohen, L. M. (1989). A continuum of adaptive creative behaviors. *Creativity Research Journal, 2,* 169–183.

Cramer, J. S. (2007). *I to myself: An annotated selection from the journal of Henry David Thoreau.* New Haven: Yale University Press.

Cropley, A. J. (1967). *Creativity.* London: Longmans, Green.

Csikszentmihalyi, M. (1988). The dangers of originality: Creativity and the artistic process. In M. M. Gedo (Ed.), *Psychoanalytic perspectives on art* (pp. 213–224). Hillsdale, NJ: Analytic Press.

Csikszentmihalyi, M. (1990). The domain of creativity. In M. A. Runco & R. S. Albert (Eds.), *Theories of creativity* (pp. 190–212). Newbury Park, CA: Sage.

Csikszentmihalyi, M. (1996). *Creativity: Flow and the psychology of discovery and invention.* New York: HarperCollins.

Eco, U. (1992). Overinterpreting texts. In U. Eco (Ed.), *Interpretation and Overinterpretation* (pp. 45–67). New York, NY: Cambridge University Press.

Eisenberger, R., & Shanock, L. (2003). Rewards, intrinsic motivation, and creativity: A case study of conceptual and methodological isolation. *Creativity Research Journal, 15*, 121–130.

Eisenman, R. (1992). Creativity in prisoners: Conduct disorders and psychotics. *Creativity Research Journal, 5*, 175–181.

Gruber, H. E. (1988). The evolving systems approach to creative work. *Creativity Research Journal, 1*, 27–51.

Gruber, H. E. (1996). The life space of a scientist: The visionary function and other aspects of Jean Piaget's thinking. *Creativity Research Journal, 9*, 251–265.

Harrington, D. M., & Anderson, S. M. (1981). Creativity, masculinity, femininity, and three models of psychological androgyny. *Journal of Personality and Social Psychology, 41*, 744–757.

Henrickson, G. P. (2003). Mark Twain, criticism, and the limits of creativity. *Creativity Research Journal, 15* (2/3), 253–260.

Ippolito, M., & Tweney, R. (2003). Virginia Woolf and the journey to Jacob's Room: The "network of enterprise" of Virginia Woolf's first experimental novel. *Creativity Research Journal, 15*, 25–43.

Jamison, K. R. (1989). Mood disorders and patterns of creativity in British writers and artists. *Psychiatry, 52*, 125–134.

Jones, K., Runco, M. A., Dorinan, C., & Freeland, D. C. (1997). Influential factors in artists' lives and themes in their art work. *Creativity Research Journal, 10*, 221–228.

Kasof, J. (1995). Explaining creativity: The attributional perspective. *Creativity Research Journal, 8*, 311–366.

Kaun, D. E. (1991). Writers die young: The impact of work and leisure on longevity. *Journal of Economic Psychology, 12*, 381–399.

Lindauer, M. S. (1992). Creativity in aging artists: Contributions from the humanities to the psychology of aging. *Creativity Research Journal, 5*, 211–232.

Ludwig, A. (1998). Method and madness in the arts and sciences. *Creativity Research Journal, 11*, 93–101.

Lyubomirsky, S., Sousa, L., & Dickerhoof, R. (2006). The costs and benefits of writing, talking, and thinking about life's triumphs and defeats. *Journal of Personality and Social Psychology, 90*, 692–708.

McClary, R. (2007). Healing the psyche through music, myth, and ritual. *Psychology of Aesthetics, Creativity, and the Arts, 1*, 155–159.

Merton, R. K. (1968). The Matthew effect in science. *Science, 159*, 1–8.

Parker, H. (1981). The "new scholarship": Textual evidence and its implications for criticism, literary theory, and aesthetics. *Studies in American Fiction, 9*, 181–197.

Parker, H. (1984). *Flawed texts and verbal icons: Literary authority in American fiction.* Evanston, IL: Northwestern University Press.

Pennebaker, J. W., Kiecolt-Glaser, J. K., & Glaser, R. (1997). Disclosure of traumas and immune function: Health implications for psychotherapy. In M. A. Runco & R. Richards (Eds.), *Eminent creativity, everyday creativity, and health* (pp. 287–302). Norwood, NJ: Ablex.

Piaget, J. (1970). Piaget's theory. In P. H. Mussen (Ed.), *Carmichael's handbook of child psychology* (3rd ed., pp. 703–732). New York: Wiley.

Plucker, J. A. (1998). Beware of simple conclusions: The case for content generality of creativity. *Creativity Research Journal, 11,* 179–182.

Reynolds, S. S. (2007a, April 15). Kinfolks: Falling off the family tree. *Los Angeles Times Review of Books.*

Reynolds, S. S. (2007b, October 7). Review of J. S. Cramers's *Annotated Journal of Henry David Thoreau* (Yale University Press). *Los Angeles Times Review of Books.*

Richards, R. (1990). Everyday creativity, eminent creativity, and health: "Afterview" for Creativity Research Journal issues on creativity and health. *Creativity Research Journal, 3*(4), 300–326.

Rothenberg, A. (1990). Creativity, mental health, and alcoholism. *Creativity Research Journal, 3,* 179–201.

Rothenberg, A., & Hausman, C. R. (Eds.) (1976). *The creativity question* (pp. 86–92). Durham, NC: Duke University Press.

Runco, M. A. (1988). Creativity research: Originality, utility, and integration. *Creativity Research Journal, 1,* 1–7.

Runco, M. A. (Ed.). (1991). *Divergent thinking.* Norwood, NJ: Ablex.

Runco, M. A. (1994). Creativity and its discontents. In M. P. Shaw & M. A. Runco (Eds.), *Creativity and affect* (pp. 102–123). Norwood, NJ: Ablex.

Runco, M. A. (1996). Personal creativity: Definition and developmental issues. *New Directions for Child Development, 72* (Summer), 3–30.

Runco, M. A. (1998). Suicide and creativity: The case of Sylvia Plath. *Death Studies, 22,* 637–654.

Runco, M. A. (1999). Contrarianism. In M. A. Runco & S. Pritzker (Eds.), *Encyclopedia of Creativity* (pp. 367–371). San Diego, CA: Academic Press.

Runco, M. A. (2006). Creativity is always personal and only sometimes social. In J. Schaler (Ed.), *Howard Gardner under fire: The rebel psychologist faces his critics* (pp. 169–182). Chicago: Open Court Publishers.

Runco, M. A. (2007). Creativity and education. *New Horizons in Education,* May, 96–104.

Runco, M. A. (2008). A hierarchical framework for the study of creativity. *New Horizons in Education* [www.scpe.ied.edu.hk/newhorizon].

Runco, M. A., & Charles, R. (1993). Judgments of originality and appropriateness as predictors of creativity. *Personality and Individual Differences, 15,* 537–546.

Runco, M. A., & Okuda Sakamoto, S. (1993). Reaching creatively gifted children through their learning styles. In R. M. Milgram, R. Dunn, & G. E. Price (Eds.), *Teaching and counseling gifted and talented adolescents: An international learning style perspective* (pp. 103–115). New York: Praeger.

Sigelman, C., & Rider, E. (2008). *Lifespan human development* (6th ed.). New York: Wadsworth.

Simonton, D. K. (1995). Exceptional personal influence: An integrative paradigm. *Creativity Research Journal, 8,* 371–376.

Skinner, B. F. (1983). Intellectual self-management in old age. *American Psychologist, 38,* 239–244.

Smith, W. (2007, April 15). Review of Stubbs' *John Donne: Reformed soul*. *Los Angeles Times Review of Books*.

Solomon, B., Powell, K., & Gardner, H. (1999). Multiple intelligences. In M. A. Runco & S. Pritzker (Eds.), *Encyclopedia of creativity* (pp. 259–273). San Diego, CA: Academic.

Stubbs, J. (2007). *John Donne: The reformed soul*. New York: W.W. Norton.

Tweney, R. D. (1996). Presymbolic processes in scientific creativity. *Creativity Research Journal, 9*, 163–172.

Weeks, D. J., & Ward, K. (1988). *Eccentrics: The scientific investigation*. Stirling: Stirling University Press.

Weeks, D. J., & Ward, K. (1999). Eccentricity. In M. A. Runco & S. Pritzker (Eds.), *Encyclopedia of Creativity* (pp. 613–621). San Diego, CA: Academic Press.

Whorf, B. (1956). *Language, thought, and reality*. Cambridge, MA: MIT Press.

12

Creative Cognition in Science Fiction
and Fantasy Writing

THOMAS B. WARD AND E. THOMAS LAWSON

Creative writing is a multifaceted endeavor requiring verbal skills, extensive content knowledge, and the motivation to persist in spite of obstacles. In this chapter we focus particularly on creative writing in the form of science fiction and fantasy. We begin with a presentation of a particular view of creativity, namely the creative cognition approach that emphasizes knowledge and how it is used. We then consider ways in which access to that knowledge can, on the negative side, *limit* and, on the positive side, *guide* the originality and believability of new stories that authors generate. Along the way, we also make suggestions about ways in which novice and experienced writers can produce texts that are more engaging as well as informative and compelling.

CREATIVE COGNITION

Creative cognition is an approach to understanding and fostering creativity that focuses on fundamental cognitive processes, such as retrieval, conceptual combination, and analogical mapping, and on the conceptual structures on which those processes operate to yield novel and appropriate ideas (Finke, Ward, & Smith, 1992; Ward, Smith, & Finke, 1999). Its goal is to provide a rich theoretical account of the factors that underlie the production of new thoughts; that is, the mental representations that are the raw materials of creativity in all its forms, ranging from the most mundane to the most exalted.

The creative cognition approach recognizes that conceptual structures are developed and that cognitive processes operate within a broader context of individual differences, developmental trends, and environmental influences, among other factors. There are variations in the extent to which individuals have acquired broad, domain-general knowledge about the workings of the world, as well as more specific knowledge regarding the content domains within which they might make creative contributions (e.g., Amabile, 1982, 1983; Csikszentmihalyi, 1999; Lubart & Sternberg, 1995; Sternberg & Lubart, 1995). The creative cognition approach also recognizes that differences in knowledge may be qualitative rather than merely quantitative, as when experts develop both more abstract (Chi, Glaser, & Rees, 1982) and more specific (Johnson & Mervis, 1997; Tanaka & Taylor, 1991) domain representations, and that those differences can affect the originality and practicality of newly developed ideas (Ward, 2008). Similarly, individuals differ in their ability or propensity to use both domain-general or domain-specific skills, as well as in their intrinsic motivation to do so, their openness to new experiences that might interact with their current knowledge, their perseverance in the face of obstacles, and so on (Amabile, 1982, 1983; Csikszentmihalyi, 1999; Sternberg & Lubart, 1995).

For the purposes of this chapter, we concentrate almost exclusively on conceptual structures and processes as the sources of the novel ideas that are essential to creative writing. Rather than focusing at the level of interacting systems as in confluence models of creativity (e.g., Amabile, 1983; Csikszentmihalyi, 1999; Sternberg & Lubart, 1995), we illustrate how a set of cognitive operations that are, in principle, available to most adults interact with stored concepts to produce ideas that vary in their creative potential and ultimately yield creative products in the form of science fiction and fantasy stories.

To show how people can employ basic cognitive processes in their own creative writing, we use the Geneplore model (Finke et al., 1992; Ward et al., 1999), a specific instantiation of the creative cognition approach, as an organizing framework. This model characterizes creative outcomes as resulting from two interacting phases of thought: a generative phase and an exploratory phase. In the generative phase, candidate ideas are produced that carry some level of creative potential, but are not in themselves considered to be creative products. These ideas are referred to as *preinventive* to capture this notion that they are neither creative nor uncreative in themselves. To the extent that preinventive ideas are recognized by the creative person as having potential, that person might then engage in subsequent exploratory processing to develop that potential into something that could be recognized as a creative product (e.g., a short story). Importantly, the creative process is not viewed as a simple, two-step process with one generative phase and one exploratory phase. Rather, creative endeavors of any magnitude can, and most often do, involve a continual cycle of interacting generative and exploratory phases. As we describe more fully in subsequent sections, it is the recursive nature of the generate–explore process that results in large-scale creative products.

RETRIEVING KNOWLEDGE AT MULTIPLE LEVELS OF ABSTRACTION

A fundamental process that plays a key role in creative writing is the deceptively simple one of retrieval. Paradoxically, *new ideas* have their roots in *existing knowledge*. When a science fiction author dreams up a new alien species, for example, he or she undoubtedly accesses knowledge about real living things or fictional ones encountered in reading the works of other authors. This access to knowledge could occur at many levels of abstraction, from highly specific details and facts about a given animal to very general biological principles. It could take the form of retrieving specific instances of known Earth animals (e.g., birds or dolphins), specific aliens developed by the same or other authors, more general known principles that characterize existing life forms, as well as other aspects of knowledge at intermediate levels of abstraction. The retrieved knowledge serves to guide the development of the new ideas. In this section, we show how the *level* at which an author accesses knowledge can have an effect on both the perceived originality and the believability of the new creation.

A psychological phenomenon that seems to govern the retrieval and use of existing knowledge is the *path-of-least-resistance* (Ward, 1994; Ward, Patterson, Sifonis, Dodds, & Saunders, 2002). As originally conceived, the path-of-least-resistance refers to the tendency of individuals to retrieve and use highly specific, *basic-level* instances of stored concepts when they create novel ideas within conceptual domains. In laboratory studies, for example, the predominant tendency, shown by about two-thirds of all participants, is to retrieve specific animals (e.g., elephants) and use them as a starting point when given the task of imagining alien life forms. The same tendency applies to other conceptual domains, as when people retrieve oranges and apples to form the basis of imaginary fruit, and hammers and screwdrivers to serve as models for imaginary tools (Ward et al., 2002).

Science fiction authors are not immune to the tendency to rely on Earth animals, as evidenced by the fact that content analyses of their creations reveal striking similarities to the properties of typical animals, including bilateral symmetry and the presence of legs and eyes, with the latter often represented symmetrically in heads at the tops of bodies (Ward, 1994). Indeed, a complaint about much of science fiction is that many of the fictional creatures that exist on imagined worlds quite different from Earth, which could take on a range of wildly different forms, are nevertheless copies of Earth animals with minor modifications (Barlowe & Summers, 1979; Martin, 1976; Ochoa & Osier, 1993).

In laboratory studies, there is also a strong tendency to use humans as the base for alien creatures, especially when the creatures are described as being intelligent and capable of space travel (Ward, Dodds, Saunder, & Sifonis, 2000; Ward et al., 2002). Again this tendency is prevalent in the science fiction literature and has provoked considerable criticism for its evident lack of imagination. In noting that creatures that have evolved on other planets are unlikely to resemble humans, Ochoa and Osier (1993) went on to state that "slapping a few warts on a human will not help" (p. 161) make the creature seems more original or imaginative. Martin (1976), a notable science fiction author in his own right, went as far as to say that if an author did not make a creature substantially different from humans, he or she might just as well make them identical to humans.

There are several means of escaping from the limiting influences of the path-of-least-resistance, and indeed the best science fiction writers are undoubtedly adept at accessing and deploying their knowledge in these ways (Lawson, 2007; Ward, Finke, & Smith; 1995, chapter 7). One technique that can be used in the service of devising more unusual alien creatures is to adopt an analytic approach to one's knowledge and consider the more abstract properties shared by a wide range of organisms. This approach is expressed in Ochoa and Osier's (1993) "Alien-Builder's Workshop" that lists general properties of life forms on Earth, such as bilateral symmetry, cephalization, sense organs, and movement, and asks would-be writers to consider whether those properties are necessary and whether and in what ways they could be varied. By deliberately bringing such properties to mind, an author can avoid inadvertently including properties (e.g., two eyes located symmetrically in the head at the top of a bipedal body that is taller than it is wide) that may limit the perceived originality of the alien species.

In effect, one might produce creatures that have *alignable differences* (see, e.g., Markman & Gentner, 1993) between those novel entities and Earth creatures. An alignable difference is a difference based on an underlying commonality (e.g., cars and motorcycles share the commonality of wheels but have the alignable difference of four versus two wheels). An example of this type of generation of alignable differences that illustrates this point is present in Nancy Kress's *Probability* trilogy. In that series, humans encounter an alien species that bears both similarities and differences to humans. Like humans, they possess brains and, as on Earth, their brains have been shaped by evolutionary pressures. Thus, there are common properties present and common abstract shaping principles at work. However, because the specific evolutionary pressures differ from those on Earth, the key properties of the creatures' brains also differ. Rather than the more isolated and individualized nature of human minds, this novel species experiences a "shared reality," which involves living according to a strict set of common norms. A physiological mechanism leads to head pain in any who transgress against those norms.

Another approach that allows science fiction authors to avoid the limitations imposed by the path of least-resistance is world-building, in which the author first mentally crafts a world that operates according to a particular set of principles, and then considers what properties would be true of species that populate that world (see, e.g., Clement, 1991). To the extent that the properties of the envisioned world differ from those of Earth, the features of the aliens who live their will also differ. An example of such creatures is Clement's Mesklinite, which has 36 legs, is built low to the ground, and has an extreme fear of falling. Clement designed this creature with a particular planet already in mind, one that rotates rapidly and has flattened to the shape of a disk such that gravity varies greatly from the poles to the equator.

Laboratory studies have, in fact, shown that encouraging people to think more abstractly can lead them to develop imaginary aliens that are rated as more original than those produced by people encouraged to use specific animals as a starting point or who are given no special instructions (Ward, Patterson, & Sifonis, 2004). An important feature of that study is that the participants were an unselected group of individuals from introductory psychology classes rather than experienced fiction writers. Thus, even relative writing novices can at least generate preliminary ideas for science fiction aliens that show increased originality when they access their knowledge at more abstract levels.

In a general sense, good science fiction writers regularly rely on abstract principles from the sciences, including physics, biology, and psychology, in crafting their stories. To use just one favorite example, in the *Probability* trilogy mentioned previously, Nancy Kress made use of quantum entanglement, but extended it to macro-level object entanglement in describing the operation of space tunnels that allow near-instantaneous travel around the galaxy.

Because many science fiction readers are scientifically literate, it is important that writers who employ the world-building and abstract principles approaches possess and use an accurate understanding of the relevant scientific principles. If they stretch the principles beyond accepted views in the sciences to introduce originality into the mix, it is incumbent on them to explain those variations in a way that scientifically educated readers would find believable. Readers naturally build mental models based on the narrative, and if the mental model provided by the author does not fit with a plausible interpretation of scientific theory and fact, the result will be jarring.

Interestingly, however, many science fiction readers may not have a clear understanding of the scientific principles at work. Rather, they may possess what can be called folk or intuitive theories about the workings of the world, including folk understandings of biology, physics, and psychology. Those theories guide not only their expectations in interacting with the real world but also their expectations in reading and appreciating fiction, including science fiction. Complicating a science fiction writer's task is that those theories may not always correspond to scientific theories. In fact, they often do not. Consequently, in addition to creating plausible scenarios for learned readers, writers may also need to educate less scientifically literate readers about the scientific principles at work in their stories while at the same time entertaining them without appearing pedantic.

Beyond any scientific principles however, science fiction stories have appeal largely because they deal with issues of human concern, such as desires, goals, conflicts between good and evil, moral dilemmas and interpersonal relationships. Again the *Probability* trilogy provides an example, in that the humans must get their hands on a potentially hugely destructive weapon to keep it from the xenophobic, hostile Fallers who would use it for harmful purposes. But extracting the device from beneath the planet would destroy the mechanism underlying the "shared reality" of another peaceful species, thus causing them great, irreparable harm. The moral dilemma of whether doing harm to one group in the service of preventing greater harm is justifiable creates a meaningful issue that can be considered in the context of the exotic, imagined world of the story.

One final means of introducing more originality or novelty does not involve abstraction at all. Rather it is a deliberate attempt to retrieve specific concept instances that are known to the writer but are less readily accessible than more typical ones, or to learn about and use more unusual specific instances. The world is full of wildly exotic creatures, such as those that have been discovered living near the thermal vents deep in the ocean. Rather than stopping retrieval when one has thought of a highly accessible animal, such as a dog, one could work harder at retrieving such unusual instances and use them as starting points or models for an alien species. Although the novel creature would still be based on existing knowledge, its properties would necessarily deviate in interesting ways from those of typical Earth animals.

Fitting in with existing knowledge implies that science fiction writers need to operate under some constraints tied to known physical reality. But what of fantasy writers who might be seen as free to create any sort of world free of any constraints? Although it seems intuitively reasonable that constraints may not play a constructive role in fantasy, a little reflection reveals that they can lead to fantasy stories with greater interest value. To understand this point consider "the cost of magic," a constraint that Orson Scott Card argues for. If using magic has no costs associated with it, then the "good guys" can always escape readily from any bad circumstance with no evident negative consequences and there is limited tension in the story. For example, if Frodo could have used the power of the ring at any point without the risk of being corrupted by it, then he and his companions could have easily escaped any bad situation, and *The Lord of the Rings* would not have been the gripping tale that it was. Thus constraints, particularly when they link to dilemmas of concern to humans, can serve a critical role in fantasy writing.

A ROLE FOR SPECIFICITY

Although we have stressed the role of abstraction and access to more unusual instances as means of escaping the path-of-least-resistance, we should also note that guidance by typical specific instances can also have value. An important reason for this is that readers will have their own paths-of-least-resistance (Lawson, 2007). They will expect that the creatures about which they are reading and the world they inhabit will conform to properties and principles they understand. If a writer moves too far beyond that path, there is a risk that readers will not comprehend or will reject the ideas as not fitting in with their own knowledge and expectations.

There is evidence that relying on specific known instances of concepts can result in greater practicality or believability of the idea being generated. When people were asked to design new sports, for example, those who relied on specific known ones (e.g., basketball) came up with products that were rated as less original than those developed by people who accessed more abstract forms of knowledge, but their designs were also rated as more playable (Ward, 2008). Something about the structure of the specific idea they retrieved helped them stay within the bounds that were recognized by raters as being practical.

The work on novel sports highlights another sense in which the path-of-least-resistance affects creative writing. In contrast to an idea for a novel alien or a novel world, around which an entire story might be built, a novel sport might be seen as a specific activity that would take place within a world. That is, having decided to craft a story about a group inhabiting a particular "world," one must do the hard work of envisioning the ways in which those individuals act and the day-to-day events they experience; in short, the detailed particulars that bring the world to life in the minds of readers.

The stunningly successful *Harry Potter* series by J. K. Rowling provides a multitude of examples of building in details to make a world come alive. One example is that, in spite of being a school of witchcraft and wizardry, Hogwarts is nevertheless a boarding school somewhere in England. As such, it is reasonable to suppose that its students would engage in athletic activities, and her invention of the sport of quidditch fulfilled that purpose. It is not clear whether Rowling developed the sport by retrieving and relying on properties of specific known sports, by considering more abstract principles shared across sports, or by envisioning an activity that would make sense in that particular world. However, quidditch is interesting in that it bears some similarities to known sports, such as soccer and basketball, in which two teams of the same size compete for possession of balls that must be propelled through goals or hoops guarded by a keeper. Yet, there are also major differences, such as participants flying on brooms and the presence of not one, but three types of "balls" that play different roles in the game.

Taken out of the context of the magical world of Hogwarts, quidditch would almost certainly be rated as not particularly playable. Constrained by gravity, Earth sports are, of course, played on some type of surface, not up in the air. People do not have ready access to flying brooms, and thankfully, balls do not have minds of their own and attempt to collide with players. Nevertheless, the sport works beautifully within the world Rowling so intricately created. By putting the needed pieces in place throughout the book, she guided readers down a path that made this exotic athletic activity perfectly reasonable.

So, one way to devise stories that are both original and believable at the same time is to carefully adhere to principles that readers will know to be true and will expect to find. As noted earlier, for principles that are inordinately complex or outside the experience of readers, it is important to subtly guide them by granting them at least enough understanding so that they are not distracted by trying to figure out how something could work that way. For principles that violate existing knowledge or expectation, much hand-holding may be needed to craft a world in which those counterfactual possibilities can become realities.

THE PATH-OF-LEAST-RESISTANCE IN CRAFTING SENTENCES

In developing ideas for stories and in developing scenes and chapters within the framework of a larger story, the writer clearly accesses knowledge. And it is clear that what is retrieved influences the perceived originality and believability of the story and its scenes. But this same type of structuring by ordinary retrieval processes undoubtedly comes into play in the construction of individual sentences. Just as dogs, oranges, and hammers are highly accessible instances of the categories of animals, fruit, and tools, respectively and are likely to come to mind when an individual tries to envision imaginary instances of those categories, so too are there highly accessible instances of verbs to express action, adjectives to express qualities, and adverbs to express manner. For example, in retrieving words that express the concept of moving via leg power, it is likely that *walk* and *run* are more readily accessible than *stroll* and *jog*, which in turn are more accessible than *saunter* or *amble*. Whether or not this ordering reflects the exact pattern of accessibility of such words for any given individual, the point is that some words that are exemplars of the broader concept will come to mind more readily and they will likely be the more common and potentially less expressive instances. The same applies to adjectives (e.g., big or huge versus gargantuan, behemothic, or elephantine) and adverbs (e.g., slowly versus languorously). Aside from the fact that they are more engaging items to which readers are not yet habituated, the less accessible instances tend to carry more specific meanings, allowing for the creation of more precise mental images in the mind of the reader.

An interesting facet of considering the retrieval process at the level of individual sentences is that it illustrates the utility of both more abstract and more specific aspects of retrieval. Considering the more abstract level first, any given sentence is part of a broader effort to convey a thought or create a scene. Thus, the individual words that are chosen must advance that theme. Without the bigger picture in mind, the specific instances that are used could end up being either uninspiring at best or jarring and disruptive at worst. At the same time, the words that do carry on the theme are precise ones that could even be thought of as subordinate instances of the more readily accessible terms for the same concept. So for example, sauntering can be seen as a specific instance of walking that differs from other instances, such as ambling, shambling, plodding, and strolling. A given character might be better described as "sauntering languidly" or "plodding sluggishly" rather than "walking slowly" through a particular scene. The two former phrases convey specific and distinct meanings, whereas the last is more general and less evocative. Each of the first two constructions goes beyond the most accessible words that express "slow movement by foot" to retrieve a less accessible, but more precisely descriptive term. Thus, the path-of-least-resistance and ways to overcome it can be seen as operative and relevant in a recursive way during the fine-grained production of small units of a story.

Again, skilled writers will create larger frameworks (Lawson, 2007) and use words that are consistent with the paths-of-least-resistance within readers' minds, whether in terms of complex scientific principles or the more mundane actions of characters within a story. Although specific words within categories have some chronic, overall level of accessibility, their accessibility is also influenced by the context. At the level of words for specific actions, for example, a story or scene about an oppressed, downtrodden species would reasonably be expected to lead to different movement words being accessible than a story or scene about a dominant or arrogant species. In reading through such a scene readers would presumably move down different paths with different expectations about exactly how the creatures would move. Describing the former as trudging or slogging and the latter as strutting or striding would presumably fit better with expectations than vice versa and would allow readers to continue down the paths that the writer has prepared them to go.

An additional interesting and potentially limiting feature of the path-of-least-resistance at the level of individual word selection and sentence construction is that people gravitate down the path to the basic level; that is, the level of dogs, and cars, and trees, and birds. They tend not to continue to still more specific levels, such as collies, Toyota Camrys, white birches, and robins. Yet to create vivid pictures in the reader's mind, it is essential to describe scenes at least at the level immediately subordinate to the basic level, if not at even more specific levels. A man standing by a tree is vastly different from a muscular balding man in button-fly jeans and a white sleeveless t-shirt lurking in the dappled shade of a weeping willow. Writers must develop the tendency to move beyond the path-of-least-resistance to more precise levels of concepts. In some cases doing so might require learning more specific words, but in others, it may simply be a matter of retrieving known, but relatively less accessible specific terms.

COMBINING CONCEPTS

One means of overcoming the narrowing influence of individual, highly accessible concepts is to use conceptual combination, the merging of two concepts that have previously been separate in the writer's mind or in the minds of readers. Several aspects of conceptual combination make it a powerful technique. The first is that it is a process readily available to virtually all humans. Even young children produce and comprehend combinations of words they have never heard before. Thus, even novice writers ought to be in a position to use this strategy.

The second aspect of combinations that makes them powerful writing tools is that unexpected properties and possibilities can arise when concepts are put together, particularly if the components being combined are in some way discrepant. Conceptual combinations are the classic case of the whole being greater than the sum of its parts. Much as hydrogen and oxygen alone are distinctly different from their mixture together in the form of H_2O, so too are separate concepts often different from their combination. In the afterword to *The Real Story*, Stephen Donaldson, the noted fantasy writer, expressed the idea eloquently when he observed, "Rather like a binary poison – or a magic potion – two inert elements combine to produce something of frightening potency" (1991, p. 223).

A third aspect of combinations that gives them power is that they can operate at many levels of abstraction and can therefore facilitate many aspects of writing. They can serve as prompts for whole stories, allowing authors to express ideas that might otherwise have lain dormant. Indeed, two remarkably similar quotes from Stephen Donaldson and Orson Scott Card illustrate writers' awareness of the centrality of combinations as prompts for stories. Donaldson (1991) stated that "a fair number of my best stories arise, not from one idea, but from two" (p. 222). Card (1990) observed, "All but a handful of my stories have come from combining two completely unrelated ideas" (p. 33). Combinations can also be triggers for scenes within a larger story, and they can be used to find just the right means of expressing a thought or feeling, as in the strongly evocative "sweet sorrow" of parting.

Donaldson (1991) describes a particularly interesting example of conceptual combination as a spark for a powerful story. He reports that he had a desire to write a story about the concept of "unbelief," the unwillingness to accept fantasy or the possibility of a fantasy world, to accept a different reality from the concrete one we normally experience around us. The idea nagged and tugged at him for several years, but he could find no concrete way to bring it to fruition in the form of a story, until one day he realized that he needed to combine unbelief with the concept of leprosy and to have his protagonist, Thomas Covenant, suffer from the disease of leprosy (Hansen's disease). Donaldson reports that the realization sparked his excitement, and he quickly set about the tasks needed to lay the groundwork for the story.

What made the combination such a powerful one for Donaldson may not be obvious for readers without clinical knowledge of the symptoms of leprosy (Hansen's disease), but a key component is that it kills the peripheral nerves that bring sensations from the extremities. The consequence is that people who have the disease and go untreated can sustain serious injuries to the hands or feet and develop infections that threaten life and limb without knowing that they have a problem at all. In severe and untreated cases, they may need to have affected parts amputated.

So consider now, as Donaldson must have, a main character who has leprosy in his real life, and who has developed a systematic approach to examining his extremities for injuries on a regular basis. He is shunned by others who ignorantly fear him. His wife has left him and he has already lost part of his hand to the disease. He blacks out as a fast-moving car is about to hit him, and awakes in a fantasy world, the Land, where he is welcomed as the legendary hero, Berek Halfhand. Consider further that there is a substance in the Land called hurtloam that apparently regenerates the nerves and restores feeling to his extremities. In many respects, his life in the Land could be better than the one he has lived in his real world, but the poignantly painful struggle in his mind is that, by accepting the Land, accepting his role, he would become complacent and give up on the surveillance procedure that has protected him up until now. In short, he is the embodiment of "unbelief" – Thomas Covenant, The Unbeliever. The palpable tension between his desire for release from his troubled life and his unwillingness to accept the apparent escape offered by the Land reveals the power of the combination that drives a truly compelling series of fantasy novels.

Donaldson's account of the origins of the Thomas Covenant story reveals several important aspects of how conceptual combination relates to story writing (Ward, 2001). Recall that, in the Geneplore model, preinventive ideas that have varying degrees of creative potential are generated in an initial generation phase, and if the creative person sees that they have a strong creative potential, that individual can explore and exploit them in a subsequent exploration phase. By his own description, Donaldson recognized the potential of the combination, noting that his brain took fire. But he also went on to say that he then spent months drawing maps, envisioning characters and scenes, and just generally engaging in the hard work of crafting a world and a story out of the initial germ of an idea. That is, although he felt the spark of illumination from the initial idea and experienced the excitement that it engendered, he nevertheless had to go on and perform the difficult task of actually crafting a tale that writers must face (Lawson, 2007).

Interestingly, one need not be a professional writer to recognize the creative potential in novel combinations. One of us (TW) regularly has his students complete an assignment in which they develop very brief stories from randomly generated adjective–noun combinations (see http://bama.ua.edu/~tward/storyweb.html). The Web-based program randomly chooses an adjective and a noun from a set of more than 5,000 words. Because the members of the pair are selected at random, the resulting combinations can seem quite familiar and prosaic (e.g., red car, large house) or unusual and suggestive (e.g., lexical diplomat, sensible agony). If students are inspired by the first combination they see, they use their interpretation of it as a starting point for a very short story. If they are not inspired, they may click a button to generate another random pair until they come upon a combination that does spark their interest. Students have a week to complete the assignment, and they regularly produce compelling and interesting stories, particularly in response to the more unusual combinations.

The fact that the students write interesting stories in response to unusual combinations suggests one means for beginning writers or even experienced ones to get a starting point when stumped for an idea for a story. The power of unusual combinations is highlighted in statements by Donaldson, who stresses that combinations of the exotic and familiar concepts are evocative, and Card, who as noted earlier, derives good stories from "completely unrelated" ideas. The computer program used in the class exercise is one means of securing unusual combinations, but any procedure that produces a reasonable number of pairs at random has the potential of yielding inspiring items.

Earlier we noted the importance of knowledge both from the writer's and reader's perspectives, and Donaldson's unbeliever reinforces those points. Donaldson was prepared to recognize the significance of combining unbelief with leprosy, because he had extensive, close-up experience with the disease. His father was a physician who worked with individuals afflicted with it. Without that background knowledge, the significance of the combination, the dynamic tension that it creates, would have been lost on him.

Without extensive knowledge, Donaldson also would not have been able to create the scenario in a way that was compelling to readers. Without the basic understanding of the nature of the disorder and how someone suffering from it might behave, readers would not have been able to grasp the terrible conflict that drove Covenant. In the context of the story, Donaldson was able to introduce the concept of visual surveillance of extremities, by which individuals who lack sensation in their hands and feet might religiously and rigorously inspect those appendages for injuries or infections. He was able to explain why Covenant had already lost part of his left hand to the disease and how people around him avoided him out of the unwarranted fear that they might catch the disease from him. Thus, Donaldson taught readers about the disease, not in an explicit way, but in the context of and in service of conveying a great story (see Lawson, 2007).

Just as the path-of-least-resistance and ways of overcoming it operate at the level of ideas for whole stories as well as at the more minute level of the phrasing of individual sentences, so too can combinations play a role at the micro-level of sentence construction. They can help convey exact intended meanings and produce precisely vivid images in the reader's mind. Just as a character might chortle, guffaw, or snicker rather than simply laugh, the person might chortle gleefully, guffaw uproariously, or snicker menacingly. Thus, combinations convey more precise meanings and can give rise to better developed mental images of a scene.

SUMMARY

We have explored the creative cognition approach as it applies to the art and craft of creative writing, specifically in the genres of science fiction and fantasy. We have tried to show how the operation of basic cognitive processes influences all aspects of writing from the initial excitement sparked by realizing the broad idea for a story; to the development of objects, scenes and events within a story; to the selection of individual words in writing a given sentence. *At all points, the outcome depends on what is retrieved, on whether the information is specific or abstract, and the extent to which it fits with the knowledge and expectations of readers.*

An important ingredient, even in the seemingly exotic realms of science fiction and fantasy, is the role of useful, knowledge-based constraints. The best writers will possess large storehouses of scientific knowledge (or sufficient motivation to acquire that knowledge). They will escape from rigid adherence to a path-of-least-resistance by accessing broader knowledge of the workings of the world, and they will craft stories that also take into account the reader's path-of-least-resistance. They will also efficiently manage their knowledge, traversing between more abstract levels to define broader goals and outlines and more specific levels to instantiate those goals in compelling ways.

REFERENCES

Amabile, T. M. (1982). Social psychology of creativity: A consensual assessment technique. *Journal of Personality and Social Psychology, 43*, 997–1013.

Amabile, T. M. (1983). *The social psychology of creativity*. New York: Springer-Verlag.

Barlowe, W. D., & Summers, I. (1979). Barlowe's guide to extraterrestrials. New York: Workman Publishing.

Card, O. S. (1990). *How to write science fiction and fantasy*. Cincinnati, OH: Writer's Digest Books.

Chi, M. T. H., Glaser, R., & Rees, E. (1982). Expertise in problem solving. In R. J. Sternberg (Ed.), *Advances in the psychology of expertise* (Vol. 1, pp. 7–76). Hillsdale, NJ: Erlbaum.

Clement, H. (1991). The creation of imaginary beings. In G. Dozois, T. Lee, S. Schmidt, I. R. Strock, & S. Williams (Eds.), *Writing science fiction and fantasy* (pp. 129–146). New York: St. Martin's Press.

Csikszentmihalyi, M. (1999). Implications of a systems perspective for the study of creativity. In R. J. Sternberg (Ed.), *Handbook of creativity* (pp. 313–335). Cambridge: Cambridge University Press.

Donaldson, S. R. (1991). *The gap into conflict: The real story*. New York: Bantam.

Finke, R. A., Ward, T. B., & Smith, S. M. (1992). *Creative cognition: Theory, research, and applications*. Cambridge, MA: MIT Press.

Johnson, K. E., & Mervis, C. B. (1997). Effects of varying levels of expertise on the basic level of categorization. *Journal of Experimental Psychology: General, 126*, 248–277.

Lawson, E. T. (2007). Cognitive constraints on imagining other worlds. In M. Grebowicz (Ed.), *SciFi in the mind's eye: Reading science through science fiction* (pp. 263–274). Chicago: Open Court.

Lubart, T. I., & Sternberg, R. J. (1995). An investment approach to creativity. In S. M. Smith, T. B. Ward, & R. A. Finke (Eds.), *The creative cognition approach* (pp. 269–302). Cambridge, MA: MIT Press.

Markman, A. B., & Gentner, D. (1993). Splitting the differences: A structural alignment view of similarity. *Journal of Memory and Language, 32,* 517–535.

Martin, G. R. R. (1976). First sew on a tentacle (recipes for believable aliens). In C. L. Grant (Ed.), *Writing & selling science fiction* (pp. 147–168). Cincinnati: Writer's Digest Books.

Ochoa, G., & Osher, J. (1993). *The writer's guide to creating a science fiction universe.* Cincinnati: Writer's Digest Books.

Sternberg, R. J., & Lubart, T. I. (1995). *Defying the crowd: Cultivating creativity in a culture of conformity.* New York: Free Press.

Tanaka, J. W., & Taylor, M. (1991). Object categories and expertise: Is the basic level in the eye of the beholder? *Cognitive Psychology, 23,* 457–482.

Ward, T. B. (1994). Structured imagination: The role of conceptual structure in exemplar generation. *Cognitive Psychology, 27,* 1–40.

Ward, T. B. (2001). Creative cognition, conceptual combination and the creative writing of Stephen R. Donaldson. *American Psychologist, 56,* 350–354.

Ward, T. B. (2008). The role of domain knowledge in creative generation. *Learning and Individual Differences, 18*(4), 363–366.

Ward, T. B., Dodds, R. A., Saunders, K. N., & Sifonis, C. M. (2000). Attribute centrality and imaginative thought. *Memory & Cognition, 28,* 1387–1397.

Ward, T. B., Finke, R. A., & Smith, S. M. (1995). *Creativity and the mind: Discovering the genius within.* New York: Plenum.

Ward, T. B., Patterson, M. J., & Sifonis, C. (2004). The role of specificity and abstraction in creative idea generation. *Creativity Research Journal, 16,* 1–9.

Ward, T. B., Patterson, M. J., Sifonis, C. M., Dodds, R. A., & Saunders, K. N. (2002). The role of graded category structure in imaginative thought. *Memory & Cognition, 30,* 199–216.

Ward, T. B., Smith, S. M., & Finke, R. A. (1999). Creative cognition. In R. J. Sternberg (Ed.), *Handbook of creativity* (pp. 189–212). Cambridge: Cambridge University Press.

PART IV

THE DEVELOPMENT

13

Writing in Flow

SUSAN K. PERRY

It is very gratifying for a researcher/practitioner to discover that her personal experience bears out the results of her own previous study. I enjoyed this fortunate circumstance recently when I wrote my first novel some years after completing a dissertation and later writing a popular trade book about successful writers and their writing processes (Perry, 1996, 1999).

My writing research consisted of interviews with a convenience sample of 76 regularly publishing writers (40 novelists and 36 poets; 43 males, 33 females). Participants included both best-selling novelists such as Jonathan and Faye Kellerman, Sue Grafton, Michael Connelly, T. Coraghessan Boyle, and Ursula LeGuin, and Pulitzer Prize, MacArthur Foundation Award, and American Book Award winning literary authors and poets such as Jane Smiley, Robert Olen Butler, Donald Hall, Octavia Butler, Philip Levine, and Mark Strand. (All attributed but uncited quotes in this article are from interviews I personally conducted [Perry, 1996, 1999].) I also read hundreds of accounts of and interviews with writers and have continued to do so.

So many of the creative writers with whom I spoke enjoyed writing so much that I decided to try it myself. I had been an independent writer of nonfiction books and articles for magazines and newspapers for the previous two decades. I wondered whether it would be possible for a writer who had until then been so scrupulous about truthfulness to make things up. Perhaps as important, would I be able to write consistently, when my usual writing to commercial specifications had lately become a form of torture?

The first thing I realized I would have to do was to find my personal keys to entering flow.

WHAT IS FLOW IN WRITING?

Flow is the altered state in which you find yourself – or recognize later that you have just come out of – when time seems to stop and the writing flows through you with little or no angst (Csikszentmihalyi, 1990; Perry, 1996).

Some of the metaphors writers gave me express a sense of travel, of having to perform a physical movement through space to get to the place of no time, no self, and, perhaps, no rationality. In everyday reality, space and time are thought of as two different concepts, which then collapse in the state of flow. Some of the metaphors refer to going down, deeper, inside, under, and below. "What I do feels like an archaeological dig," novelist Faye Moskowitz told me. "I carefully remove one layer of memory and go down deeper and then deeper. . . . At a certain depth, . . . I uncover what I could not have predicted, and then, flow begins."

Some of the other ways novelists I interviewed refer to this special state of mind and body are to speak of opening a faucet, peeling layers, of moving into a movie screen, and of entering a cave that at first seems unbreachable but that finally reveals an opening just as you are about to leave. They describe going down deeper and deeper, beyond the daylight level of thought to where unexpected material and insights usually hide. David L. Ulin, who has written novels and is now primarily a nonfiction writer and editor, said it was "like I'm dancing on a fine line of energy, able to hold a million thoughts and ideas in my head at once." A detailed description was given by novelist Judith Freeman:

> You start walking into the story first in a kind of pedestrian way, a very conscious way, in which you're aware of sitting there rereading what you've written. . . . And then it really is as though you're starting to enter a landscape. . . . I see myself beginning to descend into a much more timeless, realm . . . the realm, in a sense, of pure story, pure imagination. And I can almost visualize it as walking down a series of steps that lead me into some sort of wonderful secret illuminated chamber.

The most reliable way of recognizing when you have been fully engaged and in flow is to catch yourself glancing at the clock and being surprised at how much time has passed. A tedious and unappealing task has you clock-watching as the minutes tick by all too slowly. When you are in flow, time becomes irrelevant. Many writers seek out the positive feelings unleashed by flow, when intense absorption overtakes consciousness of self. Many feel their best work comes out of a flow state, and I wanted to experience this for myself.

Finding yourself in a state of flow is often more than a fortuitous accident. Learning to enter flow is a psychological skill that writers can learn to optimize over time with increased knowledge and practice.

In this chapter, I discuss how creative writers make and experience the shift from ordinary reality to the altered reality of a flow state. I describe some of the more salient factors that lead writers toward becoming fully absorbed in writing, among which are intrinsic motivation, getting feedback, regular writing rituals, and audience (un)awareness. Finally, I describe some of the strategies that writers, including myself, have used to optimize writing in flow.

MOTIVATION AND WRITING IN FLOW

Creative writing seems to flow most readily when it is intrinsically driven. Research has shown that an intense interest and involvement in an activity for its own sake, with little or no thought of future rewards, lead to positive feelings, persistence, creativity, and flow. That intrinsic motivation may be undermined when extrinsic rewards, such as evaluation pressure or competition, are introduced (Hill & Amabile, 1993).

Despite conflicting results that have come from studies of whether extrinsic rewards increase or decrease creativity, depending on how creativity was defined and the salience of the reward involved, it does appear that when one sees a task as a means to an end, engagement may be lessened and creativity decreased (Condry, 1977; Eisenberger & Selbst, 1994; Hennessey & Amabile, 1988). Task engagement directly relates to the likelihood of entering flow.

Extrinsic motivators, however, may combine with intrinsic ones to make flow even more likely, so long as the extrinsic push does not come to feel like an effort at control by someone else (Hennessey & Amabile, 1988). This may help explain why external deadlines are often helpful in raising the level of one's internal motivational state. When writers set their own deadlines or mini-deadlines, they may feel more intrinsically motivated (Bandura & Schunk, 1981). When they set standards to measure themselves against, they thus fulfill the need for immediate feedback posited by flow theory. More on that soon.

However, at least one theorist (Weisberg, 1993) mentioned novelists such as Twain and Dickens who published in monthly serials, seemingly an extrinsic motivator. Hennessey and Amabile (1988) suggested that those eminent in and knowledgeable about a domain have developed means of dealing with the potentially negative effects of extrinsic rewards. Negative feedback may be able to increase motivation, for example, if it is seen as a challenge or as purely informational by an intrinsically motivated person. And, of course, highly autonomous individuals, who are very intrinsically motivated, might also be highly motivated to achieve compensation for their work (Amabile, Hill, Hennessey, & Tighe, 1994). For confirmation, ask almost any writer (except for poets, who are paid rarely or only minimally).

FEEDBACK AND FLOW

Staying in flow requires getting feedback (Csikszentmihalyi, 1990), which enables writers to know when they are approaching mastery and they can sense self-efficacy. However, writers usually do not get outside feedback until the work is complete or nearly so, and thus they must learn to provide it for themselves. Intrinsically motivated individuals seem to be better able to provide this self-initiated feedback, though many of the writers I interviewed were not able to describe exactly how they manage to accomplish this task.

Novelist Margot Livesey told me that she reads aloud whatever she writes, adding, "If a character is sitting in a room, or pruning a hedge or fixing a bicycle or sitting on a bus, I try to see that character both internally and externally as clearly as possible. I might begin writing a scene with three dozen details of the bus journey, then decide that only two of them really further the novel, and are therefore to my mind what is needed."

Many writers merely sense that they are on the right track. If that sense of rightness is missing, sooner or later they will change their direction.

WHO WILL READ IT (AND WHO CARES)

Most writers are only partially aware of their eventual audience of readers, at least until they are ready to revise what they have written. When they are most fully engaged and in flow, thoughts of the audience tend to be below the level of conscious awareness. Writers' practices range from never thinking of the audience at all to being quite clear as to when it's "safe" to visualize their readers without inhibiting their creativity. For instance, novelist Susan Taylor Chehak said, "What I try to do, rather than my [writing for an] audience, because that's a very frightening term to me, the idea of strangers, that scares me, but I try to divide myself in half, on the one hand writing for myself the audience, reading as if I were the reader, and then, on the other hand, writing, just writing, rather than thinking of some objective person with glasses in a chair sitting in front of the fire reading my book."

Even during the revision process, writers say they think of the audience only in the interests of clarity, rather than being concerned about the potentially critical judgment of others. "I value clarity so highly," said writer Bill Mohr. "I feel that if I put words that are interesting enough together, the audience will follow."

Of course, writers who have an expectation of being published and being read find ways to incorporate their audience into themselves in such a way that it is not inhibiting. Rather it is part of the ongoing process of making choices as to what will work. Ursula K. LeGuin wrote, "Consciousness of audience while writing is fatal to the work." And, more humorously, science fiction author David Gerrold said, "I sort of imagine them [the faceless masses] as a crowd with torches and pitchforks. I've met them – I do speaking at conventions and I kind of imagine that room."

Some, perhaps to counteract the negative possibilities, purposely imagine positive, nurturing audiences, a good friend or fantasy reader, or intelligent (i.e., intuiting what the writer is trying to accomplish) though faceless masses. Others devise audiences of their own imagining to help clarify their thinking. Sometimes the quandary is very much on the conscious level, as though the writer is arguing in his or her mind with market forces. Will this be acceptable to its intended audience? And if not, should I write it anyway? More paradoxically, some incorporate the sense of audience into themselves, becoming writer and reader at once, shifting imperceptibly back and forth throughout the creative process.

FROM RITUAL TO FOCUS

Many of us have a tendency to procrastinate about writing. We figure we will start the project (or write the next section) when we have answered every e-mail, completed every important phone call, done just a bit more "necessary" research, or cleared the overstuffed in box, each sliver of paper seemingly calling out to be handled *now*. There is the impulse to say to oneself, "I'll just get them all over with once and for all and *then* sit down and be creative."

This method actually works for some writers, such as Janet Burroway (1980, p. 187): "It seems as if I have been stripping everything carefully away for several weeks to clear my self for the *ceremonial* undertaking of the commitment." More commonly, though, you will not be able to "clear the decks" completely. If you wait for the perfect time to write, it is guaranteed not to come. To lure yourself into flow, it is necessary to consider priorities. I asked the creative writers in my sample how exactly they let go of everyday concerns and lose themselves in the delicious mental hideaway of flow, and I got a surprising variety of responses.

One of the insights I gained was that everyone has a ritual. Some of them did not even know they had a ritual associated with writing, but they all did, however simple and basic that ritual might be. Novelist Susan Taylor Chehak described her routine this way:

> Making sure that everybody's cared for and everybody's full and set and nobody needs me. It's because there's a certain amount of revving up that takes time, and you can't just get into it. You don't just go into that state. And I've usually left the work in some way that there's something to go to, that's left hanging. I would purposely leave something that I would probably be mulling over while I'm whipping mashed potatoes.

Novelist Judith Freeman put it this way: "It's as though you just have to go through certain kinds of acts and warm-ups, but really it's just preparing yourself by familiarizing yourself once again with these people, this place, beginning to enter it in a little more pedestrian way. That might take anywhere from 15 minutes to 45 minutes."

What's going on here? When you do the same thing each day before writing, you are getting your brain and body used to it. This is one habit that is very good for you. Instead of wasting a lot of time deliberating, "Should I write today? Should I write now or later? Maybe I should just read this letter first," what happens is that you simply start writing. This sounds simple and in a way, it is. If you choose a particular time to write each day (or 3 days a week, or whenever) and then go through your personal routine, the switch to starting your writing and entering a flow state becomes automatic. No matter how wildly creative or erratic the rest of your life is, this is one area in which habit helps.

My own ritual is nonvarying – and utterly boring to describe. I get up, get dressed, eat breakfast, and have coffee while I read most of the local newspaper. Then I sit down at the computer, beginning with seeing if the outside world still exists (the *New York Times* updates every 10 minutes). Then I check a few carefully chosen RSS feeds to literary blogs and answer those e-mails that are quick and easy (I put the rest into a holding file so they do not distract me). Then it is time to reread some of what I did the day before or skip around the bits and pieces of my novel-in-progress until I find an entry point.

A number of famous writers claim to have written while under the influence of alcohol, a mood-altering substance that might ease flow entry by silencing the internal critic (Goodwin, 1988). Writers find the particular schedule that works best for them, with more apparently preferring to write in the morning than later in the day, many with the help of coffee. Anne Dillard recalled, "To crank myself . . . I drank coffee in titrated doses. It was a tricky business, requiring the finely tuned judgment of a skilled anesthesiologist. There was a tiny range within which coffee was effective, short of which it was useless, and beyond which, fatal" (Dillard, 1989, pp. 49–50). But a few writers believe they only write well when they are fatigued. Gore Vidal's practice is my favorite and most succinct writerly ritual: "First coffee, then a bowel movement. Then the muse joins me" (Clarke, 1981, p. 311).

Part of the purpose of a writer's ritual is to focus attention inward, which is always made easier by eliminating distractions. Some do this by carving out a sense of solitude for their writing time, whether that entails strict aloneness or merely psychically cutting themselves off from the activity around them. Some writers claim they need to face a wall or a boring scene, though others can shut themselves off even in the midst of a coffee shop.

For some, once the beginning of the story is captured, focus is easy and flow follows. Amy Tan said, "I focus on a specific image, and that image takes me into a scene. Then I begin to see the scene and I ask myself, 'What's to your right? What's to your left?' and I open up into this fictional world. I often play music as a way of blocking out the rest of my consciousness" (Epel, 1993, p. 284).

As useful as it is to have a beginning ritual, writers often have a specific way of ending the day's writing that makes the next session's flow entry that much easier. For example, a common strategy is to stop in the middle of something. A writer might complete a first-draft scene that simply begs to be revised the next day. Those revisions may then send the writer forward into new material. Others purposely stop in the middle of a scene, allowing their subconscious to keep mulling over the story while they go about other business.

VARIETIES OF FLOW

Is some flow deeper or heavier than another flow? Some writers have the ability to sustain their focus for long periods of time, whereas others enter and leave flow more frequently, writing in spurts and then taking a break of whatever length of time to rejoin reality. However, it is not inevitably true that a longer, more consistent flow is a deeper flow.

It seems to me, as a person who experiences flow only in short bursts, that how one experiences flow is part and parcel of one's personality. I am a light sleeper, for example, and I am not comfortable sitting still for too long a time – unless what I am focusing on is unusually engaging – and thus it seems consistent that I am one of those who typically leaves flow readily when my attention is distracted by my surroundings. My own physiological responses dictate how I will experience flow, but it *is* flow, nonetheless.

Adding to the subjective flavor of flow is the fact that some writers believe the editing is the hardest part of their work, regardless of whether they say they are in flow then or not, whereas others claim that editing is the easiest, most emotionally thrilling part. Writing in different genres can also affect flow entry for a particular individual, and some writers say they have a harder time when writing nonfiction than when writing either poetry or fiction.

Moreover, some writers apparently experience flow as something they get into after crossing a gate or doorway or line, like flipping an on/off switch, or as more like moving or settling along a continuum, somewhat the way light changes during dusk. Clearly, your metaphors relate to your personal experience of flow. Therefore, when writers who are feeling blocked or having trouble even getting started ask me for advice, I suggest they purposely change their flow metaphor. For example, imagine you can get past the wall in front of you by walking around it. Or, better yet, see the wall that blocks you as simply a filmy bubble that looks solid but that will burst at the slightest touch; in other words, by simply sitting down and beginning to put words, *any* words, on paper.

Flow may change its depth, according to the perception of the writer, depending on variables such as time of day or stage of the creative process. "If I postpone it, I probably won't avoid it, but I can't get into it as deeply," claimed novelist Nancy Kress. "It's very hard for me to get into it when I know I have a shortened amount of time. It doesn't feel as complete, as deep," said Gerald DiPego, many of whose novels have been made into movies. Interruptions, such as family members' requests or the much-loathed telephone, may pull a writer from a deep flow to a lighter one, making it difficult to get back in deeply. As Carol Muske explained, "Whatever happens, it does take me a while to resurface, to figure out 'what world is this?' People call it scatterbrained, which is a very telling word. I have to do one thing at a time, ultimately, but I'm still conscious of the other things on my mind."

An interesting side note was that I and only one other writer in my study do not much mind the telephone. She gets in and out of flow readily, and as for me, I probably do not get in deeply enough for brief interruptions to disturb me.

Evidence for the continuum theory of flow was offered by novelist Nancy Kress: "I'm in the work right away, if it's going well, but it will be not a completely submersed flow state right away. It'll be more conscious in the beginning. If I'm lucky – it doesn't always happen – somewhere around, oh, I don't know, 20 minutes or a half hour, I'll get really with it."

A common distinction among different kinds of flow states is that between first-draft flow and revision flow. Some say they get into a deeper flow while writing first drafts and only enter a semi-flow or light flow state while revising their work. Others believe there is no real difference between one kind of flow and another, especially if the writing process is one of going back and forth between first-draft composition and editing.

Another distinction made by my respondents was between the kind of flow (or absorbedness) they experienced in their primary creative writing and their other writing, which might be nonfiction, essays, or, for a poet, fiction. Said Kress, "I never get into a flow state when I'm writing nonfiction. And I can write it with a lot more interruptions, and just pick it up again. It doesn't matter. I used to write corporate copy and I don't think I ever once got into flow with that." That was my own experience with most of my previous journalistic writing.

Let me give the final thought on this topic to poet (and my husband) Stephen Perry: "Sometimes you don't get to kiss the angels; you just get a hand job from the muse."

PHYSICAL EXPERIENCE OF FLOW

It is difficult, if not impossible, to notice one's body during an altered state in which the self, both body and mind, is lost to conscious awareness. Nevertheless, some writers did notice some physical effects of being in flow, and many of them had something to say about what it felt like to exit flow. Some writers mentioned particular physiological effects, such as increased thirst and heart rate, breathing through the mouth, and gazing as though watching a movie.

Other writers described paradoxes in which their awareness of physiological changes meshed with the mental/emotional changes common to flow. According to Carol Muske, "People will ask me questions when I'm trying to focus in, and . . . sometimes I won't even answer their questions, or I won't know what I've said. It's like being on automatic pilot. It's as though there's this other presence that one goes into or one becomes. I feel that beginning to happen, and I get irritable because I want to get into this state."

After exiting flow, writers usually feel different physiologically and sometimes psychologically as well. It is not unusual for a highly focused writer not to notice hunger and thus to skip a meal or two. Some will also not notice feeling tired. They may tense up while writing, and the hunger and tiredness catch up with them when they stop writing. Remember that the body has disappeared from awareness. Again, this state was described well by novelist and poet Carol Muske: "After those six or seven hours of 'lost time,' I will suddenly come to and I'll be hunched over the keyboard. Sometimes I literally start to gasp for air, and I realize I haven't been breathing. My leg's gone to sleep. I'm literally cut off from my body." The well-known mystery writer Jonathan Kellerman mentioned having to consciously relax his breathing: "It's just that feeling of coming out of the hypnoidal state, of leaving one world and entering another."

But as expected, not all writers react alike. Although some end up drained, novelist Ethan Canin reported experiencing the opposite: "I notice that my anxiety is decreased after I'm finished." Novelist Judith Freeman explained the positive postflow feelings this way: "That room is really, in a sense, like a mine where one goes and mines certain things. And I think just like you can feel tired by a day of strenuous work where you've been picking at some little vein, you can also be exhilarated when you actually strike it rich."

LEARNING TO FLOW

One of the most liberating ways of thinking about writing fiction is that there is no one right way to approach a project. Each writer finds what works for him or her, some experimenting with different methods of entering flow and with various methods of doing the actual composing and other writers falling immediately into a pattern that works for them and then sticking with it almost religiously.

Outlines and self-imposed deadlines, such as planning to write 1,000 words a day or committing to write one scene a day, in order, are helpful for some writers. Considering my own proclivities – more rational than intuitive, more likely to read Cynthia Ozick than James Joyce; creative, yes, but not out-of-left-field creative – I was initially surprised at how appealing to me was the system used by one writer of what she calls "time travel-romantic-historical fantasias." Bestselling author (and PhD biologist) Diana Gabaldon's "chunk" or "kernel" method results in engrossing and wryly humorous novels that have an intense fan base. What she does is start anywhere and she writes anything that relates to her projected story. Then she writes anything else, whatever she feels like writing at the moment. Say she wants to set some scenes in Scotland (she did). When the mood struck her to describe the town, she put a description of the town into the computer. Later she felt like writing a funny love scene or a conversation between a serving maid and a stranger. She then wrote those.

Gabaldon described her process like this:

> I don't normally write any of the stuff that I write from the beginning
> and work straight through. I will pick up some bit of resonance, I call it a
> kernel; in terms of fiction it's a very vivid image or line of dialogue or an
> emotional ambiance (in nonfiction it's a striking idea or turn of phrase),
> but anything like that that I can put on paper easily, I put that down
> first. And then you've got something to stand on when you're working
> backwards and forwards. In its own good time, the first sentence will
> come along and you can put it where it belongs.

Gabaldon further explained that her chunks, although not located next to
each other in the finished book, eventually start sticking together and forming
a kind of framework. Once the connected chunks become a long enough
sequence, say one that might run 150 pages (her books are many hundreds of
pages long), she is more able to see what is going to happen next. She explained,
"They would be long sequences connected to each other like continents rising
out of the ocean. First you just see the tips of the islands, the volcanoes coming
up, but then as the whole land mass rises, the contours become evident. You
can see where one valley leads into the next mountain." She lures flow by
writing only what is relatively easy and enjoyable at the time. She mentions
that she might initially avoid an emotionally challenging scene, but eventually
it would have the context she needed and it, too, would become easier and flow
out of her.

Gabaldon's methods are an example of the way writers are able to transform an activity physically or psychologically by either concentrating on some
previously overlooked portion of the environment or the activity or by varying
the way they do the activity. Writers use a variety of strategies in an effort
to regulate their attention and motivation so they can persist in what might
otherwise sometimes be a boring activity.

Ways to enter flow can be learned. "It's like developing any specific set of
muscles," said Maurice Sendak (Epel, 1993, p. 231). Writers get better at it over
the years, becoming able to will themselves into flow without worrying about
whether or not it will happen.

Changing their attitudes can be the key to flow for some writers. Whether
or not there is a specific set of traits that characterize the creative writer, individuals who wish to enhance their creative side can do so by adopting the
habits and attitudes of successful (that is, consistently writing) writers. Such
attitudes influence directly how they act on a day-to-day basis.

My studies had shown that openness of mind and looseness of thinking
were assets for a creative writer. Some of the ways I pursued those attributes
(whether or not they were native to me was not relevant) was to read a great
many interviews with writers. That helped me envision the wide variety of
ways for a writer to think and behave.

I began noticing how often I am tempted to say "No," as well as the occasions that caused me to say or think "I can't do that" or "I shouldn't do that." Were the risks real or imagined? As I like to tell writing students, writing entails no risks at all. (On the other hand, publishing *may* in rare instances be risky, but that is a concern for much later and not relevant to freeing up one's creativity.)

Learning to reserve judgment is good practice for not prejudging one's own work. Whenever I visit an art museum now, or look at architecture, or hear music I am not used to, I try to see what I can discern in each work of art that made someone find it worthy.

It suited my temperament to extend my work day, so that rather than forcing myself to achieve a lot in only 2 or 3 hours, I could continue to jump up and do other things and yet return to my main task repeatedly and get a lot done over a longer period of time.

The more ways a writer is motivated to write, the better. Otherwise it is tempting to stop writing. One method that has worked for many is to find ways to increase the novelty and challenge of a writing project. Challenge can mean trying something you have never done before; for example, Diana Gabaldon once gave herself the challenge of writing a "triple-nested flashback."

Other ways to increase the engagement factor are to write from a different point of view, such as the point of view of the bicycle or the dog or the new immigrant, or to begin a story in a way that is new to you. For example, I have tried beginning a piece of writing with an anecdote, or a fake journal entry, or a letter to an old teacher.

For my own first novel, I used a variety of techniques to stay engaged, choosing the ones that offered just enough challenge but not too much of a feeling of being in over my head. When I reread the manuscript some months after completing it, it is as though I was not "myself" when I wrote it, but rather someone who managed to summon more creativity than I am usually able to do. To the extent that is true, I give much of the credit to having learned how to write in flow.

REFERENCES

Amabile, T. M., Hill, K. G., Hennessey, B. A., & Tighe, E. M. (1994). The work preference inventory: Assessing intrinsic and extrinsic motivational orientations. *Journal of Personality and Social Psychology, 66*(5), 950–967.

Bandura, A., & Schunk, D. H. (1981). Cultivating competence, self-efficacy, and intrinsic interest through proximal self-motivation. *Journal of Personality and Social Psychology, 41*, 586–598.

Burroway, J. (1980). Opening nights: The opening days. In J. Sternberg (Ed.), *The writer on her work* (pp. 187–215). New York: W. W. Norton.

Clarke, G. (1981). *Gore Vidal*. In G. Plimpton (Ed.), *Writers at work: The Paris Review interviews, fifth series* (pp. 283–311). New York: Penguin.

Condry, J. (1977). Enemies of exploration: Self-initiated versus other-initiated learning. *Journal of Personality and Social Psychology, 35*, 459–477.

Csikszentmihalyi, M. (1990). *Flow: The psychology of optimal experience.* New York: HarperCollins.

Dillard, A. (1989). *The writing life.* New York: Harper & Row.

Eisenberger, R., & Selbst, M. (1994). Does reward increase or decrease creativity? *Journal of Personality and Social Psychology, 66,* 1116–1127.

Epel, N. (1993). *Writers dreaming.* New York: Carol Southern Books.

Goodwin, D. W. (1988). *Alcohol and the writer.* Kansas City, MO: Andrews and McMeel.

Hennessey, B. A., & Amabile, T. M. (1988). The conditions of creativity. In R. J. Sternberg (Ed.), *The nature of creativity: Contemporary psychological perspectives* (pp. 11–38). Cambridge: Cambridge University Press.

Hill, K. G., & Amabile, T. M. (1993). A social psychological perspective on creativity: Intrinsic motivation and creativity in the classroom and workplace. In S. G. Isaksen, M. C. Murdock, R. L. Firestien, & D. J. Treffinger (Eds.), *Understanding and recognizing creativity: The emergence of a discipline* (pp. 400–432). Norwood, NJ: Ablex.

Perry, S. K. (1996). *When time stops: How creative writers experience entry into the flow state. Dissertation Abstracts International, 58*(8), 4484.

Perry, S. K. (1999). *Writing in flow: Keys to enhanced creativity.* Cincinnati: Writer's Digest Books.

Weisberg, R. W. (1993). *Creativity: Beyond the myth of genius.* New York: W. H. Freeman.

14

Writer's Block and Blocked Writers: Using Natural Imagery to Enhance Creativity

JEROME L. SINGER AND MICHAEL V. BARRIOS

NATURAL IMAGERY AND CREATIVE PRODUCTION

Creative writing, whether in literature or science, may well seem like an enjoyable pastime to its readers, but it most certainly involves hard work, intense concentration, and periods of uncertainty and blockage for even the most productive of its practitioners. No wonder the ancient Greeks and Romans called on specific deities or immortals like the Muses to guide them past inevitable hesitancies into more freely flowing streams of thought. Even the Christian poet Dante sought the aid of the pagan epic poet Virgil as his leader through his literary traversal of the realms of the afterlife. Such breakthroughs into creative production often come about through vivid daytime fantasies or suggestive night dreams that we now can recognize are natural human occurrences and not necessarily visitations from Olympian deities.

Many anecdotal reports by creative scientists, artists, and writers suggest that periods of creative impasse can be terminated by the occurrence of vivid day or night dreams (Garfield, 1974; Shepard, 1978; Singer, 1975, 2004). Albert Einstein described how his waking fantasies of himself or some alter ego traveling through space at the speed of light and then picturing the consequences of such actions opened the way for his development of his theory of relativity. Niels Bohr described how learning of his son's involvement in an act of petty thievery led to his trying to reconcile his nearly simultaneous feelings of anger and disappointment about the boy with his fatherly feelings of love and protectiveness. The image often reproduced in psychology texts of a drawing of an old crone that when stared at for a few moments reverses into a lovely young girl then came to his mind. As he contemplated this representation of perceptual ambiguity, he found himself linking these images to a scientific problem that had been troubling him and he saw a way to develop his influential theory of complementarity in quantum theory (Bruner, 1986). Years before, Michael Faraday, relatively unschooled in mathematics, attributed his own contributions to electromagnetic theory to visualizations of forces that

225

"rose up before him like things" (Koestler, 1964). The chemist Friedrich August Kekulé's oft-cited dream of a snake-like creature that "got hold of its own tail" led him to break an impasse in his research and to demonstrate that benzene is structurally a closed carbon ring (MacKenzie, 1965). Numerous more recent examples in the sciences of the ways in which spontaneous imagery led to scientific or technological breakthroughs are provided by Root-Bernstein and Root-Bernstein (1999) in their *Sparks of Genius.*

If we turn to the arts, comparable examples present themselves. The British novelist Graham Greene, in an interview aired on National Public Radio on September 15, 1980, told of how a vivid night dream about an especially intriguing personality led him to overcome a prolonged period of blockage in his writing. On awakening he was able to begin and to sustain work on a novel. The Baroque composer Giuseppe Tartini reported that he had a dream in which he handed his violin to the Devil, who then performed a beautiful piece. Tartini awoke and, inspired by the image, went on to compose what he believed was his finest work, the "Devil's Trill Sonata" (Garfield, 1974). The contemporary writer Joan Didion, has reported that her novels develop from "pictures in my mind" and that these images seem to directly guide both the structure and the language of her works (Shepard, 1978). The Root-Bernsteins describe a series of instances of writers from Charles Dickens to Amy Lowell, Wyndham Lewis, J. R. Tolkien, Vladimir Nabokov, and Tennessee Williams who relied strongly on visual and auditory imagery to help them break through impasses into the development of poetry, plays, or novels. They cite how Tennessee Williams developed his most famous play, *A Streetcar Named Desire*, when a spontaneous mental image captured his attention. It was of a single woman of mature years sitting all alone by a window with moonlight streaming in on her desolate face. She had been stood up by the man she planned to marry (Root-Bernstein & Root-Bernstein, 1999, p. 55).

From a scientific perspective, we need not attribute to supernatural visitations such breakthroughs from creative impasses to productive expressions following vivid dreams or waking imagery. In the past half-century we have seen the development of a body of research on the stream of human consciousness that can provide testable hypotheses and formal theory on the way normal patterns of daydreaming or sleep mentation may lead to imagery that can evoke creative reconstructions from the *prepared minds* of artists or scientists (Antrobus, 1999; Baars, 1997; Epstein, 1999; Singer, 1995, 2006). In this chapter we address the phenomena labeled as "writing blocks" by the psychoanalyst Edmund Bergler (1950a, 1950b) and, more recently, elaborated on by Hatterer (1966) in a clinical paper, by Leader (1991) in a thorough historical and literary review, and by Acocella (2004) in a somewhat skeptical article. Here we describe research that employs systematic statistical methods to examine ways of classifying types of blockage and then identifying particular personality patterns of individual writers susceptible to such inhibitions in their writing efforts. We then describe research on a psychological form of intervention with blocked authors that makes use of the individuals' own capacities of image production.

We began this chapter by citing some brief anecdotes in which scientists or creative writers overcame temporary impasses in their productivity after experiencing seemingly spontaneous vivid day or night dreams. We wish to stress again our belief that such sudden interventions are not supernatural events but rather natural occurrences as part of the mind-wandering and the stream of consciousness that characterize all human ongoing thought (James, 1890/1950; Klinger, 1999; Mason et al., 2007; Singer, 1975, 1995, 2006; Sternberg, Grigorenko, & Singer, 2004). Very recent work by Malia Mason and her collaborators has examined what our earlier research labeled as stimulus-independent thought and demonstrated its occurrence under conditions of reduced executive demands for mental solutions or physical activities. These investigators have also studied brain function using functional magnetic resonance imagery (fMRI) and found evidence of the so-called default conditions under which brain areas become active under circumstances when focused action demands are temporarily reduced. They concluded that mind-wandering (1) may enable the person to sustain "an optimal level of arousal"; (2) may foster "spontaneous mental time travel," thus permitting some integration of past, present, and future experiences; (3) may represent an evolved or learned capacity for multitasking; or (4) occurs because the "mind may wander simply because it can" (Mason et al., 2007, p. 394).

BLOCKED WRITERS – CHARACTERISTICS AND SUBTYPES

Some years ago we undertook an empirical study of blocked writers. We collected a sample of professional writers reporting a current and longstanding block on a specific writing project toward which they were devoting continuous attention and effort. Our goals included developing a broad understanding of the ways in which variables such as task characteristics, life circumstances, emotional trends, and imagination-related cognitive abilities might intersect within the phenomenon of writer's block. We sought to identify the broad factors that differentiate blocked writers from nonblocked writers and that contribute to the susceptibility to and severity of writing blocks. We also sought to identify subtypes of blocked writers, hypothesizing that significant factors may cohere with differing patterns and prominences within subsets of a population of blocked writers.

We recruited a total sample of 45 writers. The sample contained writers of many sorts, including writers of journalism or nonacademic nonfiction ($n = 5$, 11%), academic prose of a scientific or empirical nature ($n = 6$, 13%), academic prose in the arts and letters ($n = 11$, 24%), technical or instructional material ($n = 2$, 4%), prose fiction ($n = 16$, 36%), scripts for stage or screen ($n = 3$, 7%), and poetry ($n = 2$, 4%). Approximately 53% of the total sample might be viewed as working within a nonfictional writing genre, whereas approximately 47% were working within a fictional or artistic genre. The average age of this sample was 37, and 82% of the members of the sample enjoyed some current or previous period of documented writing-related professional success. The remaining 18% were early-career writers without established markers of career success. Thirty-three of the 45 writers reported an impasse on a current writing project that they considered to be of central importance to their careers. These impasses or blocks, by our definition, included objective indications of nonprogress in their work and subjective complaints of an incapacity to write. These writing difficulties were of at least 3 months' duration, with an average duration in the sample of 23 months. This group of 33 constituted our blocked sample. Twelve of the 45 recruited writers reported no unusual difficulty in writing. These writers were not significantly different from the blocked sample on dimensions of age, gender, marital status, occupational status, or educational level, and the distribution of fiction and nonfiction writers in this unimpaired group was not significantly different from that in the blocked group. This group of 12 constituted our nonblocked sample.

One phase of our research with these writers entailed extensive structured interviews and the administration of questionnaires. Among the questionnaires were 20 widely available, well-validated measures of personality, psychopathology, and cognitive ability. In addition to these, we administered 37 face-valid and internally reliable new scales specifically pertaining to the context, process, and content of the writing process. Technical features of the various measures are available in Barrios (1987).

Comparison of Blocked and Nonblocked Writers

A discriminant model contrasting blocked and nonblocked writers indicates that, taken together with other critical characteristics, blocked writers are significantly more likely than nonblocked writers to report low levels of positive and constructive mental imagery as measured by the Imaginal Processes Inventory (Huba, Aneshensel, Singer, & Antrobus, 1981). They also report a lower level of vividness in their current work-related mental imagery activity. Blocked writers also report that the writing project itself is intrinsically more difficult than others, requires greater novelty for successful completion, and requires higher levels of fantasy or dramatic content.

Mood and affect constitute significant factors in discriminating blocked from nonblocked writers. Depression and anxiety, in the form of symptoms of obsessive-compulsive disorder (OCD), are particularly prominent among blocked writers, as compared to nonblocked writers. This salience of OCD symptoms, such as unproductive repetition, self-doubt, perfectionism, and procrastination, is consistent with observations and anecdotes throughout the clinical literature (Gapinski, 1999–2000). Blocked writers present themselves as worried, self-doubting, and highly constrained by rigid rules and standards for their work. The relatively higher incidence of depressive symptoms is accompanied by high levels of reported self-criticism and lower levels of work-related feelings of excitement, pride, or joy. Interview data suggest that some of the blocked writers are mildly to moderately depressed prior to the onset of their block. More pronounced, however, is the finding that nearly all of the blocked writers find the experience of prolonged incapacity to write to be in itself quite depressing. Further complicating the work process, the blocked writers report an aversion to solitude, seemingly as an avoidant response to work-triggered dysphoria and feelings of helplessness.

Blocked and nonblocked writers also seemed to differ in their assessments of the quality of their social lives and the stability of their current life circumstances. Blocked writers expect a more substantial disruption of their current life as a result of completing their writing project than do nonblocked writers. For some, the block may serve to forestall a life transition that is contemplated with fear or ambivalence. Blocked writers are less likely than nonblocked writers to report an attachment to their current professional roles and relationships. They report lower levels of ambition. They also report more active disdain and dissatisfaction with colleagues and available role models. The blocked writers present an impression of holding on tightly to the uncomfortable status quo while simultaneously complaining about it.

Overall, blocked writers as compared with nonblocked writers appear to be more unhappy with themselves and the people around them. Depression, self-hate, guilt, and an inability to be alone with themselves are augmented by dissatisfactions with professional roles, disinterest with the work itself, and disdain for available role models. The persistence of writing blocks also appears to be strongly associated with a relatively poor capacity for constructive daydreaming or vivid work-related mental imagery. Finally, a writing project that is relatively highly demanding and that requires substantial imaginative skill is likely to intensify or prolong a block; such projects appear to overtax the blocked writer's constricted range of cognitive skills and depleted resources of self-esteem. Altogether, discouragement and disenchantment, coupled with a rigid, obsessive-compulsive coping style, appear to distinguish the blocked writer from the nonblocked writer.

Typology of Blocked Writers

In our contacts with the sample of blocked writers we were impressed with the apparent heterogeneity of the group. Writing blocks appeared to be subjectively experienced in a variety of ways, and there appeared to be numerous situational and behavioral pathways through which writers developed and maintained their blocks. Acknowledging this diversity, we sought to identify patterns of personality and experience that might characterize distinctive types of blocked writers.

To establish empirically derived types of blocked writers, we performed an obverse factor analysis of extensive questionnaire data from the 33 blocked writers. Obverse factor analysis – also known as transposed factor analysis or q-technique factor analysis – possesses several qualities to recommend it for research applications such as ours. It is an analysis in which subjects load on factors within a variable space, the obverse of the more typical r-technique factor analysis in which variables load on factors within a subject space. Obverse factor analysis is appropriate to the data of our research because it can effectively accommodate the large number of variables and relatively small number of subjects being studied. The result of this analysis is the identification of types of subjects, in this case types of blocked writers. Four essentially orthogonal types were extracted. Each type possessed sufficient numbers of univocally loading subjects to permit interpretation. These univocally loading subjects were identified as type-definers. To interpret the types, subjects' standardized scoring coefficients were correlated with the variables that had been entered into the analysis. Interview data obtained from type-defining subjects were cautiously employed in the service of providing nuance and coherence to the interpretation of the types (Barrios, 1987).

Type 1: The Dysphoric/Avoidant Type

This type of blocked writer expresses a wide variety of acute emotional distress. Questionnaire data indicate that high levels of multiple dysphoric experiences are associated with writing, including anger, fear, confusion, self-criticism, and fatigue. Relative to other blocked writers, there is also a striking absence of positive emotions in relation to writing; there is an absence of joy, excitement, pride, confidence, and interest. Generalized, phobic, and social anxieties are prominent. Depressive symptoms, guilty-dysphoric daydreams, and a high propensity for distractibility are frequently noted. These writers possess vivid imaginative capacities, but these qualities are not presently effectively employed in the service of writing. Rather, they appear to intensify aversive ruminations. Unhappy with the vivid dysphoric content of their imaginations and experiencing difficulty in imposing and maintaining structure in their writing projects, these writers avoid the quiet solitude of work.

An examination of interview data for a type-defining Type 1 writer provides an impression that is consistent with the factor analytic findings above. Matt is a single man in his early thirties who, at the time of our interview, had published three novels and a large number of articles and short stories. He is an articulate, soft-spoken man with a look of weary sadness in his face. He has been at work on his fourth novel for longer than 1 year and has been unable to progress beyond the first chapter. His editor has grown concerned about the lack of progress and has pressured Matt into a series of deadlines that have gone unmet. Despite his willingness to promise a completed book, he privately doubts his ability to ever finish it. The novel, set in ancient times, is outlined to feature a perplexed, enervated, and disillusioned protagonist who is seeking to cope with the complex cultural, social, and interpersonal challenges of a decaying civilization. The pessimistic themes of this project appear to be painfully mood congruent for Matt, complicating his tolerance for sustained absorption in his work.

Matt dates the onset of his writing difficulties to an abrupt and unforeseen disappointment over a woman with whom he was in love. Grief, outrage, and helplessness evoked by this painful loss appear to aggravate his work-related turmoil. He describes himself as having longstanding difficulty with trust in relationships and reports that his one prior experience of writer's block occurred in the aftermath of having been rejected by a woman. Like other Type 1 writers, he describes an early family history containing significant elements of deprivation and emotional trauma. In Matt's account, writing fiction has consistently served a function, especially during childhood and adolescence, of providing a refuge, an alternative imaginative world that is safely distant from his unhappy home life. Matt continues to see the process of writing as the single recourse available to him amidst his current unhappiness in relationships. Unfortunately, this former refuge has become yet another distressing entanglement. Writing, in his view, is his only hope for reinstating some sense of balance, yet he now finds himself flooded with anxiety and gloom when he isolates himself to work. Furthermore, he now feels pursued and tormented by an unhappy publisher.

Both psychometric and interview data suggest that, although writing remains life's primary activity for these Type 1 writers, it is no longer experienced as life's primary reward. Writing now precipitates intolerable states of anxiety, discouragement, and depletion, and its rewards have grown to be very few. Whereas writing was once a source of self-esteem and personal excitement, it now seems to expose these writers to profound self-doubt.

Among these writers, past interpersonal losses and humiliations contribute to current depressive experience. This demoralization appears to interfere with their capacity to concentrate on writing. At the same time, the loss of writing as a means of self-soothing and self-empowerment seems to threaten still further their sense of equilibrium in life. These writers have become intensely lonely and isolated people. The writing project, although dreaded and resented, has become their central companion in day-to-day life.

Type 2: The Guilty/Interpersonally Hindered Type
This cluster of writers is notable for having been less susceptible to writing disruptions in the past than the other types. They are noteworthy for their good work habits, their persistence, and their continuing capacity for positive and constructive daydreaming. When blocked they report relatively low levels of

enjoyment in their writing, and they acknowledge significant levels of hostility and irritation toward others. Whereas the process of writing is not currently enjoyable, they describe a highly positive attitude toward their writing project, reporting that it is both interesting and financially rewarding. In addition, they note that their current writing project is highly connected to the quality of their relationships with other people in their lives and that they are finding it difficult to justify their involvement in writing to significant other people.

Interview data seem to confirm the high prominence of interpersonal factors in this type of blocked writer. Sharon is a married woman in her mid-forties who, after marrying and having children, "drifted" into a career in business. Several years later, she "drifted" into a teaching job at a university school of business, and ultimately into a tenured professorship. At present, she is working on a book that she believes is likely to make her very well known in her field. Although she is keenly interested in her work, she now reports that she is having difficulty finishing this book and sending it to her publisher. She states that she repeatedly finds reasons to work on other projects, such as topically related articles that are shorter and perceived to be less important to her career.

Sharon speaks in strikingly passive and unambitious terms regarding her career. It is noteworthy that Sharon did not enter academia until after her husband had failed to receive tenure in a separate field at a different university and had embarked on a new career of his own in a nonacademic setting. Sharon has a very explicit worry about the possible negative consequences of her career success, particularly about the consequences of her publication of a book. The focus of her worry is on what this event may mean for her marriage. Her husband once aspired to write a book, but he did not succeed in doing it during his academic career. She acknowledges considerable concern about her husband's potential envy and resentment in relation to her successful completion of her book. She fears that her professional achievements will inevitably elicit feelings of self-doubt and shame in him and that in consequence she may be confronted with her own feelings of guilt and discomfort. Sharon acknowledges that she feels good when she is achieving her professional goals and is well regarded by colleagues, but she is not at ease with the possibility of being singled out for her accomplishments.

It is perhaps important to note that Sharon grew up in a family where only certain very traditional, family-centered accomplishments were supported among women. Her family actively opposed her pursuit of a college degree. Through the support of her high school teachers and counselors, she received a college scholarship, but faced censure and rejection from her family. At a young age she faced hard choices regarding the potential negative consequences of her own ambitions. As she speaks of these experiences now, she expresses strong feelings of anger and sadness, and she consciously worries that these painful past experiences may complicate her current relationship to her husband.

The difficulties of Type 2 writers seem to be strikingly interpersonal and to be characterized by severe self-inhibition. These writers seem to be caught between the desire for personal achievement and a subjective sense of duty to a spouse, a parent, or a child who is perceived as vulnerable. These writers seem to be highly attuned to other people. They find themselves shrinking away from becoming an object of envy to others. They seem most able to permit themselves to succeed when their success appears to be incidental and unintentional. The challenge posed by their current project is that it poises them on the brink of surpassing others. They face a difficult dilemma regarding whether they must sacrifice their own career opportunities and prerogatives for the sake of keeping others comfortable. They fear large-scale success and suspect that self-assertion may prove interpersonally destructive (Horner, 1972).

Type 3: The Constricted/Dismissive/Disengaged Type

Results of the obverse factor analysis indicate that Type 3 writers are somewhat more severely blocked than other types. These writers deny the involvement of anxiety or anger in their writing efforts. They deny interest in or attachment to their work colleagues, and they dismiss the possibility of benefit to their writing from their association with knowledgeable co-workers. These writers seem to be lacking in creative or inventive aptitude, and they are struggling with a writing project that seems to demand the high levels of originality that they lack.

Interview data seem to reinforce this general picture of constriction, disengagement, and limited creative resources. George is a graduate student in drama. Although he began his training in hopes of becoming an actor, he was told early on that he had only limited aptitude for acting. In consequence, he transferred to a program in drama criticism, and he is currently working on a thesis so that he can find what he hopes will be a "decent-paying" academic job. He denies distress, disappointment, or feelings of nearly any sort pertaining to his change in career direction. His expressive style is at once bland, nonspecific, and seemingly indifferent. He has not formed friendly relationships with faculty or other students in his new program. He asserts that he is only interested in getting his degree. He states that he is a good writer who has been consistently praised, but adds, "Writing was never what I really wanted to do." Despite the hope of finding substantial extrinsic reward for completing his thesis, he has not been able to generate much excitement or interest in his project. He seems half-heartedly to have hoped that writing criticism would offer him personal fulfillment, but instead has found the work dull and unsatisfying.

Type 3 writers describe a basic detachment from their work. They place a low value on the process of writing itself. These writers also create an impression of having relatively limited access to their emotional and imaginative experience. Inner experience is described in stereotyped language. These individuals seem dismissive and cynical about their colleagues and their own careers. They seem to invest minimal energy in creating a written product.

Type 4: The Angry/Disappointed Type

This type of blocked writer is characterized by the expression of a high level of negative emotion. Feelings of hostility, negativism, and resentment, are accompanied by writing-associated behaviors such as breaking, smashing, kicking, and throwing things and by growing irritable and short-tempered with other people. Type 4 writers are inclined to use alcohol or drugs when writing. Compared to other blocked writers, these writers report relatively high levels of anxiety, depression, somatic complaint, and paranoid or psychotic ideation. This type of writer has achieved the lowest level of occupational status among the four types, yet reports the highest level of striving for interpersonal attention and extrinsic reward for writing activities. These writers are highly distractible and report that their current project is highly demanding.

Howard is a Type 4 writer in his thirties who is writing a novel based on his past personal adventures as a young, self-styled urban hipster and cultural critic. He is a man who very early in life showed great promise as a writer. While still in his early twenties, he won a prestigious award for his writing and was given a grant to study abroad. He published his work in a number of widely recognized literary publications, but since his early days of high promise and acclaim, Howard's career as a writer has declined steadily and decisively. By Howard's account, his current novel constitutes an urgent attempt to get back to his "old self," to regain an idealized self who now seems to be lost to him. He is currently a discouraged and angry man who feels saddled with a difficult family life, severe financial worries, and a once hopeful future that is now seemingly out of his reach. He yearns to reclaim the public attention and carefree hopefulness of his earlier years.

Type 4 writers appear to be preoccupied with concerns about their own identity and worthiness. Their concerns are largely narcissistic. Much of their struggle lies outside the task of writing and focuses on the preservation of an idealized image of themselves. These writers have often had past experiences of success or acclaim, but now feel that their former comfortable status has been threatened or stolen.

Type 4 writers appear to be engaged in a search for a better self or a "lost self." They seek to regain attention and admiration. Their pronounced anger seems to contain elements of indirect self-blame for not living up to their ideals and aspirations. They feel burdened by an early success that they feel they have failed to sustain. These writers seem to be working to fend off despair and emptiness. Writing is looked to as the difficult path of escape from their current unhappiness. They continue to write in an effort to reinstate a former golden age and to bolster their fantasies of future reward and recognition by others.

Table 14.1. *Comparison of types of blocked writers*

	Type 1	Type 2	Type 3	Type 4
Feared Consequence of Work Involvement	Chaos	Betrayal	Arousal	Disappointment
Primary Affect or Expressive Mode	Anxiety/ Depression	Guilt/Inhibition	Detachment/ Constriction	Shame/Rage
Central Difficulty	Impaired Ability to Structure and Modulate Thoughts and Feelings	Ambivalence about Actualizing Personal Ambitions	Detachment from Own Imaginative Resources, Emotions	Failure to Actualize Personal Ambitions
Interpersonal Relatedness	Avoidant, Self-Isolating, Grieving	Attuned to Expectations of Others	Politely Indifferent, Disengaged	Impatient, Seeking Affirmation

Comparison of the Four Types of Blocked Writers

Table 14.1 summarizes and compares the characteristics of the four types of blocked writers across four dimensions of experience. We propose that these dimensions are helpful in clarifying strong relationships between Type 1 and Type 3 writers, and between Type 2 and Type 4 writers.

Type 1 and Type 3 writers appear to be characterized by difficulties of affective and ideational modulation. Type 1 writers appear to have insufficient distance and control in relation to their work: They are overwhelmed and immobilized by dysphoric thoughts and feelings. Type 3 writers appear to have excessive distance and control in relation to their work: They appear to be constricted, withdrawn, and out of touch with the potentially vitalizing aspects of their work. Difficulties of undercontrol and overcontrol appear to characterize these types. To a large degree, these types seem to be related to Schachtel's (1959) autocentric and allocentric modes of functioning; raw, unmodulated and poorly differentiated emotional experience is prominent in Type 1, whereas stereotyped, emotionally blunted, and hyperconventional functioning is prominent in Type 3.

Type 2 and Type 4 appear to be characterized by their differential focus on relationships and images of the self. Type 2 writers are distracted from productive work by their preoccupation with issues of self in relation to others. Type 4 writers are distracted from work by their preoccupation with issues of self-worth and self-definition. Type 2 is concerned with enhancing self while maintaining an uncomplicated relatedness to others. Type 4 is concerned with enhancing self through obtaining admiration and acclaim from others. To some degree, these types seem to be related to Blatt and Shichman's (1983) dual configuration model of personality development; concerns involving the pursuit and maintenance of interpersonal contact and nurturance seem operative in Type 2, whereas concerns about competency, status, and identity seem operative in Type 4.

Having identified the forms of writers' blockages in production and the different personality styles that characterize such blocked writers we turn next to presenting our approach to intervening to help these individuals regain their writing paces. We know from the work of Bergler (1950b) or Hatterer (1966) cited earlier that the broader personality approach through psychodynamic therapy may be useful over a relatively long course of sessions. In contrast, our intervention focuses more narrowly on using the basic human workings of imagery and ongoing thought as a short-term intervention. It reflects the values of imagery described in Singer (2006).

GUIDED IMAGERY AS A SHORT–TERM INTERVENTION

Imagery and Daydreaming in Creative Activity

The key to a short-term intervention as a catalyst for resolving an impasse in creative efforts is first of all the recognition that the imagery of such stimulus-independent thoughts can only be useful to the *prepared mind*. The psychoanalytic treatments of Bergler (1950b), Hatterer (1966), and others summarized in Leader (1991) may have been useful in helping creative individuals overcome longstanding difficulties relating to early childhood conflicts or even more recent interpersonal difficulties. Stretching across relatively lengthy time periods, such intervention has helped some creative individuals manage their drinking or other counterproductive living habits. In some cases, as reviewed by Acocella (2004), cognitive behavioral therapy or practical tape-recorded lessons may be useful in getting beginners started in a field of writing or other creative endeavor. In contrast, a short-term intervention of the type we describe that draws on encouraging awareness of one's imagery processes and fosters waking dreams is designed for the individual who is experienced in producing work in a given area and who is already something of an expert in his or her field.

In effect we are proposing that creative writers or scientists are continuously playing and replaying sequences of thought oriented toward the goal of generating a "product." Even though they may run into an impasse in their efforts and may either in frustration or with some inherent wisdom shift their thoughts or activities to some other direction, their stream of waking or even sleeping thought (especially in REM cycles) continues to produce images and associations relevant to what Klinger (1990, 1999) has called "current concerns." According to Klinger, "daydream-like activity – unbidden, undirected, drifting – represents a kind of human mental baseline. This activity automatically fills in the mental spaces not pre-empted by directed, working thought"

(Klinger, 1999, p. 33). In the research of Antrobus and Singer (Antrobus, 1999; Singer, 2006), Giambra (1977a, 1977b) and, most recently, Mason et al. (2007), we find such thought labeled as task-unrelated intrusive thought (TUITs) or stimulus-independent thought (SITs) for operational purposes in specific experiments. The acronym TUIT is whimsically designed in part to suggest the possible linkage to the term "intuition," which sometimes in popular usage seems to reflect an almost mystical phenomenon but which we propose is a process firmly rooted in the brain-based characteristics of normal ongoing thought. The flow of thought that we notice as mind-wandering or daydreaming or our recall of night dreams may involve brief conscious reconstructions, new associations, or the reshaping of mental schemas and scripts, but these soon seem forgotten as our attention is attracted by external stimuli or the return to seemingly higher priority mental activity. In the intervention experiments we now describe, we sought to recover some of the apparently forgotten reformulations that emerged briefly in awareness during the fleeting daydreams or sleep mentation of potentially creative persons. Our general hypothesis was that many of these brief experiences had occurred originally quite consciously, but had subsequently seemed to be forgotten because the forms in which they occurred – as dreams or daydreams – were interfered with by the pressure of more urgent concurrent mental or physical tasks.

Waking Imagery, Hypnotic Dream, and Rational Discussion Interventions

Our first study was carried out more than 25 years ago with a group of 48 men and women who had responded to an advertisement calling for persons who were experiencing a creative block in an area of artistic, literary, or scientific professional productivity (Barrios & Singer, 1981–1982). They were carefully screened so that we could be sure they could carefully describe their impasse. The block had persisted for at least 3 months in almost all of the participants. These individuals averaged 37 years in age and were predominately white, with 15% representing identifiable ethnic minorities.

The approach we took in this formal experiment was based on earlier findings initiated by Joseph Reyher, who showed that encouraging individuals to engage in experiences of free waking imagery yielded increased emotional or "drive-related" responses as well as signs of heightened creativity (Reyher, 1978). An experiment by Gur and Reyher (1976) showed that, after imagery "training," hypnotized individuals asked to produce dream experiences then obtained higher scores than control subjects on one of Torrance's creativity measures. A careful subsequent study by Dave (1979) followed up Reyher's approach. It drew on anecdotes of dream-derived solutions of creative problems such as Kekule's of the benzene ring. Dave worked with adults who were experiencing a variety of creative blocks. Using quasi-hypnotic methods with half his participants, Dave encouraged these persons to generate several dreams related to their creative product and to continue such dreams over the following week. To control for "placebo" or attention effects, Dave offered a portion of his control participants a form of treatment that involved very focused, logic-oriented, and purely verbal exploration of their blocks. Still another control group merely engaged in activity unrelated to their problem. The hypnotic-dream-induced group showed greater creative problem solution than did the two control groups.

The study we conducted was designed to determine whether hypnotic induction was really critical to generating imagery or dream-like productions or whether we could get comparable or even better results by simply encouraging our blocked professionals to form relatively spontaneous vivid or dreamlike waking imagery without some of the seemingly mystical or "spooky" features most people still associate with hypnosis. We therefore made use of a set of procedures developed by Barber and Wilson (1979) that encourage active and conscious production of mental imagery. We divided our 48 participants into four groups: waking imagery intervention, hypnosis-induced dream intervention, and two control groups. One control group engaged in a tightly focused, practical discussion of difficulties encountered in their creative projects. The other group, a "pure" control group, met for the same amount of time and the same number of sessions as the other groups and allowed individuals to describe their problems to a nondirective authority. At the end of the 2-week period, this last group of 12 individuals was evaluated with the same outcome measures as the other three groups for ethical reasons. The 12 individuals were then randomly assigned to one of the other three treatment groups and underwent either the intervention procedure of waking dream, hypnotic dream, or rational problem analysis. We hypothesized that the waking imagery technique might yield the best results, followed by the hypnosis group, and then possibly that some of those in the rational discussion group would show some gains.

All of our participants received a battery of questionnaires gathering demographic information and also answered questions about the characteristics of their blockages, their expectations of the treatment, their interpersonal relationships, and their history of similar impasses. They also filled out psychological questionnaires measuring their capacity for Absorption, a good predictor of suggestibility (Tellegen & Atkinson, 1974); their daydreaming patterns on the Short Imaginal Processes Inventory (Huba et al., 1981); their Public or Private Self-Consciousness styles (Fenigstein, Scheier, & Buss, 1975); their predisposition to Social Anxiety (Fenigstein et al., 1975); and their general intelligence (Jastak & Jastak, 1964). The specific form of intervention was described to each individual prior to its onset. As in all experimental research, we of course obtained signed informed consent documents from each participant.

A fully detailed account of the specific procedures we employed in each group and the descriptions of tests, statistical analyses, and outcome measures are available in Barrios and Singer (1981–1982). Let us briefly describe here the approach taken in the three intervention groups. The waking imagery condition called for participants, seated in a dimly lit, quiet room, to close their eyes and then to go through the imagining of 10 images from the Barber and Wilson scales (1979); for example, mentally producing some exquisite music, imagining and exploring a nature setting in slow motion. They then were told, "Now some images will come into your mind's eye. Please describe them to me as you see them." After each participant produced and described three such images, he or she was asked to generate a dream or dream-like image and to allow it to develop more fully. Then they were encouraged to picture or otherwise represent mentally the various elements of their blocked project and to signal when they had appeared. At this point they were to create a vivid dreamlike experience without actively incorporating their project elements but allowing them to emerge as if they had a life of their own. When the participant signaled that the dream was developed and recounted it, he or she was encouraged to allow similar dreams or waking images to occur each of the next seven nights.

The hypnotic dream group underwent a procedure closely similar to that of the waking imagery group, except that the relaxation exercises and instructions to participants closely followed the steps of a hypnotic induction. No specific reference was made to the word "hypnosis," but the suggestions and their sequence were those employed in experimental and clinical studies of hypnosis. Both conditions called for the participants to rate the vividness of their dream images at the conclusion of the sessions.

By contrast, the rational discussion condition took place in a well-lit room and was presented as a mutual problem-solving situation. The experimenter explained how distracting thoughts and seemingly irrational impulses might lead one away from careful focus on identifying and then overcoming the participant's block to making progress with his or her project. The experimenter frequently reflected or rephrased the participants' verbalizations and tried to keep the discussion focused on the presented problem and on possible solutions. The discussion lasted as long as 1 hour, averaging closer to 45 minutes. As indicated above, the pure control condition paralleled the rational discussion group, but was primarily built around the blocked individual's description of the problem and comments, with the experimenter assuming primarily a nondirective stance.

Outcomes of the First Intervention Study

A series of ratings and discussions with our participants took place after the first week and then after the second week of the study. We were able to ascertain that our general hypothesis was reasonably well supported. Ratings by the participants of their satisfaction with the outcomes of the procedure indicated highest scores for the waking imagery participants followed by the hypnotic induction group, then the rational discussion group, with the lowest ratings coming from the control group. This ordering was statistically reliable, but further analysis showed that only the two groups focusing on production of images were statistically superior to the controls. The control participants who were subsequently assigned to one of the three other groups all showed a statistically reliable improvement in their scores after they were exposed to the interventions.

We conducted various other analyses to determine if participants' expectations of their procedure group might have determined the outcome, but these beliefs had only a very slight influence. The most reliable predictors of which individuals would demonstrate gains in overcoming their blocks proved to be primarily the specific procedure to which they had been exposed. The predisposition to have better scores on the measure, High Attentional Control of Imaginal Processes, and having a creative block that had less impact on interpersonal relationships also had an influence on the outcome. Poorer effects were associated with the length of time the block had persisted and the participants' own lower level of general intelligence. We found that the best predictors of success with the waking imagery exposure condition came from those persons who had a predisposition to engaging in Positive-Constructive Daydreaming, held higher expectations for a good outcome, were more intelligent, and had been able to overcome blocks in the past. In the rational discussion condition the participants with the best outcomes were those who had a predisposition to Good Attentional Control of their Imaginal Processes, were less prone to Guilty or Dysphoric Daydreaming, and had devoted more time in the past to overcoming blocks. For the hypnotic induction participants only a higher occupational level was a predictor of success, in addition to following the experimenter's imagery instructions.

In general our results suggest that helping individuals generate imagery and sustain it over a week's time proved extremely useful in helping persons overcome their blocks. The results were also most effective for persons who have some predisposition to controlling and enjoying positive constructive fantasies and who are less prone to guilty, hostile, or anxious daydreams. Some examples follow of individuals who managed to make significant progress in overcoming blocks through either of the two imagery-fostering interventions.

A young college professor who was approaching a review for receiving tenure had been blocked in publishing her research since completion of her dissertation. Despite receiving good evaluations for teaching and college service, she faced the classic "publish or perish" risk in academia. She seemed excited and energized by the waking imagery procedures. On follow-up she found herself taking a playful approach to writing and begun an article describing her research. Soon afterward she showed us an article she had completed that had been accepted for publication.

A painter had been blocked for several years following the death of her mother. A painting she had been working on at that time that seemed frightening and disturbing kept recurring in her thoughts. After receiving the waking imagery treatment, she reported that she had begun a number of relatively simple color and texture painting experiments that she found enjoyable and encouraging. Not long afterward she retrieved the disturbing earlier painting from her basement and was able to rework it so that its colors and imagery evoked a sense of calmness and peace in her emotions. The painting now hangs in her home and she believes she has "discovered a well inside."

Another participant, this time in the hypnotic induction group, was a published poet and writer of nonfiction articles. She was blocked in undertaking a desired fictional work. With each image she produced in the treatment process, she began to envision more elaborate action and dialogue sequences for a short story. Then she was able from her imagery to generate a conflict among characters that enlivened the plot. In the follow-up period she was considerably pleased with her story and also reported that she had become more productive in writing poetry.

Still another example drawn from a participant in the waking imagery approach is of an architect who had been assigned the task of designing a large indoor-outdoor educational center for a particular handicapped population. He was paralyzed by trepidation and could not seem to begin, even though the formal requirements were within his area of expertise. During the waking imagery session, he was able to empathize vividly with the kinds of people who would be using the facility. He began to imagine the general physical atmosphere, the breezes, the sunlight, and other physical properties of the setting. At the follow-up he indicated that the session had been helpful to him in developing a design and an outline of the project. Several weeks later he called to tell us that he had presented his proposals to the project administrators, who proved to be very pleased. They were delighted with the very designs he had visualized in his imagery sessions.

In summary, our first intervention study provided reasonable evidence that exposing blocked individuals to ways of generating and attending to their imagery and ongoing consciousness might serve to loosen their cognitive-affective inhibitions and suggest new avenues for pursuing their scientific or artistic goals. We also had evidence that these gains could be accomplished without the more complex and somewhat controversial procedures of hypnosis. This led us to the second intervention, which focused primarily on literary blocks and also was based on the analysis we had conducted of the patterns of such blocks and on the particular kinds of persons who manifested writing hesitancies.

Imagery Intervention with Writers Blocked in Artistic, Nonfiction, or Critical Projects

In our second study we identified 45 writers who could be divided into an experimental group of 33 individuals who met our criteria of blockage and, as controls, 12 writers who had no significant current or past blockages in their productivity. This sample included approximately equal numbers of fiction and nonfiction writers and is the same one that provided the basis for the four factor analytically derived types of blocked writers described earlier. Each writer in the sample was currently working on a writing project of significant importance to his or her career. Among blocked writers, the average length of work disruption was 23 months. Characteristics of this sample are more fully described in the second section of the chapter. A detailed account of the means of procuring participants and the specific natures of the blockages is available in Barrios (1987).

As in the first intervention study, we sought to assess the effects of guided mental imagery activities on the work production of blocked writers. We employed a within-subject methodology, using repeated measures of a face-valid Writing Difficulty Scale (corrected Cronbach's alpha = .92) to assess objective and subjective elements of progress. The order of presentation of treatment conditions was balanced across blocked and nonblocked groups to control for possible confounding effects.

Experimental procedures were essentially identical for both the blocked and nonblocked groups. All participants were contacted by phone, screened for appropriateness, and scheduled to have two meetings with the experimenter. On average, each session lasted for about 2 hours and 40 minutes. At the first session, subjects were asked to describe their current writing project and their rate of progress on it. They were then given a lengthy questionnaire battery. After completion of the questionnaire, half of the samples of blocked and nonblocked writers were interviewed at length regarding a wide range of past and present experiences. This interview invited writers to reflect on five general areas of their lives: (1) the history of their involvement with writing; (2) the history and nature of their primary interpersonal relationships; (3) the nature and extent of their personal achievements, frustrations, and ambitions; (4) the phenomenology of writing and attempting to write when blocked; and (5) the specific nature and context of their current writing project.

Approximately 2 weeks after the interview session, the same two subsets of the blocked and nonblocked samples again met with the investigator for another 2- to 3-hour session. At the beginning of this meeting, subjects again filled out the Writing Difficulty questionnaire. After completing the questionnaire, subjects participated in an expanded waking imagery session similar to that in our first study (Barrios & Singer, 1981–1982). In brief, this session involved asking participants (1) to sit quietly in a dimly lit room with eyes closed and to focus on making themselves physically relaxed; (2) to describe, when asked at intervals of 2 minutes, the contents of their ongoing thoughts or fantasies; (3) to immerse themselves in the series of mental imagery exercises that form the basis of the Creative Imagination Scale (Barber & Wilson, 1979); (4) to repeatedly visualize or otherwise "experience" the elements of their current writing project; and (5) to repeatedly permit themselves to generate "dreamlike experiences" inspired by the recently examined elements of their writing projects. To assess the effects of this procedure on the writers, subjects were contacted by phone 2 weeks after participating in the waking imagery session. At this phone contact, subjects again were administered the Writing Difficulty Scale.

As noted earlier, an effort was made to control for order effects. Therefore, the second half of the blocked and nonblocked samples participated in two sessions identical to those described immediately above, but they undertook them in reverse order. Thus, after a brief description of their writing projects and completion of the lengthy battery of questionnaires, they participated in an imagery session in Session #1. Two weeks later, in Session #2, the participants were interviewed at length about a wide range of their personal and writing-related experiences. Like the first cohort of subjects, this group also received a 2-week telephone follow-up after Session #2.

Outcome of the Intervention Study

At the outset of this study, we had hypothesized that exposure to one's imagery and the generation of waking dreamlike thought (the experimental condition) would produce a significant improvement in writing effectiveness for our participants. We also proposed that this improvement would be of greater magnitude for our participants than any gains they might make just from having participated in the interview session alone. Both expectations were supported.

We conducted various statistical analyses to be sure that, even though all participants did reduce their scores on our measure of writing difficulty after the straightforward interview condition, the effects of being exposed to the waking imagery experimental condition yielded statistically reliable gains greater than mere participation in the study procedure itself. In effect, whether the participants underwent the interview before the imagery or the imagery before the interview, the improvement they made in writing difficulty was clearly greater after practicing imagery and then generating the waking dreams.

Having shown the advantageous effect for writers of our experimental condition, we then sought to determine what personal qualities of the writers and what special circumstances were most likely to predict a positive response to the imagery session. Here we resorted to the use of change scores – initial work difficulty scores minus postimagery work difficulty scores – to assess the personal characteristics or contingent circumstances that combined to predict improvement after the imagery exercise. Using a stepwise multiple regression statistical analysis and entering the same variables we had used in our analysis of block severity, we found a highly significant prediction effect. Writers who showed a good response to our imagery exercises were likely to be highly motivated, self-confident, and introspective. They were also more likely to tolerate workplace anxiety reasonably well, to show less anger as a part of their emotional palette while writing, and also to display less confusion during that task. They seemed less dependent on others for support and were also more likely to have set themselves fairly well-defined goals in what they would be writing.

If we examine the treatment outcomes for all four of the types of blocked writers described earlier and summarized in Table 14.1, we find that each type showed gains in reducing writing difficulty after exposure to the waking imagery exercise. This finding confirms the results from the first intervention study in demonstrating the potential of essentially one session of imagery exploration. We have reason to believe, however, that the members of Type 3 who were more constricted in their natural resort to daydreaming and imaginative thought might benefit from more extensive training in identifying and elaborating their imagery capacities. Type 1 and 4 participants also consistently indicated that they would prefer more extensive exposure to the "treatment" even though they made good gains after the single session. It seems likely that, given the frequent indications of loneliness among our writers, future intervention efforts might best offer more sessions, and indeed, treatment of blocked writers in small group sessions might be worth considering.

In summary, our second intervention study points up the value for writers of imagery exercises and demonstrates the power of using waking-dream generation, focused around specific blocks or goals, for reducing difficulties in expression. We can consider that further research with persons blocked in other artistic tasks such as choreography, sculpture, painting, or even musical composition might be worthwhile. However, it would be folly to propose that our waking imagery intervention could help inexperienced writers or beginning students suddenly produce creative fiction. Good writing of fiction, scholarly works, or criticism is built on a foundation of a rich vocabulary, wide reading, and hours of practice in written expression. These studies do corroborate the evidence from accumulating research that suggests that most people in the course of their daily stream of consciousness or the reworking of such ongoing thought in night dreams are inherently more creative than they realize. Clinical therapy has shown that increased attention to one's thought stream, fantasies, and dreams may heighten creative approaches to issues of daily life (Singer, 2006). The research of Robert Sternberg and his group on "successful intelligence" has indicated the value of training individuals in creativity through imagery and role playing, and this approach demonstrates possibilities for clinical application as well as for increasing originality in work situations (Kaufman & Singer, 2003–2004; Sternberg & Grigorenko, 2000). We believe that the studies described here that use imagery to help trained professionals overcome difficulties in writing may also be useful eventually for constructive expansions of creative accomplishments in a variety of work and artistic settings.

REFERENCES

Acocella, J. (2004, June 14). Blocked. *New Yorker, 80*(16), 110–129.

Antrobus, J. S. (1999). Toward a neurocognitive processing model of imaginal thought. In J. A. Singer & P. Salovey (Eds.), *At play in the fields of consciousness* (pp. 3–28). Mahwah, NJ: Erlbaum.

Baars, B. J. (1997). *In the theater of consciousness*. New York: Oxford University Press.

Barber, T. X., & Wilson, S. C. (1979). Guided imagining and hypnosis: Theoretical and empirical overlap and convergence in a new creative imagination scale. In A. A. Sheikh & J. T. Shaffer (Eds.), *The potential of fantasy and imagination* (pp. 67–88). New York: Brandon House.

Barrios, M. V. (1987). *Writer's block and blocked writers: Description and intervention*. Unpublished doctoral dissertation, Yale University, New Haven CT.

Barrios, M. V., & Singer, J. L. (1981–1982). The treatment of creative blocks: A comparison of waking imagery, hypnotic dream and rational discussion techniques. *Imagination, Cognition & Personality, 1*, 89–109.

Bergler, E. (1950a). Does writer's block exist? *American Imago, 7*, 43–54.

Bergler, E. (1950b). *The writer and psychoanalysis*. New York: Doubleday.

Blatt, S. J., & Schichman, S. (1983). Two primary configurations of psychopathology. *Psychoanalysis and Contemporary Thought, 6*, 187–255.

Bruner, J. (1986). *Actual minds, possible minds*. Cambridge, MA: Harvard University Press.

Dave, R. (1979). Effects of hypnotically-induced dreams on creative problem-solving. *Journal of Abnormal Psychology, 88*, 293–306.

Epstein, S. (1999). The interpretation of dreams from the perspective of cognitive-experiential self-theory. In J. A. Singer & P. Salovey (Eds.), *At play in the fields of consciousness* (pp. 51–82). Mahwah, NJ: Erlbaum.

Fenigstein, A., Scheier, M. F., & Buss, A. H. (1975). Public and private self-consciousness: Assessment and theory. *Journal of Consulting and Clinical Psychology, 43*, 522–527.

Gapinski, K. D. (1999–2000). Imagery in obsessive-compulsive disorder: Implications for symptoms and treatment. *Imagination, Cognition and Personality, 19*, 351–365.

Garfield, P. L. (1974). *Creative dreaming*, New York: Simon & Schuster.

Giambra, L. M. (1977a). Daydreaming about the past: The time setting of spontaneous thought intrusions. *The Gerontologist, 17*, 35–38.

Giambra, L. M. (1977b). A factor analytic study of daydreaming, imaginal process, and temperament: A replication on an adult male life-span sample. *Journal of Gerontology, 12*, 675–680.

Giambra, L. M. (1995). A laboratory method for investigating influences on switching attention to task-unrelated imagery and thought. *Consciousness and Cognition, 4*, 1–21.

Gur, R. W., & Reyher, J. (1976). Enhancement of creativity via free imagery and hypnosis. *American Journal of Clinical Hypnosis, 18*, 237–249.

Hatterer, L. J. (1966). *The artist in society: Problems and treatment of the creative personality*. New York: Grove Press.

Horner, M. (1972). Toward an understanding of achievement-related conflicts in women. *Journal of Social Issues, 28*, 157–175.

Huba, G., Aneshensel, C. S., Singer, J. L., & Antrobus, J. S. (1981). Development of scales for three second-order factors of inner experience. *Multivariate Behavioral Research, 16*, 181–206.

James, W. (1950). *Principles of psychology*. New York: Holt. (Original work published 1890)

Jastak, J. F., & Jastak, S. R. (1964). Short forms of the WAIS and WISC vocabulary subtests. *Journal of Clinical Psychology Monographs, 20*(18), 167–199.

Kaufman, S. B., & Singer, J. L. (2003–2004). Applying the theory of successful intelligence to psychotherapy training and research. *Imagination, Cognition & Personality, 23*, 325–355.

Klinger, E. (1990). *Daydreaming*. San Francisco: Tarcher.

Klinger, E. (1999). Thought flow: Properties and mechanisms underlying shifts in content. In J. A. Singer & P. Salovey (Eds.), *At play in the fields of consciousness* (pp. 29–50). Mahwah, NJ: Erlbaum.

Koestler, A. (1964). *The art of creation*. New York: Macmillan.

Leader, Z. (1991). *Writer's block*. Baltimore: Johns Hopkins University Press.

Mackenzie, N. (1965). *Dreams and dreaming*. London: Aldus Books.

Mason, M. F., Norton, M. I., Van Horn, J. D., Wegner, D. M., Grafton, S. T., & MacRae, C. H. (2007). Wandering minds: The default network and stimulus-independent thought. *Science, 335*(5810), 393–395.

Reyher, J. (1978). Emergent uncovering psychotherapy: The use of imagoic and linguistic vehicles in objectifying psychodynamic processes. In J. L. Singer & K. S. Pope (Eds.), *The power of human imagination* (pp. 51–94). New York: Plenum.

Root-Bernstein, R., & Root-Bernstein, M. (1999). *Sparks of genius*. New York: Houghton Mifflin.

Schachtel, E. (1959). *Metamorphosis*. New York: Basic Books.

Shepard, R. N. (1978). The mental image. *American Psychologist, 33*, 125–137.

Singer, J. L. (1975). *The inner world of daydreaming*. New York: HarperCollins.

Singer, J. L. (1995). Don't be afraid to daydream. *Reader's Digest, 106*(2), 77–80.

Singer, J. L. (2004). Concluding comments: Crossover creativity or domain specificity? In R. L. Sternberg, E. L. Grigorenko, & J. L. Singer (Eds.), *Creativity: From potential to realization* (195–223). Washington: American Psychological Association.

Singer, J. L. (2006). *Imagery in psychotherapy*. Washington, DC: American Psychological Association.

Sternberg, R. S., & Grigorenko, E. L. (2000). *Teaching for successful intelligence*. Arlington Heights, IL: Skylight Training & Publishing.

Sternberg, R. J., Grigorenko, E. L., & Singer, J. L. (Eds.). (2004). *Creativity: From potentiality to realization*. Washington, DC: American Psychological Association.

Tellegen, A., & Atkinson, G. (1974). Openness to absorbing and self-altering experiences ("absorption"), a trait related to hypnotic susceptibility. *Journal of Abnormal Psychology, 83*, 268–277.

15

Pretend Play, Emotional Processes, and Developing Narratives

SANDRA W. RUSS

Pretend play sets the stage for the creative writer. So many processes that are important in creative writing occur in the play of childhood and are developed in the arena of pretend play. Pretend play involves imagination, fantasy, storytelling, emotional expression, becoming absorbed in the moment, being spontaneous, taking risks, understanding the perspectives of others, and experiencing the joy of creation. Individuals who are able to engage in pretend play as children should be able to access these processes as adults during the writing process.

This chapter reviews processes in pretend play that are important in creativity, with a specific focus on emotional processes and creative writing. Although pretend play in children is a long way from creative writing in adults, nevertheless basic elements of the creative process occur in play. We can study these processes and learn about how play can help foster these elements. As in many areas of creativity, both case studies of creative writers (Wallace, 1989) and research studies offer valuable information. This chapter includes theory, research, and case examples that illustrate creative processes in creative authors.

PRETEND PLAY AND CREATIVITY

One of the best definitions of pretend play is by Fein (1987). She conceptualized pretend play as "a symbolic behavior in which one thing is playfully treated as if it were something else" (Fein, 1987, p. 282). A block becomes a telephone, for example. Pretend play involves the use of fantasy, symbolism, and make-believe. Fein also thought that pretense is charged with feelings and emotions, so that affect is intertwined with pretend play. Krasnor and Pepler (1980) believed that play involved nonliterality, positive affect, intrinsic motivation, and flexibility. These elements and many others that occur in play are important in the creative process. Many scholars in the area of pretend play have stressed the relationship between play and creativity. For example, Fein (1987) viewed play as a natural form of creativity. Vygotsky (1930/1967) thought that the creative imagination originated in children's play. Singer and Singer (1990) stressed the interaction of cognitive and affective processes in play that are important in creativity. Sawyer (1997) conceptualized pretend play as improvisational. Play is unscripted but has loose outlines to be followed. Improvisation is important in adult creativity.

In the field of creativity, a distinction is usually made between the creative product and the creative process. The creative product is the output of the individual, which can be judged as to the amount of creativity it exhibits. There is a consensus in the field that a product must be original, of good quality, and appropriate to the task (Sternberg, Kaufman, & Pretz, 2002). The creative process refers to the many cognitive, affective, and personality processes within an individual that are involved in the creative act. Individuals who are high on some of these processes will have a higher likelihood of producing a creative product. Different profiles of creative processes are likely in different domains of creativity. For example, Feist (1999) concluded that some personality traits are domain-general and some are domain-specific. Sternberg and Lubart (1996) discussed the complexity involved in generating a creative act. They reviewed confluence approaches to creativity involving multiple components that must converge for creativity to occur. Some of these components occur in pretend play.

There is some consensus about the processes involved in the creative act. Russ (1993) reviewed the research literature and described the cognitive, affective, and personality processes associated with the creative ability. A few of the cognitive processes are insight (Vandenberg, 1980), divergent thinking (Guilford, 1968), and transformation abilities (Guilford, 1968). Insight refers to the ability to see the solution to a problem. Sternberg (1988) developed a three-facet model of insight and synthesizing ability involved in creative thinking. Divergent thinking refers to the ability to generate a variety of ideas (Guilford, 1968). Transformation abilities involve the capacity to shift sets in problem solving and reorder information. Affect is also important in creativity. Csikszentmihalyi (1990) defined an optimal "flow" experience occurring when an individual is totally involved in an activity, feels a deep sense of enjoyment, and is optimally challenged. Related to the flow concept is intrinsic motivation. Amabile (1983) has demonstrated the importance of intrinsic motivation in creativity. For those who are intrinsically motivated, the love of the work drives the creative process. Other affective processes related to creativity are openness to emotional experiences (both positive and negative) and access to affect in fantasy, memories, and images (Russ, 1993, 2004).

Pretend play comprises a variety of cognitive and affective processes that can be observed and measured (Russ, 2004). Many of these processes are similar to those that have been identified as important in creativity. Russ proposed that cognitive processes in play include organization (the process of telling a story with a logical time sequence), divergent thinking (the process of generating a number of different ideas), symbolism (the process of transforming objects into representations of other objects), and fantasy/make-believe (the process of engaging in "as if" play behavior). Affective processes include the expression of emotion, expression of affect content themes, comfort and enjoyment in the play experience, and emotion regulation and modulation of the affect in the play (the process of containing the emotion within the narrative). Russ (1987, 2004) developed the Affect in Play Scale (APS), a standardized play measure, to assess these cognitive and affective processes that occur in play. Research findings with this measure are discussed later in this chapter.

Creative writers often refer to and remember pretend play events in their childhood. Stephen King remembers that his earliest memory "is of imagining I was someone else . . . the Ringling Brothers Circus Strongboy" (King, 2000, p. 18). He was about 2 1/2 or 3 years old at the time. He was dragging a concrete block across the floor and imagined standing on it in the center ring and being dressed in an animal skin. He then fell and the pain was intense. The memory stayed with him. At this young age, his imagination was active in pretend play. Mark Twain engaged in make-believe play at age 7 with his friends. He would assign them roles and dialogue that he drew from legends, such as those about Robin Hood (Powers, 2005). At that early age, he was practicing with dialogue and understanding different perspectives. Ingmar Bergman remembered the importance of playing with a magic lantern at 9. Putting on puppet productions of plays was an important part of his childhood (Rothstein, 2007).

AFFECT AND THE CREATIVE PROCESS

Five affective processes have emerged that are important in creativity based on theory and the research literature (Russ, 1993, 1999).

1. *Openness to affect states*: This is the ability to feel the affects and specific emotions as they occur. Individuals differ as to how much they can experience both positive and negative affect states.
2. *Access to affect-laden thoughts and fantasy*: This is the ability to think about ideas, images, and fantasies that include affect. Thoughts involving affect themes such as aggression, sex, affection, or fear illustrate this blending of affect and cognition. The psychoanalytic concept of primary process (discussed later) is an example of this type of cognitive-affective process.
3. *Affective pleasure in challenge*: This process involves the excitement and tension that come with identifying a problem or mystery.
4. *Affective pleasure in the creative act*: This is the tendency to take deep pleasure or joy in completing an artistic production or solving a problem in a new way.
5. *Cognitive integration and modulation of affective material*: This is the ability to control, think about, and regulate the affective events one experiences

and not be swept away by them. Although more of a cognitive than an affective process, it does reflect an interaction of cognition and affect and is important in the creative process.

Other types of affect systems important in creativity are often referred to as broad motivational systems. For example, intrinsic motivation (Amabile, 1990) is the motivation that comes from within the individual to perform the task. Conflict resolution and sublimation come from the need to resolve an internal conflict or, in the case of sublimation, to channel one's energy into a specific creative endeavor. The concept of an unresolved conflict or desire driving creative acts is a psychoanalytic one that has little empirical support, but has much clinical anecdotal material underlying it.

THEORIES OF AFFECT AND CREATIVITY

Different theories of creativity speculate about how affect is involved in creativity. What are the mechanisms at work with these different affective processes, and are they different in different domains of creativity?

Historically, the first theory of affect and creativity was psychoanalytic. Its key concept is primary process thinking. Sigmund Freud (1915/1958) first conceptualized primary process thought as an early primitive system of thought that is drive-laden and not subject to rules of logic or oriented to reality. An example of primary process thinking is the kind of thinking that occurs in dreams. Dreams are illogical and not oriented to rules of time and space, and they frequently include affect-laden content and images. Holt (1977) categorized the drive-laden content in primary process as oral, libidinal, and aggressive. Access to primary process thought was hypothesized to relate to creative thinking because associations are fluid and primitive ideas and images can be used. Martindale (1989) stated, "Because primary process cognition is associative, it makes the discovery of new combinations of mental elements more likely" (p. 216).

Kris (1952) introduced the concept of regression in the service of the ego, which emphasizes the importance of being in control of primary process thought. He postulated that creative individuals could regress, in a controlled fashion, and access primary process thought. Regression is an important concept because it holds that the individual could go back to a primitive mode of thought and use it for an adaptive, creative purpose. The individual could evaluate the loose, primitive associations and images and use them adaptively.

Creative writers often describe getting in touch with the primary process mode of thinking. One example I have discussed previously (Russ, 1993) is that of the comedian Robin Williams, who described this process as follows:

> And sometimes there are times when you're just on it – when you say the muse is with you and it's just flowing and that's when you know that the

well is open again and you just put in the pipe and you stand back and say "yes" – you're in control but you're not – the characters are coming through you (as cited in Culbane, 1988).

A recent interview with the playwright Harold Pinter by Lahr (2007) presented another example of this process of being in control but not being in control. His play *The Homecoming* begins with this sentence: "What have you done with the scissors?" Pinter said,

> I didn't know who was saying it. I didn't know who he was talking to. Now, the fellow he was talking to – if he had said, "Oh, I've got them right here, Dad," there would have been no play. But instead he says, "Why don't you shut up, you daft prat?" Once that's said, there's a spring of drama, which develops and follows its own course. I had no idea what the course was going to be. I hadn't planned anything. In the back of my mind, I think I knew there was another brother going to come back. I think I saw them quite early in a big house, with the doors being taken down, leading to a stairway. I saw them moving in that space. (p. 67)

In this passage, Pinter describes the process of letting the material come to him without a tight evaluative or logical component. He was comfortable enough with that process to let it happen.

Jorge Luis Borges, the Argentine writer, also described the feeling of not being in control (Russ, 1993). As Beard (1983) pointed out, Borges often used the passive tense in discussing his writing, as in the following:

> Suddenly I feel something is about to happen. Then I sit back and get passive, and something is given to me. I received a beginning and an end. When I have a subject, the subject tells me the style that he needs. When I write, I forget my own prejudices, my own opinions. The whole world comes to me. (pp. 7–8)

There is substantial evidence that access to primary process thought relates to creativity in adults (Russ, 1993; Suler, 1980). There are strong findings for this relationship with male populations and mixed findings with female populations. In children in my research program, primary process expression on the Rorschach was related to creative thinking in boys (Russ & Grossman-McKee, 1990). Again, there were mixed findings with girls. When we investigated the relationship between primary process on the Rorschach and primary process in play, we found that children who had more primary process expression on the Rorschach had more primary process in their play, more affect of all types in their play, and higher fantasy scores than children with less primary process expression on the Rorschach. This finding shows consistency in the construct of affective expression in fantasy across two different types of situations. In addition, primary process expression in play, in both boys and girls, was related to a divergent thinking task (Russ & Grossman-McKee, 1990).

What do the descriptions of creative writing and primary process have in common with children's pretend play? Play is a place where children become comfortable with this kind of free-flow process. They experience the pleasure involved in thinking about and manipulating the primitive ideas and images involved in primary process thinking. And play serves a purpose in helping children integrate this content into manageable bits.

Themes of affective content or primary process material are expressed in play, although emotion may or may not accompany the content. Waelder, in 1933, conceptualized play as a leave of absence from reality. It is a time to let go and let primary process thinking occur. Winnecott (1971) also recognized that play is a deeply pleasurable process that involves instinctual material. He stated that in play "the child puts out a sample of dream potential" (p. 51). Children express many types of raw emotion in play. They express affect-laden cognition like oral, aggressive, and libidinal content that is prevalent in primary process thought. Puppets eat, action figures hit each other, and dolls pat, hug, and dance together.

Russ (1987) proposed that primary process thought is a subtype of affective content in cognition. Primary process is content around which the child has experienced early intense feeling states. Learning to regulate these intense emotions and affect-laden thoughts and images is a major developmental task. Children vary widely as to whether this content is thought about, how it is expressed in fantasy and play, and how it is integrated into imagination. How this early affective content is dealt with may affect the amount and kinds of memories that are encoded.

Erikson (1963) introduced the concept of mastery in play. Children use play to gain mastery over traumatic events and everyday conflicts. Play is thus a major form of conflict resolution. Waelder (1933) described the child as repeating an unpleasant experience over and over until he or she gains mastery over the event. Play is a "method of constantly working over, and, as it were, assimilating piecemeal an experience which was too large to be assimilated instantly at one swoop" (p. 218). The child has "digested" the event, to use Waelder's analogy.

As mentioned earlier, psychoanalytic theory also emphasizes the importance of unresolved conflicts in motivating the individual to engage in creative work. For example, unrequited love will be expressed in a poem or the loss of a loved one will be written about to help resolve the loss. The motivation to transform one's own pain into artistic creations that have universal appeal is thought to be an important factor in creative work.

Fein's (1987) view of affect as intertwined with pretend play and creativity also makes an important theoretical contribution. She viewed play as a natural form of creativity. She studied 15 master players (children who had excellent play abilities) and identified characteristics of play that were common among these good players. Two noteworthy characteristics are referential freedom and affective relations.

Referential freedom in play is the "as if" quality displayed when one object is treated "as if" it were another or one person functions as if he or she was someone else. Object substitutions and transformations occur in play. Fein theorized that transformations occur when a representational template is mapped onto persons or objects in the environment. These representations can then be manipulated and are detached from practical outcomes in play.

Symbolic units represent affect relations such as fear of, love of, anger at, etc. Fein proposed an affective symbol system that represents real or imagined experience at a general level. These affective units constitute affect-binding representational templates that store information about affect-laden events. The units are "manipulated, interpreted, coordinated, and elaborated in a way that makes affective sense to the players" (Fein, 1987, p. 292). These affective units are a key part of pretend play. Fein hypothesized that divergent thinking abilities such as daydreams, pretend play, or drawing can activate the affective symbol system.

One of Fein's major conclusions was that creative processes cannot be studied independently of an affect symbol system. An affective symbol system is activated in pretend play and probably facilitated through pretend play.

Another theoretical approach to affect and creativity has been within a cognitive-affective interaction framework. Much of the research within this framework has used a mood induction paradigm in which a specific mood state is induced by having participants watch a film or think about a memory that is happy or sad. For example, Isen, Daubman, and Nowicki (1987) found that induced positive affect facilitated creativity. They concluded that the underlying mechanism is that positive affect cues positive memories and a large amount of cognitive material. This process results in defocused attention and a more complex cognitive context that, in turn, result in a greater range of associations and interpretations. Studies with induced negative affect have had mixed results, depending on the amount of negative affect and the type of task (Vosburg & Kaufmann, 1999). One of the main conclusions from this experimental work is that the involvement of emotion broadens the association process, which facilitates creativity.

An interesting theoretical model is the emotional resonance model of Getz and Lubart (1996). In this model, they described endocepts, which represent emotions attached to concepts or images in memory. These emotional memories are partially interconnected and can activate one another. Endocepts attached to concepts resonate with one another. When stimulated, endocepts trigger other memories and associations and influence creative problem solving.

Another theoretical concept that has implications for the play and creativity relationship is that of conceptual blending (Fauconnier & Turner, 2002). Conceptual blending is the complex cognitive process of combining and fusing different ideas, thoughts, images, and mental representations. It is central to creative artistic work. Fauconnier and Turner proposed a set of principles and rules that are involved in the many different types of blending that occur. They described the mechanisms by which associations and concepts become fused. Affect can be a combinatory element. Children demonstrate the different types of blendings and fusions in their artistic expressions and, although not formally studied, one could speculate they occur in pretend play as well.

Deacon (2006) conceptualized aesthetic experience as a function of an intrinsic shift in motivational structure that favors combinatorial associative exploration. This process involves combinatorial freedom in manipulating mental representations and their emotional correlates with respect to one another. Deacon discussed symbolic play as unique to humans; it enables the taking of a "representational stance" during which mental representations and their emotional correlates can be manipulated without serious conse-quences. The play frame is a safe one. The similarities between these ideas and Fein's descriptions of master players are striking. Deacon went on to state, "Aesthetic cognition may involve representational manipulation of emo-tional experiences" (p. 38), and this feature differentiates humans from other primates. Sophisticated human emotions are emergent synergies of blended cognitions and emotional experiences that the mind transfigures by symboli-cally re-representing them. Deacon thus augmented the conceptual blending construct by linking it to emotional states. The play experience is the beginning of the lifelong process of manipulating cognitions and emotional experiences.

EMPIRICAL FINDINGS

There is a large body of research in the play and creativity area. Individual differences in creative processes can be identified in children, and many of these processes are experienced and developed in pretend play (Russ, 1993, 2004; Saracho, 2002). Both cognitive and affective processes that are important in creativity occur in play.

Insight, a cognitive process that is important in creative problem solving, can be facilitated through play. In a review of experimental studies of insight and play, Vandenberg (1980) concluded that play facilitated insightful tool use and enhanced motivated task activity. For example, in a classic study, Sylva, Bruner, and Genova (1976) had one group of children play with objects, a second group observed an experimenter solve a problem, and a third control group was only exposed to the objects. Significantly more children in the play and observation groups solved the problem than in the control group. The play group was more goal oriented than the other groups in the task and was more likely to piece together the solution.

Divergent thinking has been identified as one component of creativity and is important in many domains (Runco, 1991). Play should be related to divergent thinking because in play children generate a variety of ideas and recombine ideas and symbols. In essence, play is practice with divergent thinking (Singer & Singer, 1990). In addition, the involvement of emotion in play should increase children's access to emotional memories and broaden their associative network (Isen, Daubman, & Nowicki, 1987; Russ, 1993).

A large number of studies have found a relationship between play (usually solitary) and divergent thinking (Johnson, 1976; Pepler & Ross, 1981; Singer & Rummo, 1973). Russ and Grossman-McKee (1990) found that both cognitive and affective processes in play related to divergent thinking, independent of intelligence. Lieberman (1977) found a relation between playfulness, which included affective components of spontaneity and joy, and divergent thinking in kindergarten children. In Fisher's (1992) meta-analysis of play studies, the largest effect size was for divergent thinking.

In a longitudinal study, Russ, Robins, and Christiano (1999) found that imagination and organization of fantasy in play in first and second graders were associated with divergent thinking in the fifth and sixth grades. In this study, the Affect in Play Scale (APS; Russ, 1993, 2004) was individually administered to children in the first and second grades. The APS is a play task in which children play with puppets and blocks for 5 minutes. The play is videotaped and rated according to categories of frequency and type of affect expression, organization of the narrative and imagination, and comfort in play. The scale measures both positive affect (i.e., happiness and nurturance) and negative affect (i.e., aggression, fear). Eleven types of affect are coded. Thirty-one of the children who received the APS in the first and second grades received a divergent thinking task in the fifth and sixth grades. Imagination in play significantly related to divergent thinking ($r = .42$, $p < .01$), and this relationship remained significant after controlling for IQ. Play did not facilitate divergent thinking, but demonstrated a stable relationship to it over time. Children who showed imagination in their play in the first and second grades were better divergent thinkers in the fifth and sixth grades. When these children were in the seventh grade, we again administered the APS, this time modifying the instructions and asking the children to put on a play with the puppets. Early play was significantly related to imagination and affect expression in the play of these older children. The magnitude of the correlations was quite good for longitudinal data. The strongest correlation was for the expression of positive affect ($r = .51$). These findings suggest that the cognitive and affective processes in play that are measured by the APS are stable over time.

Recently, Russ and Schafer (2006) found a relationship between negative affect in fantasy play and divergent thinking. Children who could express negative themes in play, such as aggression or sadness, generated more uses for objects and more original uses for those objects on a creativity task. This finding indicates that the expression of negative affect in play is related to creative processes. This study also found a relationship between affect in play and affect in memory descriptions. This is an important finding that brings us to the important area of emotional processing, access to memories, and the writing process.

PRETEND PLAY AND MEMORIES

Theoretically, children who can express affect content in play and who can think about and express affect-laden cognition in pretend sword fights, cake baking, feeding activities, running from monsters, and the like should have more access in general to memories with affective content. Children use play to process emotion and the events that happen to them that have emotional content. Russ and Schafer (2006) tested this hypothesis by administering the APS to 46 first- and second-grade children. These children also received a divergent thinking test and an emotional memories questionnaire. In the memories task, the children answered nine questions about different memories – three questions each about positive memories (tell me about a time when you felt happy), negative memories (tell me about a time when you felt sad), and neutral memories. Responses were coded for amount and type of affect. There were significant relationships between play scores (organization, imagination, affect frequency, affect variety) and the amount of affect in memories. These relationships remained significant when word count and verbal intelligence were controlled. The finding that affect in play related to the amount of affect in memory descriptions suggests a cross-situational ability in children. Children who are able to express affect in play are also able to include emotion when thinking about a memory. This result is consistent with that of Russ and Grossman-McKee (1990) who found that affect in play related to the expression of affect-laden primary process content on the Rorschach; thus, the ability to express affect-laden content was cross-situational in that study as well.

The Russ and Schafer (2006) study is the first to show that play ability is related to affect in memories and to offer some evidence supporting the many theories previously reviewed that would predict this finding (psychoanalytic, affective symbol system, cognitive blending). Many more studies need to be carried out to further test and understand the mechanisms involved. It is possible that children who can use play well can store more emotional memories to begin with and also have better access to these memories than children who cannot use play to deal with emotion. Expressing negative affect in particular was important in this study.

What advantage would having a rich store of affect-laden memories and having easy access to these memories give to the aspiring writer? The poet Stanley Kunitz (2005) beautifully describes the importance of emotion in writing poetry: "The poem has to be saturated with impulse and that means getting down to the very tissue of experience. How can this element be absent from poetry without thinning out the poem?" (p.103). Many writers struggle to get to this "tissue of experience," which requires experiencing deep emotions and remembering experiences that might be painful or conflicted. Early play experiences in which the child learns to express, master, and contain emotions would help the child gain an early start in living fully. Of course, in the creative writing process, this personal emotional material is transformed into artistic productions. There too, the play experience may provide early practice with transformation events.

Ingmar Bergman used his childhood memories in his screenplays. In a 1993 interview, Bergman said,

> I have maintained open channels with my childhood. I think it may be that way with many artists. Sometimes in the night, when I am on the limit between sleeping and being awake, I can just go through a door into my childhood and everything is as it was – with lights, smells, sounds and people. . . . I remember the silent street where my grandmother lived, the sudden aggressivity of the grown-up world, the terror of the unknown and the fear from the tension between my father and mother." (Rothstein, 2007, p. A20)

Many writers have experienced the early loss of a parent or significant person in their lives (Morrison & Morrison, 2006; Pollock, 1962). Ideally, the intense emotion involved in early loss would be integrated, perhaps through play. Morrison and Morrison (2006) discuss writers who experienced the pain of early loss but who have not been able to integrate the experience for a variety of reasons. They hypothesize that these intense early memories, if repressed, can serve as a motivation for creative expression in writing. They present case conceptualizations of Emily Bronte, J. M. Barrie, Isak Dineson, and Jack Kerouac as examples of writers who were constricted in some ways by their unresolved mourning, but used their unresolved grief and identity issues in their transformative creative work.

PLAY INTERVENTIONS

Most of this research on play and divergent thinking has been correlational; therefore, one cannot conclude from these studies that play facilitates creativity. However, a causal relationship has been found between play and divergent thinking in a few experimental studies. In two important studies, play facilitated divergent thinking in preschool children (Dansky, 1980; Dansky & Silverman, 1973). In particular, Dansky and Silverman, in a well-designed study using random assignment, found that children who played with objects during a 10-minute play period gave significantly more uses for those objects than did children who imitated play or who colored pictures. In the later experimental study, Dansky (1980) found that make-believe play was the mediator of the relationship between play and creativity. Also, in the second study, play had a generalized effect in that objects in the play period were different from those in the test period. These two studies are important in that they show a direct effect of play on divergent thinking. In a review of the research literature, Dansky (1999) concluded that there were consistently positive results in studies with adequate control groups that demonstrated that play tutoring, over a period of time, did result in increased imaginativeness in play and increased creativity on measures other than play.

Russ, Moore, and Pearson (2008) investigated the effectiveness of two different play interventions on play skills in comparison with a control group. One play intervention script focused on improving imagination and organization of the narrative. The other play intervention script focused on increasing affective expression in play. In addition, outcome measures of creativity and other measures of adaptive functioning were included. It was hypothesized that both play interventions would result in improvements in all play skills when compared with the control group. Of particular interest was whether the affect group intervention would have an effect on the affect play skills and whether the imagination group intervention would positively affect imagination and organization. In addition, it was expected that both play intervention groups would have higher scores on the creativity measure (divergent thinking) than the control group.

We saw each child individually for 30 minutes for five sessions over a 2-month period. For each session the child was asked to make up stories and act them out with the toys. Children in the imagination group were presented with a set of toys including human-like dolls, blocks, plastic animals, Legos, and cars. They were asked to play out 13 possible stories with high fantasy content (e.g., someone who lives on the moon) and high story organization (e.g., what someone needs to do to get ready for school). Children were encouraged to explore alternate endings for their stories, and they were reinforced for being creative and engaging in object transformations. The specific instructions were as follows:

> I have some toys for you to play with. I want you to make up stories about different things. So, you can make up a story and play it out with the toys. Have the dolls and animals talk out loud so I can hear you.

> Make up a story with a beginning, middle, and end. Think about what will happen next in the story. Use your imagination and make up new things. Make up a story about . . .

Among the 13 possible stories were getting ready for a day at school, going to the zoo, living in a city under water, and having magic powers. We started with the more simple stories (going to the zoo) and moved to the more imaginative stories (going to the moon) over time. During the 30-minute sessions, the trainer was active, giving these standardized prompts: have a beginning, middle, and end; show details; have the characters talk; pretend something is there (use a Lego to be a milk bottle); make up different endings;

and ask what happens next. The trainer used reinforcement, modeling, and praise.

Children in the affect group were given the same set of toys as children in the imagination group, although the instructions, stories, and prompts were different. Instead of focusing on fantasy and organization, children were encouraged to express feelings and were asked to play out stories with affective content. For example, a child might have played out a story about someone who was happy because she was going to a birthday party or sad because he had lost his favorite toy. Here are the specific instructions:

> I have some toys for you to play with. I want you to make up stories about different things. So, you can make up a story and play it out with the toys. Have the dolls and animals talk out loud so I can hear you.

> Make up a story with a lot of feelings. Have the toys and dolls talk out loud and say and show how they are feeling. Make up a story about . . .

Possible storylines included a friend moves away (sad), have a birthday party (happy), get lost on the way home from school (scary), get teased at school (angry), give a present to a friend (caring), and cannot find a favorite toy (upset). We mixed affects in each session and always ended with a positive affect story. The examiners used modeling, reinforcement, and reflection of feeling states to encourage affective experimentation. They gave these standardized prompts: reflect/label feelings, ask how the dolls are feeling, have the dolls talk to each other about how they are feeling, state they are feeling this way because . . . , and ask what happens next.

Children in the control group spent their sessions putting together puzzles and coloring on coloring sheets. The puzzles and coloring sheets were of neutral scenes such as a farm puzzle and pictures of flowers and butterflies. Experimenter interaction was controlled for by using standardized prompts and encouragement unrelated to affect or imagination. For example, children putting a puzzle together might have been asked about the colors in the picture, the content of the picture, or how many puzzle pieces there were. Toy choice (i.e., being able to pick what toys to use, as in the intervention groups) was controlled for by allowing the children to choose whether they wanted to start by doing a puzzle or by coloring. They had the option of changing activities at their discretion. Here are the specific instructions:

> I have some puzzles and coloring sheets and crayons for you to play with. I want you to pick a puzzle or coloring sheet to start out with and when you are finished you can do something different. You can talk out loud about the colors in the picture and what you see.

The prompts were to ask what is in the picture, what puzzle piece is that, what color is that, and how many puzzle pieces are there. Examiners were also active in praising children for their effort and helping them with the puzzles.

The major finding of this study was that the play interventions were effective in improving play skills, with the affect play condition having a stronger impact. After baseline play was controlled for, the affect play group had significantly higher play scores on all play processes. These children had more affect in their play (both positive affect and negative affect), a greater variety of affect content, and better imagination and organization of the story than did the control group. The imagination play group also had significantly more positive affect and variety of affect than the control group. Another major finding was that, on the creativity outcome measure, significant effects varied by group. Although the individual contrast comparisons did not reach significance, inspection of the profile plots indicated that the play groups (usually the affect play group) had higher scores on the creativity measure.

The affect play intervention was the most effective intervention in improving play skills. By having children play out stories involving emotion, both positive and negative, we were able to improve play skills as measured by the APS. It is worth noting that the APS play task is quite different from the play intervention situation in that it uses only a few props (two puppets and a few blocks), whereas the intervention used a variety of toys. In addition, the instructions for the APS are very unstructured ("play any way you like"), whereas the play intervention was quite structured and the child was directed to make up stories with specific themes. Thus, the finding that play changed on the unstructured outcome play measure suggests that the effect of the play intervention would generalize to a natural play situation. Future research should investigate this question.

The finding that the affect play group intervention increased both affective expression in play and cognitive abilities of imagination and organization of the story suggests that involvement of affect also influences processes of imagination and fantasy. To express emotion, the child had to call on storytelling and imagination. Developing a narrative around the emotion may be a powerful process for children. The imagination play group had a significantly greater frequency of positive affect and variety of affect. That the imagination play group intervention improved positive affect and resulted in a wider range of affect expression suggests that using one's imagination involves positive affect. This finding is consistent with results from the creativity research in which positive affect facilitates creativity and imagination (Isen, Daubman, & Nowicki, 1987).

The finding that both play group interventions increased the positive affect in play is important. Pretend play is fun for most children and may stimulate positive affect themes such as stories about having fun, being happy, and caring about others. This result could have implications for mood regulation in children.

Interestingly, the play intervention in this study was to make up stories, some with affect and some without. There are many similarities to the writing process. An interesting study would be to compare the effects of a making up a story play intervention and a making up a story writing intervention. An important outcome measure to add would be a creative writing component in addition to the play outcome and divergent thinking measure.

CONCLUSION

Theory, descriptions of the writing process by creative writers, and research in the play and creativity area all point to the importance of play in the development of creativity and of processes that are important to the creative writer. Not only does pretend play involve and facilitate divergent thinking – the ability to generate a variety of ideas and associations – but it also involves affective processes that are important to the creative process. We can speculate as to how play helps facilitate the processing of emotions, which in turn helps the child feel comfortable with emotion and develop a rich store of memories. Pretend play would be a resource for the budding writer to utilize. In addition, the joy of the play experience can be rediscovered in the creativity of the act of writing.

REFERENCES

Amabile, T. (1983). *The social psychology of creativity.* New York: Springer.

Amabile, T. (1990). Within you, without you: The social psychology of creativity and beyond. In M. Runco & R. Albert (Eds.), *Theories of creativity* (pp. 61–91). Newbury Park, CA: Sage.

Beard, D. (1983, May 22). Jorge Luis Borges: What else can I do but write? *Plain Dealer,* pp. 1–7.

Csikszentmihalyi, M. (1990). *The psychology of optimal experience.* New York: Harper-Collins.

Culbane, J. (1988, January 10). Throw away the script. *Plain Dealer,* pp. 1–5.

Dansky, J. (1980). Make-believe: A mediator of the relationship between play and associative fluency. *Child Development, 51,* 576–579.

Dansky, J. (1999). Play. In M. Runco & S. Pritzker (Eds.), *Encyclopedia of creativity* (pp. 393–408). San Diego: Academic Press.

Dansky, J., & Silverman, F. (1973). Effects of play on associative fluency in preschool-aged children. *Developmental Psychology, 9,* 38–43.

Deacon, T. (2006). The aesthetic faculty. In M. Turner (Ed.), *The artful mind* (pp. 21–53). Oxford: Oxford University Press.

Erikson, E. H. (1963). *Childhood and society.* New York: W. W. Norton.

Fauconnier, G., & Turner, M. (2002). *The way we think: Conceptual blending and the mind's hidden complexities.* New York: Basic Books.

Fein, G. (1987). Pretend play: Creativity and consciousness. In P. Gorlitz & J. Wohlwill (Eds.), *Curiosity, imagination, and play* (pp. 281–304). Hillsdale, NJ: Erlbaum.

Feist, G. J. (1999). The influence of personality on artistic and scientific creativity. In R. J. Sternberg (Ed.), *Handbook of creativity* (pp. 273–296). New York: Cambridge University Press.

Fisher, E. (1992). The impact of play on development: A meta-analysis. *Play and Culture, 5,* 159–181.

Freud, S. (1958). The unconscious. In J. Strachey (Ed. & Trans.), *The standard edition of the complete psychological works of Sigmund Freud* (Vol. 14, pp. 159–215). London: Hogarth Press. (Original work published 1915)

Getz, I. & Lubart, T. (1999). The emotional resonance model of creativity: Theoretical and practical extensions. In S. Russ (Ed.), *Affect, creative experience and psychological adjustment* (pp. 41–56). Philadelphia: Bruner/Mazel.

Guilford, J. P. (1968). *Intelligence, creativity and their educational implications.* San Diego: Knapp.

Holt, R. (1977). A method for assessing primary process manifestations and their control in Rorschach responses. In M. Rickers-Ovsiankina (Ed.), *Rorschach psychology* (pp. 375–420). New York: Kreiger Publisher.

Isen, A., Daubman, K., & Nowicki, G. (1987). Positive affect facilitates creative problem solving. *Journal of Personality and Social Psychology, 52,* 1122–1131.

Johnson, J. (1976). Relations of divergent thinking and intelligence test scores with social and nonsocial make-believe play of preschool children. *Child Development, 47,* 1200–1203.

King, S. (2000). *On writing.* New York: Scribner.

Krasnor, I., & Pepler, D. (1980). The study of children's play: Some suggested future directions. *New Directions for Child Development, 9,* 85–94.

Kris, E. (1952). *Psychoanalytic explorations in art.* New York: International Universities Press.

Kunitz, S. (2005). *The wild braid.* New York: W. W. Norton.

Lahr, J. (2007, Dec. 24). Demolition man. *New Yorker,* pp. 54–69.

Lieberman, J. N. (1977). *Playfulness: Its relationship to imagination and creativity.* New York: Academic Press.

Martindale, C. (1989). Personality, situation and creativity. In J. Glover, R. Ronning, & C. R. Reynolds (Eds.), *Handbook of creativity* (pp. 211–232). New York: Plenum.

Morrison, D., & Morrison, S. (2006). *Memories of loss and dreams of perfection.* Amityville: Baywood Publishing.

Pepler, D., & Ross, H. (1981). The effects of play on convergent and divergent problem solving. *Child Development, 52,* 1202–1210.

Pollock, G. (1962). Childhood parent and sibling loss in adult patients: A comprehensive study. *Archives of General Psychiatry, 2,* 295–305.

Powers, R. (2005). *Mark Twain.* New York: Free Press.

Rothstein, M. (2007, July 31). Ingmar Bergman, master filmmaker, obituary. *New York Times,* pp. A1, A20.

Runco, M. A. (1991). *Divergent thinking.* Norwood, NJ: Ablex.

Russ, S. (1987). Assessment of cognitive affective interaction in children: Creativity, fantasy and play research. In J. Butcher & C. Spielberger (Eds.), *Advances in personality assessment* (Vol. 6, pp. 141–155). Hillsdale, NJ: Erlbaum.

Russ, S. (1993). *Affect and creativity: The role of affect and play in the creative process.* Hillsdale, NJ: Erlbaum.

Russ, S. (1999). Play, affect and creativity: Theory and research. In S. Russ (Ed.), *Affect, creative experience and psychological adjustment* (pp. 57–75). Philadelphia: Bruner/Mazel.

Russ, S. (2004). *Play in child development and psychotherapy: Toward empirically supported practice.* Mahwah, NJ: Erlbaum.

Russ, S., & Grossman-McKee, A. (1990). Affective expression in children's fantasy play, primary process thinking on the Rorschach, and divergent thinking. *Journal of Personality Assessment, 54,* 756–771.

Russ, S., Moore, M. E., & Pearson, B. L. (2008). *Effects of play intervention on play skill and adaptive functioning: A pilot study.* Manuscript submitted for publication.

Russ, S., Robins, D., & Christiano, B. (1999). Pretend play: Longitudinal prediction of creativity and affect in fantasy in children. *Creativity Research Journal, 12,* 129–139.

Russ, S., & Schafer, E. (2006). Affect in fantasy play, emotion in memories, and divergent thinking. *Creativity Research Journal, 18,* 347–354.

Saracho, O. N. (2002). Young children's creativity and pretend play. *Early Child Development and Care, 172,* 431–438.

Sawyer, P. K. (1997). *Pretend play as improvisation.* Mahwah, NJ: Erlbaum.

Singer, D. G., & Singer, J. L. (1990). *The house of make-believe: Children's play and the developing imagination.* Cambridge, MA: Harvard University Press.

Singer, D. L., & Rummo, J. (1973). Ideational creativity and behavioral style in kindergarten age children. *Developmental Psychology, 8,* 154–161.

Sternberg, R. (1988). A three-facet model of creativity: In R. Sternberg (Ed.), *The nature of creativity* (pp. 125–147). Cambridge: Cambridge University Press.

Sternberg, R., & Lubart, T. (1996). Investing in creativity. *American Psychologist, 51,* 677–688.

Sternberg, R. J., Kaufman, J. C., & Pretz, J. E. (2002). *The creativity conundrum.* New York: Psychology Press.

Suler, J. (1980). Primary process thinking and creativity. *Psychological Bulletin, 88,* 144–165.

Sylva, K., Bruner, J., & Genova, P. (1976). The role of play in the problem-solving of children 3–5 years old. In J. Bruner, A. Jolly, & K. Sylva (Eds.), *Play* (pp. 244–257). New York: Basic Books.

Vandenberg, B. (1980). Play, problem-solving, and creativity. *New Directions for Child Development, 9,* 49–68.

Vosburg, S. D., & Kaufmann, G. (1999). Mood and creativity research: The view from a conceptual organizing perspective. In S. Russ (Ed.), *Affect, creative experience, and psychological adjustment* (pp. 19–39). Washington, DC: Taylor & Francis.

Vygotsky, L. S. (1967). *Imagination and creativity in childhood.* Moscow: Prosvescheniye. (Original work published 1930)

Waelder, R. (1933). Psychoanalytic theory of play. *Psychoanalytic Quarterly, 2,* 208–224.

Wallace, D. (1989). Studying the individual: The case study method and other genres. In D. Wallace & H. Gruber (Eds.), *Creative people at work* (pp. 25–43). Oxford: Oxford University Press.

Winnicott, D. W. (1971). *Playing and reality.* London: Tavistock.

16

The Healing Powers of Expressive Writing

JANEL D. SEXTON AND JAMES W. PENNEBAKER

Over the past 20 years, the value of expressive writing has made the transition from anecdotal folk wisdom to a large and growing body of scientific research. Specifically, expressing thoughts and feelings about a traumatic event can improve one's mental and physical health (Frattaroli, 2006; Pennebaker, 1997; Smyth, 1998). As social and health psychologists, we give an overview of this line of research that began in the 1980s and has continued to proliferate up to the present. We now know that writing can have an impact on a broad range of physiological, physical, and mental states across many types of people. Non-health-related benefits have also been uncovered, and these are discussed as well. After describing the standard expressive writing paradigm and its application to creative writers, we discuss the role that language plays in this picture, including how language use can predict health benefits.

THE EXPRESSIVE WRITING PARADIGM

The procedure is simple and straightforward: Participants are asked to reflect on their deepest thoughts and feelings about a traumatic event. In the original studies, participants were randomly assigned to write about either an emotional topic or a control topic for 15 to 20 minutes each session for three to five sessions completed over the course of several days or weeks. One writing session was completed per day, and participants were often given the freedom to decide what time of day to write. For those in the experimental group, the following instructions were given:

> For the next (3) days, I would like for you to write about your very deepest thoughts and feelings about the most upsetting event of your entire life. In your writing, I'd like you to really let go and explore your very deepest emotions and thoughts. You might tie your topic to your relationships with others, including parents, lovers, friends, or relatives, to your past, your present, or your future, or to who you have been, who you would like to be, or who you are now. You may write about the same general

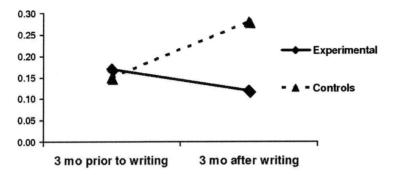

Figure 16.1. Monthly health center visits: Across four studies.

issues or experiences on all days of writing or on different topics each day. All of your writing will be completely confidential. Don't worry about spelling, sentence structure, or grammar. The only rule is that once you begin writing, continue to do so until your time is up.

No feedback is typically given to participants, and all participants are assured that their writings will be held in strict confidence. Figure 16.1 shows health improvements as measured by visits to the student health center, collapsed across four studies combined (Pennebaker & Beall, 1986; Pennebaker, Colder, & Sharp, 1990; Pennebaker & Francis, 1996; Pennebaker, Kiecolt-Glaser, & Glaser, 1988). Interestingly, participants in the control group actually get sicker over time, whereas those in the experimental group maintain their health over time. Expressive writing can be thought of as a preventive health measure in this sense: Those who write are less likely to get sick. This is especially apparent when studies are conducted in the fall with follow-up in the winter cold and flu season.

After establishing the basic effect, other lines of research opened up that sought to uncover the physiological mechanisms underlying this effect of writing on health. For example, participants were brought in to the lab and asked to write about either an emotional topic or a control topic. Their blood was then drawn and tested for the lymphocyte (white blood cell) response to the mitogen phytohemagglutinin (PHA). PHA stimulates the proliferation of helper cells, and blastogenesis is the measurement of the proliferation of lymphocytes in response to mitogen stimulation. It can be thought of as a rough measure of immune functioning, as greater white blood cell activity in response to a foreign body is an indicator of good immune system functioning. It was found, as predicted, that persons who wrote about an emotional topic evidenced greater blastogenic activity than those who wrote about a control topic (see Figure 16.2; adapted from Pennebaker et al., 1988).

A number of physiological improvements have been uncovered as well, in addition to increased blastogenesis after writing. Several studies examined

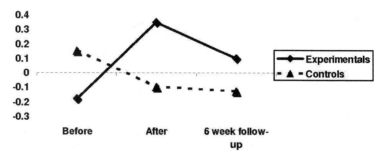

Figure 16.2. Mean mitogen response (PHA).

indicators of immune system functioning. One such study looked at the level of hepatitis B antibodies in medical students after a vaccine (Petrie, Booth, Pennebaker, Davison, & Thomas, 1995). Others found an increase in natural killer cell activity (Petrie, Fontanilla, Thomas, Booth, & Pennebaker, 2004), changes in CD-4 (t-lymphocyte) levels (Petrie et al., 2004), and links between writing and changes in salivary cortisol (Sloan, Marx, & Epstein, 2005).

A broad range of other health improvements have been observed in the numerous studies conducted using the writing paradigm. These include not only reduced physician or health center visits but also fewer missed work days among employees (Francis & Pennebaker, 1992), reduced symptoms and medication use among pain and asthma patients (Smyth, Stone, Hurewitz, & Kaell, 1999), fewer days spent in the hospital after a surgery (Solano, Donati, & Pecci, 2003; Taylor, Wallander, Anderson, Beasley, & Brown 2003), improvements in systolic and diastolic blood pressure (McGuire, Greenberg, & Gevirtz, 2005), and improved sleep quality (De Moor et al., 2002). In terms of mental health, writing has resulted in a reduction in depression and rumination (Lepore, Fernanadez-Berrocal, Ragan, & Ramos, 2004) and an improvement in self-image (Seagal & Pennebaker, 1999).

Beyond health improvements, a variety of other benefits have been discovered through expressive writing. Students who completed the writing exercise earned higher grades compared to their peers (Pennebaker et al., 1990), and those laid off from their jobs were quicker to acquire a new one (Spera, Buhrfeind, & Pennebaker, 1994). In an examination of how writing may improve functioning, one study found an improvement in working memory (Klein & Boals, 2001). Working memory is the ability to pay attention to something while being distracted. People with high levels of stress have poorer working memory function. The reasoning is that stressful memories, because they are coded differently, are more accessible and consume attentional resources. Writing may recode these memories in such a way that they do not interfere with other tasks.

Several meta-analyses have examined the expressive writing paradigm. The first (Smyth, 1998) found a moderate effect size ($d = .47$), including both physical and psychological improvements. A later report contradicted this finding and concluded there is insufficient evidence showing that expressive writing improves physical and mental outcomes (Meads, Lyons, & Carroll, 2003). Another meta-analysis found benefits for health, especially physical health ($d = .19$; Frisina, Borod, & Lepore, 2004).

Most recently, a large meta-analysis of more than 140 expressive writing studies found that expressive writing does have a small but significant effect ($r = .075$; Frattaroli, 2006). Larger effects are found for studies that used participants who had experienced a trauma, that followed participants in the short term, that had participants write at home as opposed to in a laboratory setting, that had more lengthy disclosure sessions (at least 15 minutes per session and over at least three sessions), and that had participants write about a recent trauma. This is good news for creative writers who are more likely to write at home and over extended sessions.

The meta-analysis also included a thorough examination of the moderators of the writing process, shedding light on how to maximize the effectiveness of writing for the benefit of health. Clearly a host of mechanisms account for the benefits of writing, and no single explanation is sufficient (Pennebaker & Chung, 2007). One such moderator is stress level: Those who begin writing with a greater degree of stress are more likely to experience improved physical health. This stands to reason, although it is surprising that this group does not show improved psychological health relative to their less stressed counterparts. Similarly, writers with a preexisting health condition show greater health benefits than their healthier peers. Another interesting and important finding is that, when writing instructions are more directed and structured and when participants are instructed to write about a previously undisclosed trauma, a somewhat greater psychological benefit is obtained (Frattaroli, 2006).

Importantly, the benefits of expressive writing do not discriminate – the effectiveness of the paradigm has been found across diverse groups. Samples have included college students, maximum-security psychiatric inmates, unemployed engineers, Holocaust survivors, and also patient cohorts who suffer from ailments such as chronic pain, arthritis, asthma, breast cancer, and posttraumatic stress disorder. Labs across the world have found benefits, including those in the United States, Mexico, the Netherlands, Spain, Italy, and New Zealand. Although professional writers as a group (especially poets) tend to have worse health outcomes (Kaufman & Sexton, 2006), expressive writing can still be a useful tool to gain benefits.

There is an intriguing versatility in gaining benefits from expressive writing that carries a direct and positive application to authors, especially creative writers. For example, in one study, participants benefited from writing not about a trauma they had actually experienced, but about an imaginary trauma supplied by the experimenters (Greenberg, Wortman, & Stone, 1996). It seems that the psychological work required to process such emotions is helpful even when they have not been experienced firsthand. In another study, writers found positive effects when they wrote about their "best possible selves" (King, 2001) or even about positive experiences (Burton & King, 2004). Clearly, it is not necessary to take on a literal or journal style of writing to find gains from written expression.

WHY AND HOW DOES EXPRESSIVE WRITING WORK?

Documenting improvements after writing has proven to be much easier than gaining an understanding into how and why it works, although a variety of studies have shed light on this question. It is known that writing generally does not bring about health improvements through a change in health behaviors, such as exercise and alcohol consumption. It is also known that people do not benefit from writing simply because of a release of emotion (a cathartic effect).

Several theories have been proposed to explain the mechanism. One of these, called the emotional inhibition theory, posits that not talking or writing about an important event is a form of inhibition, which requires physiological work. Inhibition can thus be seen as a long-term low-level stressor. This is an intuitive theory, a favorite among lay people, and is reminiscent of a Freudian interpretation. However, it has been found that simple venting does not bring about positive changes. In fact, studies have shown that when people are asked just to write about emotions as opposed to cognitions, they do not benefit (Pennebaker & Beall, 1986).

A second explanation is the emotional expression or exposure theory. In this line of thinking, directly confronting an emotional upheaval can result in emotional changes leading to habituation and extinction. This mechanism is similar to prolonged exposure therapy. The emotions associated with a trauma become dulled and do not carry the same weight, thereby reducing anxiety and helping improve daily functioning. There is support for this theory in the literature, which shows that symptoms of trauma are reduced by writing and having more extended writing sessions (hence more exposure) is linked to better health outcomes (Frattaroli, 2006; Lepore, Greenberg, Bruno, & Smyth, 2002).

Another theory is that writing helps people by bringing about an improvement in self-regulation. Self-regulation is the ability to recognize and manage one's emotions, which allows for greater self-control and mastery of emotional states. Self-regulation is closely related to aspects of emotional intelligence and makes for a more predictable, controllable environment. This theory has received some support in the literature and is a promising direction for future research (Cameron & Nicholls, 1998; King, 2002).

A fourth explanation is cognitive restructuring/adaptation. This theory argues that cognitive changes result from writing, including labeling, structuring, and organizing traumatic events. These changes make a trauma easier to manage psychologically by helping people make sense out of confusing and upsetting events in their lives. This theory sees writing as a meaning-making process. Constructing a coherent story from a traumatic event can be a critical element of writing. This last theory has mixed support and needs to be tested more adequately (Pennebaker & Seagal, 1999).

Some caveats are worth mentioning. Although varied sets of detailed writing instructions have successfully brought about healthful effects for writers, it is important not to impose constraining instructions (i.e., write only about your emotions, not your thoughts about the event). Limiting or circumscribing the natural unfolding that writing can bring is not as helpful as giving writers a free rein to express themselves fully. In addition, one of the critical features of the expressive writing paradigm is a pretense of anonymity, coupled with an absence of feedback. Although social support can be quite helpful in the midst of an upheaval, it carries a risk of negative social support and perceived judgment. Writing is a process of self-exploration, to be carried out without an audience. Finally, although daily journaling may be helpful to some, those who do journal are no more healthy than those who do not (Pennebaker, 1997a). Perhaps this is because those who journal regularly have a need to do so, making them different in some way from those who do not journal. Although a randomized study has not been published to our knowledge in which participants are randomly assigned to journal or not, perhaps those who do write on their own would be worse off if they did not journal. Regardless, expressive writing should be undertaken when the need exists, as opposed to becoming a forced routine. Similarly, writing immediately after a traumatic event may not be as helpful as writing about it after some time (several months) has passed.

PATTERNS OF LANGUAGE USE

One way in which the emotional expression and cognitive restructuring theories can be tested is by examining the writing samples for themes, trends, and stylistic patterns. To do this, Pennebaker and colleagues (Pennebaker, Francis, & Booth, 2001) developed a program called Linguistic Inquiry and Word Count (LIWC), which is a way of systematically assessing writing samples. LIWC is a computer-based text analysis software program that counts the rate of words that appear in a number of categories as a function of the total number of words in a given writing sample. LIWC contains 72 word categories, such as self-references (e.g., I, me, we), positive and negative emotion words, insight words (e.g., realize, understand), and causal words (e.g., because, therefore). This approach was designed to help identify linguistic patterns and their relation to health.

Using LIWC, it has been discovered that people are relatively consistent in how they write or talk. In other words, there is somewhat of a language

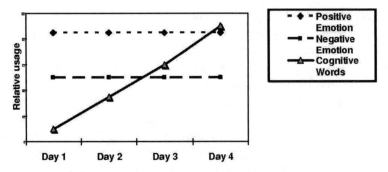

Figure 16.3. Language dimensions predicting health.

"fingerprint." This consistency is found in the use of emotional words, the use of big words, and the use of past-tense words (Pennebaker & King, 1999). Language can also be linked to health. For example, people who use the first-person singular tend to be more depressed and less healthy. Negative emotion words are linked to alcohol and tobacco use. In a specialized study of poets, references to self and death versus first-person plural (we, us) references were associated with committing suicide (Stirman & Pennebaker, 2001).

Patterns that predict improved health include a high rate of positive emotion words, a moderate rate of negative emotion words, and an increase in the number of cognitive words (e.g., because, although) over the days of writing (Pennebaker & Chung, 2007; see Figure 16.3.) The picture that emerges from this pattern of results is one in which the person who benefits from writing is expressing a good deal of positive affect, but acknowledging the negative as well, and is making meaning of events.

Although no randomized studies of language use and health have been published, it is more plausible to assume that language is the result of a depressed or unhealthy state rather than the cause of it. Evidence for this assumption can be found in a paper chronicling New York City Mayor Rudy Giuliani's patterns of language use before, during and after major changes in his life. After some significant upheavals, his use of "I" went up considerably and then later dropped back down (Pennebaker & Lay, 2002). Another finding using linguistic analysis is that those who change their use of the first person from singular to plural (e.g., from "me" to "us") also experience more benefits. This reflects a shift in perspective and a movement toward social integration.

SUMMARY

In summary, expressive writing is a useful tool to help people cope with traumas. Language patterns reveal a unique linguistic fingerprint that not only differs from person to person but also is associated with health as evidenced by relationships with depression, doctor's visits, and smoking. Personal traumas wreak havoc on people by undermining normal cognitive functioning and disrupting social relationships. Although not a panacea, writing can help people move toward healing in the face of an upsetting event. Putting our upheavals into words transforms our experiences and sets into motion new ways of coping. Such expression helps formulate our "stories" as individuals and can serve as a catalyst to better health. Although there is work left to be done to understand the mechanisms involved, we know that writing about traumas reduces the need to inhibit thoughts, emotions, and behaviors; helps organize thoughts about a traumatic event; frees up working memory; and allows for closer social relationships. Expressive writing is a promising and cost-saving approach for helping persons cope with upheavals.

REFERENCES

Burton, C. M., & King, L. A. (2004). The health benefits of writing about intensely positive experiences. *Journal of Research in Personality, 38,* 150–163.

Cameron, L. D., & Nicholls, G. (1998). Expression of stressful experiences through writing: Effects of a self-regulation manipulation for pessimists and optimists. *Health Psychology, 17,* 84–92.

De Moor, C., Sterner, J., Hall, M., Warneke, C., Gilani, Z., Amato, R., et al. (2002). A pilot study of the effects of expressive writing on psychological and behavioral adjustment in patients enrolled in a phase II trial of vaccine therapy for metastatic renal cell carcinoma. *Health Psychology, 21,* 615–619.

Francis, M. E., & Pennebaker, J. W. (1992). Putting stress into words: Writing about personal upheavals and health. *American Journal of Health Promotion, 6,* 280–287.

Frattaroli, J. (2006). Experimental disclosure and its moderators: A meta-analysis. *Psychological Bulletin, 132,* 823–865.

Frisina, P. G., Borod, J. C., & Lepore, S. J. (2004). A meta-analysis of the effects of written disclosure on the health outcomes in clinical populations. *Journal of Nervous and Mental Disease, 192,* 629–634.

Greenberg, M. A., Wortman, C. B., & Stone, A. A. (1996). Emotional expression and physical health: Revising traumatic memories or fostering self-regulation? *Journal of Personality and Social Psychology, 71,* 588–602.

Kaufman, J. C., & Sexton, J. D. (2006). Why doesn't the writing cure help poets? *Review of General Psychology, 10,* 268–282.

King, L. A. (2001). The health benefits of writing about life goals. *Personality and Social Psychology Bulletin, 27,* 798–807.

King, L. A. (2002). Gain without pain? Expressive writing and self-regulation. In S. J. Lepore & J. M. Smyth (Eds.), *The writing cure: How expressive writing promotes health and emotional well being* (pp. 119–134). Washington, DC: American Psychological Association.

Klein, K., & Boals, A. (2001). Expressive writing can increase working memory capacity. *Journal of Experimental Psychology: General, 130*(3), 520–533.

Lepore, S. J., Fernanadez-Berrocal, P., Ragan, J., & Ramos, N. (2004). It's not that bad: Social challenges to emotional disclosure enhance adjustment to stress. *Anxiety, Stress & Coping: An International Journal, 17,* 341–361.

Lepore, S. J., Greenberg, M. A., Bruno, M., & Smyth, J. M. (2002). Expressive writing and health: Self-regulation of emotion-related experience, physiology, and behavior. In S. J. Lepore & J. M. Smyth (Eds.), *The writing cure: How expressive writing promotes health and emotional well-being* (pp. 99–117). Washington, DC: American Psychological Association.

McGuire, K. M. B., Greenberg, M. A., & Gevirtz, R. (2005). Autonomic effects of expressive writing in individuals with elevated blood pressure. *Journal of Health Psychology, 10*, 197–207.

Meads, C., Lyons A., & Carroll D. (2003, May). *The impact of the emotional disclosure intervention on physical and psychological health – a systematic review*. Report No. 43. Birmingham, UK: West Midlands Health Technology Assessment Collaboration.

Pennebaker, J. W. (1997a). *Opening up: The healing power of expressing emotion*. New York: Guilford.

Pennebaker, J. W. (1997b). Writing about emotional experiences as a therapeutic process. *Psychological Science, 8*, 162–166.

Pennebaker, J. W., & Beall, S. (1986). Confronting a traumatic event: Toward an understanding of inhibition and disease. *Journal of Abnormal Psychology, 95*, 274–281.

Pennebaker, J. W., & Chung, C. K. (2007). Expressive writing, emotional upheavals, and health. In H. S. Friedman & R. C. Silver (Eds.), *Foundations of health psychology* (pp. 263–284). New York: Oxford University Press.

Pennebaker, J. W., Colder, M., & Sharp, L. K. (1990). Accelerating the coping process. *Journal of Personality & Social Psychology, 58*(3), 528–537.

Pennebaker, J. W., & Francis, M. E. (1996). Cognitive, emotional, and language processes in disclosure. *Cognition & Emotion, 10*(6), 601–626.

Pennebaker, J. W., Francis, M. E., & Booth, R. J. (2001). *Linguistic Inquiry and Word Count (LIWC): LIWC2001*. Mahwah, NJ: Erlbaum.

Pennebaker, J. W., Kiecolt-Glaser, J., & Glaser, R. (1988). Disclosure of traumas and immune function: Health implications for psychotherapy. *Journal of Consulting and Clinical Psychology, 56*, 239–245.

Pennebaker, J. W., & King, L. A. (1999). Linguistic styles: Language use as an individual difference. *Journal of Personality and Social Psychology, 77*, 1296–1312.

Pennebaker, J. W., & Lay, T. C. (2002). Language use and personality during crises: Analyses of Mayor Rudolph Giuliani's press conferences. *Journal of Research in Personality, 36*, 271–282.

Pennebaker, J. W., & Seagal, J. D. (1999). Forming a story: The health benefits of narrative. *Journal of Clinical Psychology, 55*, 1243–1254.

Petrie, K. J., Booth, R., Pennebaker, J. W., Davison, K. P., & Thomas, M. (1995). Disclosure of trauma and immune response to Hepatitis B vaccination program. *Journal of Consulting and Clinical Psychology, 63*, 787–792.

Petrie, K. J., Fontanilla, I., Thomas, M. G., Booth, R. J., & Pennebaker, J. W. (2004). Effect of written emotional expression on immune function in patients with Human Immunodeficiency Virus infection: A randomized trial. *Psychosomatic Medicine, 66*, 272–275.

Seagal, J. D., & Pennebaker, J. W. (1999, March). *Writing and social stigma: Benefits from writing about being a group member*. Presented at the annual meeting of the Society of Behavioral Medicine Conference, San Diego.

Sloan, D. M., Marx, B. P., & Epstein, E. M. (2005). Further examination of the exposure model underlying the efficacy of written emotional disclosure. *Journal of Consulting and Clinical Psychology, 73*, 549–554.

Smyth, J. M. (1998). Written emotional expression: Effect sizes, outcome types, and moderating variables. *Journal of Consulting and Clinical Psychology, 66*, 174–184.

Smyth, J. M., Stone, A. A., Hurewitz, A., & Kaell, A. (1999). Effects of writing about stressful experiences on symptom reduction in patients with asthma or rheumatoid arthritis: A randomized trial. *Journal of the American Medical Association, 281,* 1304–1309.

Solano, L., Donati, V., & Pecci, F. (2003). Postoperative course after papilloma resection: Effects of written disclosure of the experience in subjects with different alexithymia levels. *Psychosomatic Medicine, 65,* 477–484.

Spera, S. P., Buhrfeind, E. D., & Pennebaker, J. W. (1994). Expressive writing and coping with job loss. *Academy of Management Journal, 37*(3), 722–733.

Stirman, S. W., & Pennebaker, J. W. (2001). Word use in the poetry of suicidal and non-suicidal poets. *Psychosomatic Medicine, 63,* 517–523.

Taylor, L., Wallander, J., Anderson, D., Beasley, P., & Brown, R. (2003). Improving chronic disease utilization, health status, and adjustment in adolescents and young adults with cystic fibrosis. *Journal of Clinical Psychology in Medical Settings, 10,* 9–16.

PART V

THE EDUCATION

17

How Rewards and Evaluations Can Undermine Creativity (and How to Prevent This)

JOHN BAER AND SHARON S. MCKOOL

Since the seminal publication of Amabile's (1983) *Social Psychology of Creativity*, creativity researchers have been aware of the negative impact that rewards and evaluations can have on creative performance. Her work, in turn, was rooted in well-established findings on the effects of extrinsic motivation on intrinsic motivation, as described in *The Hidden Cost of Rewards* (Lepper & Greene, 1978). Although Amabile's basic idea has been refined and qualified to some extent (see, e.g., Amabile, 1996; Baer, 1997b, 1998b), the core insight remains: Extrinsic constraints, such as rewards and evaluations, tend to drive out intrinsic motivation.

This often puts composition teachers in a difficult position, because (a) the development of writing skills often requires feedback on performance (i.e., students' work must be evaluated) and (b) students sometimes need to be bribed to do things they do not wish to do (i.e., students may sometimes need to be offered rewards to get them to write). This tension is part of a larger conflict between enhancing creativity more generally and helping students acquire skills and content knowledge (Amabile, 1983, 1996; Baer, 1997a, 2002, 2003; Kaufman & Baer, 2002, 2005, 2006); that conflict, in turn, is part of the larger question of the relationship between learning content and learning to think more effectively (see, e.g., Chi, Glaser, & Farr, 1988; Glass & Holyoak, 1986; Hirsch, 1996; Johnson-Laird, 1983; Karmiloff-Smith, 1992; Paul, 1990; Simon & Chase, 1973; Woolfolk, 2006). It is also related to questions about the possibilities of the transfer of learning and of teaching to promote such transfer (see, e.g., Gage & Berliner, 1992; Mayer, 1987; Perkins & Salomon, 1988; Salomon & Perkins, 1989; Woolfolk, 2006).

Although there is much in this area that remains to be discovered, it is safe to say that thinking depends heavily on knowledge, that mistakes in critical thinking are more often the result of incorrect factual knowledge than a lack of general problem-solving skills, and that teaching for transfer requires a great deal of context-specific training or practice in any domain to which transfer is desired. It appears that content knowledge is essential to thinking, that teaching content-free thinking skills is impossible, that higher level thinking requires the automatization of lower level skills, and that to improve students' thinking in a given domain, students must learn a great deal of factual content about that domain as well as a variety of domain-specific cognitive skills. All of this is especially true of creative thinking (Baer, 1993, 1994a, 1994b, 1996, 1998a, 2003; Hirsch, 2000; Kaufman & Baer, 2006; Simonton, 1994, 2000; Weisberg, 1988, 1993, 2003, 2004, 2005).

As in other areas, in writing it is also true that students need a great deal of skill and knowledge if they are to become creative writers. They need to learn about such tools of the trade as plotting, character development, and dialogue, and they also need to develop skills in such mundane but essential areas as grammar, spelling, and punctuation. They need to know something (and often a great deal) about whatever topic is their subject; they need to know how to use figurative language effectively; and they need to know such seemingly trivial but inescapable things like how to use quotation marks. The list of skills and knowledge that writers need could go on and on – on top of which, writers need to be creative.

The focus of this chapter is on how some of the most effective ways to teach skills and content knowledge can undermine creativity and how to mitigate this effect. The word "mitigate" is perhaps weaker than some might wish. Readers interested in helping students become more creative writers might wonder if we could simply stop doing *anything* that might undermine creativity. But although it would be lovely if we could simply banish such techniques and replace them with more enlightened approaches, the world (and human psychology) does not always conform to our wishes. Regretfully, the solution is more complex, and it will involve doing some things *some of the time* that we know will diminish creativity, at least in the short term, to make possible higher levels of creativity in the future.

In its simplest terms, the intrinsic motivation theory of creativity says that people are more creative when they do something simply because they find it intrinsically interesting – that is, when it is something they have chosen to do just because they derive pleasure or even joy from doing it – and they are less creative when they do something because they are extrinsically motivated, such as to earn a reward (Amabile, 1983). This concept seems rather innocuous and perhaps even obvious at first blush. But it does not just say that being intrinsically motivated leads to more creative behavior. It is also saying – and Amabile (1983, 1996) and others (Baer, 1997b, 1998b; Hennessey, 1989; Hennessey & Zbikowski, 1993) have shown this decisively in a number of very interesting studies – that when people do things in order to earn rewards, they become less creative; and when they do things that they think will be evaluated in some way, they become less creative; and when they do things to please someone else, they become less creative. In fact, these studies have shown that many of the things teachers do every day – things most teachers think are essential parts of what they do – decrease students' creativity. That is certainly troubling.

All the available evidence suggests that intrinsic and extrinsic motivation tend to compete inside us, and when they are both present, intrinsic motivation tends to be the loser. Extrinsic motivation drives out intrinsic motivation, so when we offer our students rewards for doing things or when we evaluate their work, we are both increasing their extrinsic motivation *and* driving out or diminishing their intrinsic motivation for those activities. We are making the things they once found interesting *less* interesting, less worth doing for their own sake. We are also causing them to be less creative in the ways they perform those activities, as least in the short term.

One might wish that we could simply decide no longer to evaluate students' work and to give up offering rewards of any kind, but doing so is not really feasible. It would make it difficult – probably impossible – to do much of what we know we must do as teachers, including teaching our students the skills and content that we know they need to be better writers. Sadly, the same things that tend to diminish creativity are the very things that tend to increase competence. Students need feedback on their performance to improve their skills, and they often need some kind of extrinsic motivation, like rewards, to keep working when they otherwise would simply stop. So they very often need extrinsic motivation to learn.

This is where teaching for creativity and teaching to learn skills and knowledge sometimes need to part company. Teachers who care about both developing students' creativity *and* helping students acquire a broad background of skills and content knowledge are sometimes forced to make difficult choices.

Before suggesting some guidelines for making those choices, an important distinction between short-term and long-term impact on creative performance needs to be noted. Doing something for a reward or doing something in the anticipation of receiving an evaluation of some sort is likely to diminish students' creativity on whatever it is they are working on. This is true in composition and it is true in any other potentially creative endeavor. But the skills and knowledge acquired by continuing to practice or study even when one has no intrinsic motivation may provide the knowledge and skills one will need in the future to do something in a more creative way than is possible now. Similarly, the skills acquired by receiving feedback on (or evaluation of) one's performance on a task like writing an essay or designing an experiment may help one do a more competent job, and perhaps even a more creative job, on similar tasks in the future.

So perhaps, one might argue, teachers should simply not worry about the negative impact of feedback and rewards; perhaps we can quiet these concerns by reminding ourselves that the skills and knowledge our students are acquiring will some day allow them to be more creative. But although there is some truth to that position, simply ignoring what we know about creativity and extrinsic and intrinsic motivation is a rather dangerous kind of burying one's heads in the sand. Evaluations and rewards *do* lower both intrinsic motivation and creativity, and if fed a steady diet of these extrinsic constraints, students' intrinsic motivation and creativity are likely to suffer long-term negative consequences.

So what is a teacher to do? There are some things one can do, but in many cases they are not easy. The first thing one needs to keep in mind is the goal or objective for a given lesson. What Amabile's (1983, 1996) research tells us is that we cannot have it both ways, at least not at the same time. If our goal in a particular lesson is skill development or knowledge acquisition, then we need to give ourselves permission to do some things that we know make extrinsic motivation salient and depress creativity. And if our goal is to encourage creativity, then we need to avoid doing things that will increase extrinsic motivation and try to do whatever we can to increase intrinsic motivation.

A teacher's magazine several years ago published a cartoon poking fun at a teacher for being blind to her students' creativity. In this cartoon, a student is daydreaming some delightful and very creative things in the middle of a lesson. The student's thinking is loosely related to the topic of the lesson, but it is clearly not the kind of thinking that is likely to produce a correct answer to the teacher's question. The teacher interrupts to remind the student that "Creativity Time" is not for another hour.

It seems obvious that this teacher does not know much about creativity. And yet, she was doing something right. She knew her objective for the current lesson was *not* creative thinking, and she had set aside time in which that *would* be her goal. So although no one would recommend the kind of rigidity that this cartoon was depicting, we will nonetheless do a better job of both helping our students learn the content and skills they need *and* develop their creativity and their intrinsic motivation if we try to pursue those two different goals at different times.

Here is an example. When teaching writing, we want students to learn a number of skills, and we (sometimes) want them to write imaginatively. These goals are at odds because one requires an emphasis on extrinsic motivation – evaluation, in this case – and the other requires an emphasis on intrinsic motivation, which would require us to avoid evaluation. Doing a little of each will not work because extrinsic motivation will tend to drive out intrinsic motivation. But we *can* do both if we do them at different times. When working on skill development in writing, we can let students know that their work will be evaluated, let them know the criteria that will be applied, and then evaluate using those criteria. Other times we can tell them that although they must do the writing assignment, they will get credit simply for doing it and there will be no further evaluation.

Although this suggestion may sound radical, there are instructional practices used in schools today that have the potential to encourage creativity while also teaching students the skills necessary to express their ideas creatively. Writer's Workshop is one of those practices. In this workshop approach, teachers first demonstrate new ideas about writing for their students before students are asked to write themselves. This demonstration or modeling of skills is often referred to as interactive writing (Gipe, 1998), in which teachers model the skills of writing through mini-lessons. Then comes the "hand-over" phase in which the understandings and strategies that emerge during this interaction between a more competent person and a less competent person gradually become internalized in the learner's mind (Bruner, 1986). Once internalized, students are able to use these newly acquired skills to express themselves more creatively. If the demonstration of skills, with its own set of objectives and purposes, can be viewed as separate from student's writing, then students can learn a number of skills (and be held accountable for the mastery of these skills in isolated contexts) and then be free to use these skills if and when needed to express their ideas creatively.

When you use this approach, you can let your students know you are looking forward to reading (or hearing) their stories (or whatever it is they are writing), but at the same time promise them that you will not evaluate their work. And then keep your promise. Do not praise or criticize, do not correct or point out any errors, and do not suggest any changes or things they might try next time. What you need to do is simply not comment at all, beyond saying that you enjoyed reading what they wrote. After a while, students will come to believe you. This will allow them, when you tell them that you will be evaluating their work, to concentrate on skills and focus on doing things "right"; and it will free them up to write more imaginatively, if with less technical correctness perhaps, when you tell them that their work will not be evaluated. In this way their interest in writing will not get buried beneath a constant expectation of evaluation.

Will some kids abuse the license that a no-evaluation promise confers? Of course they will. Let's be honest: We know that whatever we do, some kids will find cracks to fall (or squeeze themselves) through. But sometimes we need to allow the students who want to do as little as possible to get away with it, in order not to punish those students who have the kind of intrinsic motivation that we wish all our students had.

As part of the no-evaluation pledge, it is important to remember that evaluations can be both positive and negative, and both kinds are to be avoided. A few general positive comments about enjoying the story are probably harmless, but any detailed evaluation, even if positive, is an evaluation nonetheless and has the same detrimental impact on creativity. In a study that Amabile (1983) reported, some students received positive, but genuine, feedback on one writing assignment, whereas others received no feedback. On the next assignment, the students who had received the positive feedback wrote less creative stories. When we anticipate evaluation – something that is natural to expect when we have been evaluated in a similar context in the past – it has a negative impact on creative performance. Students will be wary of promises not to evaluate – having spent time in classrooms, most students have quite naturally come to believe that everything they do will be evaluated – and it will take time to convince them of the sincerity of the no-evaluation promise. You do not want to undermine that trust by occasionally violating the rule so that you can give some positive feedback.

Having students write "just for fun," as it were, will take time away from writing assignments aimed at developing skills, but probably not as much as one might fear. These activities are likely to increase students' intrinsic motivation to write (or at least help counter the diminishment of such motivation that tends to occur in schools), and they will not take a large amount of time away from the kind of work we know is necessary to learn skills and content knowledge; that is, work that is evaluated so that students can use this feedback to improve their performance. And even if these activities do not promote creative writing, do not we want at least to try to send our students the message that writing is fun?

It is important to note that it is not always possible to remove every trace of extrinsic constraints on students, and in such cases one wants to reduce their salience as much as possible. A teacher might require a three-page short story but not evaluate its content beyond "evaluating" whether or not the student indeed wrote a three-page story of some kind. (One might further "evaluate" the language to censure offensive language.) But the freedom from evaluation should be as broad as possible if one wants to encourage intrinsic motivation and creativity.

There are also things teachers can do when evaluating students' writing that will lessen the harmful effects of evaluation without weakening its beneficial (i.e., skill developing) potential. Amabile's research (1983, 1996) suggests that it is the way students interpret the feedback they receive that determines its effects. Feedback that is viewed as evaluation – a person with greater authority or knowledge telling a novice what he or she should be doing, or judging the value of the student's work based on the expert's standards, even when that evaluation is positive – tends to be viewed as controlling, and that kind of evaluation reliably reduces intrinsic motivation (and the expectation that one will receive such evaluation negatively affects creative performance). But feedback can also be viewed as information that allows the student to achieve his or her own goals, which makes it empowering rather than controlling. To the extent that evaluation is viewed by students as empowering, there is evidence that it may not have a negative impact on creativity at all (Eisenberger, Pierce, & Cameron, 1999; Eisenberger & Rhoades 2001; Eisenberger & Shanock, 2003). In such cases it does not reduce intrinsic motivation or cause even a short-term decline in creativity.

An example of this kind of feedback occurs during a revision conference as part of a Writer's Workshop approach to writing. Here the teacher understands that his or her role is to listen to the students read their piece of writing and comment only if asked by to do so. Students are asked to come to the conference prepared to tell the teacher what they feel they have accomplished with the piece of writing and what they need from the teacher in terms of assistance. Other than this, the teacher does not point out any errors or make any suggestions. When students do not fear being evaluated, they are much more comfortable telling the teacher their perceived needs. This allows the students to have ownership over the writing and in that way become more intrinsically motivated to write.

There is no guarantee that the way we intend our feedback to be taken is the way students will in fact take it, of course, but there is at least one reliable guideline: Feedback that focuses on the work itself is less likely to reduce intrinsic motivation than feedback that is focused on the writer (the student). Noting, for example, that "the way that suspense is manipulated in this story keeps readers engaged" focuses on the work, whereas stating that "the way you use suspense to engage readers shows you have real talent as a writer" focuses on the writer. The difference might seem small, but these kinds of differences have produced significant differences in the creativity of subsequent endeavors. More specific, focused feedback is both more useful and effective in skill development and more likely to be interpreted by students as informative (rather than evaluative). It is information that is empowering rather than controlling (or at least it is more likely to be seen that way).

So it is possible to cause less harm by the way we provide evaluative feedback, but evaluation is, inevitably, sometimes going to be taken as evaluation that is more controlling than empowering, and that perception will reduce both intrinsic motivation and creativity. And even if we as teachers become very skilled at the ways we provide feedback, other evaluators whom students will encounter will certainly be less, shall we say, enlightened. Can we not protect student writers from the potential harm of such evaluations?

We can. The term that Hennessey and her colleagues use is "inoculation." For older students who enjoy writing, we can explain the negative effects of extrinsic motivation and teach them to remind themselves how much they like writing, even when their work is being judged. This may sound simple, and it is. And it has been shown to work (see, e.g., Hennessey & Amabile, 1988; Hennessey, Amabile, & Martinage, 1989; Hennessey & Zbikowski, 1993). Of course, students must be intrinsically motivated for this approach to work, but if a student does not like writing (i.e., has no intrinsic motivation to write), then teaching them about writing cannot kill their (nonexistent) intrinsic motivation.

Younger (primary grade) students may have trouble understanding this idea, but we can do the reminding ourselves. Asking students to brainstorm things they like about writing (e.g., getting to write about things they are interested in or liking to create interesting characters) and saying things like

"I know sometimes writing can be discouraging, but I know how much you enjoy writing" can help (and teachers can use items from that brainstorming list later, when reminding students of their love of writing).

We can also advise older students how they can manage their motivations. None of us likes every part of even our favorite activities, and sometimes we need to reward ourselves (extrinsic motivation) for doing those irksome but necessary tasks. When we are doing the creative stuff, we do not want to think about evaluations and possible rewards, but when it starts to feel like work and we just want to plow through it somehow, extrinsic motivation may be the best (because it is the only) kind of motivation we have working for us. For example, a student who wants to write a story that is set in another time period might need to do some research to learn more about that time period. Doing that research might not be interesting to her, but she can help motivate herself to do it by remembering that it will help her do something she *does* find interesting – telling a compelling story. (We ourselves confess that, although we found writing this chapter interesting and intrinsically rewarding, compiling the References in appropriate APA format is something that required significant doses of extrinsic motivation.)

Learning when and how to monitor (and to take action to adjust) one's own motivations is an important metacognitive skill that we can teach our students (Baer, 1997a). Sometimes even things we enjoy – activities for which we have an abundance of intrinsic motivation most of the time – can feel like drudgery. For example, a student may enjoy writing, but hate proofreading. That student might find it helpful to use rewards, such as giving herself a mental high-five for proofreading her story. Or she might promise herself a more tangible reward as a bribe to get the job done.

The research of the past quarter-century on the impact of extrinsic motivation on creativity can make teaching writing skills challenging. No creative writing teacher wants to think he or she is dampening his or her students' interest in writing or diminishing their creativity in any way. There are ways to deal with this challenge, however, that can help students become both technically competent *and* creative writers. Doing so just requires (a) some knowledge of the effects of evaluations and rewards, (b) being clear about the goals and focus of a particular lesson (sometimes building writing skills, sometimes promoting creative writing), and (c) trying to present feedback in ways that empower students – all of which are parts of creative teaching.

REFERENCES

Amabile, T. M. (1983). *The social psychology of creativity*. New York: Springer-Verlag.

Amabile, T. M. (1996). *Creativity in context: Update to The Social Psychology of Creativity*. Boulder, CO: Westview.

Baer, J. (1993). *Creativity and divergent thinking: A task-specific approach*. Hillsdale, NJ: Erlbaum.

Baer, J. (1994a). Divergent thinking is not a general trait: A multi-domain training experiment. *Creativity Research Journal, 7,* 35–46.

Baer, J. (1994b). Generality of creativity across performance domains: A replication. *Perceptual and Motor Skills, 79,* 1217–1218.

Baer, J. (1996). The effects of task-specific divergent-thinking training. *Journal of Creative Behavior, 30,* 183–187.

Baer. J. (1997a). *Creative teachers, creative students.* Boston: Allyn and Bacon.

Baer, J. (1997b). Gender differences in the effects of anticipated evaluation on creativity. *Creativity Research Journal, 10,* 25–31.

Baer, J. (1998a). The case for domain specificity in creativity. *Creativity Research Journal, 11,* 173–177.

Baer, J. (1998b). Gender differences in the effects of extrinsic motivation on creativity. *Journal of Creative Behavior, 32,* 18–37.

Baer, J. (1999). Creativity in a climate of standards. *Focus on Education, 43,* 16–21.

Baer, J. (2002). Are creativity and content standards allies or enemies? *Research in the Schools, 9*(2), 35–42.

Baer, J. (2003). Impact of the Core Knowledge Curriculum on creativity. *Creativity Research Journal, 15,* 297–300.

Bruner, J. (1986). *Actual minds, possible worlds.* Cambridge, MA: Harvard University Press.

Chi, M. T. H., Glaser, R., & Farr, M. (Eds.). (1988). *The nature of expertise.* Hillsdale, NJ: Erlbaum.

Eisenberger, R., Pierce, W. D., & Cameron, J. (1999). Effects of reward on intrinsic motivation: Negative, neutral, and positive. *Psychological Bulletin, 125,* 677–691.

Eisenberger, R., & Rhoades, L. (2001). Incremental effects of reward on creativity. *Journal of Personality and Social Psychology, 81,* 728–741.

Eisenberger, R., & Shanock, L. (2003). Rewards, intrinsic motivation, and creativity: A case study of conceptual and methodological isolation. *Creativity Research Journal, 15,* 121–130.

Gage, N. L., & Berliner, D. C. *Educational psychology* (5th ed.). Boston: Houghton Mifflin.

Gipe, J.P. (1998). *Multiple paths to literacy: Corrective-reading techniques for classroom teachers.* Upper Saddle River, NJ: Prentice-Hall.

Glass, A. L., & Holyoak, K. J. (1986). *Cognition* (2nd ed.). New York: Random House.

Hennessey, B. A. (1989). The effects of extrinsic constraints on children's creativity while using a computer. *Creativity Research Journal, 2,* 151–168.

Hennessey, B. A., & Amabile, T. M. (1988). Conditions of creativity. In R. J. Sternberg (Ed.), *The nature of creativity* (pp. 11–38). Cambridge: Cambridge University Press.

Hennessey, B. A., Amabile, T. M., & Martinage, M. (1989). Immunizing children against the negative effects of reward. *Contemporary Educational Psychology, 14,* 212–227.

Hennessey, B. A., & Zbikowski, S. (1993). Immunizing children against the negative effects of reward: A further examination of intrinsic motivation techniques. *Creativity Research Journal, 6,* 297–308.

Hirsch, E. D., Jr. (1996). *The schools we need and why we don't have them.* New York: Doubleday.

Hirsch, E. D., Jr. (2000). You can always look it up – or can you? *American Educator, 24*(1), 4–9.

Johnson-Laird, P. N. (1983). *Mental models.* Cambridge, MA: Harvard University Press.

Karmiloff-Smith, A. (1992). *Beyond modularity: A developmental perspective on cognitive science.* Cambridge, MA: MIT Press.

Kaufman, J. C., & Baer, J. (2002). Could Steven Spielberg manage the Yankees? Creative thinking in different domains. *Korean Journal of Thinking and Problem Solving, 12*(2), 5–14.

Kaufman, J. C., & Baer, J. (Eds.). (2005). *Creativity across domains: Faces of the muse.* Hillsdale, NJ: Erlbaum.

Kaufman, J. C., & Baer, J. (Eds.). (2006). *Reason and creativity in development.* New York: Cambridge University Press.

Lepper, M., & Greene, D. (Eds.). (1978). *The hidden cost of reward.* Hillsdale, NJ: Erlbaum.

Mayer, R. E. (1987). *Educational psychology: A cognitive approach.* Boston: Little, Brown.

Paul, R. W. (1990). Critical thinking and cultural literacy: Where E. D. Hirsch goes wrong. In R. W. Paul (Ed.), *Critical thinking: What every person needs to survive in a rapidly changing world* (pp. 429–435). Rohnert Park, CA: Center for Critical Thinking and Moral Critique, Sonoma State University.

Perkins, D. N., & Salomon, G. (1988). Teaching for transfer. *Educational Leadership, 46*(1), 22–32.

Salomon, G., & Perkins, D. N. (1989). Rocky roads to transfer: Rethinking mechanisms of a neglected phenomenon. *Educational Psychologist, 24*(2), 113–142.

Simon, H. A., & Chase, W. G. (1973). Skill in chess. *American Scientist, 50*, 394–403.

Simonton, D. K. (1994). *Greatness: Who makes history and why.* New York: Guilford.

Simonton, D. K. (2000). Creative development as acquired expertise: Theoretical issues and an empirical test. *Developmental Review, 20*, 283–318.

Weisberg, R. W. (1988). Problem solving and creativity. In R. J. Sternberg (Ed.), *The nature of creativity* (pp. 148–176). New York: Cambridge University Press.

Weisberg, R. W. (1993). *Creativity. Beyond the myth of genius.* New York: W. H. Freeman.

Weisberg, R. W. (2003). Case studies of innovation. In L. Shavinina (Ed.), *International handbook of innovation* (pp. 204–247). New York: Elsevier Science.

Weisberg, R. W. (2004). On structure in the creative process: A quantitative case study of the creation of Picasso's *Guernica. Empirical Studies in the Arts, 22*, 23–54.

Weisberg, R. W. (2005). Modes of expertise in creative thinking: Evidence from case studies. In A. Ericsson & P. Feltovich (Eds.), *Cambridge handbook on expertise and expert performance* (pp. 761–787). New York: Cambridge University Press.

Woolfolk, A. (2006). *Educational psychology* (10th ed.). Boston: Allyn and Bacon.

18

Teaching Writing by Demythologizing Creativity

GRACE R. WAITMAN AND JONATHAN A. PLUCKER

When Grace, one of the authors of this article, was a child, she asked her father – an English professor – to read the same books aloud so many times that he eventually committed the narration to audio tape. These stories wove in her mind a tapestry of successive events that unfolded in her imagination. Characters accomplished wild and courageous feats the likes of which she could only dream of emulating, and wondrous things zipped in and around the narration.

For most children and student writers, it is this power of stories – to captivate and bewitch – that inspires their own attempts to create narratives of their own. However, this belief in the magical power of stories simultaneously cultivates in any aspiring artist, but perhaps especially in writers, the sense that they must be hit with a kind of lightning-like inspiration to be able to conjure a text like those that inspired their own novitiate efforts at writing.

This belief mirrors one of the major misconceptions plaguing creativity research. Recently, Plucker, Beghetto, and Dow (2004) suggested that a primary challenge facing the field of creativity research remains the myth that "people are born creative or uncreative" (p. 85). In a similar vein, Sternberg and Lubart (1999) have expressed concern about the "mystification of creativity."

In this chapter, we examine how this "mystification of creativity" has been derived from a traditional theoretical emphasis on instances of eminent creativity and, further, how this focus has influenced the belief systems of creative writers about their capacity to produce written creative texts, or products. To accomplish this task, we delve into an investigation of the pedagogical manuals of creative writing to discover how their advice reveals the way that perpetuation of this myth has influenced the belief systems of creative writers.

However, with the rise of interest sparked in everyday creativity, the field of theoretical inquiry has expanded in ways to consider a more comprehensive understanding of creativity as a concept. This expanded focus allows us to conduct a more complex inquiry into the *process* of creative writing itself. Our concentration on the more everyday tasks involved with the creative writing process should illuminate the nuances of the relationship between the creative process and the creative person; specifically, we chose this focus because much of the creative writing pedagogical literature describes the significance of a creative writer developing a creative writing *persona*, or a unique conception of him- or herself *as a writer*.

Subsequently, we concentrate on how this writing persona evolves as a writer gains more experience with both the field and the domain of creative writing. In keeping with this focus on the creative writing process, we also hope to uncover how the individual's relationship to the creative writing field can have an undeniable impact on the evolution of this writing persona. By extension, the interaction between the individual and the field actually has a significant impact on the creative writer's process; therefore, the predominance of an emphasis on eminent creativity actually influences the way that creative writers *write*, because of their own beliefs about the interaction between the unconscious inspiration that produces their raw material and their conscious efforts required to revise that material. Because creative writers often believe that they have a certain lack of control over their own ability to write creatively, our evaluation of the creative writing process, along with our expanded focus on instances of everyday creativity, examines ways that our reconsideration of the process itself could be a means by which to break down the predominance of the mystification of creativity, thereby lessening its dominion over creative writers and the creative writing field.

THE INEVITABLE OVERSHADOWING OF EMINENT CREATIVITY

Historically, creativity research has often focused on instances of eminent or "Big C" creativity, the type of creativity exalted in the *public* domain – highly visible acts or occurrences of creativity that sparkled so brightly that they almost could not help but draw attention to themselves. Earlier experimental inquiries derived, at least in part, from the assumption that only certain individuals could execute creative acts or actually be "creative." This belief perpetuated a theoretical focus on instances of eminent psychology or a study of creativity that investigated the personalities of and products created by individuals collectively agreed on by society as being creative. This collective emphasis proves to be important because of Csikszentmihalyi's (1988) theory about how the field can determine which writers and what texts become exalted as quintessential exemplars of eminent creativity.

Weisberg (1993) proposes that the rise of interest in creativity theory could be linked to the presumption that "creative thinking is the result of extraordinary thinking processes, processes that are somehow qualitatively different from the 'ordinary' thinking that we all use for our daily activities" (p. xii). Weisberg labels this belief as the "genius myth." Seemingly, it would appear to be more interesting to study the processes of "geniuses" and also to participate in the belief that such theoretical inquiries could illuminate the mysterious phenomena of creativity. However, the dominion of this "mystification of creativity" within the larger milieu of the intellectual realm has created a theoretical dilemma, referenced by Plucker et al. (2004) in their assertion that earlier research in creativity studies revolved around a "traditional accent on eminent creativity," as opposed to an evaluation of more everyday instances of creativity, such as those that might occur in a fourth-grade classroom, for example.

As a result, not only have the investigations of social scientists been influenced by this phenomenon but creative individuals themselves have also cultivated beliefs about their *own* creative activities based on this stereotype. This focus inherently blocks a fully comprehensive consideration of the smaller, seemingly more mundane, or "ordinary" tasks that must be completed as part of any creative process. By evaluating how the beliefs of creative writers could have influenced their actual creative habits and practices, both social scientists and creative writers can benefit from a more comprehensive consideration of creativity. The increased focus on more "common" creative events found in research such as that of Richards (2007a) and Runco (2007), has brought studies of everyday creativity (or "little c") creativity to the forefront of investigational inquiries.

Thus, if social scientists subscribe to the belief that creativity actually occurs *only* in lightning strikes of unpredictable inspiration, their attempts to investigate experimentally such a seemingly mystical phenomenon will remain hampered by this assumption. To engage in the most extensive analysis of the creative process, they must recognize and even propagate the proposal that these presumably "ordinary" acts actually can have great significance on the larger creative process.

FROM THE PRIVATE TO THE PUBLIC: THE POTENTIAL INFLUENCE OF THE RISE OF THEORETICAL INTEREST IN EVERYDAY CREATIVITY

Richards (2007a) offers many perspectives about the potential benefits derived from an expanded focus in creativity research. Her research encompasses inquiries that investigate everyday creativity in much greater depth. After all, individuals employ creative thinking in an infinite number of different ways as part of their regular routines. Richards' text illuminates the value to be found in instances of seemingly ordinary thinking because it highlights the crucial role that ostensibly mundane tasks play in the larger creative *process*.

An expanded horizon of inquiry into everyday creativity can include experiments that simultaneously take into account the significance of day-to-day events of creative thinking and how they fit into a longer sequence of acts or events that form the creative process. This expansion could provide much-needed information for individuals who aspire to produce creative products. If they understand the importance of these smaller acts within the larger trajectory of the creative process, they could streamline the development of creative techniques as a result of their increased awareness. Such an expanded understanding could, in turn, influence the beliefs held by people attempting to pursue traditionally creative activities, including the act of writing creatively.

If, for example, aspiring writers approached their craft with the understanding that they were not simply subject to the whims of an "Ah-ha!"-like moment of inspiration, they might realize that they possess much greater control over their finished product, allowing them to experience a greater freedom *during* their process of writing creatively. More mundane tasks involved with writing – such as research and revision – could be understood within the larger context of the writing process, and writers engaged in these less glamorous yet crucial steps could work through them in a mindset enlightened by their understanding of how such actions contributed to the larger process of writing creatively.

Richards grounds her evaluations in a reconsideration of the role that an individual's belief system plays within the larger project of constructing an identity. In this respect, a writer's *beliefs* about her own capacity to be creative play an extremely important role in the larger creative process. As Richards states, everyday creativity "operates beyond survival and 'deficiency' needs, moving us toward realizing our higher human potential, and even forwarding our ongoing development" (2007b, p. 27). Richards grounds her hypotheses and evaluations within a larger context based on the precepts set forth by Maslow in his self-actualizing hierarchy.

Runco (2007) proposes that there exists a redemptive potential to be found in studying everyday creativity, primarily because it could bring to light the significance that creativity has in the lives of people on a daily basis. In fact, Runco even suggests that creativity should be considered a domain in its own right, as people do indeed use their creative abilities on a continual basis in their daily lives.

However, he also hypothesizes that such instances of everyday creativity could result in some individuals in particular domains eventually constructing creative products that could earn them the distinction of being recognized as eminently creative. According to this mode of thinking, eminent and everyday creativity can be conceived of as two locus points along a developmental continuum. Some individuals cultivate their creative skills in a specific domain, perhaps one collectively agreed on as being a traditionally creative discipline – for example, music, the visual or performing arts, mathematics, the sciences, and writing. These individuals can potentially gain *public* notice for their abilities and accomplishments – and, in fact, the press or notoriety that is linked to their creative feats actually *itself* imbues them with the label of being considered eminently creative. Again, this reference to the social context invokes Csikszentmihalyi's (1988) focus on the collective and social paradigms associated with creativity. Such occurrences of creativity could *only* become eminent as a direct result of having gained public or collective attention and agreement about being "eminent."

To have such a notable level of distinction conferred on them, though, these individuals first had to cultivate their creativity as an everyday occurrence. As Runco observes, "All creativity starts on a personal level (with interpretations, discretion, and intentions) and only sometimes becomes a social affair" (2007, p. 97). Thus, Runco identifies "personal creativity" as a description of "creativity in terms that apply to every person but also bridges eminent and everyday creativity" (p. 97). By investigating instances of everyday creativity, social scientists can arrive at a clearer understanding of how this process itself occurs – how creativity evolves from the "personal level" to the "social affair" of the creative acts and products of recognizably eminently creative individuals.

THE CREATIVE WRITER'S BELIEF SYSTEM: DEFINING THE NUANCES OF THE CREATIVE WRITING PROCESS

During the last several decades, social scientists and others interested in studying creativity often designed and implemented studies that used a nebulous conception of creativity, one derived from the myriad of ideas bound, sometimes loosely, to the term "creativity." In response to the perceived lack of a standard definition of creativity, Plucker et al. (2004) offered the following definition: "Creativity is the interaction among *aptitude, process, and environment* by which an individual or group produces a *perceptible product* that is both *novel and useful* as defined within a *social context*" (p. 87). This definition will prove helpful because it is applicable to our inquiry in the following three ways:

1. The emphasis on the *interaction* among the "aptitude, process, and environment" in which a creative writer operates underscores the dynamic quality of this relationship, as well as its constantly changing nature. For our purposes in this chapter, highlighting this dynamic quality allows us to engage in an in-depth discussion about how the interplay among these three variables *transforms and evolves* as the creative writer gains more writing experience *as a writer*. In short, the writer's cognizance about and understanding of his own aptitude remain inevitably influenced by his familiarity with the process of writing and by his participation in the environment, or field of creative writing (i.e., with other writers – both more and less experienced than himself, as well as instructors, publishers, and the like). In addition, the writer's perception of herself *as a writer* also evolves as the writer's career develops, and her awareness of her own aptitude equally becomes influenced by her understanding about the writing process as it occurs for her, within the larger environment of the creative writing field.

2. By delineating this definition of creativity, our discussion inevitably gives rise to the interaction among these three variables, particularly as they become manifested in the individual who *is* the aspiring creative writing student. For our purposes, the variable of "process" mentioned by Plucker et al. (2004) becomes our initial focal point, because the pedagogical manuals for creative writing stress this component of a writer's development. After all, the writer's actual process of writing creatively (stories, poems, etc.) unquestionably shapes the final *perceptible product* that is created; just as significantly, the writer's process of development as a writer certainly derives from the interplay among these three variables. Thus, in this chapter, we drawn on the process component of the operational definition of creativity and further subdivide this phenomenon of process into two related yet distinct entities: (1) the writer's practice and (2) the writer's process.

3. The writer's practice comprises the following idea: All writers – both beginners and those with more experience – engage in the *practice* of creative writing by incorporating writing itself into their regular lives. An individual who chooses to engage in the act of creation is employing the capacity to compose words in new combinations and escape the bounds of conventional thinking. To invoke the old adage, a writer is one who writes. Therefore, the *practice* of creative writing could be defined as the commitment or motivation of an individual to compose some sort of creative literary product (i.e., poetry, fiction, play, screenplay, memoir, etc.) and to do so repeatedly over time, to the extent that the individual can produce a finished and perceptible creative product.

Similarly, the writer's process remains inextricably intertwined with his practice: If an individual cultivates this writing practice – makes it a regular activity over the course of an extended period of time – then this individual could be said to participate in an ongoing writing *process*. When an individual writes creatively, she evolves *as* a writer. The individual's repeated choice to incorporate the writing process into her regular activities foments the development of that individual's persona as a writer. In essence, the individual comes to think of herself as a writer or as one who writes. This point may appear facile but it becomes significant because of the dynamic quality of development itself. As a writer gains more experience in the practice of writing, the process simultaneously transforms as well.

This focus logically introduces the question of a writer's self-perception of himself as a writer: Specifically, a writer cultivates a *writing persona* or *writing identity*. As an individual evolves as a writer, the sum of that individual's experiences while writing creatively and interacting with others associated with creative writing shapes that person's self-perception of himself as a writer. The creative writing *process* could thus be described as an individual's repeated engagement in the act of writing creatively, over an extended period of time, to the extent that the writer gains increased knowledge about the existing literary texts that might have an impact on the audience's reception of that aspiring writer's own work. In addition, the term *process* could signify the deeper cultivation of the individual's conception of herself *as a writer*; that is, the individual's formulation of her own writing persona, or the perceived set of characteristics or effective practices that have allowed that individual to successfully compose at least one creative text and perhaps several texts.

Obviously, the practice serves as a unit of sorts within the overall trajectory of the writer's process; yet, an examination of the practice at various moments during the process allows us to examine how it evolves. If we investigate several instances of this practice and consider them as successive plot points along the larger continuum of a writer's development *as a writer*, then we can gain a clearer picture of how a "writerly" identity develops. Our study of the pedagogical manuals for creative writers helps illuminate the beliefs of established writers themselves and also how these beliefs influence the advice and guidance that they pass along through such manuals, which are commonly used as seminal texts in many university undergraduate creative writing classes.

CREATING ART: DEVELOPING A CREATIVE PERSONA

In the pedagogical manuals on creative writing, much of the focus for an aspiring writer is on the writer's sense of herself *as a creative writer*. Not only must an aspiring writer operate with the objective to create actual creative writing products but it also proves helpful for him to cultivate a particular type of persona. In this regard, any investigation of the creative process necessarily includes an examination of the development of this creative persona. By taking this focus, we hope to illuminate some of the nuances between process and person.

In Frank Conroy's (2002) discussion of the processes that unfold within a fiction writing workshop at the University of Iowa, he focuses on the unique character of the individual writer. As he states, the "Iowa Workshop attempts to respond to what each student brings, and each student is unique. The briefest look at the variety in the work of the student – to say nothing of the famous graduates – is the proof" (pp. 110–111). He emphasizes the idea that art cannot be "made by learning a set of rules and applying them" (p. 111). If each individual is different, a set of potential "rules" would not only be interpreted differently by each writer but also would potentially be used by each writer in vastly different ways. Conroy's focus on the writer *as an individual* invokes a similar theme emphasized by John Gardner (1983) in his seminal work *The Art of Fiction*. Gardner asserts that the creative writer's "authority" remains inextricably linked to his "trustworthiness as a judge of things, [or] a stability rooted in the sum of those complex qualities of his character and personality (wisdom, generosity, compassion, strength of will) to which we [the readers] respond" (pp. 8–9). The creative writer's capacity to produce and convey a story that will continuously hold the reader's attention is rooted in this ability to communicate these qualities of his "character and personality."

These ideas underscore the significance of Runco's (2007) conception of personal creativity, which is made up of three distinct components: (1) *discretion,* or "deciding when to construct original interpretations and when to conform instead"; (2) intentions, which "reflect the values that motivate creative efforts"; and (3) the capacity to "construct original interpretations of experience" (p. 92). From this definition, it remains clear that an undeniable linkage exists between a person's self-perceptions and the creative process he enacts. Thus, the way that an aspiring creative individual views himself plays a crucial role in his development as a creative writer and also in his written products. This relationship represents the cyclical and dynamic nature of both the creative process itself and the nature of development inherent in the trajectory of a person's evolution as a creative individual.

To this end, a recurring theme in the pedagogical manuals is the transition from a person thinking of herself as a reader to conceiving of herself as a writer. For example, in the opening vignette, Grace became intoxicated with the power of stories to open up magical worlds in her imagination. When the visual images of words on the written page launched her cognizance into far-off and distant (or at least, unfamiliar) settings and lands, her enthusiasm for this experience cultivated in her an unquenchable love of reading. From this love of reading, she also grew to have an equally strong fascination with writing.

Ironically, the same magic that surrounds stories themselves – and proves most alluring to potential young writers – also exists as one of the challenges facing the writing teacher. That is, student writers can become so intoxicated with the magic of stories that they believe only certain people possess the power to create such influential narratives. The very term "magic" seems to suggest something intangible, a power that lies beyond the reach of intentional control. This power could arguably be compared to the way that some individuals view themselves as being "creative," whereas other people just as avowedly swear by their own lack of any identifiable creative potential. Such a theme also reflects the dominion granted to beliefs derived from an emphasis on instances of eminent creativity.

Woven in and through an individual's engagement with both reading and writing remains a sense of mystery attached to these processes, seemingly linked to the ephemeral magical power of stories themselves. As a reader, it can become difficult to detach one's self from the experience of reading in order to cultivate analytical abilities about exactly *how* the words on the page become translated into these magical images that unfold in one's mind. It remains an almost greater challenge, therefore, for an aspiring writer to learn how to transform his conception of himself *as a reader* – that is, as a receiver of such stories – to being a writer or the creator of these stories.

The difficulty in making this transition could be grounded in the fact that the belief that creative writing can be *taught* is still a relatively new development in the realm of academia. Conroy (2002) described the evolution of this belief, that creative writing could be a viable discipline in which universities could actually award a degree. He suggested that the term "writers' workshop" has only been in existence some 60-odd years and that it derives from the decision of the University of Iowa's Board of Regents to accept "creative" theses to fulfill course requirements for certain advanced degrees (p. 98). Only when it became an accepted idea that individuals could be instructed about a creative power or process could a forum for such educational practices be developed. However, it is important to note that the very existence of the practice of teaching creative writing suggests that creative writers themselves believe that the practice and process involved with writing can be acquired and are not, therefore, simply something inborn in people.

This subtext reveals the considerable influence that the myth of the mystification of creativity has had over both social scientists and artists themselves, including creative writers. On a certain level, the very existence of pedagogical manuals designed to guide the aspiring creative writer actually undercuts the validity of this fascination with occurrences of eminent creativity. The conventional classroom procedures that take place in a creative writing workshop similarly emphasize the significance of the potential steps that aspiring writers can take to cultivate their creative writing ability. By engaging in daily tasks in a repetitive fashion, they can apply the lessons learned through such a practice to their knowledge of creative texts, ability to produce such texts, and confidence in themselves as persons capable of repeatedly constructing such texts. By engaging in these instances of everyday creativity, they can actually transform their belief system about their own creative abilities as *part* of the process of their development *as* creative individuals.

THE WRITER'S NARRATIVE: EXPLANATION OF ACCUMULATED PERCEPTIONS IN THE CREATIVE WRITING WORKSHOP

In the creative writing workshop, students interested in fiction writing come together in a small group to engage in "practice" sessions of writing exercises and to exchange their own short stories and other literary endeavors. Through this forum, students first learn to identify the basic elements of stories – character, plot, theme, narration – and ascertain how to replicate these respective elements by reading examples of successful stories and then modeling their own attempts after these examples.

As students engage in this process, they "practice" writing in the same way that a musician rehearses on an instrument. They work through smaller examples of potential material in an effort to understand and be better prepared for how the various elements of fiction can be combined to create more complex narratives. Short exercises centered around the development of character, plot, and narrative voice serve as the writer's equivalent to the scales and arpeggios of the musician. When successful writers discuss the unique conditions of their respective "processes" and the role that creativity plays in the development of their stories, they often create a narrative that describes how they move from a certain moment of inspiration to a fully developed story.

Obviously, beginning writers would construct a rather different narrative about themselves than would ones with more experience. Perhaps most importantly, though, as writers become more adept at navigating through a more complex palette – as they move beyond the basic concepts of shape and design to considering various ways to overlay or emphasize certain parts of a story so as to more clearly convey a particular theme – their narrative about their creative process should evolve accordingly. In addition, this self-conceived narrative can actually influence their self-conception as writers, and their evolving understanding of their own creative process could thereby have an impact on the final products that they create.

Many writers perpetuate the belief that their inspiration occurs somewhat mysteriously, that the creative process itself occurs almost unconsciously. However, writers and writing manuals also focus on the *process* of creative writing, despite the authors' own beliefs about the mystification of creativity. Creative writing manuals often break down the writing process by describing the significance of a certain component of fiction (e.g., plot, character, setting, beginnings, endings, etc.) within the larger context of the story. They also stress the way that a writer's creative process can develop as the writer becomes exposed to more examples of writing. The ability to analyze other creative writing models – or stories – augments the writer's own writing process. Such an emphasis implicitly supports the idea that creative writing can be both taught and learned. This idea could be considered corollary to the practice of demystifying the act of creation itself; that is, many individuals who might not believe that they possess any creative prowess soon realize the fallacy of this assumption when they become trained how to incorporate their analytical powers into their own creative processes.

EXPRESSING PERSONAL CREATIVITY: HOW A WRITER'S BELIEF SYSTEM INFLUENCES THE EVOLUTION OF THE WRITING PERSONA

Although it might seem like a rather elementary concept, it is important to note that a writer's belief system is an integral component of his or her *self.* Among the pedagogical manuals on creative writing, one of the most notable commentaries about the significance of the concept of "self" in relation to the development of a writer's writerly identity can be found by returning to *The Art of Fiction* (1983) by John Gardner. He emphatically stresses the importance of writers cultivating a strong sense of faith or confidence in their own ability to produce a creative text. Gardner proposes that the facet of a writer's personality that is a crucial component of being able to develop this sense of confidence is the ability to have "absolute *trust* in his own aesthetic judgments and instincts" (p. 9). Gardner identifies this sense of trust in one's own abilities as being the source of the writer's potential "force," and furthermore, he asserts that this trust is itself founded partially on the writer's "intelligence and sensitivity," as well as on his or her "experience as a craftsman" (p. 9).

Seemingly, stability of character and personality, and intelligence and sensitivity, remain inextricable, but the crucial linkage between these two factors ultimately exists as the writer's *absolute trust* in her own ability. To cultivate this ability, Runco's theory of personal creativity can again be applied, as he identifies "ego strength" as one of the most important components of any aspiring creative artist or writer. As he states, "An individual with mature and resilient ego strength is the most likely to stand up for his or her own perspective" (p. 100). This characteristic, he suggests, is the most likely to result in "a realistic expression of one's self," and he proposes that this personal trait should be a "first priority . . . if creative self-expression and the fulfillment of potential are desired" (p. 100). This proposal extends the third component of his definition of personal creativity, the "capacity to construct original interpretations of experience" (p. 92). By exerting the "force" to be found in a strong "faith" or sense of confidence in one's self, writers can most successfully cultivate their "intelligence and sensitivity" to serve them in the creative process; by extension, they can sustain a stable "character and personality" to bolster their capacity to serve "as a judge of things."

This "force" can also be used as a metaphor to describe the dynamic processes that underlie the writer's sense of self. After all, it is this impetus to produce a creative text that fuels the writer's drive to actually write. Perhaps the most crucial area to explore is *how* a creative writer manages to translate the abstract concepts and ideas in his mind into tangible creative products that can be presented to the world. In the same writing manual, Gardner further extrapolates,

> Art depends heavily on *feeling*, intuition, taste. It is *feeling*, not some rule, that tells the abstract painter to put his yellow here and there, not there, and may later tell him that it should have been brown or purple or pea-green. It is *feeling* that makes the composer break surprisingly from his key, *feeling* that gives the writer the rhythms of his sentences, the pattern of rise and fall in his episodes, the proportions of alternating elements, so that dialogue goes on only so long before a shift to description or narrative summary or some physical action. The great writer has an *instinct* for these things. . . . And his *instinct* touches every thread of his fabric. (emphases added, p. 7)

This emphasis on feeling – and, to a lesser extent, on instinct – coincides with the idea of a writer's "character and personality," in the sense that Gardner makes reference to seemingly unconscious impulses on the part of the writer.

The writer cannot rely on rules because art inherently relies on creativity, and the concept of creation implicitly invokes a break with existing axioms. As Gardner (1983) states, "Invention, after all, is art's main business, and one of the great jobs of every artist comes with making the outrageous acceptable" (p. 8). The writer's capacity to control the various alternating elements of his fiction, or to retain control over the overarching structure of the work, becomes inextricably intertwined with the fabric of his story.

But this fabric is not something that arises magically overnight, like some sort of golden thread that instantly materializes in the whipping turns of a fairy tale; rather, the "fabric" must be prepared (brainstormed), treated (researched), and created initially (first draft), but then augmented, revitalized, ripped apart, and sewn back together again (revision). Only after the fabric's material has been visited again and again (and again) can the final product appear as the magnificent and multilayered series of plot twists and character development that eventually comprise the finished pages of a story.

Of course, such a finished product inevitably erases all the struggles, the hardships, and the inevitable effort involved with thinking and producing and creating – the very steps involved in the *process* of creating a story. So it comes as little surprise to both writers and their readers that this act – the creative act – frequently becomes mystified, made mysterious, or appears rather opaque and inaccessible.

To combat this notion, Robert Olen Butler (2005) directly addresses the confluence between unconscious invention and conscious revision in his seminal writing guide *From Where You Dream*. In it, he first relates that there exists in the mind of every writer a voice that struggles to squelch that writer's impulse to create. He labels this voice a "self-conscious metavoice" (p. 19), and he describes the difficulty for any writer to subdue, much less silence, the constant presence of this voice. He describes it as "analytical garbage running through your mind . . . , [as] a voice about the voice [or] talking about [one's] own consciousness" (p. 20). It remains necessary for any creative writer, but perhaps especially a novice one, to find a way to silence this critical voice of which Butler speaks. Only in this way can a writer truly discover a *means* of constructing "original interpretations of experience." After all, by making her product absolutely personal, a writer can likely best cultivate the sense of trust in herself as discussed by Gardner.

Butler actually suggests that writers can use the creative process *itself* as a way to translate abstract conceptual images in the mind into a tangible creative product. As he explains, "One of the ways of understanding your unconscious is by realizing that in order to get into it you have to actually stop that garbagey analytical reflex voice in your head and induce a kind of trance state. . . . Psychologists call it the 'flow state,' being in the flow" (pp. 20–21).

Through this state of being in flow, a creative writer can successfully access the innovative associations conceptualized in his unconscious intellectual processes, to bring forth onto paper the raw material of a rough draft, which is, of course, the first step in the larger process of constructing a written creative text. To immerse one's self in the state of flow, a writer must squelch this voice; in fact, this task is one of the most important to accomplish throughout the writing process, no matter the writer's experience level.

Butler's advice is echoed by the counsel offered by Anne Lamott (1995) in her text *Bird by Bird*, which many creative writing teachers use as a textbook or guide. In particular, her chapter entitled "Shitty First Drafts" proves useful in illuminating the importance of revision and its role in the writer's creative process and practice. She states that "all good writers" inevitably create "shitty first drafts" (p. 21). After all, just as a painter cannot work without a canvas, and a sculptor requires the rough-hewn rock from which to hone a masterpiece, the writer also needs initial material to polish and refine.

Lamott continues that this process allows all writers to "end up with good second drafts and terrific third drafts" (p. 21). She avowedly demystifies the "fantasy of the uninitiated" (p. 21) by explicitly contradicting the assumption that "successful writers" who are "getting their books published and maybe even doing well financially . . . sit down at their desks every morning feeling like a million dollars, feeling great about who they are and how much talent they have and what a great story they have to tell" (p. 21). Such writers, she states, never "take in a few deep breaths, push back their sleeves, roll their necks a few times to get all the cricks out, and dive in, typing fully formed passages as fast as a court reporter" (p. 21). Instead, they face the daily challenge of "pulling teeth" (p. 22), because "the right words and sentences just do not come pouring out like ticker tape most of the time" (p. 22). She even offers the example of a writer who "sits down every morning and says to himself nicely, 'It's not like you don't have a choice, because you do – you can either type or kill yourself'" (p. 22). Her words undercut the assumption that all worthwhile creative writing should result from a lightning-like strike of inspiration, and they further call into question the myth-like presumption that creativity can only occur in certain gifted individuals during mysterious instances that result in eminent products.

As Sawyer (2006) observes,

> Our [creativity] myth tells us that creativity emerges in a burst of inspiration from the unconscious, [so] we naturally think that the inspired first draft is the best. . . . But this is a false creativity myth; professional writers know that the first draft often needs heavy editing. Very few writers can attain their best without subjecting this spontaneous work to careful, tedious, time-consuming review and editing. (p. 207)

Lamott's description of the "fantasy of the uninitiated" reflects Sawyer's idea that this representation of the writing process is merely a reflection of a "fantasy" issued forth by "Hollywood": As he states, "In our romantic conception of creativity, the words pour onto the page in a burst of inspiration. But that's Hollywood, not real life" (p. 207). This "fantasy" of eminent creativity is annihilated by the very everyday tasks and exercises that Lamott and other creative writing manual authors describe as part of the writing process of *any* writer, both novice and experienced.

Indeed, through the very adjective that Lamott selects for the act of creating some initial material for a story, she adroitly identifies the dual-edged nature of the initial stages of the creative writing process. She suggests that, for herself and most of the other writers she knows, "writing is not rapturous" (p. 22). In fact, she admits that "the only way [she] can get anything written at all is to write really, really shitty first drafts" (p. 22). However, quickly on the heels of this assertion, she further describes this first draft as the "child's draft, where [a writer] let[s] it all pour out and then let[s] it romp all over the place, knowing that no one is going to see it and that [the writer] can shape it later" (p. 22). Her word choice of "child" suggests that this act of completing an initial draft could almost be described as fun, in the sense that, during this stage of the process, the writer gets to prance through all the various original spectacles that might arise from the imagination.

In this sense, it seems that the creation component of the writing process – that is, the task of setting words down on paper to describe the images unfolding in the creative writer's head – actually serves as a viable means through which the writer can enter Csikszentmihalyi's (1990) state of flow. As Perry (2005) describes it, "In flow . . . time seems to disappear. Theory mandates that a flow state is entered when . . . you have the sense that your personal skills are suited to the challenges of the activity" (p. 23). Further, she invokes Csikszentmihalyi's own findings that "every flow activity . . . provided a sense of discovery, a creative feeling of transporting the person into a new reality" (p. 23). If creative writers move into a "new reality," then they can "discover" the means by which to "construct [an] original interpretation" of their experience *through* the creative process.

Through this romping in the experience of creating the "child draft," a writer can best produce what Lamott terms as "clutter" (p. 28). As Lamott continues, this clutter actually comprises "wonderfully fertile ground" (p. 28), because it serves as raw material that can then be refined, shaped, and altered until it attains a high level of refinement and polish. And it is within this "clutter" that the writer "can still discover new treasures under all those piles, [to] clean things up, [to] edit things out, [to] fix things, [and to] get a grip" (pp. 28–29). Such clutter fulfills its useful purpose in giving the writer the rough material to shape, and then the process of organizing begins, to "clean things up [and] edit things out" (p. 28). Only by remaining in the presence of such "clutter" can a writer engage in the other component of the writing process: revision. As Lamott states, "Tidiness suggests that something is as good as it's going to get" (p. 28), and in fact, the very term makes her "think of held breath, of suspended animation, while writing needs to breathe and move" (p. 28). Her description highlights the dynamic quality of the creative writing process – the need for writing to "breathe and move"; too often, this dynamism becomes lost in an evaluation of the more static and reified final product of the creative writing text.

OVERALL TRAJECTORY OF THE CREATIVE WRITING PROCESS

The primary goal of any novice writer is to increase her understanding about how to best revise her own raw material into the refined strands of a polished story. As she gains more experience with the various tribulations and challenges involved in constructing a story, she simultaneously has the opportunity to cultivate a greater capacity for analysis. In this sense, it becomes of the utmost importance for any novitiate writer to become perhaps even more accomplished as a reader. With this ability, he will automatically experience greater success in his writing. After all, a creative writer's experience as a craftsman – Gardner's third consideration – remains extricable from that writer's own experiences of reading.

When a writer encounters a larger amount of creative work, then she becomes exposed to a larger breadth of material – various genres, narrative strategies, etc. – that she can then draw from as part of her palette. The writer can then incorporate these elements into his own work to blend them into a new entity, an original work of fiction. Through this exposure, the aspiring writer can construct a scaffold with which to analyze and evaluate *how* other writers have accomplished their seemingly impossible feats. By extension, the writer acquires a better grasp about how to revise her *own* stories so that they can more clearly convey a particular thematic intention.

So that creative writers can become exposed to a vast array of works, many creative writing programs encourage students to cultivate the ability to read creative texts with a critical eye. By analyzing the work of other creative writers, students become much more adept at revising their own work. When they trust their own ideas and can effectively identify a theme that arises in their work, they can develop those portions of their story that best illustrate this theme. Subsequently, they can revise their own work more successfully so that the final draft or product best conveys their larger objective. This practice of honing a writer's analysis through a particular approach to reading further allows writers to simultaneously develop a sense of absolute trust in their own work, so that they become more successfully equipped to exert a particular creative force *through* their writing.

To accomplish this task, the creative writer (especially those who specialize in fiction) must inhabit two writerly roles. First, *during* the process of creation, especially at an initial stage, the writer must be willing to produce material that does not emerge fully polished, but that must undergo stages of revision before it can become anything approximating a quality story. This willingness corresponds with a personality characteristic important to creativity, a tolerance for ambiguity. Second, the writer must be able to cultivate a rational faculty for *analysis*, which enables the development of the intellectual tools necessary to engage in an effective revision process of the work. Thus, the way that a novitiate creative writer's creative process develops becomes important. Ideally, the writer gains greater confidence or has a stronger trust in his own capabilities. She must learn to trust her own analytical ability, so that she can determine the best way to revise the initial unpolished material into something more refined – from those beginning, rough-hewn weavings into the thicker, stronger threads of a developed fabric or tapestry.

The beginning writer must become familiar with the successive experience of initially producing a malleable text and then cultivating the analytic prowess to successfully revise this text. As part of this experience, the writer should also become aware of his assumptions *about* this process and how they have influenced his capacity to effectively execute this process. Both Gardner and Conroy emphasize this multifaceted quality of the creative writing process. As Conroy states, the Iowa Writers' Workshop "asserts that it is *process* that counts" (p. 113). In a certain sense, Conroy describes the process in a way that suggests its inextricability *from* the writer's identity as an individual. He describes the cyclical nature of the writing process itself in his summary of the events that comprise life in the Writers' Workshop:

> All the work is necessary to move ahead, hence it is all valuable. Every writer creates weak, middling and strong work. No one ever knows when lightning will strike, and we are all, much of the time, waiting for it. But we are not passive. We write, we struggle, we take risks. We work to be ready for the lightning when it comes, to be worthy of it, to be able to handle it rather than be destroyed by it. (Success has ruined more writers than failure.) Writing, sayeth the workshop, is a way of life. You either sign on or you don't. (p. 113)

Seemingly, the writer's propensity both to cultivate and sustain a sense of "absolute trust" in her own ability and judgment remains dependent on the writer making the *writing process* itself an inherent component of her life. Csikszentmihalyi (1990) suggests that "happiness . . . is a condition that must be prepared for, cultivated, and developed privately by each person. People who learn to control inner experience will be able to determine the quality of their lives, which is as close as any of us can come to being happy" (p. 2). Csikszentmihalyi's discussion of flow invokes the significance that an individual's control over her own consciousness can have on the development of her abilities and path in life. His emphasis echoes the focus of both Conroy and Gardner on the writer's status *as an individual* and the *unique* quality of the creative writer's work. When a writer has made the practice of writing a part of her identity or has enacted Runco's personal creativity, she can more easily conceive of ideas that genuinely and accurately illustrate her own ideas, concerns, and themes. Through this development, the writer stands a much greater chance of producing something both original and that also conveys a sense of the writer's writerly and readerly identities, which arguably remain inextricable from one another.

Conroy discusses how creative writers begin to gain cognizance about how their prior assumptions can influence their creative writing process. As he explains, even the most promising young writers – or those students accepted into the prestigious Writers' Workshop at the University of Iowa – "tend to cling to the texts that got them into the workshop in the first place, [as they remain] deeply and understandably worried that the magic might not strike again, that the magic is unpredictable" (p. 112). This idea of "magic" arises from their own embedded beliefs that they themselves possess little to no control over their own capacity to produce quality literary work. Conroy continues that the students "mistakenly think that only their strong work is significant and that their weaker work is a total waste of time. They fear being exposed as imposters" (pp. 112–113). His discussion illustrates the idea that even effective creative writers often fall victim to the belief that the "magic" to create may leave them. They might believe that they can only be struck by lightning once and that, despite their success, they might actually be a creative imposter.

In this kind of evaluation of their own abilities, such writers initially fail to acknowledge the role played by their own critical abilities in their revising process. However, as they become exposed to more literature of a certain quality and their critical faculty evolves, they gain a greater confidence in their ability to take chances in the creative process. The most effective writer arguably cultivates his instinct about the larger pattern of his own fiction, especially in relation to those existing stories that he has already read and analyzed. It is the writer's knowledge of and level of comfort in dealing with this underlying pattern that allow her to know when to break from convention or from what has come before. The writer must be able to trust or have faith in her capacity to produce original material and to successfully present unconventional material in the framework of a story. The writer's perception of herself *as a writer* must match the level of competence she has actually achieved. She must remain aware of how much her own writing and revising abilities have evolved, as a result of the development of analytical prowess in reading.

When Conroy suggests that "success" has ruined more writers than failure, he speaks to the anxiety that a writer experiences about whether he will be able to *replicate* the instance of one (or even numerous) successes. A writer's sense of faith in himself should remain as stable as possible, though of course, every creative act inevitably includes moments of hesitation and uncertainty. Michael Chabon himself writes about this conundrum in his book *Wonder Boys*, as Kirschling (2007) reports in an interview with the author. The book represents Chabon's first novel since his freshman success with *The Mysteries of Pittsburgh*, and a major character in *Wonder Boys* reflects on the difficulties of trying to repeat one's initial success. Somewhat ironically, Chabon's constructed narrative invokes his own challenges as a fiction writer. In this respect, the story that his main character *tells himself* becomes almost as significant as the story he attempts to pen as his second novel. On a certain level, the main character almost becomes intimidated by his own persona as a revered writer. After Chabon won the 2001 Pulitzer Prize for his *The Amazing Adventures of Kavalier and Clay*, he admitted that he finally discovered his secret love of comic books. Chabon successfully identified his own anxiety about being able to replicate his early level of acclaim and actually channeled this emotion into a primary theme of his fiction (in *Wonder Boys*). As he gained greater faith in his own ability, he was able to produce a fictional work that proved a stronger illustration and exploration of a genre that most genuinely interested him – comic books. The trajectory of Chabon's own conception of himself as a writer (and by extension, as a reader – for example, of comic books) suggests the importance of Conroy's discussion about the mysterious "lightning" of inspiration and creative power and ability.

Chabon's revelations appeared only after he had dedicated countless hours to his ability – as both a reader and a writer – to gain experience as a craftsman. Just as a musician must rehearse the minute details of technique until reading music becomes almost instinctual, the beginning writer must equally engage in smaller tasks that cultivate an almost instantaneous response about the most effective way to construct a literary text. This idea also corresponds with Butler's (2005) commentary about the "flow state" experienced by writers during the writing process. Butler compares this state to the "muscle memory" experienced by athletes when they are "in the zone" (p. 21), and he extends this metaphor to suggest to aspiring writers that, for them, it's "not muscle memory; it's dream space, it's sense memory" (p. 21). This comparison invokes Runco's ideas about personal creativity, because words and phrases that arise as a result of a writer being in a state of flow could arguably result in a creative written text that most fully expresses original interpretations of experience. If a creative writer engages in everyday tasks that comprise the more mundane components of the creative writing process, then the accumulation of these habits – the action of repeatedly *writing* creative texts – builds up the writer's "sense memory" muscles in the same way that an athlete builds tone to serve him on the playing field. Finally, the agglomeration of these habits come to be strung together in the individual persona of the writer himself, to form a pearl-like strand of his ability to effectively and repeatedly construct creative texts.

CREATING A SUBJECTIVE REALITY: INTELLECTUAL TOOLS FOR
WORKING WITHIN THE CREATIVE WRITING FIELD AND CULTIVATING
A WRITERLY IDENTITY

To create a "subjective reality" in which a writer could *consciously* order her "different goals and intentions" associated with writing, she would need to learn the method of writing that would most effectively facilitate her capacity to invent original ideas through the medium of words. Just as importantly, she should gain awareness about how to later revise her work so as to whittle away the excess material and hone it into the fine points of a streamlined and polished story. To explore how best to accomplish this task of learning, we return to the ideas espoused by Sternberg and Lubart (1996) that served as a theoretical foundation for our operational definition (Plucker et al., 2004).

Specifically, Sternberg and Lubart propose that a multidisciplinary approach to creativity research proves most fruitful because it resists the proclivity of the unidisciplinary approach that reduces creativity to particular characteristics (of individuals, or related to outcomes), and then presents this data as comprehensively representing the entirety of creativity and the creative process. In their article, they laud investment theory as one of the more comprehensive multidisciplinary approaches to creativity research. According to this methodological approach, creativity requires a confluence of six distinct but interrelated resources: intellectual abilities, knowledge, styles of thinking, personality, motivation, and environment (p. 684). Sternberg and Lubart further classify the resource of intellectual abilities into three separate but necessary characteristics or abilities:

> a) the synthetic ability to see problems in new ways and to escape the bounds of conventional thinking, (b) the analytic ability to recognize which of one's ideas are worth pursuing and which are not, and (c) the practical-contextual ability to know how to persuade others of – to sell other people on – the value of one's ideas. The confluence of these three abilities is also important. (p. 684)

The first two, in particular – the synthetic ability and the analytic ability – prove to be crucial components of both the writer's practice and process of creation. Much of the literature that offers recommendations about ways and methods to foster the creative writing process focuses on the writer's capacity to conceive of novel ideas and then to discriminate among these various inspirations to produce creative products that can be accepted as contributions to the existing literary corpus. Thus, the synthetic ability and the analytic ability are key components of the creative resource, as they prove essential especially for the revision process.

Just as important, however, is the writer's capacity to understand how to balance the inventive stages of the writing process, in which the raw material of stories is produced, with the more intentional segments of the process that focus on revision, at which time the writer works to shape words with a more deliberate objective in mind. Clearly, the synthetic ability corresponds more closely with the inventive stage, and the analytical ability proves most useful in the revising process. To more clearly elucidate the nuances of these two phases, the Geneplore model proves useful to consider.

As Finke, Ward, and Smith (1992) explain, the Geneplore model, based largely on a foundation that explores creative cognition theories, consists of two distinct processing components: a generative phase followed by an exploratory phase (p. 17). In the first stage, the generative or inventive phase, the individual constructs mental representations, labeled preinventive structures, which have various properties that promote creative discovery (p. 17). These properties are then used during the second phase, the exploratory phase or the revising portion of the model, in which the creative individual seeks to "interpret the preinventive structures in meaningful ways" (p. 17). As Finke and colleagues note further, these "preinventive structures can be thought of as internal precursors to the final, externalized creative products and would be generated, regenerated, and modified throughout the course of creative exploration" (p. 17). Overall, these phases are enacted in a recurring cycle, in the sense that the "resulting creative cognitions can be focused or expanded according to task requirements or individual needs by modifying the preinventive structures and repeating the cycle" (p. 18). In addition, the final product itself can be modified during the cycle at any time, in both stages – the generative (inventive) stage and also the exploratory (revising) stage (p. 18).

The characteristics of this model correspond closely with the two stages of the creative writing process, as it is described in the pedagogical manuals. In addition, the cyclical nature of the model, as well as the flexible manner in which it can be used, certainly serves as a quintessential model for describing the interaction between the more unconscious stage of penning the "child draft" described by Lamott and the more deliberate task work required for revision, or the editing of Lamott's "clutter." The Geneplore model certainly serves our purposes well for considering the larger structure of the creative writing process, but to illuminate further the nuances of the interaction between the individual and his field and domain, Csikszentmihalyi and Sawyer (1995) provide an extremely helpful model. The pedagogical creative writing manuals traffic in the vocabulary of an understanding of the synthetic and analytical abilities as couched in the context of a narrative – or the accumulated perceptions of an individual, as derived from her experiences with the creative writing field and domain.

In Csikszentmihalyi and Sawyer's study, they focus on the "A-ha!"-like moment of inspiration, which they label as an "insight." This unit of analysis ostensibly focuses on the moment of an instant, but the comprehensive approach that Csikszentmihalyi and Sawyer take proves useful to our purposes because of the way they consider this single moment within the larger context of the social interactions that have led up to, have inevitably affected, and perhaps even precipitated its occurrence. As they state, "When we look at the complete 'life span' of a creative insight in our subjects' experience, the moment of insight appears as but one short flash in a complex, time-consuming, fundamentally social process.... These reports [about the moment of insight] usually are embedded within a more complex *narrative*, a *story* that describes the effort preceding and following the insight, and the overall sense of these *complete narratives* stresses the salience of social, interactional factors" (emphasis added; p. 331). The fact that Csikszentmihalyi and Sawyer label these larger considerations as a "narrative" and a "story" underscores the way that a writer constructs a writerly persona – that is, he does so *through* a *narrative* that he creates about his larger experiences with creative writing. This narrative – a story of sorts, in and of itself – concretizes and reifies the writer's accumulated perceptions about his experiences with the creative writing field and domain. Subsequently, the writerly identity that a writer cultivates remains strongly influenced by such perceptions, and, in fact, a writer's own beliefs about what he could accomplish could ultimately remain hampered by his beliefs, as they remain embedded in this narrative. For example, if he believes his work can only be spawned from an uncontrollable lightning bolt of inspiration, then he might doubt his own ability to replicate past successes in the future, instead of cultivating the strong sense of trust in himself and his own work that is so heavily emphasized by Gardner.

Conversely, if a writer believes she has more control over the outcome of her own work and constructs a narrative – and by extension, a writerly persona – that underscores this sense of control, then she stands a much better chance of succeeding in the creative writing field (again, invoking Csikszentmihalyi's conception of the term). Sternberg and Lubart (1999) relate in Sternberg's *Handbook of Creativity* (1999) that personality attributes that help foster creativity include self-efficacy, a willingness to overcome obstacles, taking sensible risks, and tolerating ambiguity (p. 11). If a writer understands that he maintains greater control over the final creative product, then he can be willing to overcome obstacles and tolerate ambiguity much more easily; in the same vein, this certainty allows him to take sensible risks, all of which will increase his self-efficacy and confidence as a writer or his faith in himself – his own judgments, creative decisions, and abilities.

In essence, the writer's own writerly persona becomes the point of stability that preserves a sense of continuity across her forays into the two stages of invention (generative) and revision (exploratory). Through the stability of the writer's writerly persona, she can exert the force to be found in trusting herself and can thus maneuver much more effectively between the inventive and revision stages, as she enacts this dynamic process, as explained by the Geneplore cyclical model. By extension, she can also more easily construct the "subjective reality" required for the state of "flow," which will then imbue her experiences of the creative process with the positive effects of "flow" that Csikszentmihalyi describes.

THE INFLUENCE OF THE SOCIAL REALM ON THE CREATIVE INDIVIDUAL

Thus, the writer's own constructed narrative about his own creative practice, or experience of the writing process, holds an undeniable influence over the actions that he takes to produce a polished story. Like any artist, the writer must strike a particular balance between risk and security. A writer must trust himself enough to risk producing original material, but then should draw on his own analytical powers and reading experiences to remain consciously aware of the strengths and weaknesses of this material. A writer must make a writing practice part of his life, but simultaneously understand the tribulations and challenges inherent in this practice. Anne Lamott further describes the overall practice according to the various stages of revision, as she suggests,

> Almost all good writing begins with terrible first efforts. You need to start somewhere. Start by getting something – anything – down on paper. A friend of mine says that the first draft is the down draft – you just get it down. The second draft is the up draft – you fix it up. You try to say what you have to say more accurately. And the third draft is the dental draft, where you check every tooth, to see if it's loose or cramped or decayed, or even, God help us, healthy. (pp. 25–26)

Writing the first draft – the "child draft" – could be compared to the experience of "flow" described by Csikszentmihalyi (1990). A creative writer who becomes immersed in the experience of "flow" is more easily able to associate a positive affect with creative writing. If a writer remains conscious of the particular components of creative writing that she finds more challenging (e.g., dialogue over description), then the process of writing can be made easier by her willingness to acknowledge and practice her areas of difficulty. Through such conscious acknowledgments, a writer can remain aware of how best to enact her synthetic and analytic abilities, so as to produce a strong creative product. This habit would likely prove most fruitful during the exploratory (revision) stage of the writing process. At the same time, a writer who can sustain faith in her ability can also take the risks necessary to overcome the obstacles of these difficulties, and by doing so, such a writer would also exhibit her characteristic of being able to overcome obstacles.

Csikszentmihalyi and Sawyer further note the significant influence that the social realm has on the creative process of the individual:

> The creative process involves the generation of a novel creative product by the individual, the evaluation of the product by the field, and the retention

of selected products by addition to the domain. Thus, the creative process involves a recurring circle from person to field to domain and back to the person, paralleling the evolutionary pattern of variation (person), selection (field), and retention (domain). (1995, p. 336)

This configuration closely corresponds to the cyclical model of the Geneplore model, further underscoring the significance of the individual and of the dynamic components of the creative process itself. If the individual is continuously influenced by these external factors – the domain and field – then his final creative product is inevitably affected by his exposure to various forces at play in these two entities.

The creative writer's relationship to the social context that determines the efficacy or success of her creative writing product can be described more specifically through terms taken from Csikszentmihalyi's systems perspective exploration of creativity. Specifically, Csikszentmihalyi conceives of interactions among the "individual," "domain," and "field," three entities that influence each other in an interplay of variables. As Sternberg (1999) notes, for Csikszentmihalyi, an "individual" uses the information he finds in a domain and "transforms or extends it via cognitive processes, personality traits, and motivation" (p. 10). The individual operates in relation to the "field," an entity that consists of "people who control or influence a domain, [then] evaluate and select new ideas" (p. 10). Examples of the people who comprise the domain of creative writing might be literary agents, editors, and publishers, as well as established creative writers and instructors. Sternberg (1999) further reports that Csikszentmihalyi's "domain" exists as a "culturally defined symbol system, [which] preservers and transmits creative products to other individuals and future generations" (p. 10). Csikszentmihalyi defines the domain in terms of the cultural reception of a creative product; however, in terms of creative writing, the domain could arguably be defined as the body of literary texts themselves, in the sense that any novice creative writer must inevitably engage with an existing body of literary texts (perhaps the "canon," though only in a loose conception of that potentially charged label or system of categorization).

To define these terms in relation to a creative writer's practice and process, the creative writer would, of course, function as Csikszentmyhalyi's "individual." At the outset, the individual writer would need to become familiar with the method by which she preferred to compose creative texts. She would need to engage in the *practice* of writing creatively to determine the best ways in which to inspire her synthetic ability or to conceive of new stories that transcended the bounds of conventional thinking and existing stories. To facilitate this practice, the individual writer would equally need to cultivate a practice of reading, or becoming familiar with the existing body of literary texts with which her work must come into conversation. This interaction would represent the interplay happening between Csikszentmihalyi's "individual" and her "domain." Over the course of this interplay, the individual writer would also be developing her analytic ability, or capacity to recognize which of her ideas were worth pursuing and to understand which of those ideas should be discarded. This interaction would also comprise that writer's ongoing *process*.

INVENTION AND REVISION: HOW THE SOCIAL CONTEXT OF THE CREATIVE WRITING FIELD INFLUENCES THE INDIVIDUAL'S CREATIVE PROCESS

As we have already stated, the value of a creative writer's finished perceptible product becomes determined by its evaluation by the field – the social context through which it acquires its significance within the creative writing domain or the body of existing texts with which it "converses." This collectively determined value intersects with the emphasis that Csikszentmihalyi and Sawyer (1995) place on the social context and on its influence on the creative process, despite the fact that any creative process is typically made up of the experiences of a single individual. They report that when creative individuals were "asked to describe a moment of creative insight, they typically provided extended narratives that described not just a single moment but a complex, multi-stage process, with frequent discussions of interpersonal contact, strategic or political considerations, and awareness of the paradigm, of what questions were interesting as defined by the discipline" (p. 334). In this regard, the discipline itself or the field played an undeniably integral role in the formation of the individual's understanding of his discipline and, perhaps most significantly, of his capacity to judge the existing texts of the domain.

By extension, the social context provided for the writer through her interaction with both the domain and the field also determines how she evaluates her own work and how she understands how it fits into the larger paradigm of the discipline as a whole. As Csikszentmihalyi and Sawyer note further, "In narratives about problem-finding on a long time scale, preparation was discussed in terms of apprenticeship to a field, learning the basic rules and principles of the domain" (p. 351). In the narrative that elucidates a writer's belief system about her own creative ability and prowess, the individual internalizes these "basic rules and principles" to the extent that Csikszentmihalyi and Sawyer conclude that the "periods of hard work that precede and follow a creative insight are fundamentally social, deeply rooted in interaction with colleagues and in the individual's internalized understanding of the culturally constituted domain" (p. 331). Thus, it is in the persona of the individual writer that the "rules and principles" become "deeply rooted" by means of that person's exposure to, interaction with, and understanding of the "culturally constituted domain" (p. 331).

Because of this phenomenon, Conroy (2002) first suggests to his students, in the pedagogical approach he describes, the importance of *communication* in the construction of any creative written text. Near the beginning of any creative writing workshop under his leadership, he presents three words to his students: meaning, sense, and clarity (p. 103). Because language serves as the writer's medium, it makes sense that Conroy focuses on the level of the sentence, and perhaps even the word, as the writer's building block. As he states, "When we make paragraphs, use punctuation, follow (flexibly) the rules of grammar and so forth, we are borne by the flow of that continuum. . . . Literature is a river, full of currents and crosscurrents, and when we write, we are in it, like it or not. If we grow too forgetful, we can drown" (p. 103). By this statement, Conroy suggests both the importance of paying attention to the minutest detail and of the writer's reliance on the tradition of literature that has informed his own experiences of reading. He directs his students to a potential approach they could take to their daily practice and then places his counsel within the context of them as creative individuals interacting with the creative writing domain. By focusing on the importance of communicating with one's reader, the creative writer can also keep this goal in mind as a conscious objective, which could itself serve as a guiding principle as, during the exploratory (revision) phase, he could shape the material he produced during the initial generative (inventive) stage.

Along the same lines, as a writer gains greater exposure to and understanding of the various texts that comprise the domain of creative writing, she can remain mindful of what she desires should be her own contributions to the writing tradition with which she wishes to "converse." As creative writers make the transition from being a passive recipient of written texts to readers who use a specific *analytic* ability, they can acquire a particular type of knowledge and develop the habit of reading a fictional story or poem for the purposes of analysis, instead of merely passively absorbing the material as a magically unfolding narrative. This step serves to demystify both the act of creation itself, as Conroy's advice implicitly reveals his own understanding about the teachability of creative writing and, by extension, creativity. He imparts this demystification to his students by focusing on instances of *everyday* creativity. Then, he teaches his students how to build on these moments, perhaps so as to better guide them to compose stories that will be hailed as examples of eminent creativity.

When creative writing students read the texts in the domain of their field with a more astute eye, they do so with a different purpose than merely absorbing the events of a story or images of a poem. Through this methodology, they can gain not only a much greater depth of understanding about *how* other writers achieve certain effects or results in their work but they can also expand their conception about how their own work fits into the larger domain, about how it communicates with the ideas of their writing peers and predecessors in matters of theme and other considerations. For example, in preparation for writing *The Yiddish Policemen's Union*, Chabon read certain texts, including

Jane Austen, with the explicit purpose of refamiliarizing himself with those texts that he thought should be fresh and at the forefront of his mind as he composed his own work.

As a creative writer engages in more practice and extends the time of his writing process, he arguably operates with the purpose of becoming an even more successful writer. Furthermore, if he associates a positive affect with creative writing, then this positive experience will serve as his motivation for continuing to write. Within this larger framework, Csikszentmihalyi's idea of flow and its relationship to happiness emerges as an important factor in the individual's development as a writer.

This type of preparation presents a prismatic view of Conroy's description of the writing process, that "a great deal of what makes good writing is mysterious and beyond our power to control directly, but we need not be entirely helpless in our attempts to approach the state in which we might possibly increase our chances of doing good writing" (2002, pp. 105–106). In this statement, Conroy himself remains somewhat hampered by his own conception of the writing process as "something mysterious," despite his own implicit awareness about the everyday practice of fostering development as a creative writer. He forms a narrative that reflects this assumption that any writer (perhaps including himself) suffers from a distinct lack of control over the created text. Conroy embeds in his instruction a conception of creativity that corresponds with the mystification of it as a discipline.

On the other hand, although Chabon's actual writing process remains unique to him and his writing practice, his choice of specific texts with which to refresh his memory reveals the control that a creative writer can retain over his engagement with the existing domain. Chabon's decision to read Austen and other authors in preparation for writing his latest novel reflects the power he wields over his own creative practice. He draws from the knowledge he has gained from his experiences with the writing *process* when he uses his analytic ability to select Austen over other authors whose work he has read. He understands that her themes and ideas will be most conducive to helping him use his synthetic ability to write his next novel, despite the fact that his novel "converses" to a great degree with the comic book tradition and Austen might not be the first author someone else might think of in relation to this subject matter!

In this way, these smaller lessons represent instances of everyday ways of being creative, as manifested in the cultivation of particular habits. Conroy offers an example offered by the late Kurt Vonnegut: As Vonnegut notes, "you cannot really teach a baseball player how to become a great hitter ... but you can teach him where to stand in the box, how to shift his weight during the swing, how to follow through and a dozen other things he'll need to know before he can become even a good hitter" (2002, pp. 105–106). Although a creative writing teacher cannot teach a student how to become a great writer, she *can* inform her students how to master those smaller components of which writing the text, or completing the swing, is comprised. This example underscores the importance of *practicing* writing, or perhaps teaching the mind to engage in patterns of thought processes, such as the synthetic and analytic abilities mentioned by Sternberg and Lubart. Such thought processes could be compared to the physical movements that comprise musical and athletic practices that are designed to instill in the muscles a sense of "memory" for the correct procedures by which to enact effective performances, either musical or athletic.

When muscles – both physical and cerebral – become used to working in a particular vernacular, a writer can feel more at ease in working in his particular medium. Writing may be initially performative, but the product produced in such a performance is only the seed of the work. The more difficult and integral stages of creation come into play *only* through the process of revision. Unlike a musical performance, in which a musician must practice *in order* to cultivate muscle memory like that of an athlete, the writer's artistic creation evolves in a much more tangible way. He never appears in front of his readers like a musician or a magician, but rather, the layers of effort that culminate in the material product of his written text remain necessarily eclipsed and indubitably hidden. Established authors may even capitalize on this capacity to mystify, to present such a polished *perceptible* and finished creative *product* to the field – their agents, students, peers, publishers; in sum, their readers – in order to exert their third intellectual ability, mentioned by Sternberg and Lubart: their practical-contextual ability to know how to persuade others of the value of their ideas. However, such a practice obviously perpetuates the mystification of creativity that has existed as an obstacle to aspiring creative writers.

CONCLUSION

Only after a writer has been able to break down his practice of subscribing to the mystification of creativity can he become aware that he can exert a much greater locus of control over his finished creative written text than he might have previously assumed. To extend the parameters of research inquiries to focus on instances of everyday creativity, social scientists need to focus on the daily tasks that can be cultivated as repeated habits. By taking such a theoretical approach, we can use Runco's concept of personal creativity to arrive at a much clearer understanding about how the repetition of such daily tasks can help cultivate in an individual creative writer occurrences of eminent creativity.

Specifically, we can use the Geneplore cognitive model to explore how the balance between the two stages of invention (generative stage) and revision (exploratory stage) make up the larger cyclical system of the creative process itself. In turn, as a creative writer gains a greater familiarity with the various rules and policies of the discipline of creative writing, then she will be able to cultivate her analytical abilities to the extent that she can judge her own products according to the terms delineated by the social context of the creative writing field. As a result, she will be able to refine her own practice of revision, and her final polished product will more accurately correspond with the aesthetic standards of the creative writing discipline. Only by bringing a kind of public attention to these more frequently occurring instances of everyday creativity at work can we gain a more comprehensive understanding of how such tasks can be eventually identified as exemplars of eminent creativity.

REFERENCES

Beghetto, R., & Kaufman, J. C. (2007). Toward a broader conception of creativity: A case of "mini-c" creativity. *Psychology of Aesthetics, Creativity, and the Arts, 1*(2), 73–79.

Butler, R. O. (2005). *From where you dream: The process of writing fiction.* New York: Grove Press.

Conroy, F. (2002). *Dogs bark but the caravan marches on.* Boston: Houghton Mifflin.

Csikszentmihalyi, M. (1988). Society, culture, and person: A systems view of creativity. In R. J. Sternberg (Ed.), *The nature of creativity: Contemporary psychological perspectives* (pp. 325–339). New York: Cambridge University Press.

Csikszentmihalyi, M. (1990). *Flow: The psychology of optimal experience.* New York: HarperPerennial.

Csikszentmihalyi, M., & Sawyer, K. (1995). Creative insight: The social dimension of a solitary moment. In R. Sternberg & J. Davidson (Eds.), *The nature of insight* (pp. 329–361). New York: Cambridge University Press.

Finke, R., Ward, R., & Smith, S. (1992). *Creative cognition: Theory, research, and applications.* Cambridge, MA: MIT Press.

Gardner, J. (1984). *The art of fiction: Notes on craft for young writers.* New York: Vintage Books.

Kaufman, J. C., & Baer, J. (Eds.). (2005). *Creativity across domains: Faces of the muse.* Mahwah, NJ: Erlbaum.

Kaufman, J., & Baer, J. (Eds.). (2006). *Creativity and reason in cognitive development.* New York: Cambridge University Press.

Kirschling, G. (2007, May 11). The new adventures of Michael Chabon. *Entertainment Weekly.*

Lamott, A. (1995). *Bird by bird: Some instructions on writing and life.* New York: Anchor Books.

Perry, S. K. (2005). Flow and the art of fiction. In J. C. Kaufman & J. Baer (Eds.), *Creativity across domains: Faces of the muse* (pp. 41–58). Mahwah, NJ: Erlbaum.

Plucker, J. A., Beghetto, R. A., & Dow, G. T. (2004). Why isn't creativity more important to educational psychologists? Potential pitfalls and future directions in creativity research. *Educational Psychology, 39,* 83–96.

Richards, R. (Ed.). (2007a). *Everyday creativity and new views of human nature: Psychological, social, and spiritual perspectives.* Washington, DC: American Psychological Association.

Richards, R. (2007b). Everyday creativity: Our hidden potential. In R. Richards (Ed.), *Everyday creativity and new views of human nature: Psychological, social, and spiritual perspectives* (pp. 25–54). Washington, DC: American Psychological Association.

Runco, M. (2007). To understand is to create: An epistemological perspective on human nature and personal creativity. In R. Richards (Ed.), *Everyday creativity and new views of human nature: Psychological, social, and spiritual perspectives* (pp. 91–108). Washington, DC: American Psychological Association.

Sawyer, K. (2006). *Explaining creativity: The science of human innovation.* Oxford: Oxford University Press.

Sternberg, R. J. (1999). *Handbook of creativity.* New York: Cambridge University Press.

Sternberg, R. J., & Davidson, J. E. (Eds.). (1995). *The nature of insight.* Cambridge: Cambridge University Press.

Sternberg, R. J. & Lubart, T. (1996). Investing in creativity. *American Psychologist, 51*(7), 677–688.

Sternberg, R. J., & Lubart, T. (1999). The concept of creativity: Prospects and paradigms. In R. J. Sternberg (Ed.), *Handbook of creativity* (pp. 3–15). New York: Cambridge University Press.

Weisberg, R. W. (1993). *Creativity: Beyond the myth of genius.* New York: W. H. Freeman.

19

Creation and Response: Wellspring to Evaluation

GENEVIEVE E. CHANDLER AND PAT SCHNEIDER

Throughout most of the 20th century, there was often a brutal atmosphere in educational and professional writing circles. The motto governing the general environment in which writers struggled to write was: *Real writers can take it!* This was a culture in which abuse (ridicule, shaming, expressions of disgust) was often masked as "critique" and hierarchical grading (A to F, or any system that assigns success or failure to creative work) was perceived as corrective. Starting in the 1970s a popular reaction against this brutal culture emerged called "the writing process movement." It began at a grassroots level as individual teachers invented new ways to teach creative writing even before Peter Elbow's groundbreaking book, *Writing without Teachers* (1973), brought to academic attention the possibility of a nonhierarchical approach. Such an approach would create a community of peers in which mutual encouragement would replace competitive classroom response and evaluation. Since then, the movement has grown up, earned its own deserved and undeserved backlash, learned from its mistakes, and become mainstream, both in popular books and in academic theory.

Amherst Writers & Artists (AWA) has made a contribution to that history by developing a systematic methodology for the creative writing teacher or workshop leader to use in classrooms and workshops. It has been used at all levels of education – with children in preschool through graduate school, with post-PhD adults, and with a wide range of underserved populations: the homeless, the incarcerated, youth at risk, and many others.[1]

This chapter examines the writing process developed by AWA to teach and evaluate writing. It has three parts: first, a statement of theory and practice in AWA method classrooms and workshops, by Pat Schneider; second, a methodology for the evaluation of creative writing in a workshop consistent with AWA practices, by Dr. Genevieve Chandler, a professor of nursing at the University

---

[1] For a more complete list of documented populations with which the AWA method has been used, see Schneider (2003, pp. 260–261); a companion DVD is available at www.patschneider .com.

of Massachusetts who has used the AWA method both with her nursing students and in a shelter for at-risk youth; and third, a summary collaborative statement.

PAT SCHNEIDER: AWA THEORY AND PRACTICE

The deepest, truest things I know about writing – where it comes from, what it is, and what any person needs to write well – come not from my work as an academic, but from my origins in poverty and from my life as a writer and a leader of creative writing workshops and teacher trainings. Because what I have to say about the psychology of creative writing is impassioned, I think it wise to let my reader know something about my origins, which are the foundation for my perspective on creative writing.

The city of St. Louis sits in the crotch of two great rivers – the Missouri and the Mississippi. In the summer the city steams – especially if you live in a tenement building with no air conditioning and no screens on the windows. I was home from the orphanage, where the rooms around me had been clean. When my younger brother and I returned to my mother, it was to two filthy rooms on the third floor of a tenement building at 4039 Olive Street. I had come home to the seventh grade at Pere Marquette School. But now school was out.

> A knock came on my door. I had been told never, never to open the door when Mama was not at home, but the voice calling to me outside the door was familiar. As if a bolt of lightning had struck my heart, I recognized the voice of my teacher, Miss Dunn, whom I adored.
>
> It was unthinkable that a seventh-grade teacher would visit one of her students. It was unbearable that Miss Dunn had come up the dirty stairs, that she had climbed three flights, that she might see the clutter, the dirt, the shame in the rooms behind me.
>
> I opened the door just the tiniest crack, with the chain lock still in place. Yes. It was true. Miss Dunn stood in the dim light of the hallway, and she was smiling at me.
>
> I unlocked the chain, opened the door a fraction more, tried to hide the room behind me with my body. She held out a book. Gray, with blue letters. I felt faint. "Here," she said. "This is my book. I want you to have it."
>
> I took the book, but could not speak. Her book. She was giving me her book. She had told me once, when she returned a report I had written, "You can be a writer."
>
> I was unable to do anything, but cling to the door to keep from falling and to keep her from seeing inside. I read the words on the cover: DARK WAS THE WILDERNESS – By Dorothy Dunn. I looked up at her face. When I didn't speak, she said, "I know what will happen to you when you grow up."

"What?" It was my first word, and my last.

"I won't tell you now, but come and find me when you are grown, and I will tell you if I was right."

And she turned, and went back down the stairs.

When I was in my thirties, had some successes and my share of failures, but had arrived at a place where I was a writer in my own mind and in deed, I wrote to the St. Louis Board of Education and asked for the address of Dorothy Dunn. They said she died within five years of the day she had knocked on my apartment door. (Schneider, 1997, p. 3)

On the day that Miss Dunn knocked on my door, I became a writer. She named for me what I could not have dreamed for myself. She bent down into the dark that was both around me and within me and lit the fire of my own dream – and I, myself, dreamed it from then on. Dreamed it fiercely enough to find my way out of poverty.

Writers who come from economically privileged backgrounds also have a profound need for support in breaking their silence. I have learned that lesson in workshops for people with PhDs who can stun you with their verbal skills but cannot trust their own words onto paper, and for people who can neither read a book nor write a full sentence, but can move you to laughter or tears with their stories.

Writing is a communicative art form. It happens in the give and take of offering and response. The writer, in the act of putting words onto paper, reaches out, makes visible to a reader the most intimate private landscape of the mind. McGahern (2000), one of Ireland's most distinguished writers, says that every person has an inner life known to no one else and that writing comes from that inner life, but the writing itself is not alive until another person reads the words, takes them into the inner life of the reader. This is as true for fiction and nonfiction as it is for memoir. No matter what I am writing, I expose to my reader the workings of my mind – the autobiography of my imagination. As Kafka (1973) pointed out, there is no greater nakedness.

In the AWA workshop method, therefore, we recognize that vulnerability and affirm that the kind of response a teacher gives is more important to the development of a creative writer than the kind of manuscript the student offers. The response cannot be dishonest; the goal is development of voice and of craft. But the methodology of response is delicate, and a failure in response is the most common cause of failure in creative writing.

As teachers of creative writing, our first task is to evoke and affirm the craft that already exists in the language of the student. That craft is often hidden in youthful and adult writing students under layers of accumulated distrust in their own voices, but it is there, and it should be the foundation on which the writing teacher eventually teaches additional skills. The following poem was written by 10-year-old Bob Hastings, a child living in a housing project in

Chicopee, Massachusetts, in an AWA workshop for underserved children led by Enid Santiago Welch.

> WEED
>
> It is life.
> It grows from the ground.
> It is ground up like meat.
> It gives him a sharp and good feeling,
> that gives me a sharp and painful anger.
> He rolls it like a red carpet
> and licks it like a lollipop.
> My anger gets deeper
> as the smell gets worse.
> As he smokes me
> I get hotter and hotter.
> He smokes me like I'm green.

That is a good poem. "He rolls it like a red carpet/and licks it like a lollipop." Those are great similes – did anyone teach that 10-year-old about similes? Did he sit down and think, *I believe I'll use a simile now?* "My anger gets deeper as the smell gets worse. As he smokes me/ I get hotter and hotter." How subtle, how excellent a reversal, how effective a metaphor for anger! How did Bob do that? "He smokes me like I'm green." Where did he learn all that craft? Paley (1970) said, "If you say what's on your mind in the language that comes to you from your parents and your street and friends you'll probably say something beautiful." (p. 202)

There is a craft in our subconscious minds that is so wide and so deep it may in fact be infinite. Some believe that it is – and that when we create, we tap into an intelligence beyond our own. That may be, but I prefer to just stand in awe of the human mind itself, believing that everything we have seen and heard, everything we have read or watched on TV, every sensory impression that has come to us, even every dream we have dreamed – they are all recorded in the mystery of our minds. We are, each one of us, geniuses – that is what it means to be created in the image of God – or if you prefer, that is what it means to be human. Each of us has one perfect voice – perfect in its uniqueness, perfect in its exact replication of the personhood that is our own, perfect in its origin in one inexplicable individual's subconscious mind.

Exactly *there* is the wellspring of teaching or assisting someone else to be a creative writer. First, the teacher must utterly believe in the beauty and uniqueness of that primary voice – in its existence, even when he or she cannot hear it because it is so disguised by the student's *trying* to sound like a writer. Second, the teacher must help the student believe in the beauty and power of that voice, even when the student has been bullied or ignored into an utter lack of belief in its existence or in its value. Third, the teacher must patiently build on the foundation of the student's emerging confidence by inviting the student to expand his or her ability to write – an invitation that includes the teacher's excitement, partnership in exploration, and introduction of craft that stimulates the learner to want more (Schneider, 2003).

Everyone is already a writer. Writing is not like other art forms. We have been practicing the use of language since we were 1 year old – all day, every day, and even in our dreaming.

The 10-year-old boy in the projects, his illiterate adult neighbor, and the seventh-grade girl at the top of stairs that smell like urine and roach poison – all are already writers. But creativity hides when it is not safe.

The suppression of primary voice is so common in writers with privileged backgrounds and education that I often feel that most of my work in leading writing workshops for adults is *undoing* the damage our educational system and societal pressures have inflicted on creative writers. Subtly and overtly we are taught to distort and distrust what Wideman (1985) calls "the language of home," the music of our own beautifully particular voices – the innate and universal genius that Marshall (1983) calls "the poets in the kitchen." The PhD who has lost the ability to sound like anything but a PhD, the lawyer who can write only cautious, carefully considered prose, the medical doctor who gets blocked after one paragraph that is exactly the length of a medical report, and the child in elementary school who "hates writing" share this: Each distrusts her or his own voice – each tries to sound like someone else.

To say *everyone is already a writer* does not imply a dismissal of the importance of teaching craft. It simply means that we must not put the cart before the horse. Traditional methods introduce craft without understanding the importance of primary voice as the central building block for the development of craft. We try to create *ex nihilo* instead of building on a sound, sturdy foundation that lies buried under the surface. We literally throw out the very treasure we are seeking to give to our students.

It takes great patience on the part of a teacher of creative writing to look for the voice hiding within inappropriate tense changes, faulty punctuation and spelling, disorganized fragments. Correcting those errors is not what makes a creative writer. They must be corrected, but historically our methods of correction and our timing have defeated our purpose.

In AWA method practice, we follow this order of priorities:

1. The teacher believes that the student possesses at least one unique, powerful voice that is appropriate for expressing his or her own lived experience, memory, and imagination.
2. Although the teacher may not be able to detect the student's primary voice, he or she is patient in waiting for it and skilled at tempting it to reveal itself.

3. Until the primary voice appears, the teacher (a) tries to tease it out and (b) uses critique only with great restraint while honestly praising every possible thing the student does that shows skill or promise. This praise is given to specifics (fresh images, surprising elements, etc.) and in writing so the student can read positive comments more than once, away from the pressure of class or workshop presence.

4. When the student's primary voice appears it most often reveals itself in a qualitative leap of ability: a natural rhythm, a surge of grace, authority, and power (possibly without an increase in punctuation or spelling skill). The teacher recognizes and celebrates the achievement both privately and publicly, if possible.

5. The teacher teaches the student what is strong in the student's own voice and convinces him or her to believe in its value, beauty, and power.

6. The teacher encourages further writing in that voice until confidence brings the student to want correction in grammar and tense. Great care is taken by the teacher at this point to avoid confusing grammatical and syntax change with class or cultural difference, to courageously show options to the student, and to allow the student to choose changes or idiomatic speech where the writer deems it important.

7. Finally, the teacher builds on the mutually recognized and affirmed foundation of the student's own primary voice by teaching craft and offering wider options, encouraging experimentation with different voices and forms.

Now and then a teacher comes across a student whose work is so original that the teacher does not know how to offer guidance. Often that originality presents itself as "strangeness." Gardner (1983) named five qualities of great fiction. The last quality, which he said is the most important, is "strangeness." In that circumstance the teacher must not see that student writer as more gifted or as having more genius than the others. To do so is to set up a dangerous hierarchy, even though it may exist only in the teacher's mind. Rather, the teacher remembers that some other students' voices are still disguised beneath insecurity. Faced with highly unusual work, the teacher encourages the student to find his or her own way, with support and companionship and even a humble acknowledgment that "I don't know how to help you, but I love what you are doing."

Not being able to write is a *learned disability*. We have been universally taught to distrust the very thing we most need in writing: our own voices. It does not matter what class we were born into; rich or poor or somewhere in between, all of us get variations on the same theme: Our own voices are not quite good enough for writing. From teachers, from family, from friends, from editors, from critics, from our own tendency to listen to internal critics, we hear what is wrong. My own voice is too much *me*! It's too informal. It's too formal. It's too southern, it's too midwestern, it's too obscure, too personal, too political, not political enough. I should sound more like John Irving or Adrienne Rich or worse, like "famous poets of yore" – William Wordsworth, for goodness sakes!

Sawyer (2007) has said that writing is a collaborative act (see Chapter 10 in this book). I agree. Even Emily Dickinson, who is popularly known as a recluse, had her intimate – and very committed – community of support. There was Susan, next door, her most trusted critic. There was her father who gave her books, and her sister Vinnie who treasured and protected the poems she stored in the dresser drawers in her room and bound into little books with a needle and thread. And there was Mr. Higginson, who valued her even as he belittled her, calling her "my weird little poetess." Almost everyone knows someone who writes or wants to write. The teacher in the classroom, the leader of the workshop, the friend, parent, writing companion, can offer response that does not damage the delicate atmosphere in which creativity thrives.

To adequately describe the AWA method of creative writing workshop leadership is not possible in these few pages. The process, with examples and exercises, is described in detail in my 2003 book, *Writing Alone and with Others* and its companion DVD and offered as a training program for teachers and workshop leaders. At heart, the "method" is kindness and common sense. As I have said, I came from poverty, and from that perspective it seems to me that our canon of literature is a travesty. It has been and is still limited to a very narrow percentage of the voices on this planet: the economically privileged. We have begun to make inroads for women and for persons of color, but most of us who teach in traditional educational settings have not yet begun to imagine that the voices of the poor, those without formal education, are beautiful in their own right and worthy of consideration as art. AWA stands in direct opposition to that distortion. We celebrate the voices of the privileged, we take seriously matters of literary history and craft, but absolutely equally we celebrate the voices of all those who have been silenced. To do so, we believe, is ultimately to serve art and, at the same time, to heal the broken world. We say with Emily Dickinson, in whose hometown our practice originated, *Silence is all we dread./ There's Ransom in a Voice* (poem #1251; Dickinson, 1980).

Here, then, are the essential affirmations and essential practices of the AWA creative writing workshop method:

Five Essential Affirmations

1. Everyone has a strong, unique voice.
2. Everyone is born with creative genius.
3. Writing as an art form belongs to all people, regardless of economic class or educational level.
4. The teaching of craft can be done without damage to a writer's original voice or artistic self-esteem.
5. A writer is someone who writes.

Five Essential Practices

1. A nonhierarchical spirit (how we treat writing) in the workshop is maintained while at the same time an appropriate discipline (how we interact as a group) keeps writers safe.
2. Confidentiality about what is written in the workshop is maintained, and the privacy of the writer is protected. All writing is treated as fiction unless the writer requests that it be treated as autobiography. At all times writers are free to refrain from reading their work aloud.
3. Absolutely no criticism, suggestion, or question is directed toward the writer in response to first-draft, just-written work. A thorough critique is offered only when the writer asks for it and distributes work in manuscript form. Critique is balanced; there is as much affirmation as suggestion for change.
4. The teaching of craft is taken seriously and is conducted through exercises that invite experimentation and growth as well as through response to manuscripts and in private conferences.
5. The leader writes along with the participants and reads that work aloud at least once in each writing session. This practice is absolutely necessary, for only in this way is there equality of risk taking and mutuality of trust.

In a workshop or classroom where student voices are evoked, encouraged, protected, and wisely helped to grow, how does a teacher evaluate work in a way that will not do damage to the delicate and vulnerable act that is creative writing?

GENEVIEVE CHANDLER: EVALUATION

"It's not therapy, but it can be healing," Pat Schneider stated in an NPR interview after the reading of a passionate, incisive poem by a member of an AWA low-income workshop. As I listened intently to the broadcast, I thought about my years as a psychiatric nurse working with adolescents who were struggling. Whether managing an inpatient psychiatric unit or teaching in a college classroom, I had consistently seen the benefits of building on the strengths of adolescents, rather than focusing on their weaknesses. The AWA method sounded like it fit a health-focused, strength-based approach to adolescent resilience. From there my research took a turn toward writing and healing. Writing began to connect the different aspects of my faculty role, forming the web of research, teaching, and service among adolescents, empowerment, and writing. This section presents ideas on evaluating creative writing.

Evaluation of creative writing ranges from harsh critique to encouraging feedback, from red-marked papers with a grade and minimal feedback to portfolios with feedback and no grades. Though many of us who work with creative writers prefer not to have to assign a percentage or letter grade to their work, for academic classes grades are usually required and, to receive funding, evaluation results are necessary. This section reviews the feedback and eval-uation of creative writing produced in three adolescent writing interventions (Chandler, 1999, 2002; Hunter & Chandler, 1999) based on the AWA method. It also addresses the potential of grading contracts for writing classes.

Two of the writing interventions were held daily in 2-week workshops within the regular English class at a vocational high school. The other interven-tion met once a week for 10 weeks with low-income teens and college students. Both vocational school workshops included adolescents ranging from 15 to 18 years old, with an equal number of males and females; 70% were Puerto Rican, 20% African American, and 10% Caucasian. There were 11 participants in one workshop and 16 in the other. At the start of each workshop students were reticent to write, but with the safety and positive response provided by the AWA method, they quickly came around to being fully engaged in writing in response to a prompt, reading out loud, hearing the facilitator read aloud as a member of the writing group, and receiving constructive peer and facilitator responses to their writing.

The following description of the first few meetings of the smaller workshop illustrates the AWA method's power to engage every student. At our first meeting three students were absent, which their English teacher reported was not unusual. The following day all the students attended, with the absentees making a grand entrance. The three girls strutted into the classroom in high heels and form-fitting jeans, with their makeup from eye shadow to lip gloss flawlessly applied. Wrapped up in their puffy parkas, they sat in a row with their desks turned away from the class, facing the window. I started the workshop by inviting the other students to explain the AWA method to the newcomers. Several students offered their opinion of what we did on the first day, "She let us write whatever we wanted. We wrote about our life." After the explanation we began with three possible writing prompts and everyone immediately started writing. One of the prompts was to write what it would be like to be a member of the opposite sex. By the time we had all written for 15 minutes, the girls had turned toward the group and, one by one, volunteered to read out loud. With a smile on her face Angela started her reading with this sentence: "If I was a boy, life would be so easy because I wouldn't have to get up an hour early to do my makeup!" At the end of the workshop I asked why we had full attendance, and one of the girls replied, "Oh we heard, we heard something different was going on and we wanted to do this too." From that day on we had 100% attendance.

In the larger class the intervention was the same, except with more students there was more competition to read out loud. In each workshop meeting we would end with feedback on the participants' experience by using a closing ceremony. Participant opinion was part of the self-evaluation.

The evaluation method was developed according to the primary principles of the AWA method: that participants are the experts in their own experience and writing is a valid approach to sharing that experience. The goals of the AWA method with low-income and underserved populations are "to increase self esteem, enable empowerment, and evoke healing through the achievement of personal voice and the creation of a supportive community" (Schneider, 2003, p. 264). The evaluation was built on the recognition of the need to hear the voices that have been silenced by poverty, lack of education, or other hardship. Threading the voice of participants through the evaluation method of the workshop further substantiated the importance of participants' opinions.

The self-evaluation was based on verbal feedback given after every session and a written evaluation at the workshop midpoint and at the end of the 2 weeks. The verbal evaluation consisted of feedback provided by the participants, using Chinn's (2004) method of closing a group meeting. Data collection for participant formative and summative evaluations was based on Angelo and Cross's (1993) approach.

Chinn (2004) uses the term "closing" to describe a process that occurs at the end of a meeting in which all participants are invited to express their opinion about their experience. The closing process is one of the components of working effectively in groups to build community. I focus only on the closing process here but I also recommend the community-building approach developed by Chinn for facilitating healthy meetings. The closing process provides participants an opportunity to reflect on their experience of the meeting and to contribute their feedback by using one, two, or all three of the techniques of affirmation, appreciation, or appraisal:

- *Affirmation*: Using affirmation offers an opportunity to express what one has gained from the meeting. Through verbalization the individual commits to bringing this knowledge forward into his or her life. For example, an affirmation from my college/community writing group was "I am going to question more, just as Christine wrote in her narrative. I will be strong too."

- *Appreciation*: Verbalizing appreciation provides an opportunity for an individual to express gratitude for what another participant has said that contributes to that individual's knowledge or to the group's effectiveness. For example, "I really appreciate Stephanie bringing up the schedule. We all need to make it work for us."

- *Appraisal*: Chinn refers to this component as critical reflection, but I found students too shy to say anything they see as criticizing. Making an appraisal acknowledges an aspect of group function that could be improved and provides some ideas on how to improve the group process. For example, "It would be helpful to have more time to write. I feel like 10 minutes is too rushed. I can't get all my words down."

At the closing of every writing workshop, following a brief silence for reflection, participants were invited to contribute an affirmation, appreciation, or an appraisal. In the vocational classroom every member contributed

Table 19.1. *Participants' comments in the mid-workshop evaluation*

Self-esteem	Self-efficacy
I like	I like
"Writing what's on our minds."	"To write and it is helping me to write at home."
"Writing what we want to write."	
"Not being told the topic."	"I never thought of myself as a writer, I like learning about myself."
"I wish it wasn't just two weeks."	
"Remembering . . . seashells remind me that life in Vieques is very simple."	I hate writing, but I am trying."

Source: Chandler (1999), p. 75.

many comments each day, adding levity or sharing a common concern. For example, "I like the way Jesus wrote about getting his little brothers to obey his mom. I hope I can do that too," or "I can relate to Paul's story about losing something in childhood, like your father. It still hurts." In the closing ceremony each participant was able to contribute input about the experience of writing together. Having the last word provides an opportunity for group cohesiveness and leaves the individual voice in the classroom rather than out in the hallway.

The *Minute Paper* (Angelo & Cross, 1993) has been the most successful evaluation tool in my experience, whether with a small graduate research seminar or an auditorium full of undergraduates. In the workshop, the minute method was used at midpoint and at the final meeting. On 3×5 index cards students took a minute each to respond to these questions: "What worked well in the workshop?" and "What needs to be improved?" The responses to each question were coded into themes that were then grouped into two categories that emerged from the data: self-esteem and self-efficacy. Table 19.1 shows representative examples of the midpoint evaluations.

At the end of 1 week, participants recognized the workshop as an opportunity to learn about themselves. Keep in mind that these were streetwise 15- to 17-year-olds who, from all accounts, would be very resistant to learning about themselves if they were told that was the intent of the workshop. However, when self-knowledge was a byproduct of their own writing that they discovered on their own, it was welcomed. Holmes (1993) observed, "There's a connection between the ability to build a coherent story and the sense of self esteem and effectiveness that underline a strong sense of identity. In order to know who you are you need to know where you have come from, to be able to own your origins" (p. 13). In response to the writing prompts, at the beginning of each session, participants most often wrote about their origins – their family and their childhood. For example, a prompt was, "Write about something you had in your childhood that you do not have now." Without any

Table 19.2. *Participants' comments at the end evaluation*

Self-esteem	Self-efficacy
"I really enjoyed opening up and telling people a little about myself."	"These writing assignments were great! It made me express myself better on paper. It makes my schoolwork easier."
"The writing helps me remember fun things."	
"I've learned to write about my feelings, to express myself. It brought back years of memories."	My writing skills have improved. It has helped me be more creative."
"It makes me understand myself more and look back on some of the things I did wrong. It makes me realize how much I love my son and how precious memories can be."	
"It's given me a chance to talk about my life. I also like listening to other students writing and learning a little about them."	

Source: Chandler (1999), p. 75.

further direction, two of the adolescents chose to write and voluntarily read heart-felt narratives about their fathers. When the students read about their father leaving, the recognition of the experience could be seen in the other group members and their attention was riveted on the reader. The summative evaluation, Table 19.2, describes the responses of the workshop participants.

The comparison between the simple statements made after 1 week to the more reflective, involved responses that were given at the end of the 2-week workshop is noteworthy. Participants recognized the benefits of self-learning in a safe environment. In his study of the effects of writing personal essays, Allen (2000) observed, "The expression of the self and its experience through language somehow develops the whole person, so that the evidence of development appears in various things people do with their lives. Many students report not only improved academic results but improved confidence." Students reported that not only did writing in another genre come more easily, but their work also improved in other classes and "more mysterious, students credited their writing work for better performance in math and science" (p. 255).

Similarly, in their self-evaluations, participants acknowledged that their schoolwork came easier and that their homework was more creative. These outcomes alone would support expanding this type of intervention to other populations. I cannot help but recall Spiegel's (1999) observation of the effect journaling had on reducing the symptoms of asthma and arthritis: "Were the authors able to supply similar outcome evidence about a new drug, it likely would be in widespread use in a short time" (p. 1329). If more people knew of the effect of personal narrative writing, there is no question that such writing would be prescribed for more programs.

Participants in the teen group recognized the joy of learning about others through their writing. After working with students who were writing personal narratives, MacCurdy (2000) observed, "The personal essay asks students to begin a journey into themselves, but the journey will take them ultimately out of themselves and back to a community which can reestablish our common humanity" (p. 198). Similarly, in the at-risk teen response to another writing workshop using the AWA method, the journey from self to community was observed (Hunter & Chandler, 1999). The preworkshop comments were individually oriented, ranging from "I have no one to help me deal with the pain I feel" to "I have so much anger in me I am afraid I am going to hurt someone." In contrast, the postworkshop affirmations had a community flavor: "I have learned so much from everyone on how I might handle things differently" and "I find I am not much different from anyone else" (p. 245). As MacCurdy recognized, their journey went from inner self, out to others. The writing helped objectify their experience so they could separate the experience from themselves and take a look at it, improving the chance to learn from a difficult situation.

Participant formative and summative evaluations are useful tools for creative writing assessment. Facilitator responses provide information as well.

In each of the two vocational workshops there was a consistent faculty facilitator and a different graduate student co-facilitator for each session. Each graduate student provided daily written feedback. In the first week of the workshop one graduate student wrote, "At first, the students were not impressed, but as the session progressed they were relaxed, liked what they were doing and feeling good. By the end the students were all buzzing with excitement about the next day's exercise" (Chandler, 1999, p. 75). In the second week a graduate student observed that the teens did not sound like the same ones who had started just a week earlier: "Writing came easily; they were very eager and excited about sharing. I was impressed with the sensitivity to each other's writing and the feelings of closeness that came through when commenting on their peers writing" (Chandler, 1999, p. 76).

As the faculty facilitator I was amazed at the progress made in the quality and quantity of the student writing over a short period of time. I was familiar with the literature on the effect of personal narrative, but did not expect to witness the evolution from self-focus to group cohesiveness and the impact that writing in a 2-week workshop in an English class would have on their other schoolwork. Qualitative assessment (as shown in Tables 19.1 and 19.2) was the only assessment required of the workshops. However, a grading contract could easily have been put into place.

Elbow (2000), who has thoroughly studied the process of evaluating writing, concludes that there is a clear distinction between feedback, evaluation, and grading. Feedback that addresses specific concerns about the content or technicalities of the writing is essential and the most important learning strategy. Evaluation can be an aspect of feedback and grading is a narrow form of evaluation. Feedback occurs in the AWA method when participants are invited to read their writing aloud in the group. At that time the listeners are asked to frame their comments to reflect what they liked or what they remembered about the writing. The focus of the listener's comments are on the writing, not on the content of the piece. Feedback also occurs when participants hand in a manuscript and request feedback on what works and what could be changed.

Elbow suggests that reading aloud (even to yourself, but having an audience is better) with no verbal response, just attentive listening, gives the author feedback on flow, clarity, and focus. When listening to their own words, writers can hear their pieces flow and where the writing gets stuck. Feedback achieved through self or audience close listening can work well.

Evaluation can be in the form of feedback only and not tied to a grade. In fact, Elbow suggests that evaluation flows well when it is decoupled from grading. He advises that if the goal is learning then feedback is indispensable, summative evaluation is not necessary, and grading is often a deterrent. In *Everybody Can Write* Elbow (2000) offers a full explanation of the use of feedback, evaluation, and grades.

Evaluation can occur on many different levels. The most common form focuses on the technical aspects of writing, grammar, spelling, and format. The creative aspects of a piece are further developed when the evaluation focuses on elements that assist the writer in revision, such as clarity, detail, focus, energy, and thought process. When giving feedback to workshop participants, the facilitators, using the AWA method, often commented on what was clear in the writing, the strength of the focus of the piece, where they felt the energy, and how being able to follow the writer's thought process strengthened the writing. From authentic praise of the writer's words, the quality and quantity of the writing increased markedly. If required, a grading contract could provide the quantitative evaluation of the writing.

If a grading contract is to be used for the type of writing done in the intervention workshops, the contract would include specific criteria such as effort made to participate in the writing group, participation in responding to others' writing, progress in active participation and authentic, specific responses to others' writing. For example, a grade below a B would indicate not meeting all of the criteria, a B would be meeting all the criteria, and an A grade would indicate the participant went beyond the criteria. An A grade would mean the participant exhibited consistent effort, active participation, exceptional progression, increasing depth of response, and genuine efforts to assist others in improving their writing. Along with grades, feedback and evaluation should be included if an improvement in writing is expected. Grades, though, should be used along with feedback and evaluation and not by themselves.

Creative writers can be born or buried as a result of feedback, evaluation, or grading. Just as in the writing process, for evaluation the teacher response needs to be delicate and sensitive while being authentic and encouraging. Evaluation often feels like a personal judgment of the writer since, as Schneider (2003) observes, "To write is to reveal the mind at work. There is no nakedness like that nakedness (p. 26)." Evaluation needs to be from both the student and teacher, with the students being encouraged to build on the strength of their own voice. Grades should be a symbol of this creative process at work.

CONCLUSION

Our approach to the process of teaching and evaluating writing begins with developing voice through teacher response. In contrast, traditional methods of teaching start with craft, neglecting the absolute necessity of establishing a primary voice as the central building block for the development of craft. Instead of building on a sound, sturdy foundation, we have been taught to create an atmosphere of criticism and threat that is demeaning and devaluing of the writer's words. Creativity emerges from the writer feeling safe to express his or her unique voice; from nurturance through the provision of authentic, honest, encouraging feedback; and from a timely introduction to the craft.

Evaluation deserves the same sensitivity and safety as teaching the art and craft of writing. Evaluation can be conducted through feedback, evaluative statements, or grades. If the goal is more and better writing, then the evaluation must include the students' response to their experience and the teacher's clearly outlined criteria of each assignment.

The goal of the teacher or writing workshop leader is the creation of a nonhierarchical community of writers in which the teacher or leader is writing and reading new work aloud, taking the same risks she or he is asking students or workshop participants to take. In that context a teacher/leader can model the courage that self-revelation requires and, with humility and humor, make it clear to students that creative writing is always an exciting and adventurous exploration of the unknown as well as an exercise in craft.

REFERENCES

Anderson, C., & MacCurdy, M. (2000). *Writing and healing*. Urbana, IL: National Council of Teachers of English.

Angelo, T. A., & Cross, K. P. (1993). Minute paper. In *Classroom assessment techniques: A handbook for college teachers* (pp. 154–158). San Francisco: Jossey-Bass.

Chandler, G. (1999). A creative writing intervention to enhance self esteem and self efficacy in adolescents. *Journal of Child and Adolescent Psychiatric Nursing, 12*(2), 70–78.

Chandler, G. (2002). An evaluation of college and low-income youth writing together: Self discovery and cultural connection. *Issues in Comprehensive Pediatric Nursing, 25*, 255–269.

Chinn, P. (2004). *Peace and power* (5th ed.). Boston: Jones and Bartlett.

Dickinson, E. (1980). Number 1251. In T. H. Johnson (Ed.), *The complete poems of Emily Dickinson*. Boston: Little, Brown.

Elbow, P. (1973). *Writing without teachers*. New York: Oxford University Press.

Elbow, P. (2000). *Everyone can write*. New York: Oxford University Press.

Gardner, J. C. (1983). *On becoming a novelist*. New York: Harper and Row.

Holmes, J. (1993). *Between art and science: Essays in psychotherapy and psychiatry*. London: Routledge.

Hunter, A., & Chandler, G. (1999). Adolescent resilience. *Image: Journal of Nursing Scholarship, 31*(3), 243–247.

Kafka, F. (1973). Letter to Felice. In E. Heller & J. Born (Eds.), *English book* (Vol. xxv, p. 592). New York: Schocken.

Marshall, P. (1983, January 9). The poets in the kitchen. *New York Times Book Review*, p. 3.

McGahern, J. (2000). *A private world*. In an interview on the RTÉ harvest films DVD. A Humming bird/Harvest Films Production for RTÉ completed with the assistance of Bord Scannán na hÉireann.

Paley, G. (1970). Some notes on teaching: Probably spoken. In J. Baumbach (Ed.), *Writers as teachers: Teachers as writers*. New York: Holt, Rinehart and Winston.

Schneider, P. (1997). *Wake up laughing: A spiritual autobiography*. Mobile, AL: Negative Capability Press.

Schneider, P. (2003). *Writing alone and with others*. New York: Oxford University Press.

Spiegel, D. (1999). Healing words. *Journal of American Medical Association, 281*(14), 1328–1329.

Wideman, J. E. (1985, January 13). The language of home. *New York Times Book Review*.

20

Fostering Creative Writing: Challenges Faced by Chinese Learners

AI-GIRL TAN

Creative writing is an activity useful for engaging every student. To ensure that every child benefits from this activity, the creative writing program begins with the mastery of basics such as spelling, writing, and self-expression and continues with the child's acquisition of competencies in invention. In this inclusive learning context, creativity highlights the nurturing of the *constructive*, valuable, and meaningful behavior of every child (Tan & Wong, 2007). Accordingly, instruction is based on the following assumptions (Tan & Goh, 2007):

- Every individual has the potential to be creative in one or more domains (see Gardner, 1983).
- Creativity can be nurtured when the prerequisite components (i.e., motivation, knowledge, and skills) exist within the individual (Amabile, 1983) and when the individual receives ample support from his or her interpersonal and sociocultural environments (Csikszentmihalyi, 1996, 1997).
- Creative processes can be individualized (Finke, Ward, & Smith, 1992) into two phases: idea generation and exploration. During the idea generation phase, the individual proposes numerous preinventive structures, which can be ambiguous and novel. These preinventive structures can then be refined during the exploration phase with reference to the criteria of creativeness accepted for the domain.
- In a group, activities such as brainstorming, role playing, and collaborating in multimedia presentations can be facilitated in a cooperative and peer-evaluative context.
- The preinventive structures can be assessed by using the consensual assessment technique, which engages people who have expertise in the domain (Amabile, 1983) with novices who are learning to become experts (Finke, 1990).
- To facilitate creative learning, teachers should feel that they are competent in their areas of specialization (e.g., subject matter) and in the relevant

pedagogical skills (e.g., planning lessons, selecting suitable teaching models, and managing behaviors). Teachers should possess sufficient knowledge and competencies to coach and guide learning effectively. They should receive ample support from the community of practice. Furthermore, teachers should be interested in integrating creative strategies and techniques into lesson delivery and learning. They should cultivate creativity-fostering behavior and believe in nurturing their students' individual creativity.

The adjective *constructive* entails connotations such as being open to all experiences (Rogers, 1961), being ethical, having self-care and care for others, and being humanistic. In *constructive* creativity programs, teachers provide opportunities for learners to experience both internal freedom (e.g., thoughts, desires, purposes, observations, and judgments) and external freedom (e.g., speech and movement; see, e.g., Dewey, 1938/1997; Freire, 2002).

We regard creative writing programs as *constructive* in facilitating engaged learning. By using the term *constructive*, we also suggest that children are able to acquire skills to master writing and that they possess the interest to be engaged in tasks. Reviews of recent literature on creative writing indicate various benefits of engaging in creative writing. Creative writing may keep a child focused, engaged, and in attendance (Boldt & Brooks, 2006). It helps facilitate personal and professional development and learning how to value care for oneself and others. Going beyond academic writing, creative writing enables students to develop innovative ideas, discover conflicts and dilemmas, collect words and phrases, research backgrounds to the stories, and envision settings and characters, to name just a few benefits (Pople & Michael, 2006). In performing creative writing, students become active, excited, and close readers (Austen, 2005). They engage in an intensively personal endeavor and experience the broader usefulness of the skills of literature interpretation. In doing creative writing, students learn to appreciate the techniques used in literatures and texts. Students are likely to become familiar with concepts such as rhetorical devices and tell their own stories. The usefulness of creative writing in the context of wellness varies. Storytelling and journal-keeping are methods used in arts therapy. In the health care setting, creative writing can be related to "autobiographical stories told in conversation." Creative writing therapy, like other therapies (e.g., art, poetry, music, and narrative), may facilitate the use of positive coping strategies (Meekums, 2005).

THE CREATIVE WRITING PROGRAM

This chapter discusses a creative writing program that my colleagues and I designed for language teaching in a multicultural and multilingual context. We adopted a model comprising six aspects to help facilitate creative writing among Chinese learners in Singapore (Tan, 2001). Of the six aspects, three were related to enhancement of the students' *linguistic skills* (such as reading, writing, and communicating); the use of *creative techniques* (such as metaphor, simile, or *Biyu*); and the use of *appropriate assessment modes* (such as the formative or consensual assessment). The other aspects involved the teachers' and learners' *motivation to generate an ongoing task commitment* (Amabile, 1983), a *learning climate* that is critical for creativity to thrive and is creative in itself, and a *learning environment* that is supportive and caring. We included not only the consensual assessment technique (Amabile, 1983) but also Cameron's (1999) levels of analysis and representation of metaphoric language.

Linguistic competencies: Chinese-language teaching and learning have a unique history of development in Singapore. The Chinese language, being one of the four official languages in Singapore, is given the social status of "mother tongue" for students of Chinese ethnicity. By virtue of this status, students of Chinese ethnicity, regardless of their home language backgrounds, have to attend Chinese-language classes from elementary one (age: 6 years old) to high school (age: 17–18 years old). On average, an elementary school child spends about 5 hours a week, or about 20% of curricular time, acquiring linguistic expressions and competencies in school. High school students attend Chinese-language classes for about 3 hours, which is about one-tenth of the total curricular time. Two problem areas have been identified in Chinese-language learning in Singapore. First, it is claimed that "traditional" Chinese-language learning in the classroom emphasizes knowledge transmission and vocabulary memorization, which are not effective in improving students' linguistic and creative expressions. Second, some students regard Chinese-language writing as the most difficult task among the communicative skills, including listening, conversation, and reading.

Creative techniques: In Chinese-language teaching, *Biyu* (比喻) is considered as an art of rhetoric and is taught in literature appreciation. *Biyu* as a form of figurative speech comprises a sentence that contains metaphoric meaning (Cai & Guo, 2001). *Biyu* is a communicative device that allows the transfer of coherent chunks of characteristics – perceptual, cognitive, emotional, and experiential – from a vehicle that is known to a topic that is less so. Metaphors involve the mapping or transfer of information from one concept to another. They allow for the emergence of properties that are not obviously part of either the topic or the vehicle. Thus, constructing and using a metaphor are by their very nature a creative process (Finke et al., 1992). The pedagogic value of figurative uses of language is found in their potential to transfer learning and understanding from what is known to what is less known and to do so in a very vivid manner (Ortony, 1975). A major function of analogy and metaphor is to find likeness in dissimilar things and to introduce meanings beyond the objects of comparison themselves. Therefore, teaching *Biyu* may be an effective strategy for helping students with a limited vocabulary express themselves in more creative ways.

A metaphor is figurative speech that attempts, in the form of "X" is "Y," to relate two things that are different in kind as if they were both similar and identical (Khatena, 1992). The term "X" is a topic, and the vehicle of the metaphor is "Y" (Finke et al., 1992). In the metaphor "Sally is a diamond," for instance, one tries to convey in a figurative way some positive information about Sally, who is deemed to be someone who is as precious as a jewel.

The mechanisms involved in the making of creative analogies operate largely through the use of *personal analogy, direct analogy, symbolic analogy,* and *fantasy analogy* (Taylor, 1975). Personal analogy and direct analogy find relationships between two unlike phenomena; the former involves the person who is making the statement (e.g., I am as happy as a lark), whereas the latter does not (e.g., she is as happy as a lark). In symbolic analogy, a sign or symbol that has similar characteristics as the phenomenon is employed to describe the phenomenon (Khatena, 1992). To describe people who are warm, hopeful, and important to us, we may relate their dispositions to the "sun" and describe them as "they are my sunshine." In fantasy analogy, the comparison object or subject is imaginary; myths, legends, allegories, fairy tales, and the like are sources for comparison.

Alternative assessment techniques: Our creative writing program uses a natural way of providing formative feedback: Students participate in peer evaluation (Richard, 2004). It also uses another nonconventional assessment technique: the consensual assessment technique. Here, a creative product or response is considered novel and appropriate, useful, correct, or valuable to the task and learning is heuristic (Amabile, 1983). According to Amabile's (1983) consensual assessment technique, appropriate observers independently agree that the product of a response is creative. By appropriate observers, she is referring to those familiar with the domain in which the products or responses are articulated. As such, creativity can be regarded both as the quality of products or responses judged to be creative by appropriate observers and as the process by which something so judged is produced (Amabile, 1982).

Task commitment/motivation: To enhance teachers' motivation to engage in our program, we provided special training sessions to orientate them to the objectives and procedures of our study. Teachers were identified and assigned to an intervention class or a nonintervention class. Lesson plans, teaching materials, handouts, worksheets, and transparencies were designed by the researcher with input about teaching procedures from the teachers, and the creative writing articles were written by a recognized creative writer. The materials given to the teachers were meant for use in the intervention classes.

The teaching of creative writing is systematic (Smith, 2006) and is based on three levels of analysis (Cameron, 1999) that can be regarded as domain-specific processes in analyzing and representing language metaphorically. The first level, "the theory level," concerns the theoretical analysis and categorization of metaphors that are in coherence with a particular chosen logic. In the second level, "the processing level," a person produces and interprets tasks. This level concerns activities such as the activation of concepts as constructed through interactions between the person and the sociocultural environment, the processing of metaphorical language in discourse, how an interpretation of a metaphor is reached, how a metaphor is chosen, and conceptual change through encounters with metaphor. The third level, "the neural level," concerns the neurological or the neural activity that will bring about the metaphorical processing at the theory and processing levels. The neurological research likely has much to contribute to the development of congruent frameworks in metaphorical studies, though the work is still in its very early stages.

Learning environment: Creating *Biyu* is a complex process that students learn and then put into practice. In this study, teaching *Biyu* is based on Cameron's (1999) first two levels of analysis and representation of metaphoric language. Our study emphasized creating similes and metaphors (*Biyu*) and the use of personal analogy and direct analogy. It aimed to develop students' connection-making skills to go beyond merely presenting helpful comparisons. To ensure a supportive environment, we attempted to provide stimulating classroom instruction in creating metaphors by giving students a model for the process, using familiar contents to teach students the steps in creating metaphors, providing students with graphic organizers for creating metaphors, and giving them guidance as needed. They were exposed to the principles of cooperative learning and brainstorming and the importance of accepting their peers' views and deferring their judgments when their peers suggested and shared ideas.

ENGAGING THE CHINESE LEARNERS

Schedule and Design of the Study

The study involved 174 students who attended Chinese-language classes in a high school. Their ages ranged from 16 to 18 years old. Of the total, 91 were female and 83 were male. The creative writing sessions for students were conducted over 8 weeks for a total time of 8 hours and 40 minutes. The first week was used for administration of the preliminary survey (80 minutes); the second and last week were used for the administration of the pre- and posttests (80 minutes each). The intervention was conducted from the third to seventh week for these periods of time: lesson 1 (80 minutes), lesson 2 (80 minutes), lesson 3 (40 minutes), and lesson 4 (80 minutes). There was a break in the sixth week, when a total of 40 minutes was spent on creative writing, excluding the time that students spent on their homework. The design of lesson 1 was based on level 1 of Cameron's (1999) analysis, the design for lesson 2 was based on levels 1 and 2, lesson 3 on level 2, and lesson 4 on levels 2 and 3 (Tan & Goh, 2007; Teo, 2002; Teo & Tan, 2003).

Three types of *Biyu* were included in the study design:

1. *Mingyu* (明喻) refers to a form of comparison of one thing with another. The thing we aim to describe is *the topic*, and that which is used to describe it is *the vehicle*. Conjunctions such as "like," "seem," or "as" (如、像、好似) were used to link up the *topic* and the *vehicle*. Take one example, "I am as happy as a lark." In this sentence, "I" is the *topic* and "lark" is the *vehicle*. The structure is "*topic* is like *vehicle*."

2. *Anyu* (暗喻), or *yingyu* (隐喻) (Cai & Guo, 2001), attempts to relate two things of different kinds through matching either similar or identical features. In such sentences, words such as "be" "make," and "become" are meant to link up the topic and vehicle. In the example, "I am a bird released from a cage," the structure is "*topic* is *vehicle*," where "I" is the topic and "bird" the vehicle.

3. In *jieyu* (借喻) (De Francis, 1997) the topic does not appear in the sentence, and no conjunction is needed to link up the topic and the vehicle. The topic can be identified by reading the text or from the writer's background. For example, in the sentence "It is not easy to endure and survive this storm" "storm" is the vehicle to describe a difficult situation. The topic, "difficult situation," does not appear in the sentence.

Lesson 1

Duration: 80 minutes (two 40-minute sessions)

Goals: At the end of the lesson, students will be able to
- understand the term "art of rhetoric" (i.e., using language impressively)
- identify *Biyu* and its characteristics, uses, forms, and types
- determine the difference between sentences using *Biyu* and those that do not use *Biyu*
- brainstorm ideas in a group and use association techniques to create direct analogy

Materials:
- Handout
- Exercise 1

Procedure:

1. The teacher distributes the handouts and discusses the goals of learning with the class.
2. The teacher defines "the art of rhetoric" and *Biyu*.
3. The teacher then explains the characteristics of *Biyu* and uses *Mingyu* (明喻) as an example: A is like B; A – TOPIC and B – VEHICLE
4. In an exercise, students attempt to identify the topic and the vehicle.
5. The teacher then compares two sentences that express sadness: one using *Biyu* and the other without *Biyu*. The teacher then asks students to explain which sentence they like more. Next, the teacher explains the rhetorical effect of *Biyu*.

6.   The teacher continues to explain the different forms of *Biyu* – *Mingyu* (明喻), *Anyu* (暗喻), and *Jieyu* (借喻).

Mingyu (明喻) – A is like B

Anyu (暗喻) – A is B

Jieyu (借喻) – B (The topic does not appear in the sentence.)

7.   The teacher guides the students in identifying the distinctions between *Biyu* and non-*Biyu* sentences. He or she encourages them to explain the differences between the sentences.

Activity (groups of three):

1.   Students are to brainstorm and name 15 objects in 5 categories – Nature, Animals, Places, Tools/ Conveyance, and People (students are advised to use deferred judgment).

2.   Each group then chooses one object from each category, discusses its characteristics, associates it with another object or scenario, and constructs a sentence using *Biyu*. The teacher is to model the process.

Example (1): From the category, Places, "market" is chosen.

A "market" is a noisy place and it can be associated to a "classroom" when the teacher is not around.

Sentence constructed: When the teacher is not around, the classroom is as noisy as a market.

Example (2): From the category, Conveyance, "Mass Rapid Transport (MRT)" is chosen.

The "MRT" is a fast-moving vehicle and can be associated to the speed of mother's speech when she is angry.

Sentence constructed: When mother is angry, she speaks as fast as the MRT.

3.   With the understanding of *Biyu*, students can create a metaphor using "*Biyu*."

Lesson 2

Duration: 80 minutes (two 40-minute sessions)

Goals: At the end of the lesson, students will be able to

- identify phrases that use *Biyu* in a passage
- use *Biyu* to describe themselves (personal analogy)
- distinguish between appropriate and inappropriate *Biyu*

Materials:

- Transparency
- Exercise 2

Procedure:

1.   The teacher distributes the exercise that has two sections, Sections 1 and 2.

2.   In Section 1, there is a paragraph that uses several *Biyu*. Students underline the phrases that use *Biyu*.

3.   The teacher then corrects the students' answers.

4.   The teacher next flashes a transparency showing two sentences with inappropriate *Biyu*.

5.   The teacher then discusses with the students the inappropriateness of the *Biyu*.

6. The teacher then discusses the criteria of creating a good *Biyu* (i.e., appropriateness and familiarity):
    (a) There must be similarities between the topic and the vehicle. The comparison should be appropriate.
    (b) The vehicle must be something that is familiar to the reader.

Activity (groups of three):

1. In Section 2, students are to write five sentences using *Biyu* to describe themselves.
2. Students then discuss and grade the sentences written by their peers, as a group (peer evaluation).
3. Grading is done according to the following criteria: appropriateness and familiarity.

Lesson 3

Duration: One 40-minute session

Goals: At the end of the lesson, students will be able to
  • distinguish between appropriate and inappropriate *Biyu*
  • identify and analyze inappropriate *Biyu*
  • identify the topic and the vehicle and explain their similarities

Materials:
  • Exercise 3

Procedure:

1. The teacher distributes the exercise that has two sections, Sections 1 and 2.
2. In Section 1, there are 10 sentences written by students in the previous exercise. Students are to evaluate them by marking with a "tick" to indicate *Biyu* that is appropriate, and a "cross" to indicate that it is inappropriate (peer evaluation).
3. Students then discuss and analyze the sentences. The teacher guides them accordingly.
4. In Section 2, there are 10 sentences abstracted from books written by a famous local writer. Students then identify the topic and the vehicle of each sentence and also draw out their similarities.
5. The teacher then discusses the answers with the class.

Lesson 4

Duration: 80 minutes (Two 40-minute sessions)

Goals: At the end of the lesson, students will be able to
1. adopt a positive attitude toward learning *Biyu*
2. learn to evaluate *Biyu* using a rubric
3. consciously go through the process of creating *Biyu* by using a model
4. learn to elaborate on two examples of situational writing using *Biyu*

Materials:
  • Exercise 4

Procedure:

1. The teacher distributes the exercise. Students are to look at the different metaphors their peers created to describe *Biyu*. They mark with a "tick" to indicate agreement and a "cross" to indicate disagreement. The teacher

then discusses with the students the importance of having a positive attitude toward "*Biyu.*"

2. The students then divide into groups of three to assess the sentences written by their peers, using the rubric, which comprises three criteria: creativity, technique, and aesthetic. The criteria for "creativity" include the novelty of word choice, richness of imagery, and sophistication of expression. "Technique" includes appropriateness, familiarity, and meaningfulness. "Aesthetic" includes liking and beauty.

3. Students learn the process of creating a *Biyu* by using a graphic organizer. The graphic organizer contains a rhyme (in Chinese) for the *Biyu* creation process:

    > Base on the Topic
    > Choose a vehicle
    > What are the similarities?
    > What are the differences?
    > Check it out
    > Make it up

4. Students create *Biyu* and use them to express their feelings in situational writing.

Example 1: I had spent the whole evening solving a mathematics assignment given by my teacher. The next morning, I realized that the assignment was torn up by my 3-year-old brother. I was very angry and wanted to teach him a lesson.

Example 2: I had kept failing physics tests and felt very upset. My friends knew about it and volunteered to clarify my misconceptions. As a result, I scored 60 points!

External Assessment

The markers were instructed to rate the products relative to one another on the dimensions in question rather than against some absolute standard. Assessment criteria were creativity, novelty, imagination, expression, and grammar. The assessors used their subjective conceptions of *creativity* to judge the creativeness of the essay (Amabile, 1982). *Novelty* refers to new, original, and unique choice of words. *Imagination* is about the use of vivid imagery. *Expression* concerns clarity of the sentences. The right use of *grammar* is an important criterion. Twenty scripts were selected randomly from pretest and posttest essays. Independently, marker 1 and marker 2 assessed the scripts according to the criteria (creativity, novelty, imagination, expression, and grammar) using a 5-point Likert scale. For each script, parts for each of the five criteria were summed and the scores from marker 1 and marker 2 were compared. Scripts with a difference of five points between the two markers were returned to them. The researcher communicated with the markers individually to find out the reasons for these discrepancies. She then mediated the discussion with the individual markers until the difference between the total scores of the two markers for the same script was less than five points. Thereafter, the two markers continued to assess the rest of the scripts. Pearson correlation showed that the scores of the markers were significantly correlated at 0.01 significant level (2-tailed). The scores ranged from 0.4 to 0.6, which were moderately high correlated.

Knowledge of *Biyu* and Grouping

Seven questions were used to determine the students' baseline knowledge of *Biyu*. Questions 1–3 each had two similar expressions; one used *Biyu* and the other did not. The students had to identify which was a better expression. Students who chose the one with *Biyu* would be awarded one point. Otherwise, no point would be awarded. The expressions with *Biyu* were extracted from writings of recognized Chinese writers. Those expressions without *Biyu* were from the drafts of student writings (Zhang, 1998). The total score for the three questions was 3-points.

Question 4 required students to relate things and people to the word "stone." Part A of the question required students to write whatever they could think of that is related to "stone." Part B of the question required students to use "stone" to describe people.

Students who presented one relevant item in Part A would be awarded one point, those who wrote more than one relevant item were given two points, and those with more than two relevant items received three points. Items that were considered to be relevant were those related to the hard or rough characteristics of stones. Points were also allocated for items that were not commonly seen as related to the characteristics but for which students were able to explain their relevance. Three points could be awarded for each part so that the total score for this question was six.

Question 5 required students to describe themselves using *Biyu*. The sentences started with "When I was angry . . .", "When I was sad . . .", and "When I was happy. . . ." A maximum of three points could be allocated for each sentence based on these criteria: originality, fluency, flexibility, and elaboration. Sentences that fulfilled more of these criteria were awarded more points. The total score was nine for this question.

Question 6 required students to identify *Mingyu* (明喻). One point was given if they underlined correctly the simile that appeared in the question.

Question 7 comprised two parts. Part A used a short poem to test the students' ability to identify *Mingyu* (明喻) and *Jieyu* (借喻). Students were asked to underline four *mingyu* and four *jieyu* that appeared in the poem, with one point being awarded for each correct answer. Part B assessed the students' understanding by asking them to write the *topic* of a given poem. One point would be awarded if the student gave the right answer (i.e., according to the teacher). The maximum score for this question was nine. The full score for answering all the seven questions was 28.

Using these scores, students were categorized into three groups. Group 1 (G1) comprised students with the best knowledge of *Biyu* (scores ranged from 18–28). Group 2 (G2) included students with an average knowledge of *Biyu* (scores ranged from 10–17). Group 3 included students with little knowledge of *Biyu* (scores ranged from 0–12). There were 40 students in group 1, 55 students in group 2, and 79 students in group 3. Of the total, 17 (21%) of G1, 28 (35%) of G2, and 36 (44%) of G3 students received the nonintervention Chinese-language lessons, and 23 (25%) of G1, 27 (29%) of G2, and 43 (46%) of G3 students received the intervention Chinese-language lessons.

Pre- and Posttest Essays

The pre-and posttests consisted of essay writing. The questions were set according to the standard of narrative essay questions in the high school state examination – the G.C.E. A.O (Government Certificate of Examination – Advanced – ordinary [intermediate])-level examination. Each test had four essay questions. The theme for the pretest was "Making a choice." The first question was metaphoric, the second question was a statement, the third question was situational, and the fourth was an example of continuous writing in which an opening is given.

Pretest

1. 徘徊在十字路口 (Hesitating at a T – junction . . .)
2. 这个选择, 我绝不后悔! (I will never regret making this choice.)
3. 假设发生了一件事, 让你必须在朋友与道德之间作一取舍。试写出整件事情的经过, 并说明你的决定。(Imagine that an incident has happened and you need to make a choice between friendship and morality. Narrate the incident and state your decision.)
4. 哥哥埋头苦读了四年, 以优异的成绩大学毕业了。我原本以为他会稳稳当当地找一份朝九晚五的工作, 却没想到... ... (My elder brother worked very hard for four years. He finally graduated from the university with excellent results. I thought that he would find a stable job (working from 9 A.M. – 5 P.M.), but contrary to my expectations events happened with negative surprises . . .)

The theme of the posttest essay questions was "Overcoming an obstacle." The format of the questions was similar to the pretest. Students were expected to write essays of at least 500 words within 80 minutes.

Posttest

1. 这个挫折是我最好的老师 (This setback is indeed my "best teacher" . . .)
2. 困难, 我们战胜了它! (We have overcome an obstacle!)
3. 假设家里的女佣辞工回国去了, 妈妈又刚刚动了手术必须躺在床上休养两个星期, 叙述你和家人如何共同度过这段艰难的日子。(Imagine that your domestic helper tendered her resignation. Your mother just went through an operation and needed to recuperate for 2 weeks. Narrate how your family and you came together to pull through this tough period.)
4. 花了大半个六月假期精心完成了一个小组专题作业, 我正想利用仅存的三天假期好好地休息, 不料, 小组成员之一志雄竟然把开学第一天要呈交上去的作业给弄丢了......

(After spending most of the June holidays to complete a group project work, I was prepared to take a good rest in the last 3 days of the school break. However, one of our group members misplaced her/his project assignment, which was to be handed in on the first day of school.)

CHALLENGES AHEAD

Language Habits

About 93% of the participants indicated that English was their first language and that Chinese was a second language in their high school state examinations – G.C.E O (Ordinary)-level examinations. The others reported that both English and Chinese were their first languages. All of them had taken Chinese as a second language in the G.C.E A.O-level examination. Nearly two-thirds or 62.5% of the participants use the Chinese language as a tool of communication with their family, whereas 55.1% use it with friends. In addition, nearly two-thirds or 65% of the students indicated that they took up Chinese lessons because it was a prerequisite for entry into local universities. About half of the students (50%) thought that Chinese lessons can stimulate students' creativity and imagination, and 60.2% felt that the teaching methods used in Chinese lessons were usually relatively traditional.

According to the Chinese-language grading results in the G.C.E. O-level examinations, 24.4% scored A1, 28.4% scored A2, and 35.2% scored B3. In total, 89% of the students who participated in the study scored at least a B3. At least 80% perceived their listening and conversational ability to be average or good. About 70% of the students perceived their reading and writing ability to be average or good.

Whereas 65.3% of the students watched Chinese television programs more frequently than English ones, another 39.8% of them watched English programs more frequently than Chinese shows. About 5.1% of the students indicated that they watched Chinese programs as frequently as English programs.

Table 20.1. *Students' G.C.E. O-level Chinese grades according to grouping*

	A1	A2	B3	B4	C5	C6	D7/E8/F9
G1	21(52.5%)	12(30%)	7(17.5%)				
G2	13(24%)	14(25%)	22(40%)	3(5%)	1(2%)	2(4%)	
G3	9(11%)	24(30%)	33(42%)	3(4%)	2(3%)	6(8%)	2(3%)

Nearly all (93.2%) of the students read English books frequently, but only 5.1% read Chinese books frequently. Nine-tenths (90.0%) of the students read English newspapers and magazines frequently as compared to less than 10% who read Chinese newspapers and magazines frequently.

Chinese-Language G.C.E. O-Level Scores

From the O-level examinations scores – *L1R5* (adding the scores of English and five relevant subjects), all groups had *a relatively equal profile* of achievement. Specifically, in G1, 15% ($n = 6$) scored less than 10 aggregates, 20% ($n = 8$) had 11 and 13, 40% ($n = 16$) had 14 and 16 aggregates, and 25% ($n = 10$) scored more than 17 aggregates. In G2, 6% ($n = 3$) scored less than 10 aggregates, 18% ($n = 10$) had 11 and 13, 38% ($n = 21$) had 14 and 16 aggregates, and 38% ($n = 21$) had more than 17 aggregates. In G3, 8% ($n = 6$) scored less than 10 aggregates, 20% ($n = 16$) had 11 and 13, 37% ($n = 29$) had 14 and 16 aggregates, and 35% ($n = 28$) had more than 17 aggregates. More relevant to our study were the students' Chinese language G.C.E. O-level scores (see Table 20.1). About 83% of G1, 50% of G2, and 40% of G3 students scored either A1 or A2.

Descriptive statistics were computed from essay scores of the participants assigned to the intervention and nonintervention groups. We also computed the means of essay scores from the two markers. Cronbach's alpha for all the criteria in the pretest and posttest of the markers was high, at .93. The kurtosis and skewness values for all criteria were below 1.69; they were subjected to factor analysis. For the intervention group, only one factor was extracted from the criteria using principal component analysis, and direct oblimin orientation accounted for 77% and 80% of variances for the pretest and posttest, respectively. Paired *t*-test showed a significant difference between the participants' essay scores before and after the intervention. The participants' creative writing essay scores increased significantly after the intervention. The same statistical analysis was performed on the scores from the nonintervention group. The scores gave a similar psychometric structure, except for an insufficient increase (no statistically significant difference showed using the paired *t*-test) in the scores of the participants for all criteria before and after the period of teaching *Biyu*, using the normal instruction. Table 20.2 summarizes the descriptive statistics, paired *t*-test, and cluster analysis.

Table 20.2. *Mean, standard deviation, kurtosis, skewness, factor loading, and paired-t-test for the intervention group and cluster centers for all participants*

n = 93	M	SD	Kurtosis	Skewness	Factor loading	Paired *t*-test	*p*	Cluster center 1	Cluster center 2
Pretest									
Creativity	3.20	.63	.35	.21	.90	−3.52	.001	2.80	3.54
Novelty	3.12	.69	.44	.33	.88	−2.99	.004	2.67	3.50
Imagination	3.46	.71	.17	−.38	.88	−2.69	.009	3.00	3.88
Expression	3.27	.88	−.49	.15	.87	−4.38	.000	2.55	3.87
Grammar	3.07	.72	−.32	.08	.86	−5.15	.000	2.48	3.55
Posttest									
Creativity	3.45	.66	−.14	.18	.91			3.62	2.76
Novelty	3.35	.69	−.05	.01	.91			3.53	2.65
Imagination	3.67	.78	.45	−.81	.91			3.95	2.77
Expression	3.58	.77	−.90	.04	.89			3.89	2.53
Grammar	3.40	.75	−.63	−.04	.87			3.68	2.42

Cluster analysis was performed for all the criteria of creative writing scores for the pre- and posttests. The participants were regrouped into two clusters based on their scores as shown in Table 20.3. There was an increase of 2% to 3% in the scores for all groups in the intervention creative writing program. There was a drop of 3% to 6% in students in the moderate (G2) and lowest (G3) *Biyu* groups that did not receive the intervention, but had attended the normal class. Interestingly, regardless of the creative writing programs, the scores of participants with the highest scores in *Biyu* (G1) increased slightly as compared to their counterparts with moderate scores in *Biyu* (G2) and low scores in *Biyu* (G3). As indicated by the increase in the number of participants whose scores improved (see Cluster 2, pretest and Cluster 1, posttest), the

Table 20.3. *Change in clusters after attending* Biyu *classes (intervention, nonintervention)*

	Pretest Cluster 1	Pretest Cluster 2	Posttest Cluster 1	Posttest Cluster 2
G1	8(20%)	32(80%)	38(95%)	2(5%)
Intervention	2(5%)	21(52.5%)	23(57.5%)	
Nonintervention	6(15%)	11(27.5%)	15(37.5%)	2(5%)
G2	34(61.8%)	21(38.2%)	31(56.4%)	24(43.6%)
Intervenion	17(30.9%)	10(18.2%)	18(32.7%)	9(16.4%)
Nonintervention	17(30.9%)	11(20%)	13(23.6%)	15(27.3%)
G3	46(58.2%)	33(41.8%)	44(55.7%)	35(44.3%)
Intervention	23(29.1%)	20(25.3%)	26(32.9%)	17(21.5%)
Nonintervention	23(29.1%)	13(16.5%)	18(22.8%)	18(22.8%)

participants of the study with the highest scores in *Biyu* (G1) benefited from both the intervention and normal instruction.

Implications

A positive and forgiving environment: Environment and creativity have an impact on each other (Cropley, 2006; Runco, 2004). Individuals engaged in a creative task can sustain their drive longer. Chinese-language students in Singapore should not feel troubled if they make mistakes along their creative journey. Only when they are allowed to make mistakes will they achieve their ultimate creative goals successfully (Sternberg, 2007). For Chinese-language students to sense and solve problems, they need the ability to think critically about the current situation before arriving at solutions (Feldhusen & Goh, 1995; NACCCE, 1999). Students should learn to become creative critics so that they are more willing to evaluate their own ideas (Sternberg, 2003). Our creative writing program allowed the participants to acquire and master creativity-relevant skills such as brainstorming and critical thinking skills through peer evaluation. Mastery of competencies is regarded as important as it enhances confidence or self-belief in one's capacities (Bandura, 1982). In a psychologically safe but challenging environment, students generate ideas, provide constructive feedback, and adopt a positive mindset about receiving feedback. This is especially essential for language learning in a multicultural and multilingual setting, where children of different backgrounds come together under a common curriculum. From the profile of the languages reported earlier, Chinese-language learners in Singapore are likely to identify with English-language learners in terms of new knowledge and technology acquisition and with the Chinese-language learners in value transmission. The challenge for teachers and parents is to ensure a positive and supportive language environment so that children can be at ease in communicating their intent and needs in both Chinese and English.

Learning climate: Our creative writing program for the Chinese learners reflects the indispensability of developing *constructive* behavior in a *reflective* learning climate. The presence of a community of practice is essential for Chinese-language teaching and learning in Singapore in general, and for creative writing education in particular, as it ensures a shared understanding and enables all voices to be heard (Fischer, Giaccardi, Eden, Sugimoto, & Ye, 2005). Within the community of practice, the teacher learns, reflects, generates ideas, and adopts instructional strategies that enable learners to acquire autonomous forms of motivation (e.g., intrinsic motivation; Amabile, 1983). Our challenge is to ensure that creative writing for Chinese learners is facilitated in the context of reflection-*in*-action (reflection that happens in the midst of experiences; Rodgers, 2002; Schoen, 1983) or reflection-*on*-action (reflection that happens outside an experience; Rodgers, 2002; Schoen, 1983), which enhances self and professional development. This means that the creative writing intervention program should adopt Rodgers' (2002) reflective cycle, exploring the roles of presence, description, analysis, and experimentation in helping teachers reflect and attend to their students' learning in rich and nuanced ways. The minds of Chinese learners should be developed with guidance. Chinese learners should feel confident and be physically present and mentally engaged at the right place and time to collect the data important for them to master the basics, relevant skills in creative writing, and creativity-relevant skills. With this guidance, they should likely be able to complete tasks successfully.

Assessment for learning: Our creative writing programs adopted the learning for assessment approach, providing continuous or formative feedback on student achievement as a form of motivation. This was an innovative approach to learning, especially for Chinese-language teaching in Singapore. Training in using alternative and consensual assessment techniques was provided to the teachers before the start of intervention. Our challenge is to encourage the active participation of Chinese-language teachers in using various forms of assessment for learning. Chinese-language teachers in Singapore have to be convinced of the importance of investing time and effort to receive training and to develop instruction and evaluation that are developmental, guiding learners to the experiences and the assistance that they need (Cope & Kalantzis, 2000). They should also believe that the essence of assessment is to assist students who wish to learn to feel able to learn. They should further cultivate the habits of empowering students to understand the criteria of assessment and to use them to improve learning and thinking.

Multimodal learning: In today's multimedia world, the teaching of creative writing has to consider a learning that is multimodal and multiliterate (Kress, 1997). That is, the teaching of creative writing should recognize the use of verbal and written modes as well as engaging the senses to connect with the environment (Kress, 1997; NACCCE Report, 1999). In this era of technological revolution, information is presented efficiently in visual forms (Kress, 2000b). Language has become a semiotic system; the individual should not only be considered as a user but also a designer of the system. The person produces changes as a transformer and maker of new meanings. Meaning-making is done in various modes such as visual, aural, gestural, spatial, and written (Cope & Kalantzis, 2000; Kress, 2000a). Chinese-language teachers in Singapore should be encouraged to adopt the multimodal approach to teaching, which connects linguistic, visual, aural, gestural, and spatial designs (Cope & Kalantzis, 2000). Through engaging in a semiotic activity with the available design, the person could design and construct new knowledge, objects, and meaning in an innovative way (New London Group, 2000). In an expansion of our creative writing program, we incorporated the use of multimedia and integrated the multimodal approach to creative writing for a group of Tamil-language learners. The preliminary study reported some positive benefits on the learners' competencies of presenting their creative stories in written and multimedia modes (see Subramaniam & Tan, 2007).

Task-specific grouping and teaching: We used the domain-specific knowledge level of *Biyu* of the participants to form the groups, intervention and nonintervention, for our study. This was an effective task-specific grouping technique. The technique allowed us to determine improvements in Chinese-language learners whose knowledge of *Biyu* was high, moderate, or low after the intervention program or the normal teaching program. A comparison could be made among those whose initial knowledge of *Biyu* was at different levels and between those who attended the intervention and normal teaching programs. Indeed, writing represents a complex mix of skills, processes, and attributes. No single instructional approach can affect all aspects of writing. As we aspire to cultivate the creativity of every child, our challenge is to ensure that each child's engagement in individualized cognition, peer evaluation, group thinking, cooperative learning, creative writing, and multimodal representation is optimized. New knowledge gained from the use of advanced technologies such as cognitive neuroscience that provides precision in understanding the complexity of creative cognition should be integrated into the design of interventions, teaching, and learning (Abraham & Windmann, 2007).

ACKNOWLEDGMENTS

The author would like to express her thanks to Teo Ting-Ting for her early engagement in the creative writing project (2000–2003) and Benjamin Kiu for commenting on the earlier draft. The conceptions of the creative writing project were infused into the CRPP Special Project on Language, Arts, and Creativity (2004–2005). Currently, N. Subramaniam (2006–2007) is the research graduate student for the project.

REFERENCES

Abraham, A., & Windmann, S. (2007). Creative cognition: The diverse operations and the prospect of applying a cognitive neuroscience perspective. *Methods, 42*, 38–49.

Amabile, T. M. (1982). Social psychology of creativity: A consensual assessment technique. *Journal of Personality and Social Psychology, 43*(5), 997–1013.

Amabile, T. M. (1983). *The social psychology of creativity*. New York: Springer Verlag.

Austen, V. J. (2005). The value of creative writing assignments in English literature course. *International Journal of Practice and Theory of Creative Writing, 2*(2), 138–150.

Bandura, A. (1982). Self efficacy mechanism in human agency. *American Psychologist, 37*(2), 122–147.

Boldt, R. W., & Brooks, C. (2006). Strengthening academics and building community with students at-risk. *Reclaiming Children and Youth, Winter*, 223–227.

Cai, F. Y., & Guo, L. S. (Eds.). (2001). *Yuyan wenzixue Changyong Cidian*. Beijing: Beijing Jiaoyu chubanshe [蔡富有, 郭龙生编 (2001) 语言文字学常用词典 (北京：北京教育出版社)]

Cameron, L. (1999). Operationalising 'metaphor' for applied linguistic research. In L. Cameron & G. Low (Eds.), *Researching and applying metaphor* (pp. 3–28). Cambridge: Cambridge University Press.

Cope, B., & Kalantzis, M. (Eds.). (2000). *Multiliteracies: Literacy learning and the design of social futures.* London: Routledge.

Cropley, A. (2006). Creativity: A social approach. *Roeper Review, 28*(3), 125–130.

Csikszentmihalyi, M. (1996). *Creativity: Flow and the psychology of discovery and invention.* New York: HarperCollins.

Csikszentmihalyi, M. (1997). *Finding flow: The psychology of engagement with everyday life.* New York: HarperCollins.

De Francis, J. (1997). *ABC Chinese-English dictionary.* Honolulu: University of Hawaii Press.

Dewey, J. (1997). *Experience and education.* New York: Touchstone. (Original work published in 1938)

Feldhusen, J. F., & Goh, B. E. (1995). Assessing and accessing creativity: An integrative review of theory, research, and development. *Creativity Research Journal, 8*(3), 231–247.

Finke, R. A. (1990). *Creative imagery: Discoveries and inventions in visualization.* Hillsdale, NJ: Erlbaum.

Finke, R. A., Ward, T. B., & Smith, S.M. (1992). *Creative cognition: Theory, research, and applications.* Cambridge, MA: MIT Press.

Fischer, G., Giaccardi, E., Eden, H., Sugimoto, M., & Ye, Y. (2005). Beyond binary choices: Integrating individual and social creativity [Special issue]. *International Journal of Human-Computer Studies,* creativity *63*(4–5), 482–512.

Freire, P. (2002). *Pedagogy of the oppressed* (M. B. Ramos trans.). New York: Continuum.

Gardner, H. (1983). *Frames of mind: A theory of multiple intelligences.* New York: Basic Books.

Khatena, J. (1992). *Gifted challenge and response for education.* Itasca: F. E. Peacock.

Kress, G. (1997). *Before writing: Rethinking the paths to literacy.* London: Routledge.

Kress, G. (2000a). Design and transformation of new theories of meaning. In B. Cope & M. Kalantzis (Eds.), *Multiliteracies: Literacy learning and the design of social futures* (pp. 153–161). London: Routledge.

Kress, G. (2000b). Multimodality. In B. Cope & M. Kalantzis (Eds.), *Multiliteracies: Literacy learning and the design of social futures* (pp. 182–202). London: Routledge.

Meekums, B. (2005). Creative writing as a tool for assessment: Implications for embodied working. *Arts in Psychotherapy, 32*, 95–105.

NACCCE. (1999). *All our futures: Creativity, culture and education.* London: DfEE.

New London Group. (2000). A pedagogy of multiliteracies designing social futures. In B. Cope & M. Kalantzis (Eds.), *Literacy learning and the design of social futures* (pp. 9–37). London: Routledge.

Ortony, A. (1975). Why metaphors are necessary and not just nice. *Educational Theory, 25*(1), 45–53.

Pople, I., & Michael, L. (2006). Establishing a meta narrative in creative/academic writing: An exercise to help students with writing. *International Journal of Practice and Theory of Creative Writing, 3*(2), 124–131.

Richard, K. (2004). Creative writing and accountability. *International Journal of Practice and Theory of Creative Writing, 1*(1), 3–5.

Rodgers, C. R. (2002). Seeing student learning: Teacher change and the role of reflection. *Harvard Educational Review, 72*(2), 230–253.

Rogers, C. (1961). *On becoming a person: A therapist's view of psychotherapy.* London: Constable.

Runco, M. (2004). Personal creativity and culture. In S. Lau, A. N. N. Hui, & G. Y. C. Ng (Eds.), *Creativity: When East meets West* (pp. 9–21). Singapore: World Scientific.

Schoen, D. A. (1983). *The reflective practitioner: How professionals think in action.* New York: Basic Books.

Smith, H. (2006). Emerging from the experiment: A systematic methodology for creative writing. *International Journal for Practice and Teaching of Creative Writing, 3*(1), 17–24.

Sternberg, R. (2003). Creative thinking in the classroom. *Scandinavian Journal of Educational Research, 47*(3), 325–338.

Sternberg, R. (2007). Creativity as a habit. In A. G. Tan (Ed.), *Creativity: A handbook for teachers* (pp. 3–25). Singapore: World Scientific.

Subramaniam, N., & Tan, A. G. (2007). *Creative writing and affect: An intervention program for the Tamil language learners.* Graduate seminar at the Psychological Studies, National Institute of Education, Nanyang Technological University, July 30.

Tan, A. G. (2001). *Psychology of cultivating creativity.* Singapore: Lingzi.

Tan, A. G., & Goh, S. C. (2007). *Creative teaching: A positive beginning.* Singapore: Prentice-Hall.

Tan, A. G., & Wong, S. S. (2007). Constructive creativity in education. In A. G. Tan (Ed.), *Creativity: A handbook for creativity* (pp. 485–506). Singapore: World Scientific.

Taylor, I. R. (1975). A retrospective view of creativity investigation. In I. A. Taylor & J. W. Getzels (Eds.), *Perspectives in creativity* (pp. 1–36). Chicago: Aldine.

Teo, T. T. (2002). *Learning activities useful for fostering creativity.* Unpublished dissertation, National Institute of Education, Nanyang Technological University, Singapore.

Teo, T. T., & Tan, A. G. (2003). The use of *Biyu* in students' creative writing: A study on an intervention program. *Korean Journal of Thinking and Problem Solving, 13*(2), 29–39.

Zhang, D. M. (1998). *Wenxue yuyan miaoxie jiqiao.* Beijing: Zhongguo Qingnian Chubanshe. 张德明 (1998)《文学语言描写技巧》(北京：中国青年出版社).

21

Putting the Parts Together: An Integrative Look at the Psychology of Creative Writing

SCOTT BARRY KAUFMAN AND JAMES C. KAUFMAN

As should be evident from reading this book, the psychology of creative writing is complex and multifaceted, and there are many different levels in which it may be investigated. We decided to focus on five levels in this book. There is much overlap, however, among these five levels, and an understanding of one level typically increases our understanding of one or more other levels. Therefore, we would argue that a more complete understanding of the psychology of creative writing could be gained by the investigation of each of the five levels and their interactions. What are these levels?

At one level, this book tries to further our understanding of the psychology of the creative writer. What are creative writers like? Are there characteristics that differentiate them from other types of writers? From professionals in other fields? At the second level is the actual text. How can an understanding of the printed word help elucidate the psychology of creative writing? The third level is about the process. What is the creative writing process? Are there certain processes that lead to more success in creative writing? At the fourth level is the development of creative writing as well as the development of the creative writer. How can creative writing be improved? How can the actual creative writing process help people cope with stress, traumatic events, or even mental illness? And finally, at the fifth level is the teaching of creative writing in schools and workshops. What are successful creative programs like? What are the differing learning environments of the programs?

In this concluding chapter we look at the big picture by describing common themes that we have identified across multiple chapters. We hope that, through a careful reading of this book and this integrating chapter, you will have gained a deeper understanding of the psychology of creative writing and will be convinced that the study of the psychology of creative writing is worthy in its own right and that creative writing provides a good domain to study for understanding human creativity more generally.

THE WRITER

Who Is Creative?

There is a consensus among the various authors in this volume that everyone has the potential to attain at least a minimum level of creativity. Specifically, **Runco** (Chapter 11) argues that every writer is creative, because every writer interprets information in a constructive fashion. Echoes of this idea can be found in **Waitman and Plucker's** Chapter 18, in which they reference **Runco** in writing that "all creativity starts on a personal level (with interpretations, discretion, and intentions) and only sometimes becomes a social affair." These authors specifically argue for the importance of bringing to public attention the more frequently occurring instances of everyday creativity at work. Along similar lines, **Chandler and Schneider** (Chapter 19) argue that everyone is already a writer and that the teacher's role is to help the student find the voice hiding within. **Tan** (Chapter 20) also assumes that every individual has the potential to be creative in one or more domains.

Personality

Even though everyone may have the potential to achieve at least a modicum of creativity, the most creative writers may have differentiating personality characteristics. According to **Piirto** (Chapter 1), the creative writer has generic personality attributes found in other creators, but may also have some distinctive traits. She cites results from the Institute for Personality Assessment and Research (IPAR) and her own studies showing that writers prefer the *intuitive, feeling,* and *perceptive* cognitive styles of the Myers-Briggs Type Indicator. Piirto also found that writers experience high levels of emotional overexcitability. In interviews Piirto conducted, creative writers were found to have more ambition and a concern for philosophical matters; to exhibit frankness, psychopathology, depression, empathy, and a sense of humor; and to be emotional. Perhaps unsurprisingly, Piirto also argues that verbal intelligence is related to creative writing, noting that the writers she interviewed shared a love for verbal wit and had the ability to see humor where others may not. Similar linkages between verbal intelligence and humor production ability are found in **S. Kaufman and Kozbelt's** Chapter 5.

    Pourjalali, J. Kaufman, and Skrzynecky (Chapter 2) argue that creative people often take risks, have self-discipline, and are intrinsically motivated, open to experience, and unconventional. **Runco** also argues that originality is most likely when the individual is autonomous and unconventional and further that creative writers have a preference for complexity and write to work out who they are. He argues that they may need to draw on ego strength to resist social pressure to conform and to think and act in an original and unconventional fashion. Similarly, **Piirto** suggests that ego strength might protect creative writers from the fuller expression of their manic-depressive and schizophrenic symptoms.

In fact, a common theme among various contributors to this volume is the link between creative writers and psychopathology. **Piirto** states that distinguished writers tend to be schizoid, depressive, hysterical, or psychopathic. We now take up this matter further, looking at bipolar disorder and then at depression.

Bipolar Disorder

Pourjalali et al. report that creative writers have higher rates of mood disorders and anxiety. **Kohanyi** (Chapter 3) argues that from 50% to 80% of creative writers suffer from a mood disorder as compared with around 1.5% (bipolar) and 10% (unipolar) of the general population. Furthermore, student poets not diagnosed with a mental illness were found to score higher than a nonwriting control group on the manic subscale of the MMPI.

Piirto reports on a study showing that, in the faculty at University of Iowa Writers' Workshop, 80% of writers had bipolar disorder compared to 30% of the comparison group, which consisted of hospital administrators, lawyers, and social workers. Two-thirds of the faculty had sought psychiatric help, and 2 of the 30 writers committed suicide during the 15 years of the study.

It is an open question though whether people with already existing psychopathology gravitate toward creative writing or whether the trials and tribulations of creative writing cause psychopathology. The truth is probably a mix of the two (see the *Depression* section).

Piirto reports that the writers with bipolar disorder in Andreason's (1987) sample wrote during the long periods between episodes, rather than during the highs and lows, suggesting that the psychopathology may not actually be contributing to the creative writing. Andreason suggests that there may be a general creativity factor that is genetically transmitted, and that "affective disorder may be both a 'hereditary taint and a hereditary gift.'" As reported by Piirto, Jamison (1989) made a chart of the genealogies and documented manic-depressive illness in first-degree relatives of British writers. The extent to which affective disorders are beneficial to creative writing deserves future study.

Just because psychopathology is linked to creativity does not mean that it contributes to creativity. Interestingly, however, **Piirto** suggests that certain aspects of psychopathology, such as divergent thought, may be beneficial to creativity and also reports studies showing that writers and artists reported mental problems in their first-degree relatives to a greater extent than in the normal population. Therefore, although full-blown mental illness may not be beneficial to creativity, milder versions may be conducive to divergent thought. The extent to which this is true remains an open question. Whereas some research has indeed shown that schizotypy correlates with creativity among creative professionals (Nettle & Clegg, 2006), others have shown that, if you control for general intelligence and openness to experience, schizotypy does not correlate with ratings of verbal and drawing creativity (Miller & Tal, 2007).

It is also important to note that much of the research conducted in this area is quite inconsistent and spotty. The work of such mainstays as Jamison, Andreasen, and Ludwig has been ardently challenged by some scholars (Rothenberg, 1990; Schlesinger, in press). Scholars in this topic would be well advised to seek out both sides of the issue before reaching any conclusions.

Depression

Piirto reports that the presence of alcohol use and depression is common among prominent creative writers. She further suggests that suicide may be a result of the extreme sensitivity with which creative people apprehend the world. She writes, "It is as if the senses are tuned louder, stronger, higher, and so the task becomes to communicate the experience of both pain and joy." She also suggests that writers' deep empathy may be contributing to depression, as they feel for the rest of the world.

Pourjalali et al. report how artists go through a cycle of depression and rumination and argue that constant revision may *contribute* to the depression. In addition, they discuss how poets who had committed suicide were more prone to use the first-person pronoun, citing evidence that writing in a narrative form (third-person usage) is better for mental health. They wonder if depression may be prolonged if individuals ruminate about their anger or depressive symptoms. They ask how creative writers can effectively ruminate and harness their emotions in a manner that promotes effective problem solving while maintaining their inspiration.

Pourjalali et al. also discuss how depression itself might lead to rumination. They suggest that, if poets ruminate while composing or revising their poems, this train of thought may allow negative memories to be accessed faster, which may then act as negative reinforcement, causing depression or lowered affect. Therefore, according to their model, rumination may be a mediating factor between depression and creative writing. In other words, there is a correlation between depression and creative writing because creative writers may already be depressed, which may cause rumination, and this rumination is what leads to more depression. Therefore, depression may already be present among creative writers, but particular forms of creative writing, such as poetry, for which the rates of depression are the highest, may exacerbate the already existing condition because of the nature of the writing. They cite research showing that depressed individuals can overcome the tendency to ruminate by undergoing training to intentionally forget negative memories.

Pourjalali et al. also suggest that another contributor to depression in creative writers may be an external locus of control. They report that creative writers who ruminate have reported feeling less control over their lives and less hopeful about their future. They argue that the nature of writing may cause one to have an external locus of control, because writing brings with it stresses such as deadlines, publication, and public acceptance, with little security. Again, it is not clear whether a subset of writers with an external locus of control flock to creative writing because it helps them get control over their lives. Indeed, several contributors such as **Kohanyi** and **Runco** suggest that writing helps individuals gain control over their writing.

Pourjalali et al. further argue that another contributor to the depression–creative writing association might be the actual belief in the link. They report that artists held a belief that depression assisted them in creative writing and that this belief was actually associated with higher creativity. Therefore, this belief can be a double-edged sword, perhaps increasing creative output but also contributing to lowered mental health. **Sawyer** (Chapter 10) argues that, in every culture, creativity myths are propagated by writers themselves, partly because they believe them, but also because it is to their advantage to present public images that conform to the contemporary beliefs about how creativity works. **Waitman and Plucker** add that writers can exert a much greater locus of control than the mystification of creativity seems to suggest and argue that if writers do not hold the genius myth stereotype, they may feel a greater control during the process of writing creatively. **Pourjalali et al.** propose that the risk-taking personality of creative writers may be linked to an external locus of control, or a belief that both negative and positive personal events are not in their immediate control.

Women and Creative Writing

Pourjalali et al. cite research showing that female poets die the youngest of all other creative writing professionals. They argue that there may be something about poetry that brings about this result. They report how female poets experience higher rates of depression and are more likely to suffer mental illness in what is dubbed the "Sylvia Plath effect." They also report how higher stress levels are associated with female creative writers. Since females are twice as likely to suffer from a major depressive episode and are more likely to ruminate or brood when depressed, and rumination seems to be a part of the revision process, they argue that this combination of rumination, external locus of control, and chronic strain may negatively reinforce each other and prolong or bring about depressive symptoms.

Pourjalali et al. also argue that female writers may suffer more from depression because of the interpersonal demands placed on them. Similarly, **Pritzker and McGarva** (Chapter 4) report that, according to the Writers' Guild, women screenwriters have made no gains relative to male writers, and this pattern does not seem to be changing. They see the same situation for ethnic minorities. Future research should investigate the possibility that societal expectations and creative writing may affect the mental health of women and minorities.

Early Life

Pritzker and McGarva discuss research that shows that the lives of 160 exceptionally creative fiction writers were marked by an above average difficulty in childhood. They posit that the same may be true for screenwriters, noting that many experienced such difficulties as parental death or absence, childhood illness, parental divorce, family financial problems, and becoming a refugee. Similarly, in describing the sample of writers at the IPAR, **Piirto** quotes Barron's discussion of his research with creative writers; he described how difficult some writers found his questions about their past suffering.

THE TEXT

Language

Lindauer (Chapter 7) argues that there has been too much of a focus on the creative writer and that an investigation at the level of the text can gain us insight into the creative process of the writer and the way the text can engage the reader. He calls this kind of investigation "physiognomy." Lindauer states that gifted creative writers are able to use language in a way that evokes in readers affect, images, and other sensory inputs. He also argues that readers differ in the extent to which they are sensitive to these language devices. Therefore, he proposes the importance of studying individual differences in both the reader's sensitivity to literary language and the writer's ability to use such language in a way that draws in the reader to the sights, sounds, and senses of the narrative.

Simonton (Chapter 8) focuses on just such an example of exemplary literary devices by investigating the text of William Shakespeare. Simonton reviews 37 plays and analyzes them based on style, content, and impact. It seems as though as Shakespeare's career advanced, and presumably his level of expertise increased (including his ability to figure out what worked and what did not with his audience), he became less likely to use arcane words and used more colloquial words with great flexibility. Furthermore, consistent with **Lindauer**, Simonton shows that sonnet popularity is positively associated with the use of primary process imagery such as concrete experiences, sensations, and desires.

Ward and Lawson (Chapter 12) discuss how they had students develop brief stories from randomly generated adjective–noun combinations. The students produced interesting stories in response to the more unusual combinations. They suggest that combinations convey more precise meanings and give rise to better developed mental images of a scene. Such linguistic devices may be a form of physiognomy, and the use of less abstract words may have connected more with the readers (see **Lindauer**). It is also possible that the use of more precise concepts is consistent with the paths-of-least resistance already existing within the readers' minds.

Also consistent with Lindauer's idea that the more captivating narratives are those that elicit multiple sensory modes in the reader, **Tan** advocates the use of multiple modes of learning that connect linguistic, visual, aural, gestural, and spatial designs. She reports preliminary research showing that this form of instruction produces positive results.

Recurring Themes in Literature

Nettle (Chapter 6) uses an ultimate explanation to understand the text. He wonders why creative writing would have evolved in the first place, because it would not have evolved if there was not some sort of need for it. Nettle proposes that creative writing fulfills the human need to attend to imaginary narrative and that it evolved as the inevitable result of our intensely social nature, our theory of mind, and our capacity for language and potential to use language as a means of gossip. According to Nettle, imaginary representations exploit these already existing structures in humans and persist because they are good at grabbing the attention of the audience. To support his hypothesis, he discusses some common themes that have been a part of fiction writing since the beginning of humankind. He notes that most literature deals with social interactions of small groups in evolutionarily important domains such as love, sex, death, status, and alliances. Similarly, **Ward and Lawson** talk about how science fiction stories deal with issues of human concern – desires, goals, conflicts between good and evil, moral dilemmas, and interpersonal relationships.

Simonton also notes that Shakespeare's most popular plays and sonnets are more likely to discuss themes such as love, familial relationships, madness, and emotions. In fact, one of the predictors of sonnet popularity is the extent to which multiple themes are present in the work. Simonton points out that *Hamlet*, Shakespeare's most popular tragedy, exemplifies many of these themes.

Such popularity could be explained by the fact that these themes are the ones that most tap into evolved instincts, and Shakespeare was extraordinarily gifted in his use of these themes and of linguistic devices to grab the attention of the reader and elicit strong emotions. This interpretation converges with the ideas presented by **Nettle** and **Lindauer** and merits future research.

It should be noted that an emerging school of literary criticism is Literary Darwinism, which is attempting to discover the various themes in literature that relate to evolved psychological mechanisms (Carroll, 2004). Furthermore, a recent paper has postulated some more proximate (instead of Nettle's focus on distal) adaptive functions that fiction plays in people's lives (Mar & Oatley, 2008).

THE PROCESS

Stage Theories

Runco thinks that writing is best described as a process. He sees the process and product as complementary, in that the process leads to products. He argues that even if an idea does not earn recognition and fame, it can still be considered creative if it also influences the way other people think. Runco thinks that full texts may not be indicative of the author's intent or meaning, because there is often a lot of interpretation by others and texts can be misjudged and overestimated. Therefore, Runco believes that products are not the best indicator of the author's creative talent.

But what is the creative writing process? One major class of theories relating to the creative writing process involves stages. In one model described by **Lubart** (Chapter 9), the writing process is divided into three stages. The first stage is planning to write, the second stage is generating or drafting text, and the third stage is editing or revision. Lubart describes an updated model in which the stages are situated within the cognitive functions of reflection (planning), text production (turning representations into text), and text interpretation (reading and listening).

Another model described by Lubart breaks the creativity process in general into four stages: preparation (setting up the problem), incubation (no conscious work), illumination (ideas break through to consciousness), and verification (evaluating and refining ideas).

Most likely, there is no one creative process that fits everyone. **Pritzker and McGarva** talk about how writers vary in their work habits. **Lubart** mentions that there are probably a multitude of paths that can lead to a creative story. He suggests that future research ought to look at the interaction between the person and the process. Lubart wonders if further research will make it possible to identify the optimal process for a specific person, given his or her background, cognitive and personality profile, and environment. This certainly seems like a promising research direction.

Subprocess Theories

As discussed by **Lubart**, more current views of the creative writing process focus on the subprocesses that are involved in creative work. A major process theory that Lubart describes is the Geneplore model, which involves generative (knowledge retrieval) and exploratory (elaboration) processes. **Plucker**

and Waitman argue that synthetic ability relates more to the inventive stage and analytical ability is most relevant during the revising process. **Lubart** suggests that incubation, which arguably could be considered an important component of the generative stage of creative cognition, "may involve automatic spreading of activation in memory, passive forgetting of problem details or entrenched ideas that do not work, broad attention and use of serendipitous cues from the environment, or associative thinking through a random or directed combination process."

Ward and Lawson argue that the operation of basic cognitive processes plays a role in all the stages of creative writing. According to these authors, access to knowledge can limit or guide the originality and believability of new stories that authors generate. They believe that new ideas have roots in existing knowledge. According to the authors, most people have a path-of-least-resistance, in which they have the tendency to retrieve specific and common instances of a category and use that as their starting point. To overcome this tendency, writers should consider the more abstract properties shared by a wide range of organisms. The authors argue that even college students can increase their creativity when encouraged to think more abstractly and that skilled writers create larger frameworks and use words that are inconsistent with the paths-of-least-resistance within readers' minds. When principles are introduced that violate this path-of-least-resistance in the readers' minds, they argue that the writer may need to use a considerable amount of handholding to guide the reader into the new world of counterfactual possibilities by building on already existing knowledge in the minds of the reader. Similarly, **Baer and McKool** (Chapter 17) argue that writing depends heavily on knowledge, which is a necessary precondition for good creative writing.

The Importance of Revision

Multiple authors in this volume discuss the "genius myth," which views creativity as the result of extraordinary thinking processes that occur suddenly in a moment of unconscious inspiration. Both **Pourjalali et al.** and **Sawyer** report how this myth has its origins in the Romantic era. **Lubart** argues that there are usually many small moments of insight rather than one big bang. **Waitman and Plucker** talk about how it is a misconception that writers must be hit with a kind of lighting-like inspiration. **Sawyer** argues that "although unconscious inspiration plays a critical role, its role can only be understood within the context of these periods of hard work, including the hard work that precedes each spark, the hard work to elaborate the implications of each spark, and the hard work of weaving these daily small sparks together into a unified work." He mentions how even personal anecdotes describing sudden fully formed ideas, such as that reported by Coleridge, turn out to be highly exaggerated.

In contradiction to the genius myth, several authors emphasize the importance of revision. **Sawyer** mentions how writing is hard work, involves a large amount of conscious editing and analysis, and takes place over long periods of time with frequent revisions. **Pourjalali et al**. emphasize the importance of the laborious process of draft writing and countless revision. **Pritzker and McGarva** talk about how rewriting is an essential part of the screenwriting process. **Plucker and Waitman** quote Anne Lamott in saying that all good writers inevitably create first drafts that are, well, less than stellar. **Singer and Barrios** (Chapter 14) argue that creative writing involves hard work, intense concentration, and periods of uncertainty and blockage.

Therefore, according to these accounts, the most creative people devote more time to exploratory processes, put in the hard work to generate a rich conceptual knowledge base, and are constantly revising.

Waitman and Plucker see the genius myth as influencing creative writers themselves and their capacities. Specifically, they argue that writers who hold this myth may doubt their own ability to replicate past successes in the future, and they consider ways to change the process to break down the mystification of creativity. Future research should look at the impact of a belief in the genius myth and its effects on actual writing outcomes.

Mood and Creative Writing

Several authors cite research on the link between mood and creative writing. As reported by **Russ** (Chapter 15), research shows that induced positive affect can facilitate creativity by cueing positive memories and a large amount of cognitive material, which results in defocused attention and allows for more associations to be formed.

Kohanyi cites research showing that positive mood can have a positive or negative effect on creativity contingent on task requirements. She argues that positive mood may facilitate creative problem solving under high satisficing conditions (by cueing a wide variety of material), whereas negative mood may facilitate task performance for more restrictive and optimizing requirements. She also discusses research that argues that negative mood may be conducive to a rejection of conventional approaches to solving a problem and to increased problem finding. She also reports that suicidal thoughts were related to originality, a result that is in interesting in light of the studies and argument presented by **Pourjalali et al**.

The Collaborative Process

Sawyer articulates an approach that views the writing process as a function of collaboration. He adopts a *socioculturalism* view that tries to explain creative products and processes in terms of their social and cultural contexts. He argues that the stereotype of the writer sitting alone working on a typewriter is a myth based on our culture's individualist assumptions about how creativity works, as well as 19th-century Romantic notions of creativity.

Furthermore, **Sawyer** posits that much of creativity research focuses on high art forms (such as poetry), which might not be representative of the full range of the human potential for creativity. Sawyer uses jazz ensembles as an example of a product created by a group process that he calls *group genius*. According to Sawyer, this group genius involves *distributed cognition*. Sawyer argues that a psychological analysis of any one member does not provide a scientific explanation of the final product.

Sawyer also uses the example of the Inklings (C. S. Lewis and J. R. R. Tolkien), who worked closely together in the early stages of their writing careers. Again, Sawyer thinks that no explanation would be complete without a complete analysis of the social and collaborative interactions that preceded and followed each of the private bouts of writing. He discusses a promising new research program called *genetic criticism*, which investigates the evolution of manuscripts, taking into consideration the collaborative process. Similarly, **Tan** believes that, in a group, activities can be facilitated in a cooperative and peer-evaluative context.

Writing as an Adaptation

Sawyer discusses how writers adopt a problem-finding style and how the work then emerges from the improvisational act of writing and revising. Similarly, **Waitman and Plucker** emphasize how the act of writing changes and evolves as the creative writer gains more writing experience. They argue that, as writers gain more experience in writing, their writing process changes as they cultivate a writing identity. Additionally, **Runco** argues that, as a result of writing, ideas and thinking change. He argues that this process puts the person in control of the experience and that the amount of detail and exploration allowed by creative writing may be unique among the professions.

The Inner Critic

Various authors describe the role of the internal critic in creative writing. A major question is whether criticism of one's own work in the early stages can help or hurt the writer. **Lubart** reports a study showing that, out of various experimental groups, the group that evaluated quite early in their work, after only a few minutes of writing activity, typically produced more creative stories than the other groups. As Lubart points out, though, the role of evaluation may differ according to the domain. **Plucker and Waitman** argue that the writer must be willing to produce material that does not emerge fully polished. This seems similar to **Piirto's** evidence that tolerance of ambiguity is a common personality trait in creative people. **Plucker and Waitman** argue that the writer must strike a balance between risk and security and that the creative process involves a circle that goes from the person to the field to the domain and back to the person. They acknowledge that the individual operates in relation to the field, and they argue that this interaction comprises the writer's ongoing process. Taken together, it seems reasonable to conclude that a healthy dose of internal criticism is important, especially when producing work for public consumption.

Luck

Sometimes the process involved in creative writing is related to luck. A theme in **Simonton's** chapter is the role of luck in the popularity of Shakespeare's plays. Interestingly, the age at which Shakespeare created his best work, *Hamlet*, is also around the same age he created his least popular work. As Simonton points out, age does not do a very good job of predicting the success of *Hamlet*. Therefore, many factors contribute to the success of a great masterpiece; luck and timing are certainly two of them.

THE DEVELOPMENT

Flow

Flow – an altered state in which time seems to stop and writing flows through easily (see **Perry**, Chapter 13) – is perhaps one of the most coveted states for productive creative writing (Csikszentmihalyi, 1990, 1996). Unsurprisingly, multiple chapter authors discuss flow. **Pritzker and McGarva** talk about how some of their screenwriters have to get into a flow state to write their best work. Some of **Perry's** interviewees noticed that anxiety decreased during flow. Perry thinks that flow is a skill that writers can learn. To increase the chances of getting into flow, Perry suggests the use of outlines and self-imposed deadlines. She advocates increasing novelty and challenging oneself, writing from a different point of view, or beginning a story in a way that is new.

Perry also suggests reserving judgment of one's work. In Perry's interviews, those who entered flow easily said they thought of the audience only in the interest of attaining clarity during revision, rather than being concerned with the critical judgment of others. This is interesting in light of other contributors' suggestion to have a healthy dose of the inner critic (see *The Inner Critic* section). Perhaps, for times when the writer is attempting to enter flow, it is best to silence the inner critic, at least temporarily.

To enter a flow state, both **Perry's** interviewees and **Pritzker and McGarva's** screenwriters went through certain rituals before they sat down to write. The purpose of the rituals was to focus attention inward and eliminate distractions. Some played music, and some used alcohol or caffeine. **Plucker** and Waitman discuss how, through flow, the writer can access innovative associations to use in a rough draft. They also argue that the first draft may be a means through which the writer can enter flow. Indeed, **Perry** distinguishes between first-draft flow and revision flow.

Intrinsic Motivation

Pritzker and McGarva talk about how intrinsic motivation is important for screenwriters. One major component of **Runco's** model of personal creativity is intrinsic motivation. One of **Perry's** tips for increasing flow is to increase intrinsic motivation for a task. She suggests that setting deadlines may increase such intrinsic motivation. **Russ** also talks about the importance of intrinsic motivation for flow and how play is an important contributor to creativity and involves intrinsic motivation.

Baer and McKool raise the point that, although intrinsic motivation facilitates creativity, students may sometimes require extrinsic motivation in the form of rewards to help get them through difficult writing assignments. They argue that there seems to be a conflict between teaching skills necessary for writing well and the skills needed for creativity; the key to resolving that conflict is to recognize that different writing lessons have different goals and to focus on different goals depending on the activity. They therefore argue that the teacher must be willing to sacrifice creativity at times, but that it is indeed possible to protect students against the negative effects of extrinsic motivation.

Alleviating Writer's Block

Chandler and Schneider view writer's block as a learned disability. **Singer and Barrios** suggest that periods of impasse can be terminated through the occurrence of vivid day or night dreams. They view these stimulus-independent thoughts as occurring under conditions of reduced executive demands for mental solutions or physical activities. They argue that mind-wandering can help the person sustain an "optimal level of arousal." In their studies, they found that blocked writers were more likely than nonblocked writers to report low levels of positive and constructive mental imagery.

Among blocked writers, Singer and Barrios identified four subtypes. They found that some blocked writers seemed to have difficulties with emotional regulation, whereas others had difficulties with relationships and images of self. They also found depression, anxiety, and a sense of helplessness to be prominent among their sample of blocked writers. It seems that these blocked writers may have an external locus of control, which is aiding their depression, as suggested by **Pourjalali et al.**

As an intervention, **Singer and Barrios** found that encouraging individuals to engage in experiences of free waking imagery increased emotional responses. In their intervention, only the two groups that focused on production of images were superior to the controls. Helping individuals generate imagery and to sustain this ability over a week's time proved extremely useful in helping persons overcome their blocks. The intervention was most effective for those who already had some predisposition to controlling and enjoying positive constructive fantasies and were less prone to guilty, hostile, or anxious daydreams.

In a second intervention, writers who showed a good response were likely to be highly motivated, self-confident, and introspective. They were also more likely to tolerate workplace anxiety and show less anger and less confusion during the task. They argue that people in the course of their daily stream of consciousness are inherently more creative than they realize. In sum, Singer and Barrios advocate increased attention to one's thought streams, fantasies, and dreams to overcome writer's block.

Play

According to **Russ**, play is a symbolic behavior in which one thing is playfully treated as if it were something else. Pretend pay involves the use of fantasy, symbolism, and make-believe and may activate similar processes as discussed by **Singer and Barrios**. Russ proposes that affective processes play a role in play. Divergent thought in daydreams, pretend play, or drawing can activate the affective symbol system. According to Russ, creative processes cannot be studied independently of an affect symbol system. These affective processes can include expression of emotion, expression of affect content themes, enjoyment, emotion regulation, and modulation of the affect in the play. Russ argues that play is important in the development of creativity and of processes that are significant to the creative writer. She cites a study demonstrating a significant relationship between play scores and the amount of affect in memories. It is possible that children who use play can store more emotional memories to begin with and also have better access to these memories than children who cannot use play to deal with emotion.

Russ discusses another study in which children with more primary process expression on the Rorschach had more primary processes in their play, more affect of all types in their play, and higher fantasy scores than children with less primary process thought expression. Primary process thought is related to divergent thinking, and play helps children develop their primary process thought and integrate the contents into manageable bits. One such primary process that Russ argues may be important in play is conceptual blending, which may be similar to **Ward and Lawson's** ideas on the importance of conceptual combination for creative cognition. In fact, both **Lubart** and **Ward and Lawson** talk about how Stephen Donaldson, in his book, *The Chronicles of Thomas Covenant the Unbeliever*, uses the generative process of selectivity to combine the concepts of being an "unbeliever" and having leprosy.

Russ describes ways that play can improve insight, divergent thinking, creativity, and problem solving. She quotes the Singers' view that play is practice with divergent thinking. In fact, Russ cites numerous studies demonstrating the intimate link between play and divergent thinking.

In two studies reported by Russ, play facilitated divergent thinking in preschool children. Play tutoring resulted in increased imaginativeness in play and increased creativity on measures other than play. In one intervention, play was effective in improving play skills, and the affect play group had higher play scores on all play processes. The affect group had more affect in their play, a greater variety of affect content, and better imagination and organization of the story than did the control group. The affect group also had higher scores on the creativity measure.

Involvement of affect apparently influences processes of imagination and fantasy. The imagination play group was significantly better than the control in frequency of positive affect and variety of affect. Russ suggests this finding may have implications for mood regulation in children. For future research, Russ suggests comparing the benefits of making up a story as a play intervention with the benefits of making up a story as a writing intervention. We would certainly be eager to see such a study.

Positive Effects of Creative Writing

Various authors in the current volume discuss the positive effects of creative writing. **Kohanyi** notes that, when events are visited and revisited, the emotional response to the events can become dulled. More specifically, she found that those who benefit the most from writing are those who write the most intensely, for the longest amount of time, and over the longest time span.

Sexton and Pennebaker (Chapter 16) also discuss the various healing powers of expressive writing. They discuss research showing that writing can reduce depression and rumination, as well as improve self-image (it is interesting to note recent research that suggests that those particularly inclined to brood may be particularly helped by such writing; see Sloan, Marx, Epstein, & Dobbs, 2008). Also, students who participated in a writing exercise received higher grades compared to their peers and were quicker to obtain a new job after being laid off. The authors also show how writing about traumas helps writers organize their thoughts and reduces their need to inhibit strong thoughts, emotions, and behaviors.

Kohanyi also reports on researchers who looked at responses to written self-disclosure about trauma. They discuss results showing a reduction in the number of visits to health centers, higher immune functioning, decreased absenteeism, and improved grade point average. **Runco** also reports on research showing that immune systems are more effective when people have regular opportunities for written self-disclosure. **Chandler and Schneider** discuss research showing that journaling reduced the symptoms of asthma and arthritis. Although **Sexton and Pennebaker** note that daily journaling can be helpful, they also point out that those who do journal are not necessarily healthier than those who do not. They raise the possibility that those who do not write on their own would be worse off if they did journal, as those who journal regularly may have a need to do so. In addition, they suggest that it might be better to write about a traumatic event after some time has passed, instead of writing immediately after the traumatic event.

According to **Kohanyi**, "it is the exploration of thoughts and feelings associated with an experience as well as writing about topics that enhance self-regulation (including affective regulation) that result in mood and health improvements." Kohanyi also says that it is important that the topic triggers an emotional reaction, whether positive or negative, and that writers structure their thoughts into a coherent story. Kohanyi reports that participants who wrote in the first-person perspective and then switched to the third person reported feeling better than those who continued to use the first person. Similarly, **Pourjalali et al.** argue that, for expressive writing to have salutary effects, the formation of a narrative is necessary.

Similarly, **Sexton and Pennebaker** argue that the beneficial effects of expressive writing are not simply due to emotional catharsis. The benefit comes about through an improvement in self-regulation, in which the writer gains greater control of his or her emotional states.

Kohanyi found no association between engaging in creative writing and more mood variability. Writing did, however, increase positive valence and lower arousal. All writers reported that writing elevated their mood and more than half reported a decrease in arousal. Kohanyi's research concurs with earlier research that showed that, after writing, participants felt better overall, less negative, and more positive. Kohanyi thinks their writing may be more stable than controls precisely because they are writing.

Runco discusses how writing can provide an opportunity for self-expression and problem resolution more so than other domains of work because the symbol system of writing is so extensive and well known. He also argues that writing allows labeling, and thereby unambiguous problem identification and labeling a problem are useful because, once identified, the problem can be characterized and processed more easily.

THE EDUCATION

Learning Environment

Each of the creative writing programs discussed in this volume has its own unique philosophy and learning environment. **Tan** believes that creativity can be nurtured when the prerequisite components exist within the individual and receive ample support from the environment. Tan developed a creative writing program for a multicultural and multilingual context that centers on the use of various forms of metaphor and a positive and forgiving environment, where students do not feel troubled if they make mistakes. Tan argues for a psychologically safe environment, in which students generate ideas, provide constructive feedback, and adopt a positive mindset when they receive feedback. This program also makes use of cooperative learning and brainstorming and teaches students the importance of accepting peers' views. It also relies extensively on modeling, showing students example of good metaphors.

Tan's learning climate incorporates *reflection-in-action* (reflection that happens in the midst of experience) or *reflection-on-action* (reflection outside an experience). It adopts Rodgers' reflective cycle, exploring the roles of presence, description, analysis, and experimentation in helping teachers reflect and attend to their students' learning in rich and nuanced ways. The teachers believe in helping students increase their confidence. Tan also argues that teachers should feel that they are competent in their areas of specialization and in the relevant pedagogical skills. They should be interested in integrating creative strategies and techniques into lessons.

Schneider and Chandler argue for the importance of teachers helping students find their primary voice by teaching craft, offering wider options, and encouraging experimentation with different voices and forms; once students find their voice, teachers should encourage them to believe in it. This point is similar to **Plucker and McKool's** idea that self-perceptions are an important part of the writing process. They mention the importance for the writer of having absolute trust in his or her own aesthetic judgments. This trust may be similar to ego strength, which is a major component of **Runco's** model of personal creativity, as well as **Piirto's** description of the creative writer's personality. **Schneider and Chandler** also believe in a nonhierarchical spirit, confidentiality, no criticism during the first draft (unless the student asks for it), and practice (for they believe only in this way can there be equality of risk taking and mutuality of trust). One technique of Chandler and Schneider that is promising is the use of a closing process after each workshop session, in which the students affirm what they have learned that day, verbalize appreciation for the feedback of another writer that has contributed to their knowledge, and appraise a group function that could be improved.

Role of Feedback

Several authors discuss the role of evaluation in the education of creative writing. **Chandler and Schneider** argue that, until students find their own voice, the teacher should use critique with restraint. They argue that it is important that evaluation does not damage the delicate atmosphere in which creativity thrives. They suggest that creativity emerges from the writer feeling safe to express his or her own voice and that it should be nurtured through honest, encouraging feedback. They feel that evaluation deserves just as much sensitivity as teaching the writing.

Baer and McKool suggest that the teacher refrain from judgment or evaluation during the initial idea generation stage. When it comes time for evaluation, though, Baer and McKool argue that it is not feedback itself that is bad but the way in which it is delivered. They advocate the use of specific feedback and teaching students skills that will help students not be affected by others' evaluations in a negative way. **Tan** also argues that creative writing therapy may facilitate the use of positive coping strategies. **Baer and McKool** see the ability to monitoring one's own motivations as an important and teachable metacognitive skill. **Schneider and Chandler** describe a training program that Pat Schneider developed with the Amherst Writers & Artists. In this approach, the response that a teacher gives is more important than the kind of manuscript the student offers.

Evaluation

What are the different ways to evaluate creative writing? Several authors discuss different approaches.

Chandler and Schneider discuss Elbow's distinction among feedback, evaluation, and grading. According to these authors, feedback is the most important strategy. They say that grammar evaluation is the most common method, but can be helpful when the evaluation includes elements that assist the writer in revision. They also discuss the possibility of using a grading contract to evaluate writing, but only if grades represent the creative process at work. They argue that the teacher should model the courage to write him- or herself. It should be noted that Chandler and Schneider warn against confusing grammar variations with class or cultural differences, a point that we think is very important.

Tan suggests that the creative processes during the generative stage can be assessed using the consensual assessment technique (Amabile, 1996). Instructors rated (on a 5-point Likert scale) the student's product relative to one another on the following dimensions: creativity, novelty (something new, originality, and unique word choice), imagination (use of vivid imagery), expression (clarity of sentence), and grammar. Knowledge of metaphor (*Biyu*) was assessed on a rubric using these criteria: originality, fluency, flexibility, and elaboration. They also offer an option to use a graphic organizer and peer evaluation.

The purpose of assessment in **Tan's** model is to assist students who wish to learn and feel able to learn. She feels that the evaluation should empower the students to understand the criteria of assessment and to be able to use them to improve learning and thinking. Tan argues that no single instructional approach can affect all aspects of writing. The challenge is to optimize each child's engagement in individualized cognition, peer evaluation, group thinking, cooperative learning, creative writing, and multimodal representation. Tan also argues that findings from neuroscience should be used to further our understanding of creative cognition and to design intervention, teaching, and learning.

Finally, we note **Baer and McKool's** caution that when evaluation is not delivered carefully and in a compartmentalized way, students' intrinsic motivation can be diminished and their creativity subsequently decreased.

CONCLUSION

As our mutual mentor Robert Sternberg notes in the foreword to this book, creative writing and creative writers have been generally understudied in psychology. Indeed, it has been argued that psychology and the arts have a very unequal relationship. Psychology takes its materials and subject matter from the arts, but does not provide in return any particularly welcomed or suitable insights (Lindauer, 1998). One of our biggest goals in editing this book was to even up the scales a little bit. We hope that this book will be of interest not only to psychologists but also to creative writers and writing teachers. We believe that our contributors have offered invaluable insights, tips, and discussions of all aspects of creative writing and writers.

We eagerly look forward to future research and debate. We would love to see a journal devoted to the psychology of creative writing, much as there is a similar journal devoted to music (*Psychology of Music*). We are grateful for the current venues for new research on creative writing, such as *Creativity Research Journal*; *Journal of Creative Behavior*; *Empirical Studies of the Arts*; *Psychology of Aesthetics, Creativity, and the Arts*; *Imagination, Cognition, & Personality*; and many others, and we encourage interested readers to seek these journals out to find out cutting-edge research.

REFERENCES

Amabile, T. M. (1996). *Creativity in context: Update to the social psychology of creativity.* Boulder, CO: Westview.

Andreason, N. (1987). Creativity and mental illness: Prevalence rates in writers and their first-degree relatives. *American Journal of Psychiatry, 144,* 1288–1292.

Carroll, J. (2004). *Literary Darwinism: Evolution, human nature, and literature.* New York: Routledge.

Csikszentmihalyi, M. (1990). *Flow: The psychology of optimal experience.* New York: HarperCollins.

Csikszentmihalyi, M. (1996). *Creativity.* New York: HarperCollins.

Lindauer, M. S. (1998). Interdisciplinarity, the psychology of art and creativity: An introduction. *Creativity Research Journal, 11,* 1–10.

Mar, R. A., & Oatley, K. (2008). The function of fiction is the abstraction and simulation of social experience. *Perspectives on Psychological Science, 3,* 173–192.

Miller, G. F., & Tal, I. R. (2007). Schizotypy versus openness and intelligence as predictors of creativity. *Schizophrenia Research, 93,* 317–324.

Nettle, D., & Clegg, H. (2006). Schizotypy, creativity and mating success in humans. *Proceedings of the Royal Society B, 273,* 611–615.

Rothenberg, Albert. (1990). *Creativity and madness: New findings and old stereotypes.* Baltimore: Johns Hopkins University Press.

Schlesinger, J. (2004). Creativity and mental health. *British Journal of Psychiatry, 184,* 184–185.

Schlesinger, J. (in press). Creative mythconceptions: A closer look at the evidence for the "mad genius" hypothesis. *Psychology of Aesthetics, Creativity, and the Arts.*

Sloan, D. M., Marx, B. P., Epstein, E. M., & Dobbs, J. L. (2008). Expressive writing buffers against maladaptive rumination. *Emotion, 8,* 302–306.

INDEX